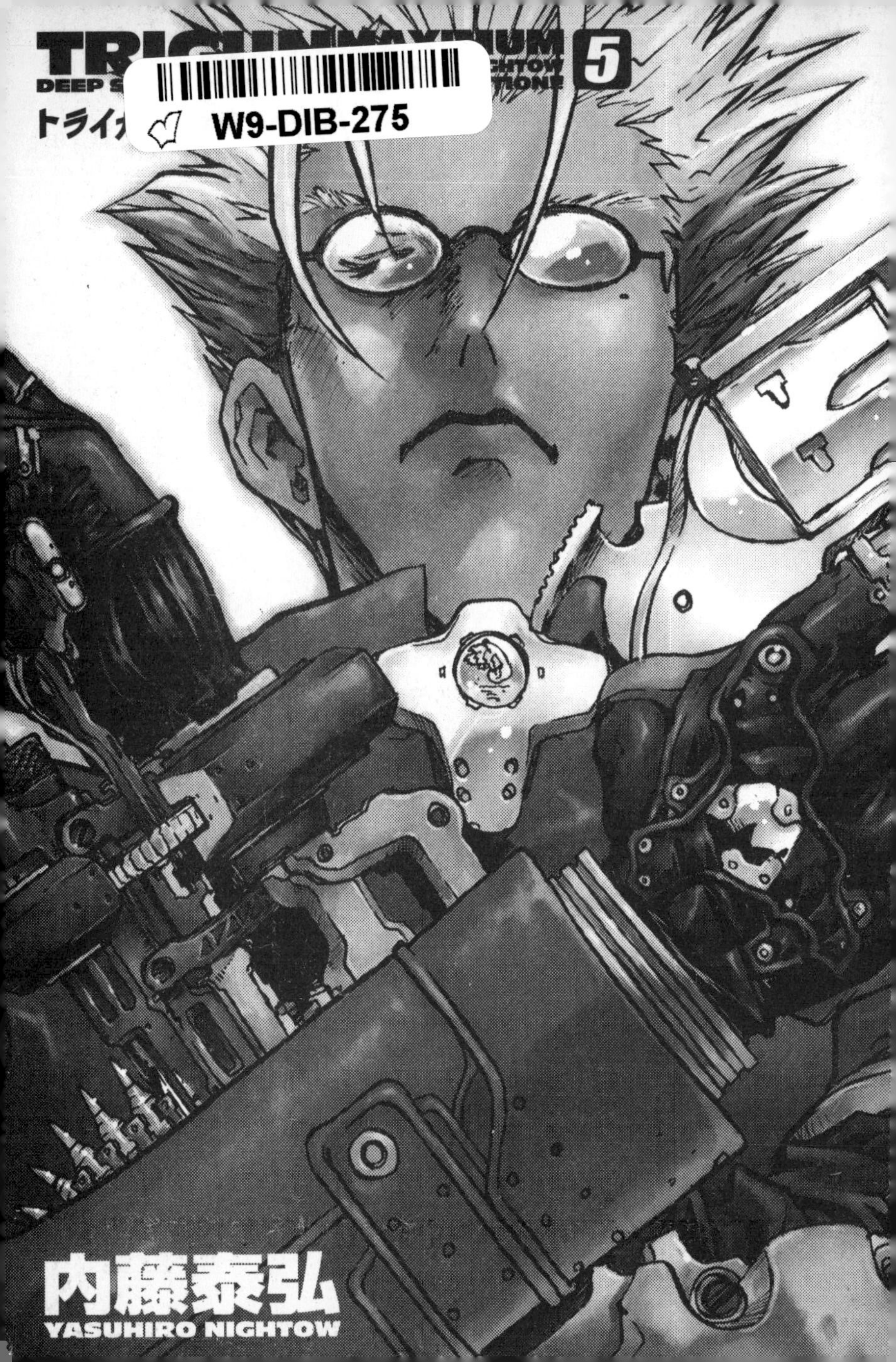
TRI... ...UM
5
DEEP S... ...GHTOW
...TIONS
トライ...
W9-DIB-275
内藤泰弘
YASUHIRO NIGHTOW

# TRIGUN MAXIMUM
### YASUHIRO NIGHTOW
### DEEP SPACE PLANET FUTURE GUN ACTION!!
# CONTENTS

TRIGUN MAXIMUM 5
BREAK OUT

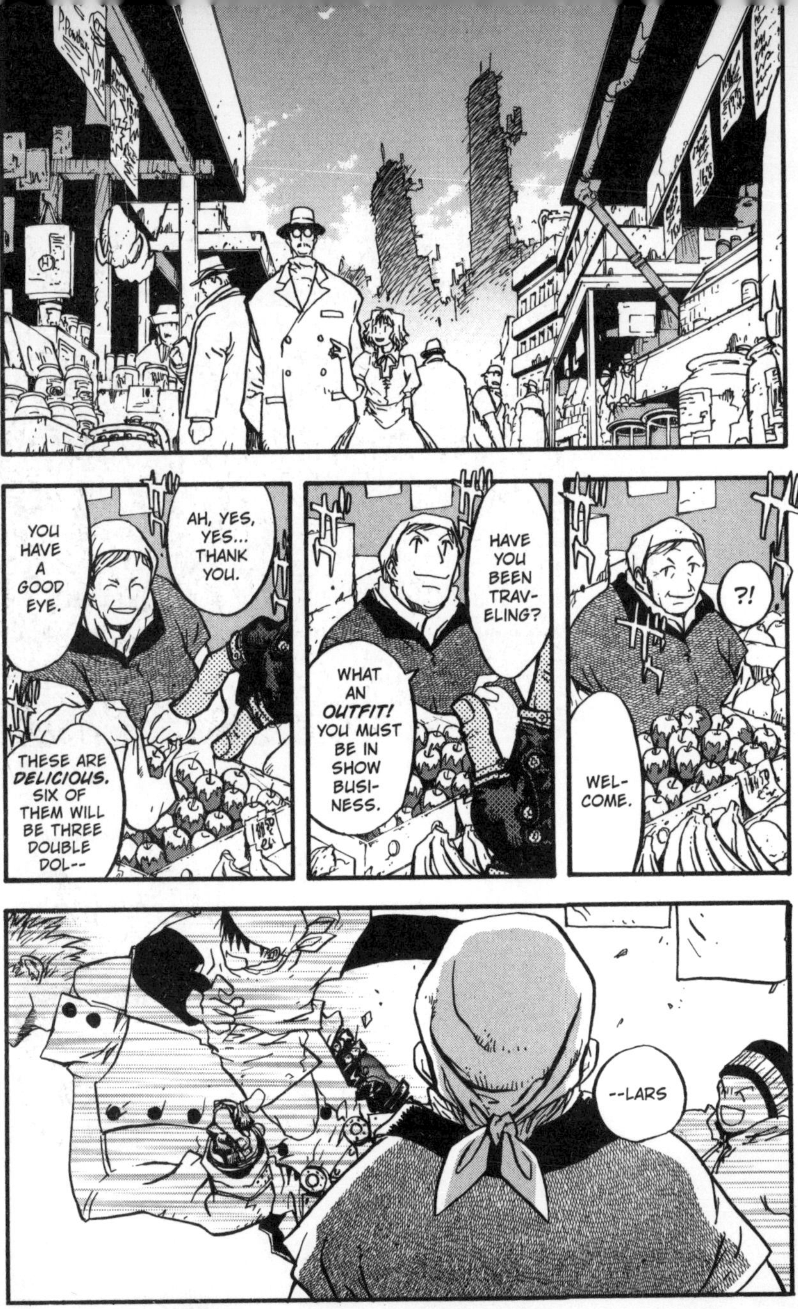
?!
WEL-COME.
HAVE YOU BEEN TRAV-ELING?
WHAT AN *OUTFIT!* YOU MUST BE IN SHOW BUSI-NESS.
AH, YES, YES... THANK YOU.
YOU HAVE A GOOD EYE.
THESE ARE *DELICIOUS.* SIX OF THEM WILL BE THREE DOUBLE DOL--
--LARS

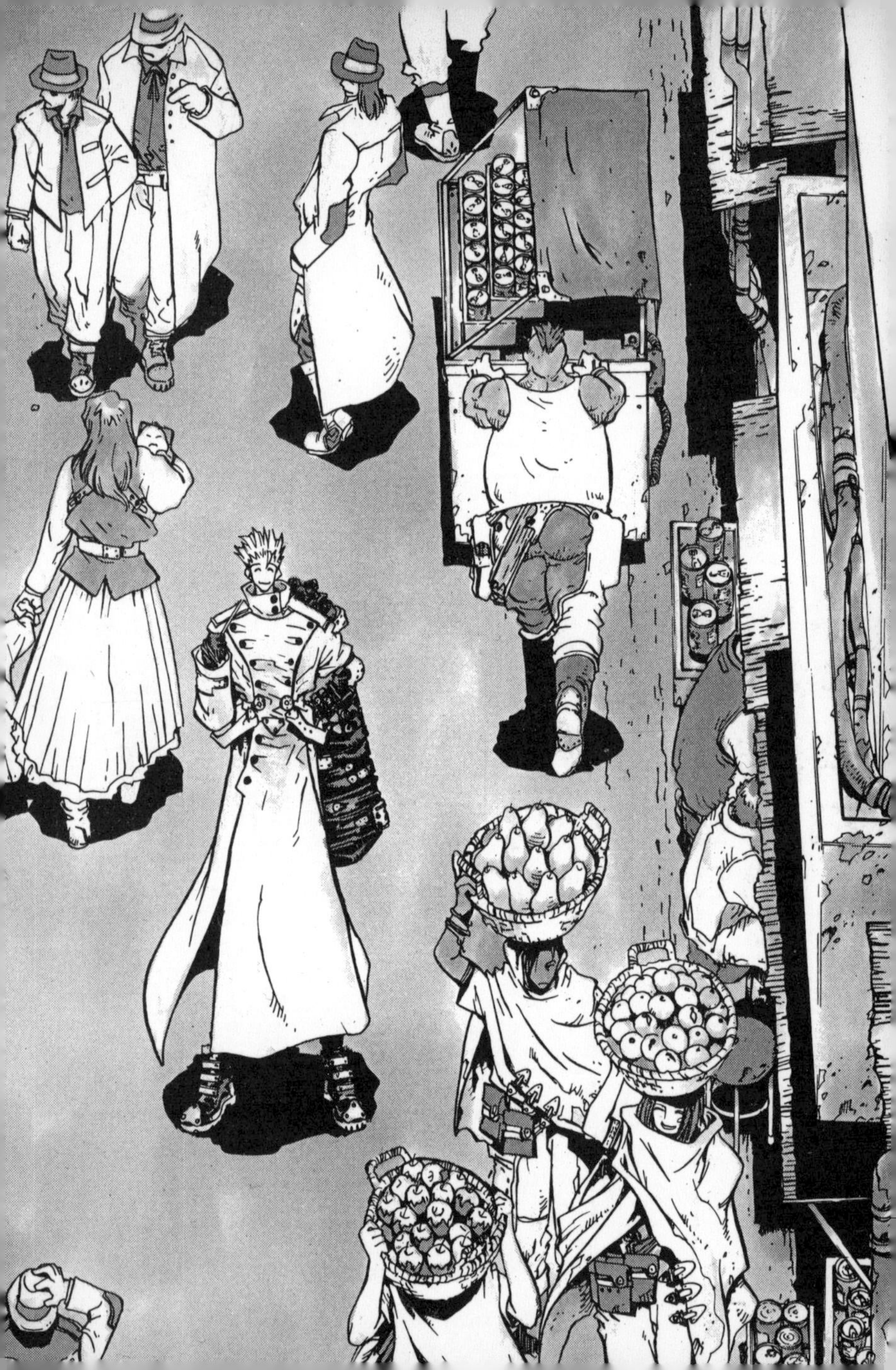

# #1.
# THE CITY.
# AND THEN THE
# BANQUET OF
# THE DOGS

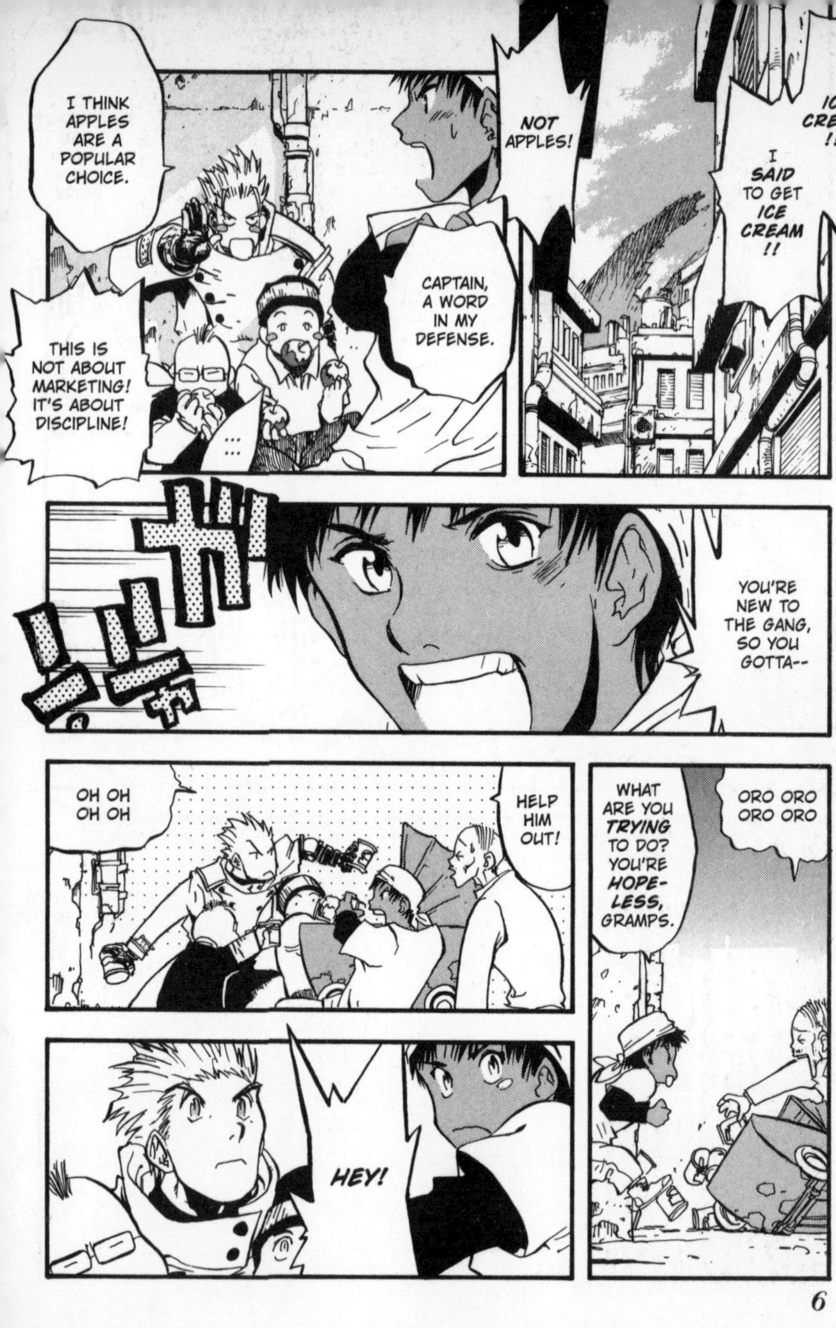
ICE CREAM!!
I SAID TO GET ICE CREAM!!
NOT APPLES!
I THINK APPLES ARE A POPULAR CHOICE.
CAPTAIN, A WORD IN MY DEFENSE.
THIS IS NOT ABOUT MARKETING! IT'S ABOUT DISCIPLINE!
...
...
YOU'RE NEW TO THE GANG, SO YOU GOTTA--
ORO ORO ORO ORO
WHAT ARE YOU TRYING TO DO? YOU'RE HOPELESS, GRAMPS.
HELP HIM OUT!
OH OH OH OH
HEY!

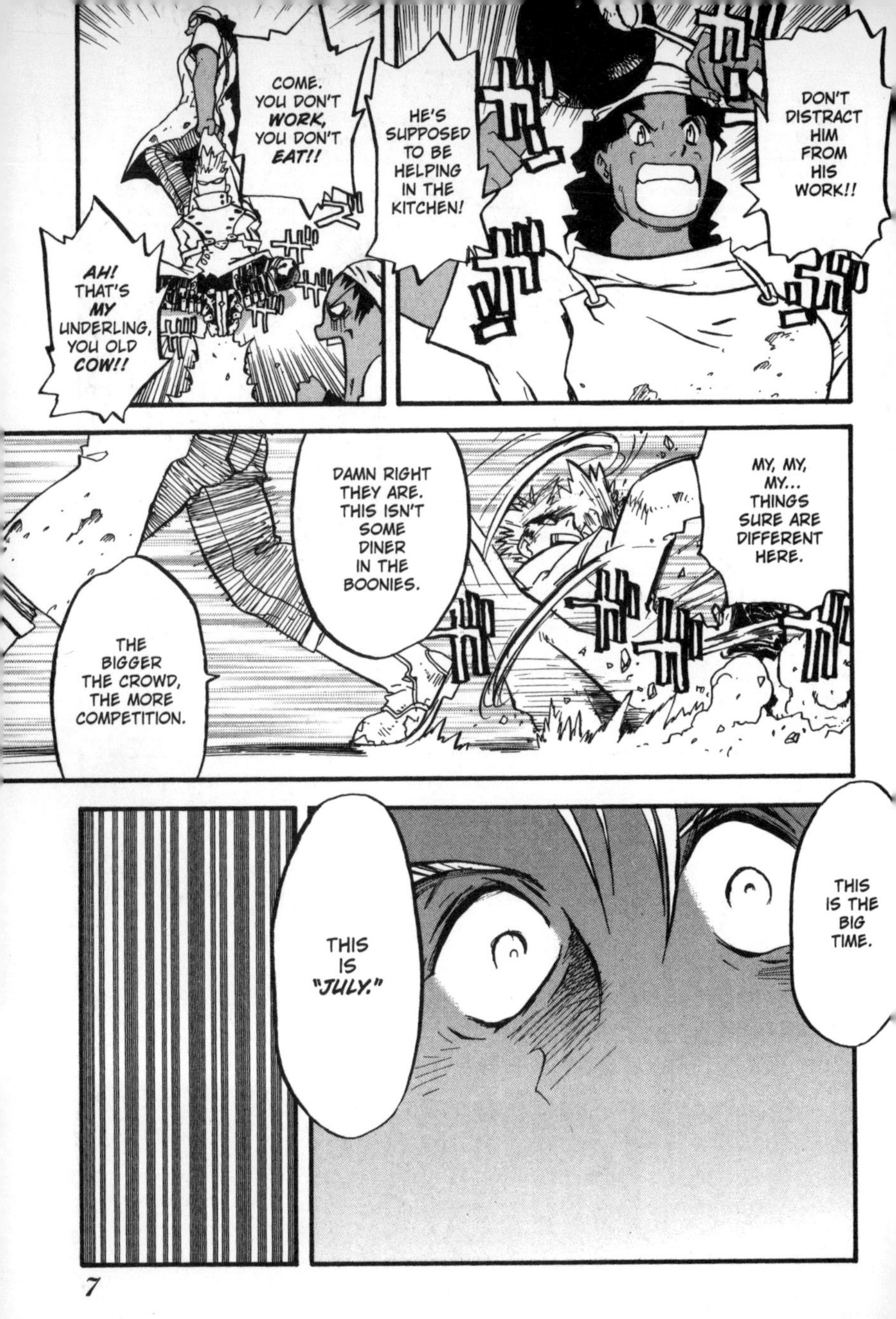
DON'T DISTRACT HIM FROM HIS WORK!!
HE'S SUPPOSED TO BE HELPING IN THE KITCHEN!
COME. YOU DON'T WORK, YOU DON'T EAT!!
AH! THAT'S MY UNDERLING, YOU OLD COW!!
MY, MY, MY... THINGS SURE ARE DIFFERENT HERE.
DAMN RIGHT THEY ARE. THIS ISN'T SOME DINER IN THE BOONIES.
THE BIGGER THE CROWD, THE MORE COMPETITION.
THIS IS THE BIG TIME.
THIS IS "JULY."

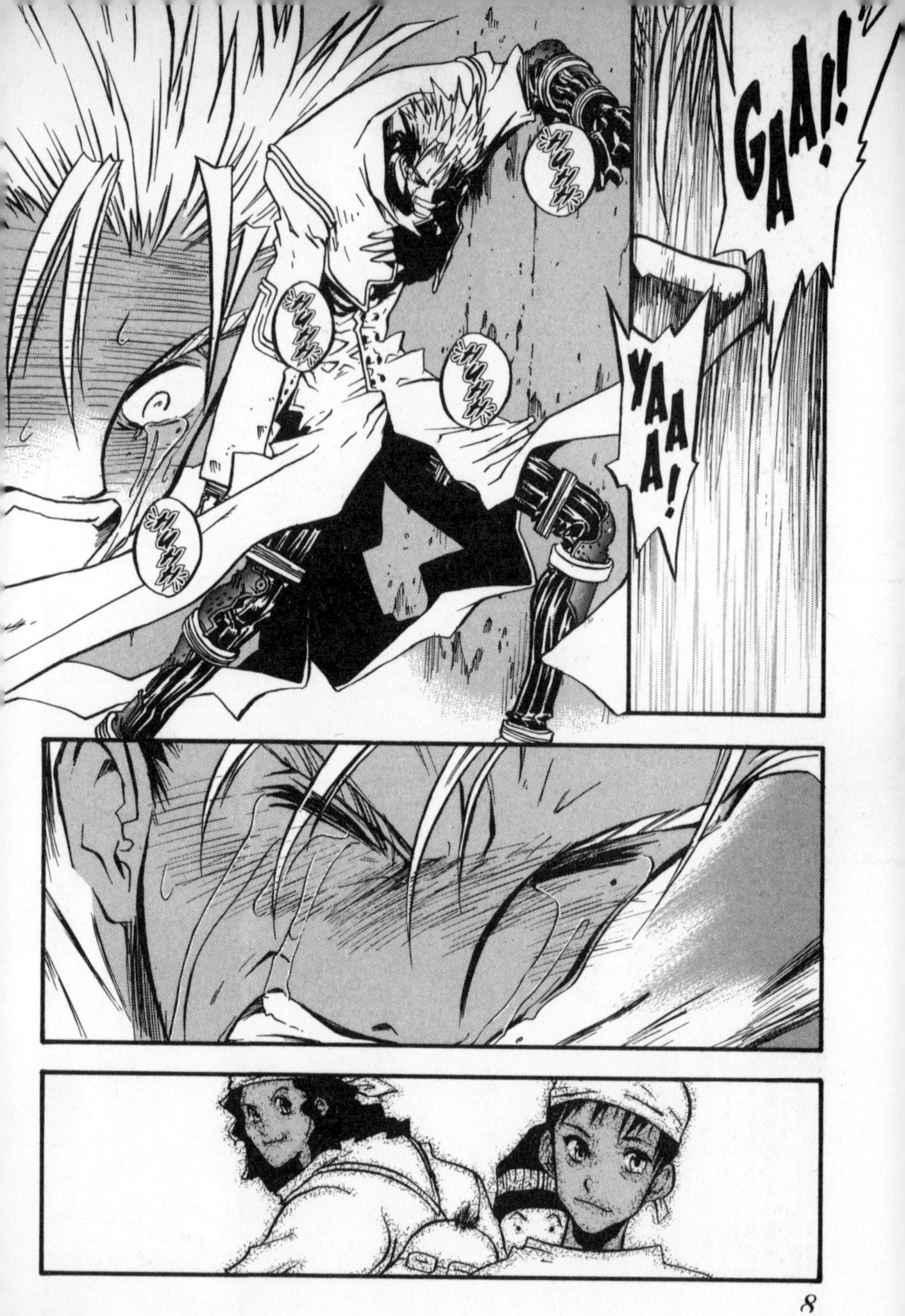
GAA!!
YAAA!
HUHH
HUHH
HUHH
HUHH

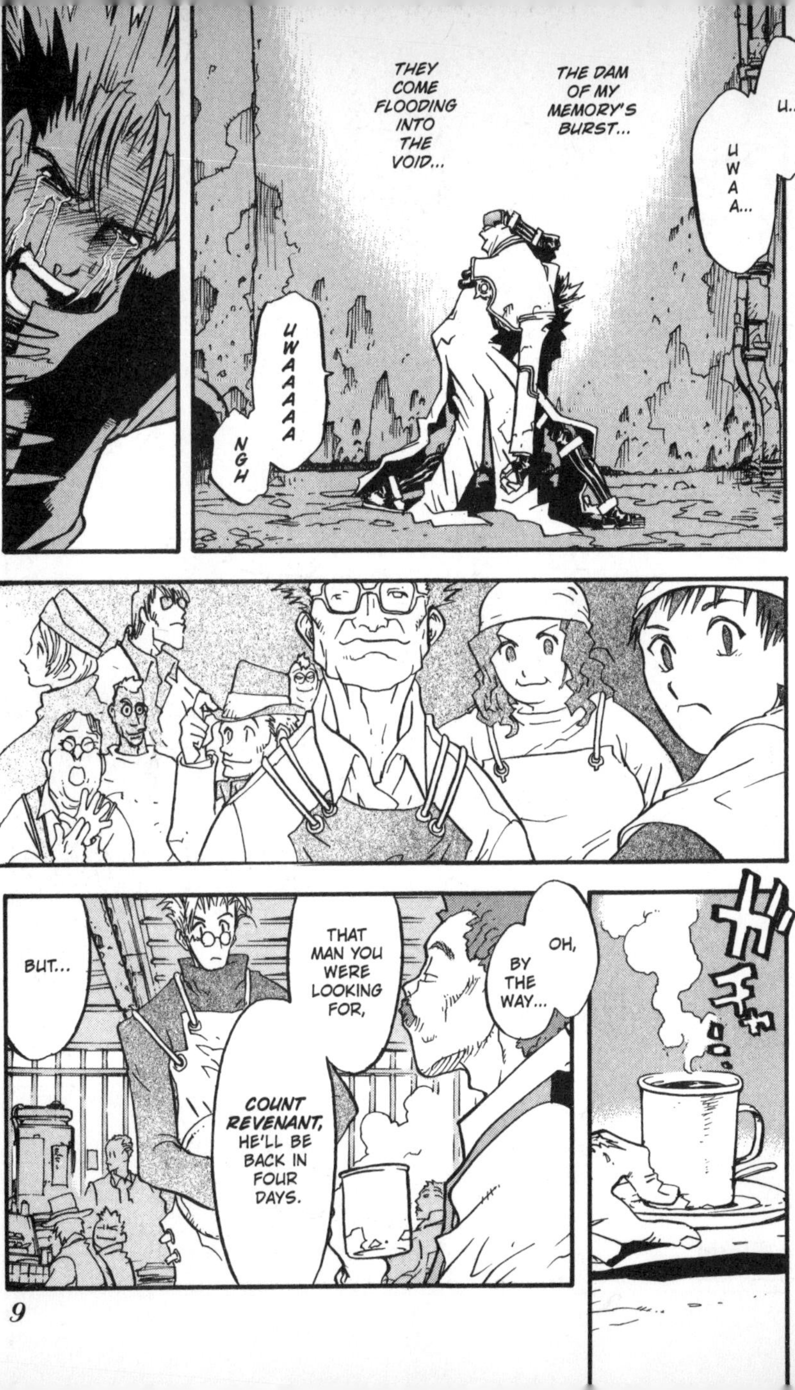
U... UWAA...
THE DAM OF MY MEMORY'S BURST...
THEY COME FLOODING INTO THE VOID...
UWAAAAAA NGH
ガチャ
OH, BY THE WAY...
THAT MAN YOU WERE LOOKING FOR,
**COUNT REVENANT,** HE'LL BE BACK IN FOUR DAYS.
BUT...

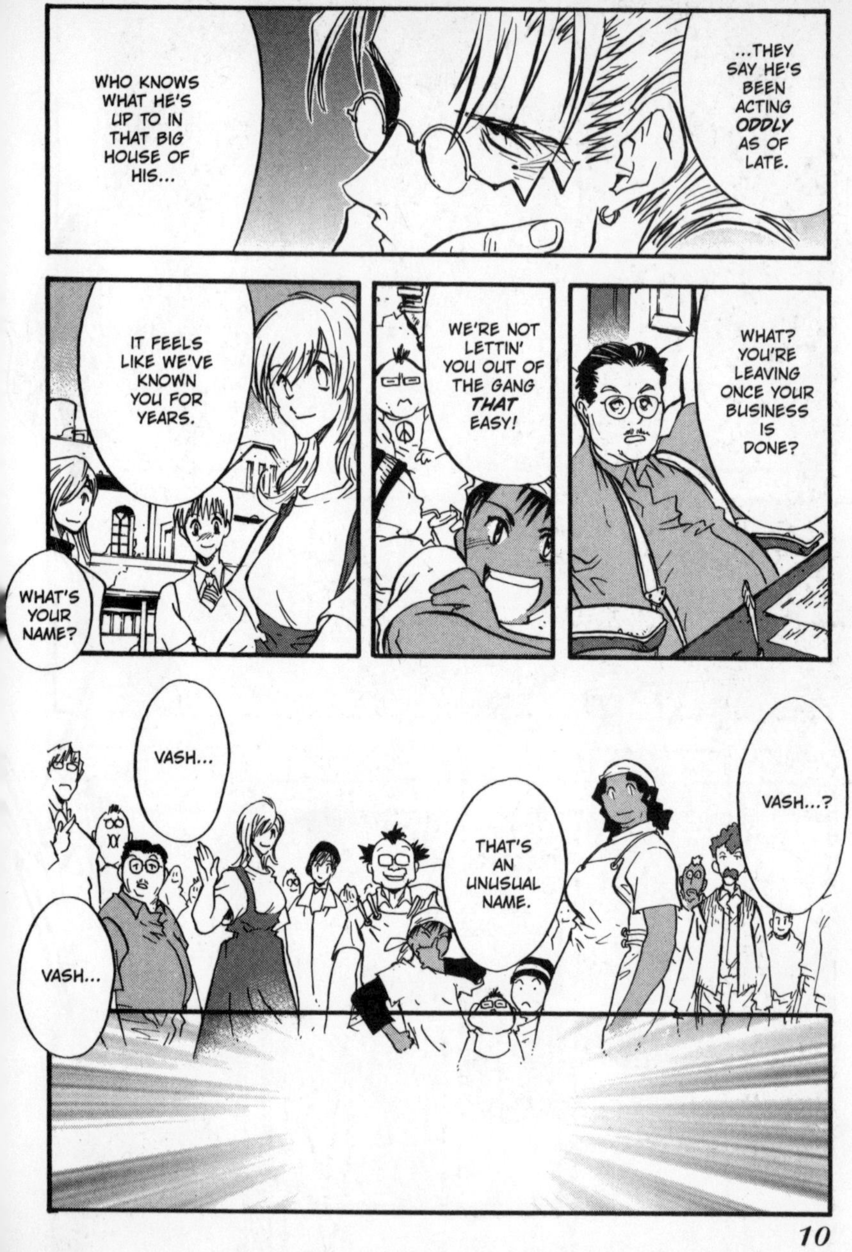
...THEY SAY HE'S BEEN ACTING *ODDLY* AS OF LATE.
WHO KNOWS WHAT HE'S UP TO IN THAT BIG HOUSE OF HIS...
WHAT? YOU'RE LEAVING ONCE YOUR BUSINESS IS DONE?
WE'RE NOT LETTIN' YOU OUT OF THE GANG *THAT* EASY!
IT FEELS LIKE WE'VE KNOWN YOU FOR YEARS.
WHAT'S YOUR NAME?
VASH...?
THAT'S AN UNUSUAL NAME.
VASH...
VASH...

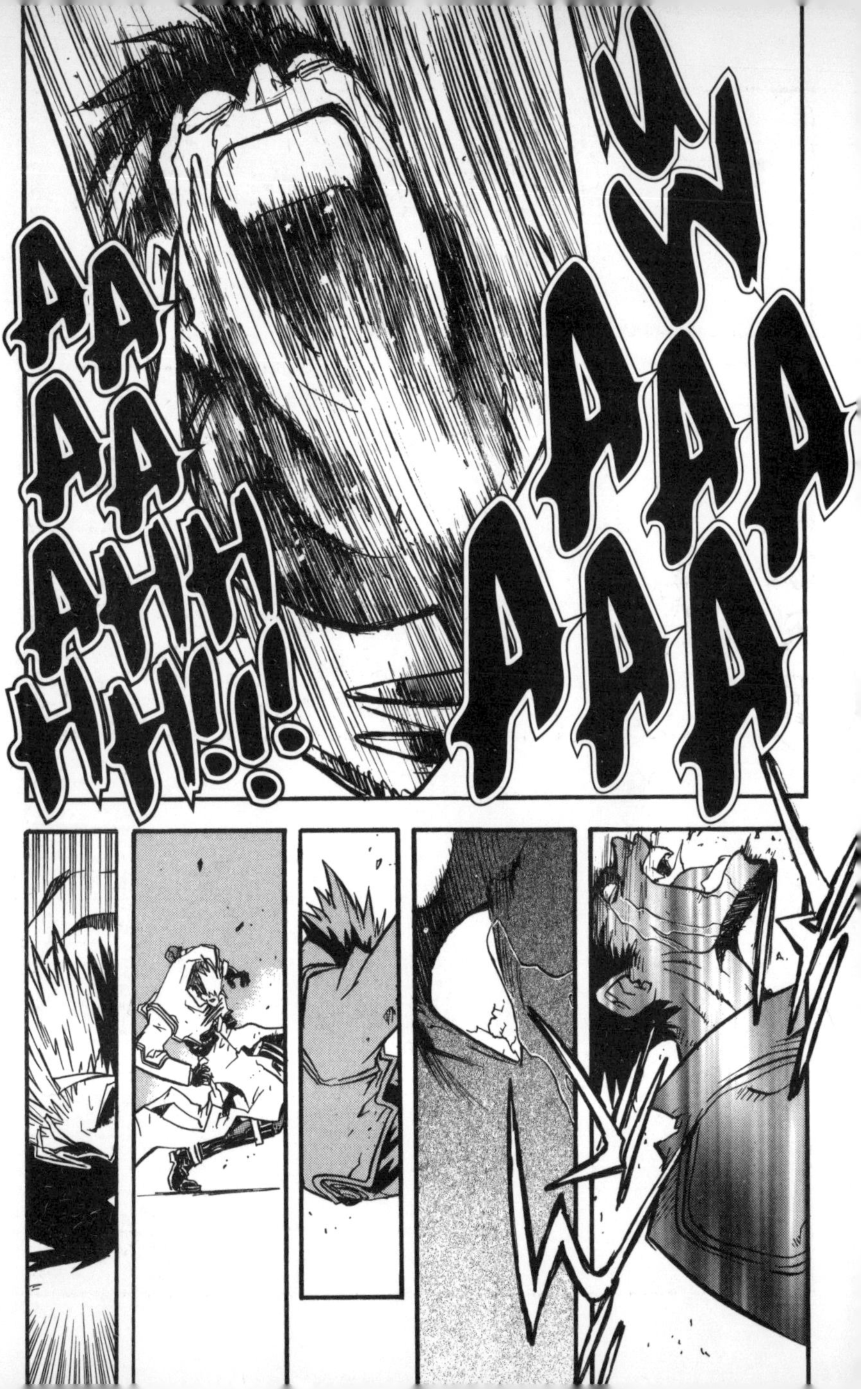
UWAAAAAA
AAAAAHHHH!!!

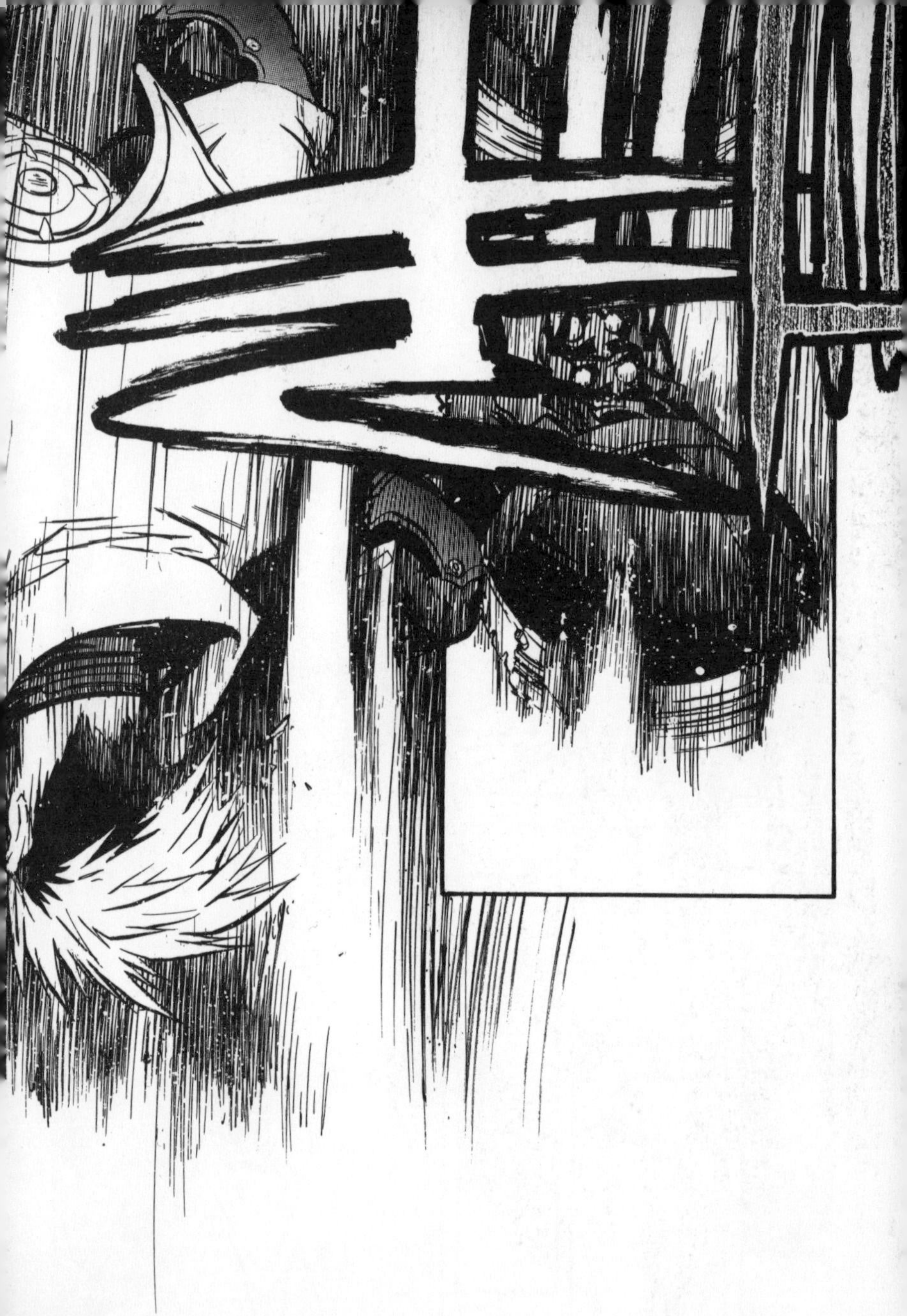

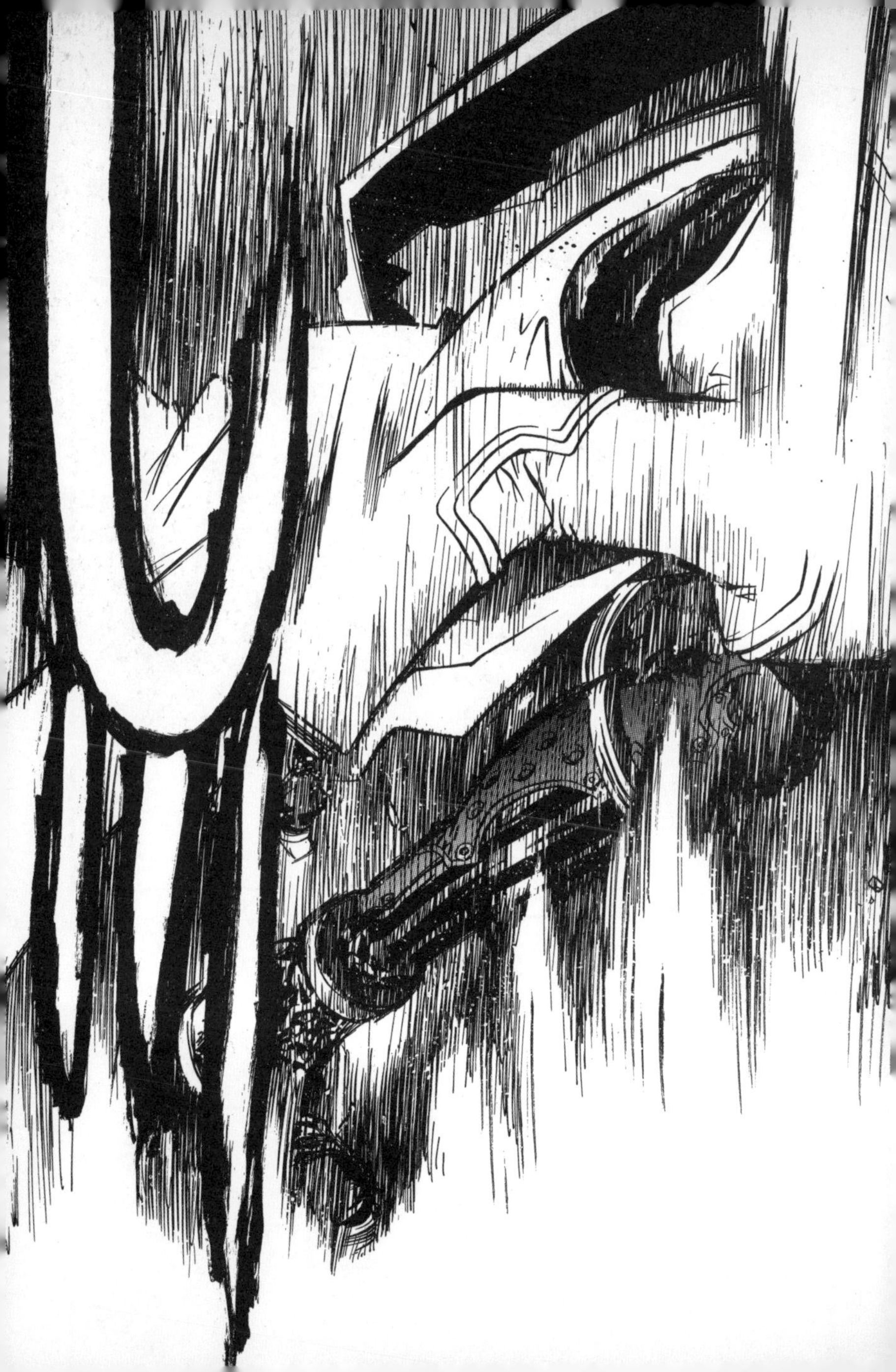

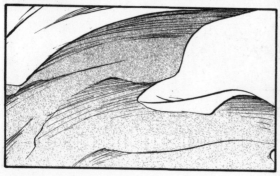

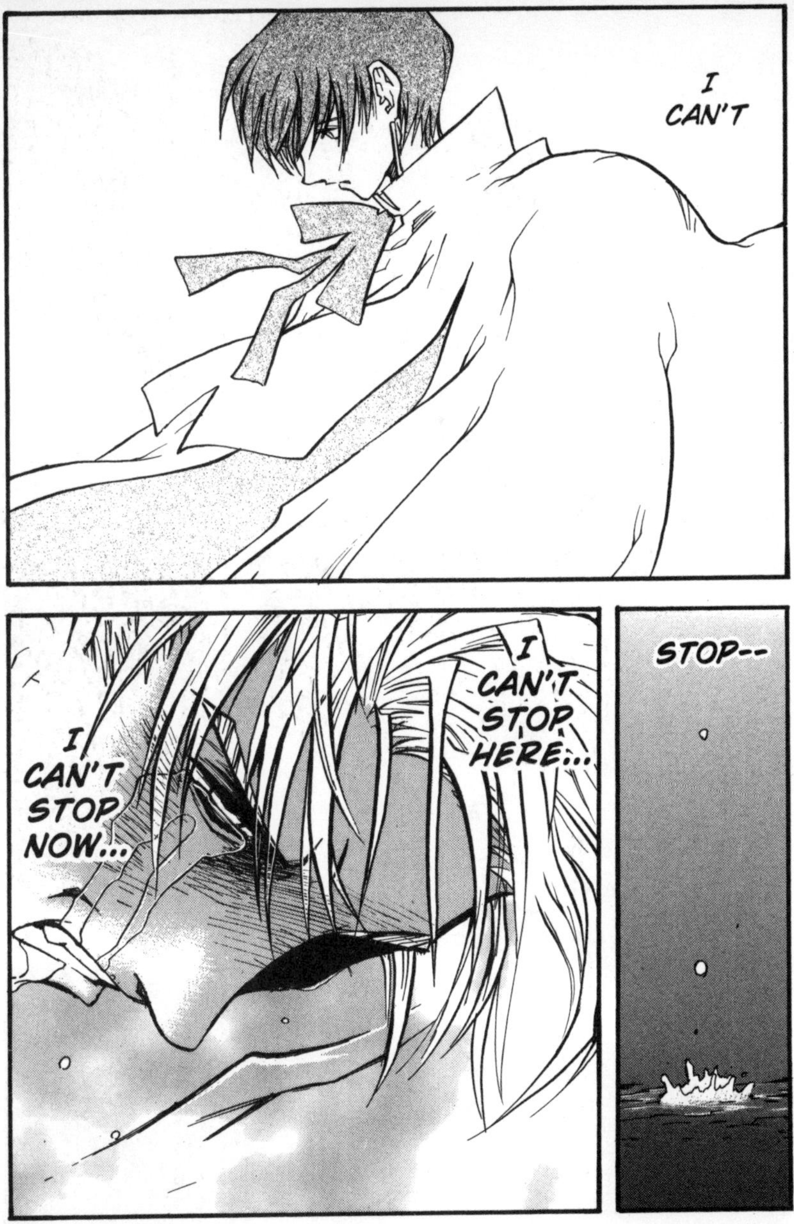
I CAN'T
STOP--
I CAN'T STOP HERE...
I CAN'T STOP NOW...

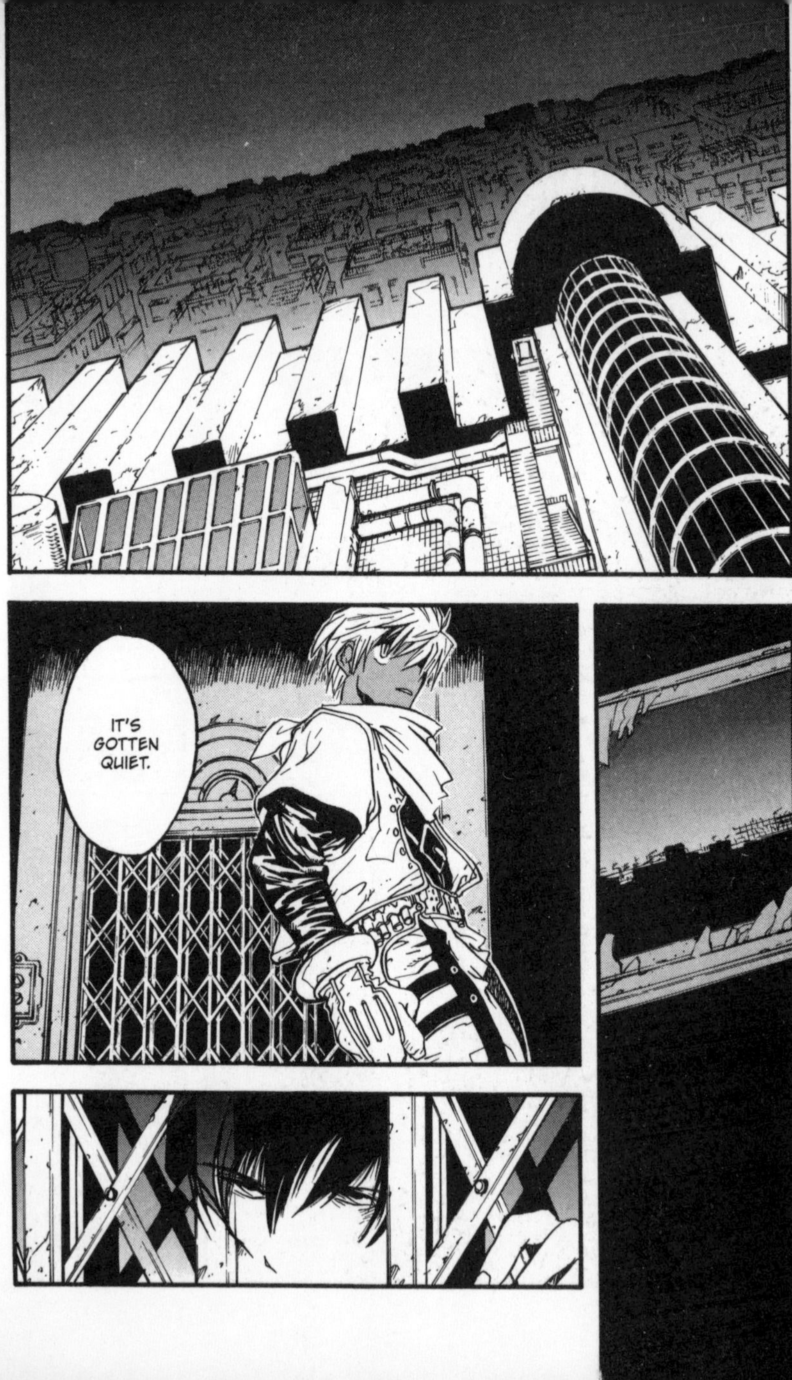
IT'S GOTTEN QUIET.

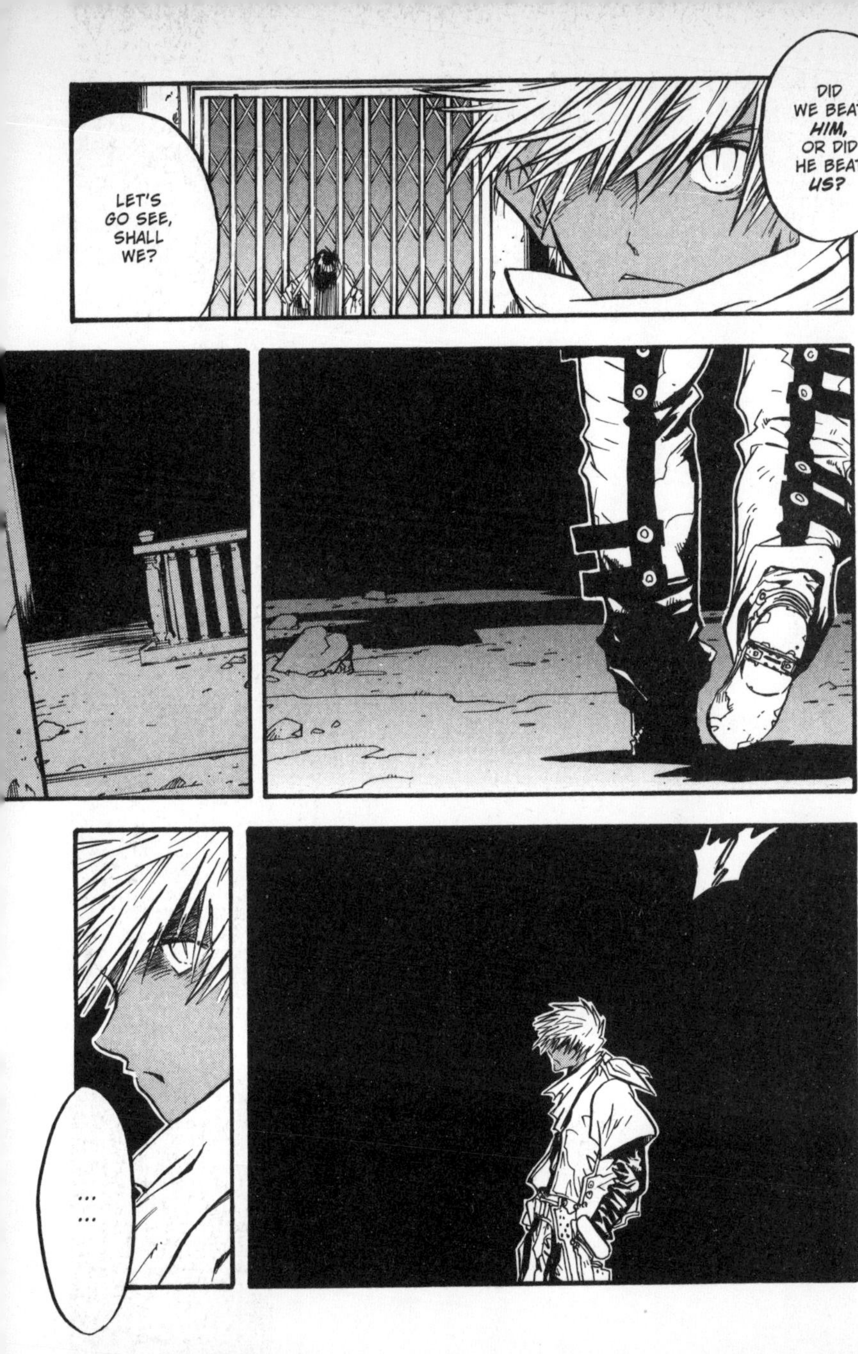
DID WE BEAT *HIM*, OR DID HE BEAT *US*?
LET'S GO SEE, SHALL WE?
... ...

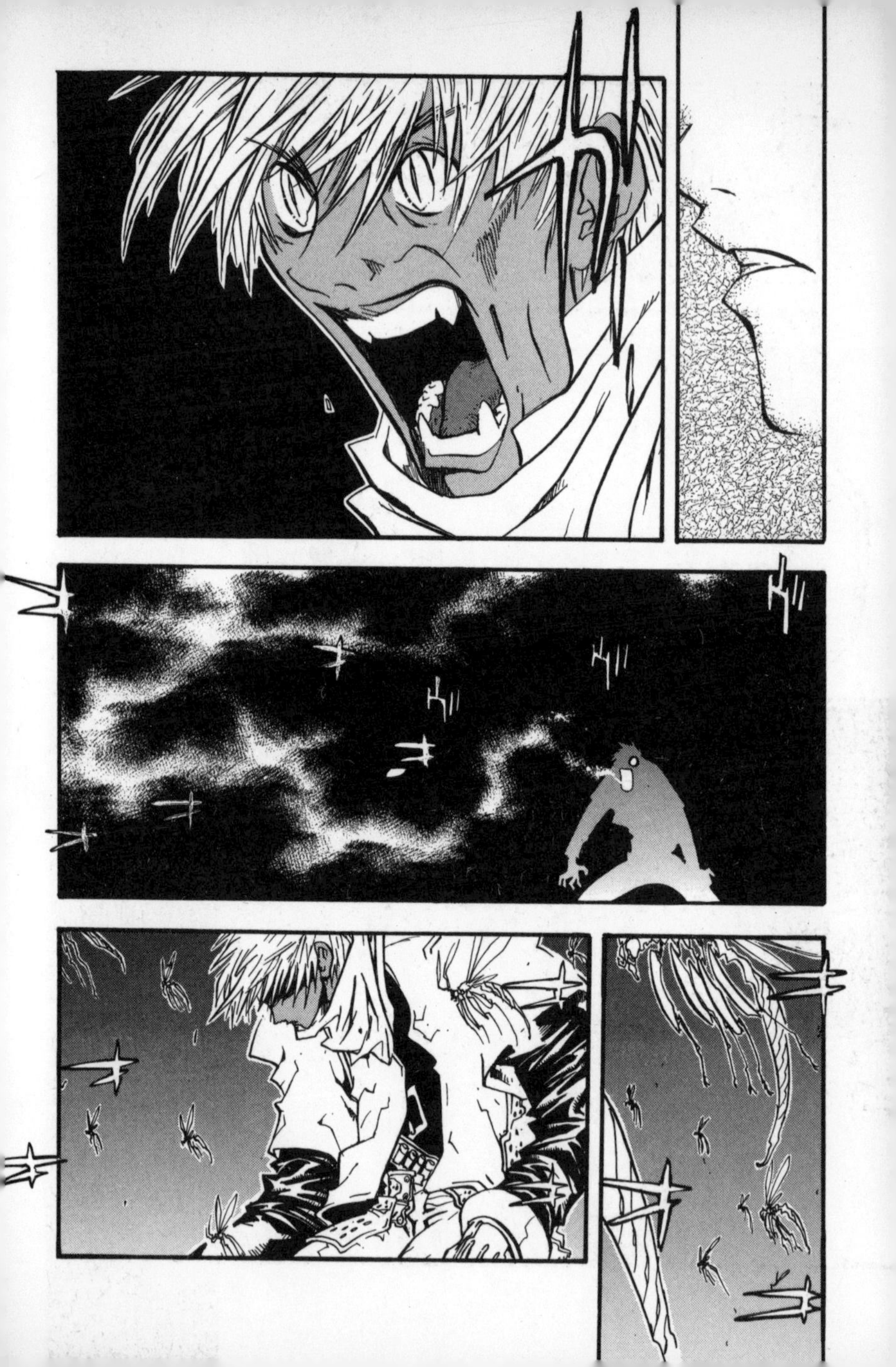

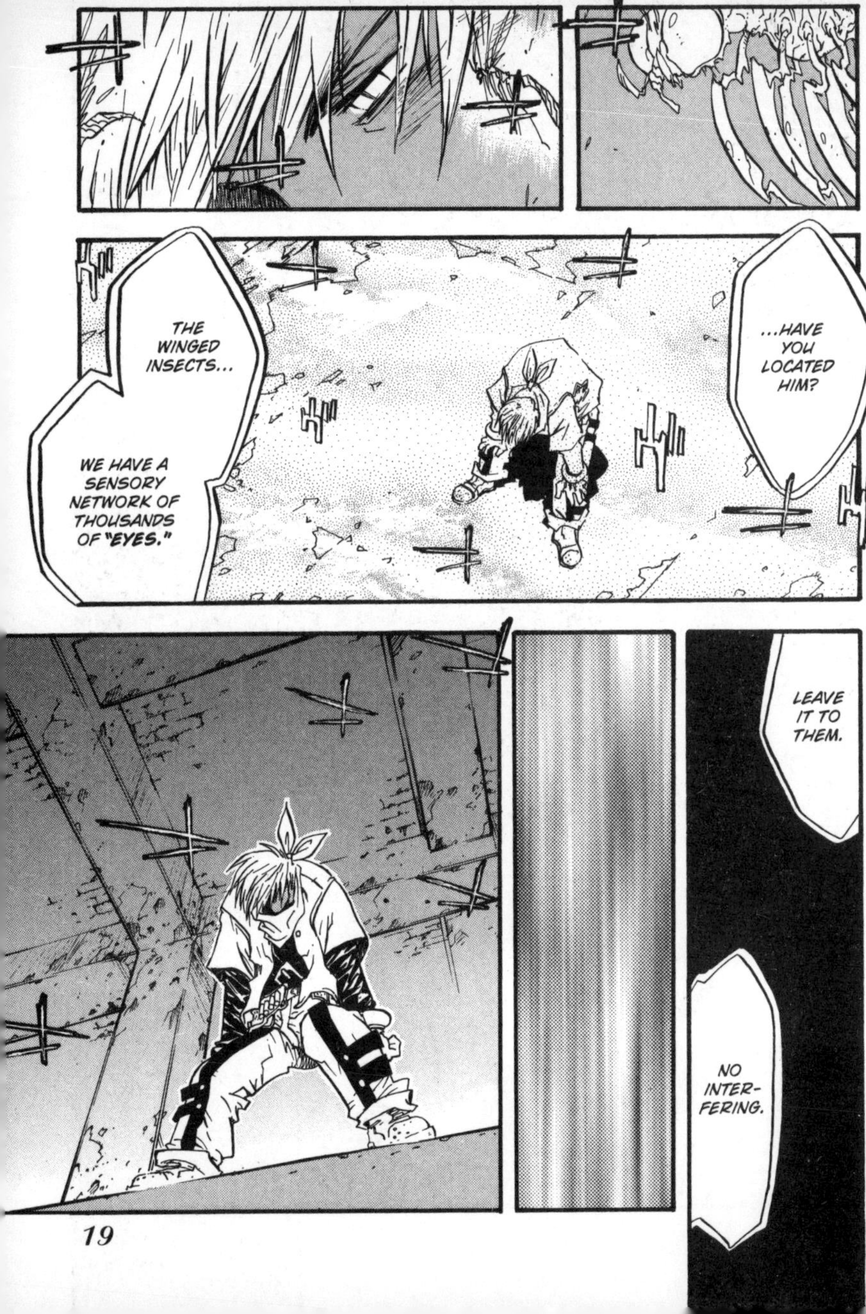
...HAVE YOU LOCATED HIM?
THE WINGED INSECTS...
WE HAVE A SENSORY NETWORK OF THOUSANDS OF "EYES."
LEAVE IT TO THEM.
NO INTER-FERING.

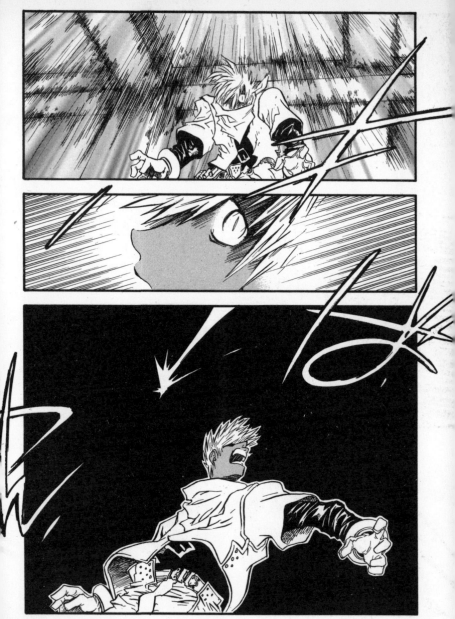

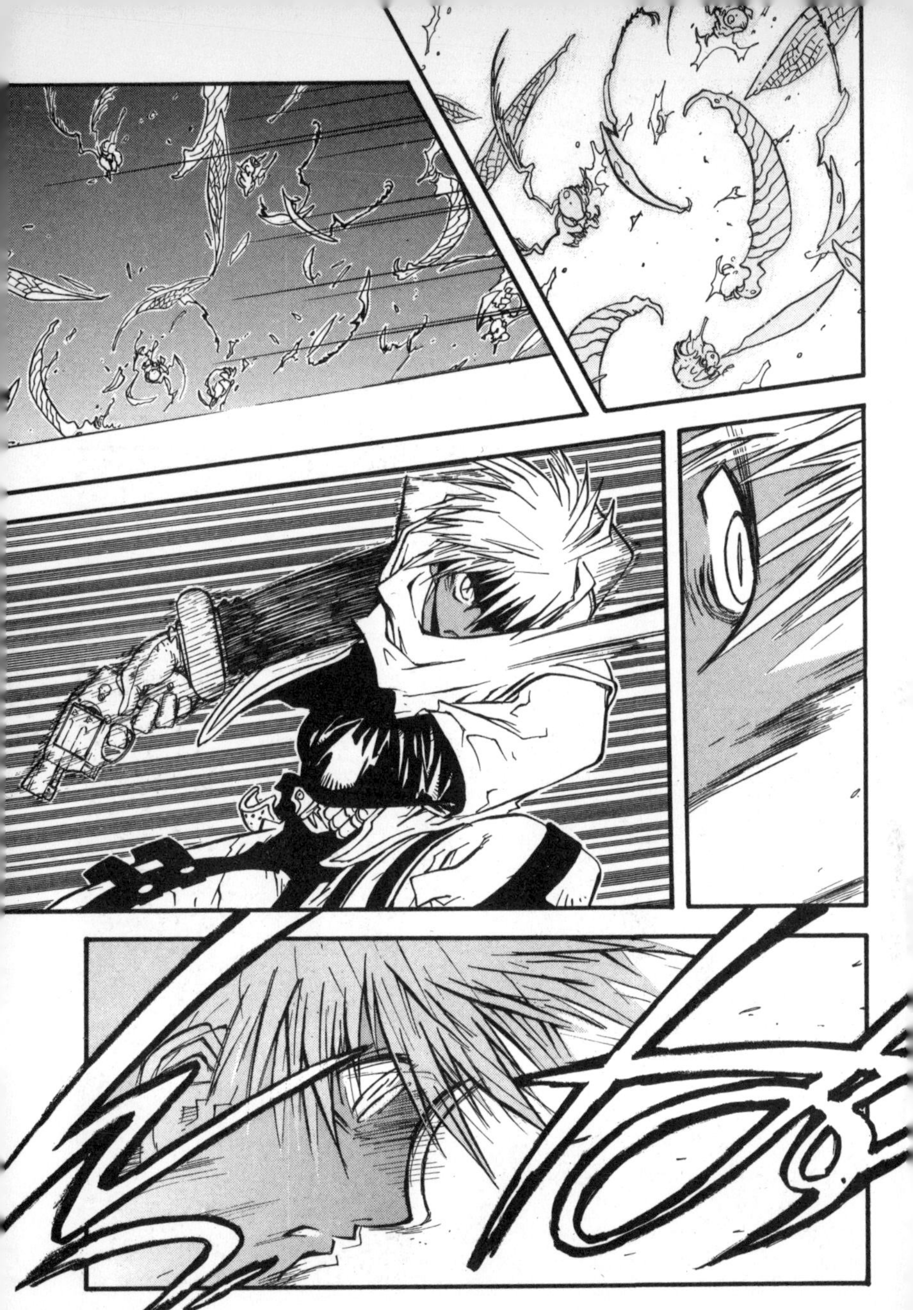

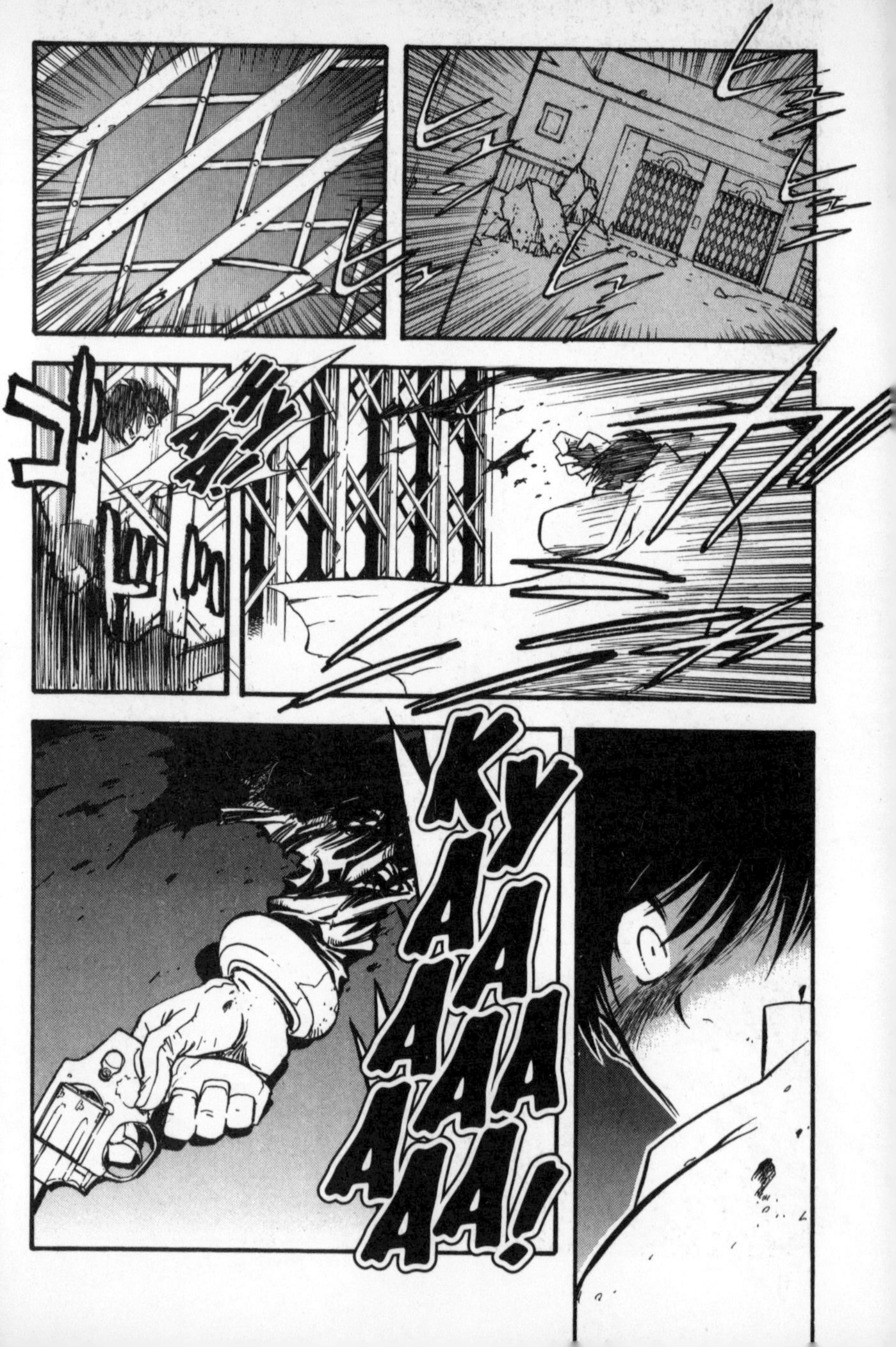
HYAA!
KYAAAAAAAAA!

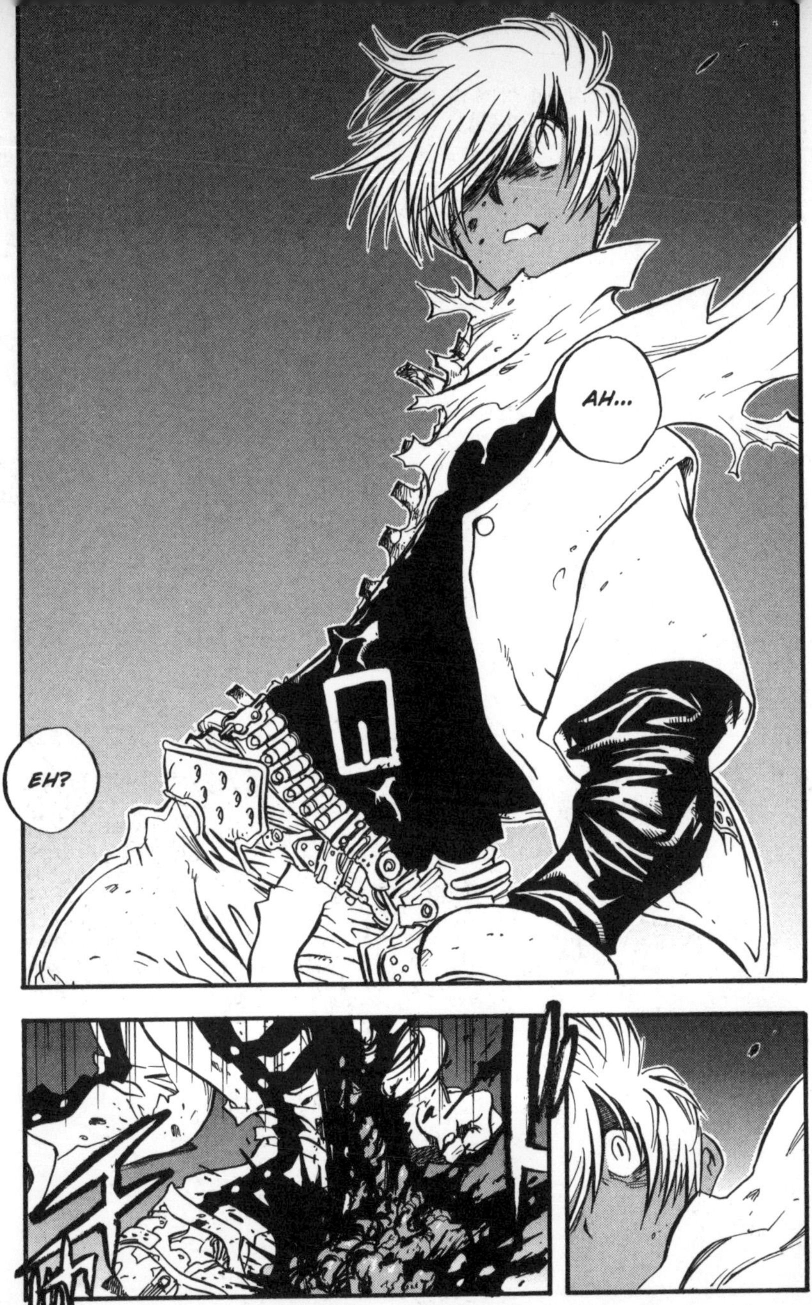
AH...
EH?

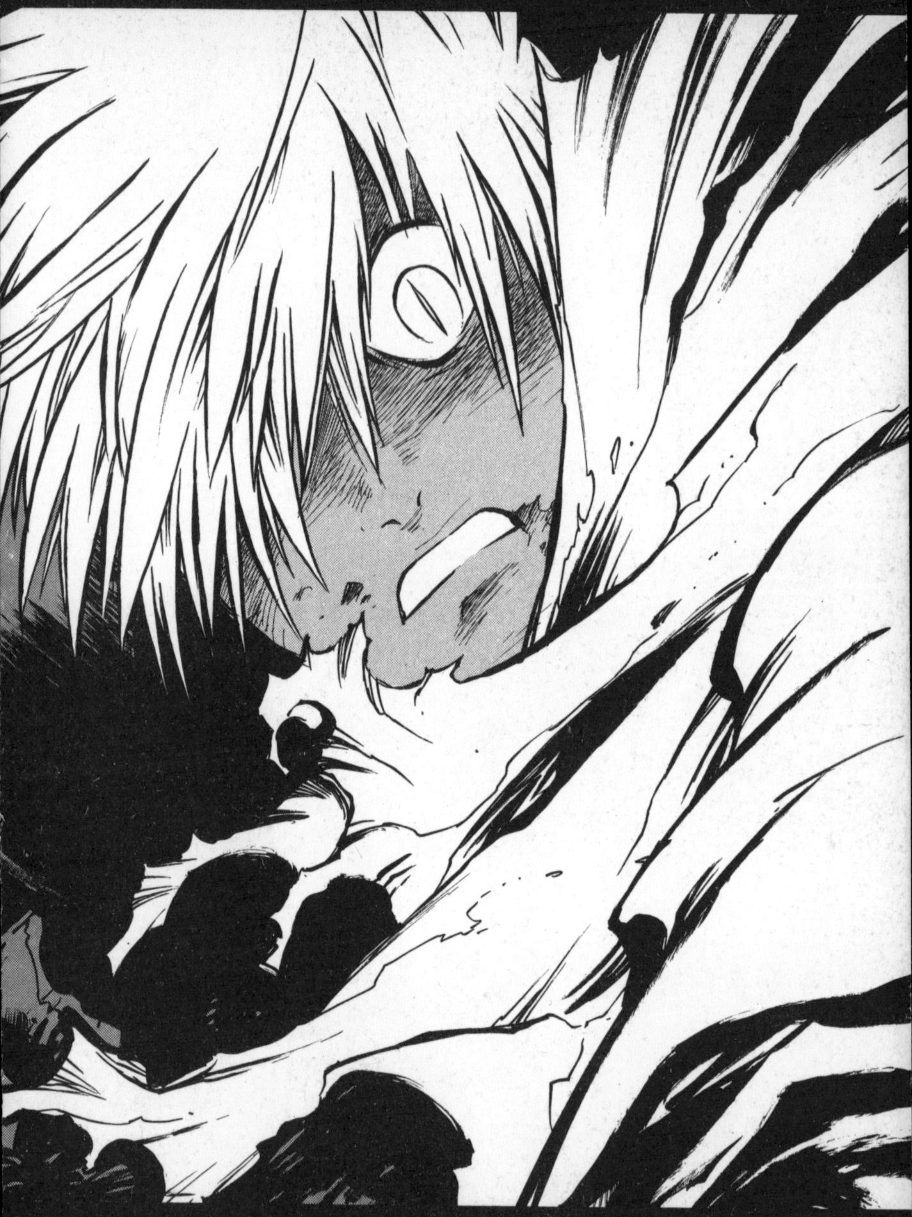

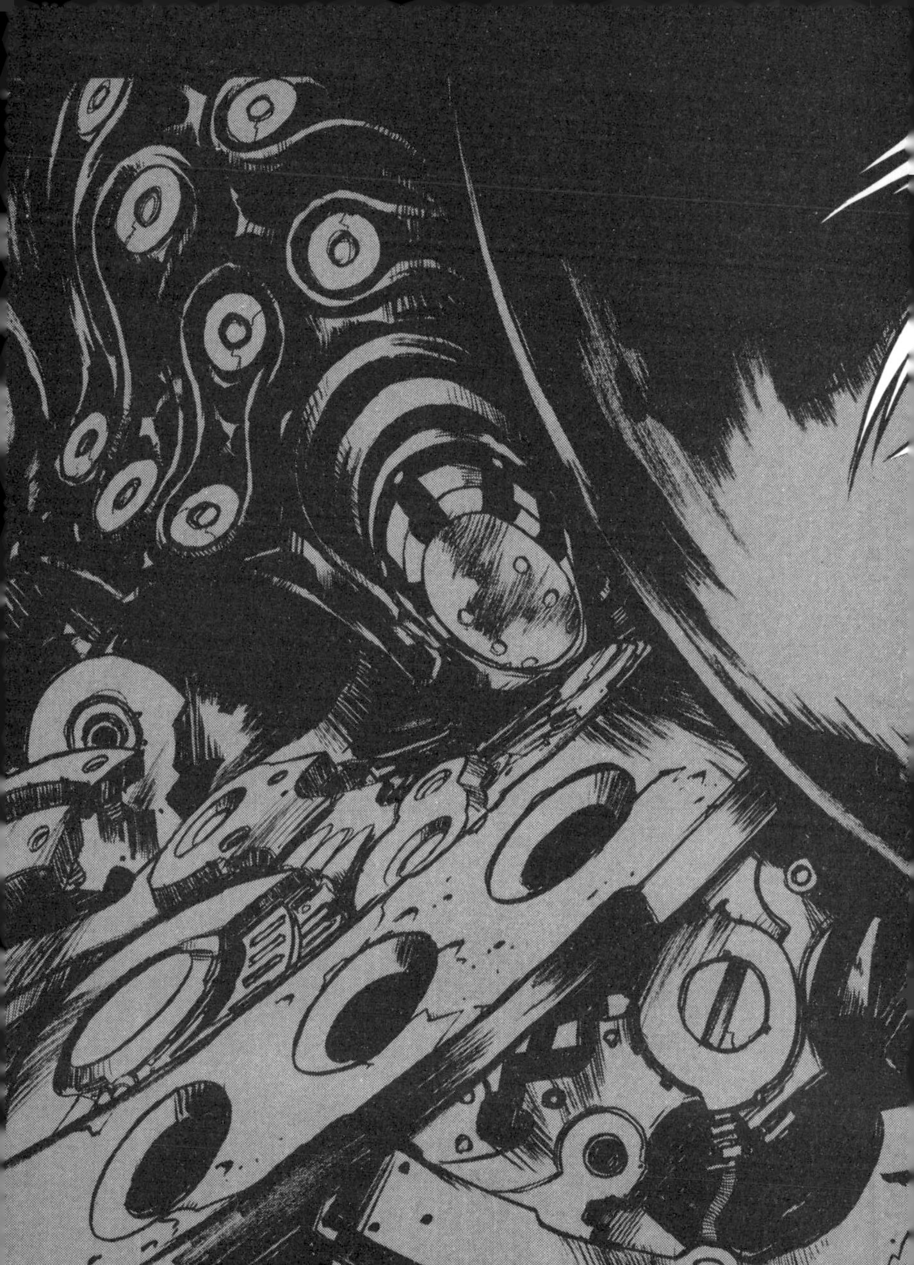

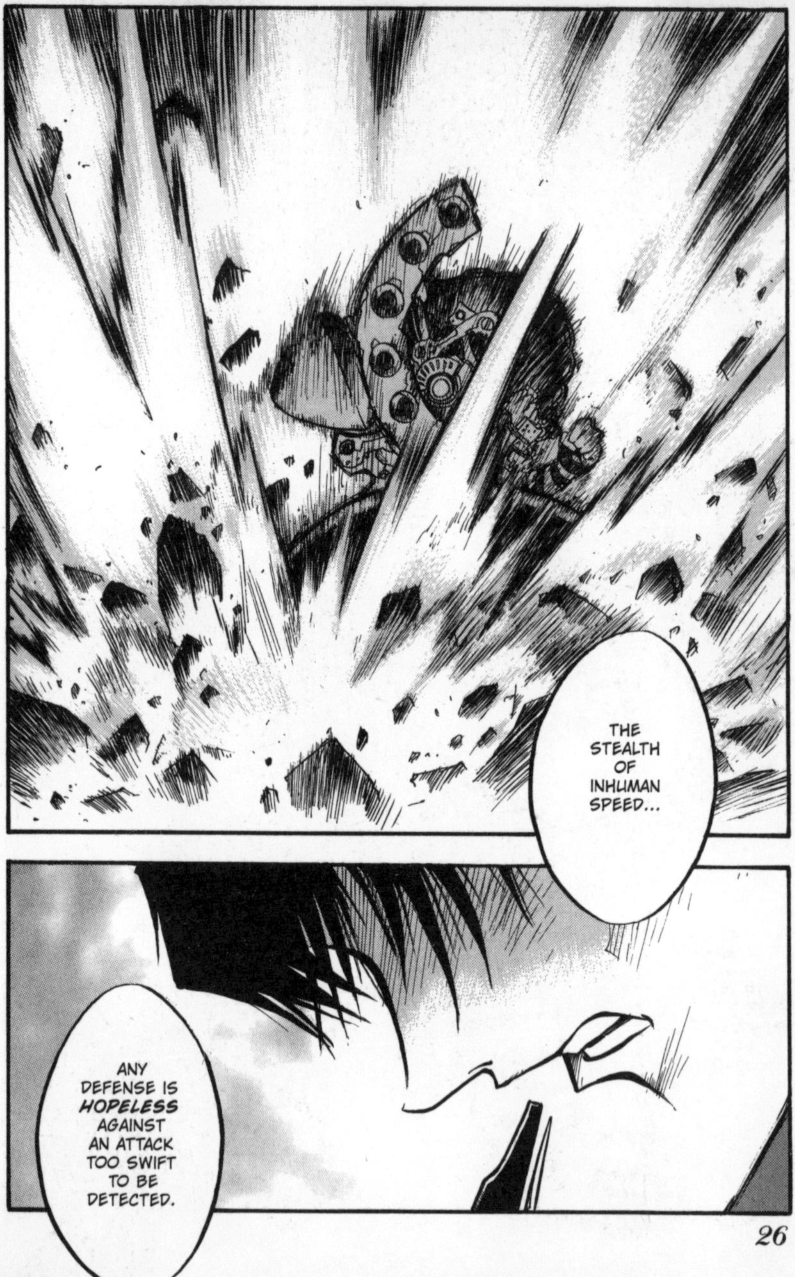
THE STEALTH OF INHUMAN SPEED...
ANY DEFENSE IS ***HOPELESS*** AGAINST AN ATTACK TOO SWIFT TO BE DETECTED.

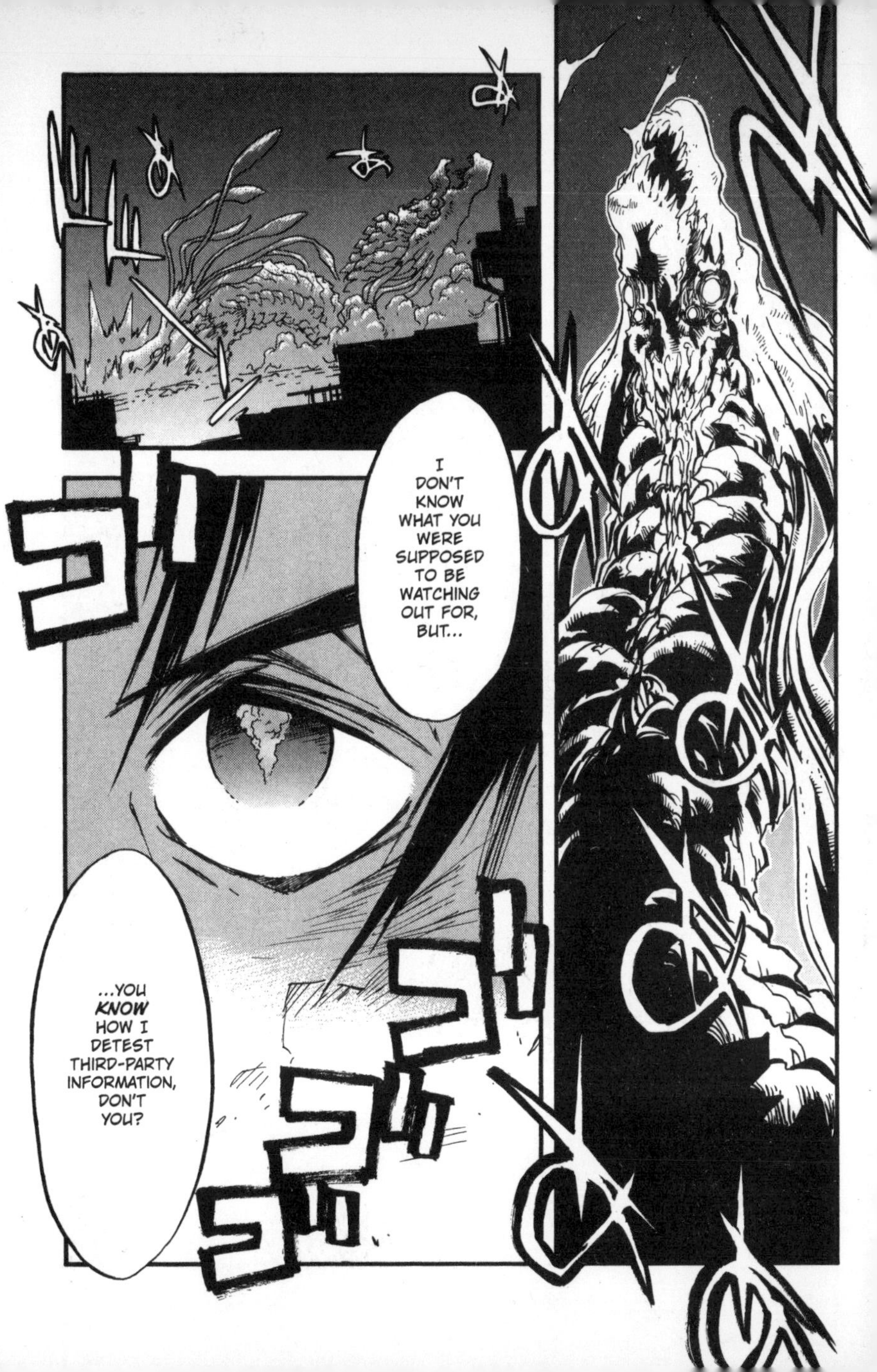
I DON'T KNOW WHAT YOU WERE SUPPOSED TO BE WATCHING OUT FOR, BUT...
...YOU ***KNOW*** HOW I DETEST THIRD-PARTY INFORMATION, DON'T YOU?

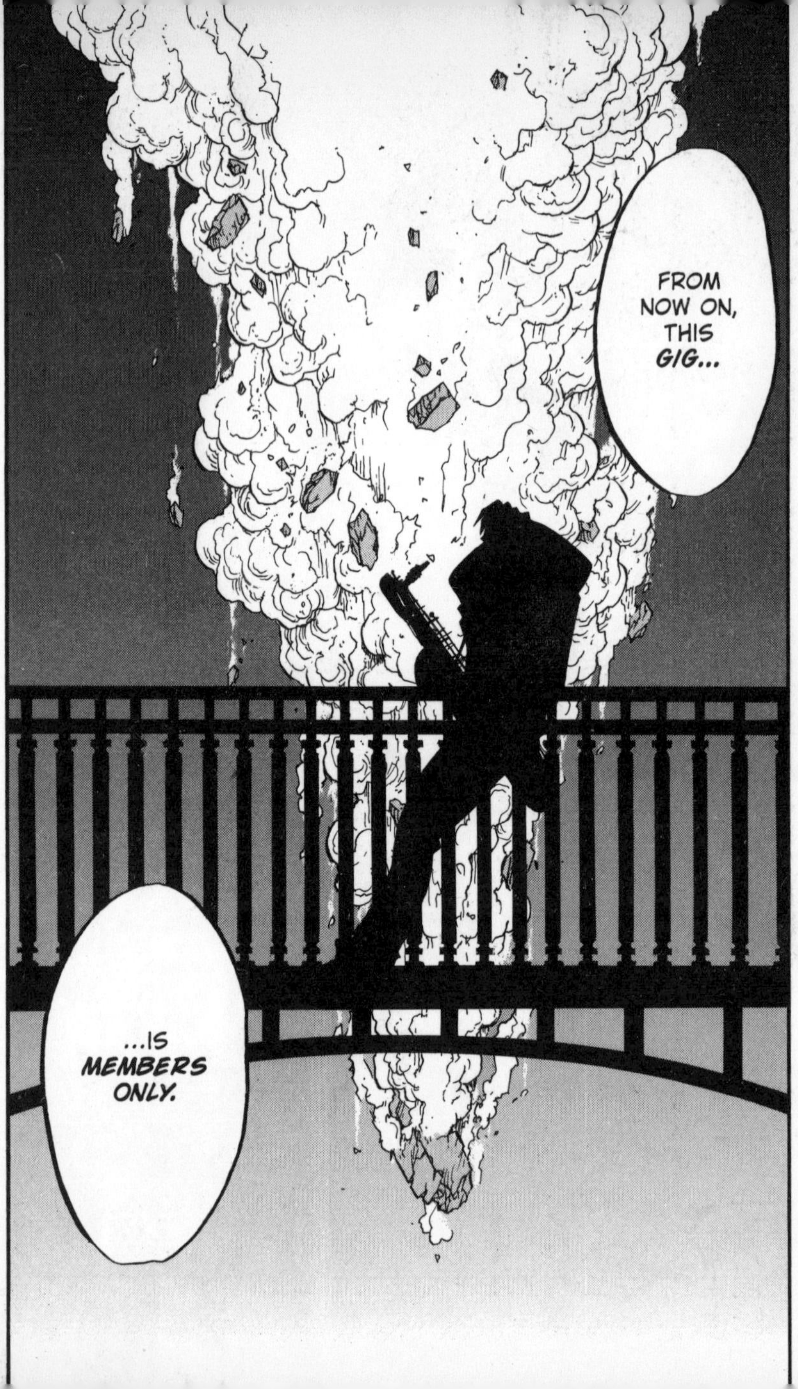
FROM NOW ON, THIS GIG...
...IS MEMBERS ONLY.

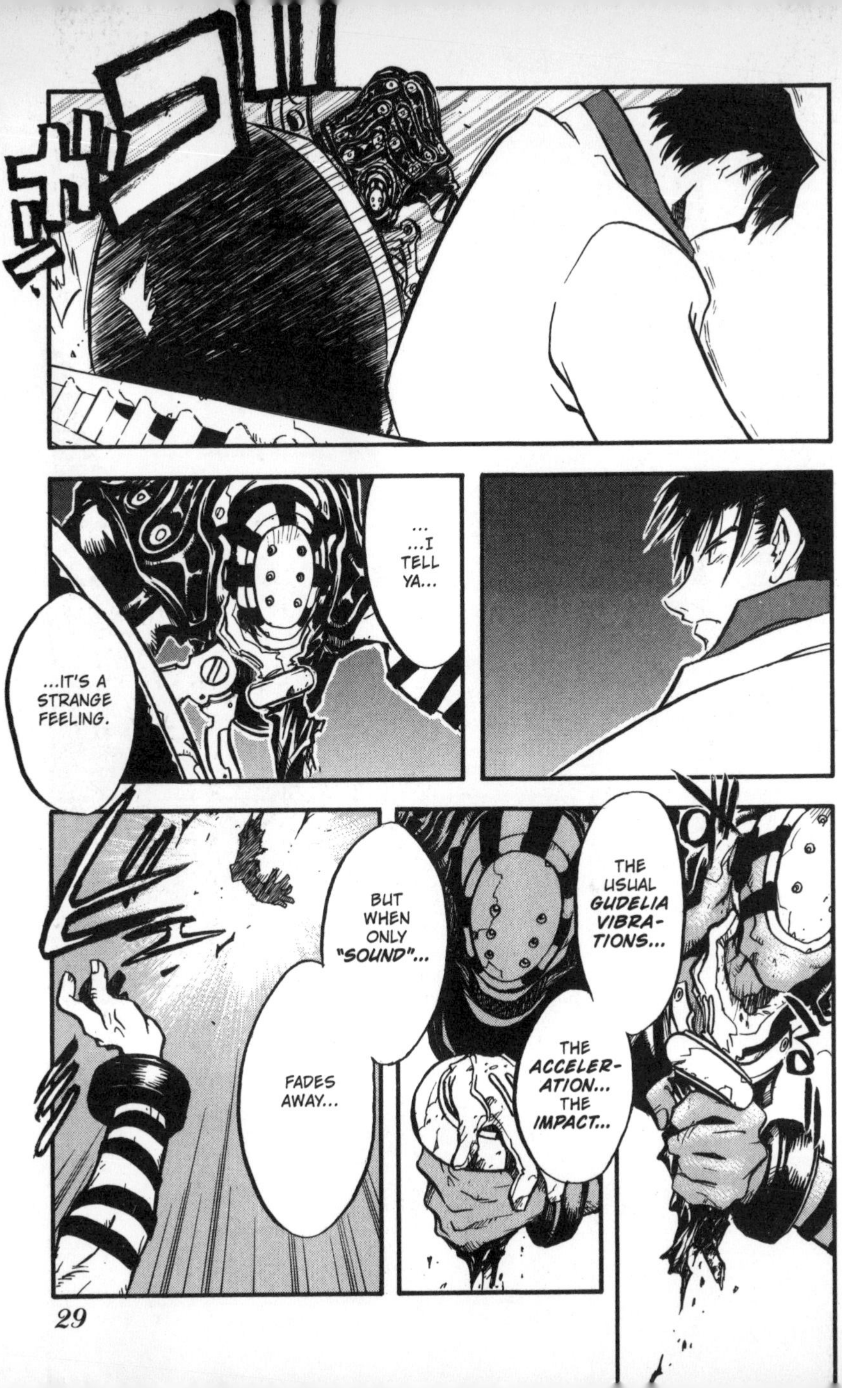
...
...I TELL YA...
...IT'S A STRANGE FEELING.
THE USUAL *GUDELIA VIBRATIONS...*
THE *ACCELERATION...* THE *IMPACT...*
BUT WHEN ONLY *"SOUND"...*
FADES AWAY...

IT'S A SIMPLE THEORY.
EVEN THE LOUDEST NOISE IS A VIBRATION OF THE AIR--
A *WAVE.*
IF IT IS MET WITH A WAVE OF PRECISELY THE OPPOSITE PHASE, IT WILL BE *COMPLETELY* NEUTRALIZED.
IN A GOOD *TUG-OF-WAR* MATCH...
...THE CENTER HARDLY BUDGES.
THIS IS THE SAME.
DON'T DIS-MISS IT SO EASI-LY...
IT'S REALLY NOT THAT SIMPLE, IS IT? HOW MANY SOUNDS DO YOU THINK **ARE** IN THIS BUILDING?
ECHOES... RESO-NANCE... IT'S FULL OF NOISE.
TO FILTER THROUGH ALL THAT INTERFER-ENCE...

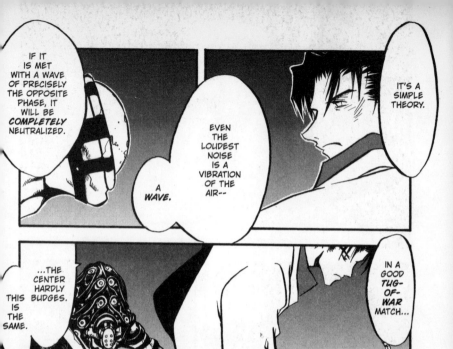

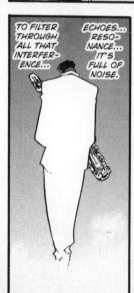

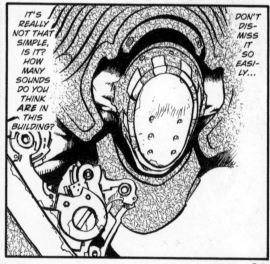

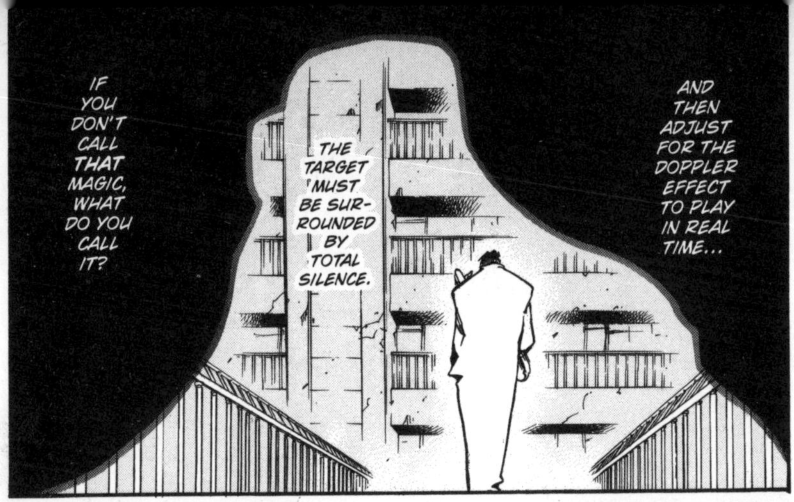
AND THEN ADJUST FOR THE DOPPLER EFFECT TO PLAY IN REAL TIME...
THE TARGET MUST BE SUR-ROUNDED BY TOTAL SILENCE.
IF YOU DON'T CALL THAT MAGIC, WHAT DO YOU CALL IT?
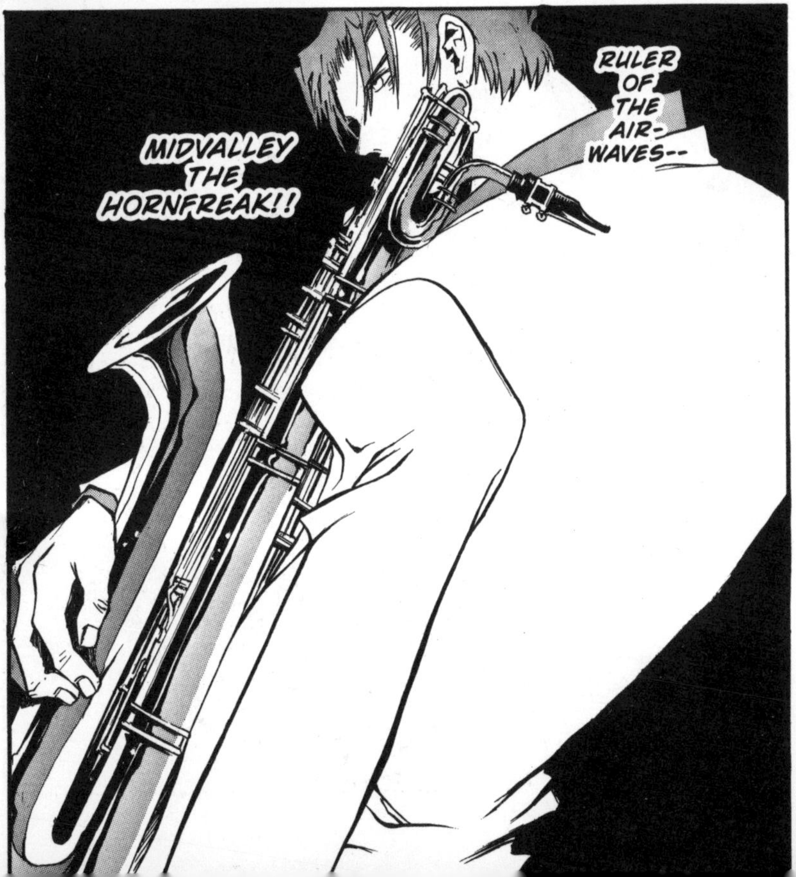
RULER OF THE AIR-WAVES--
MIDVALLEY THE HORNFREAK!!

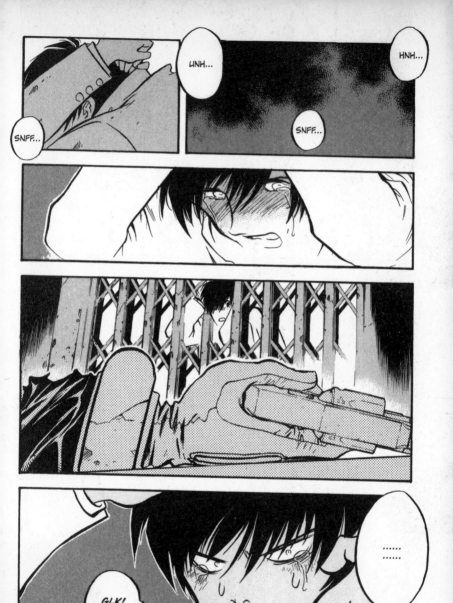

#1. THE CITY. AND THEN THE BANQUET OF THE DOGS / END

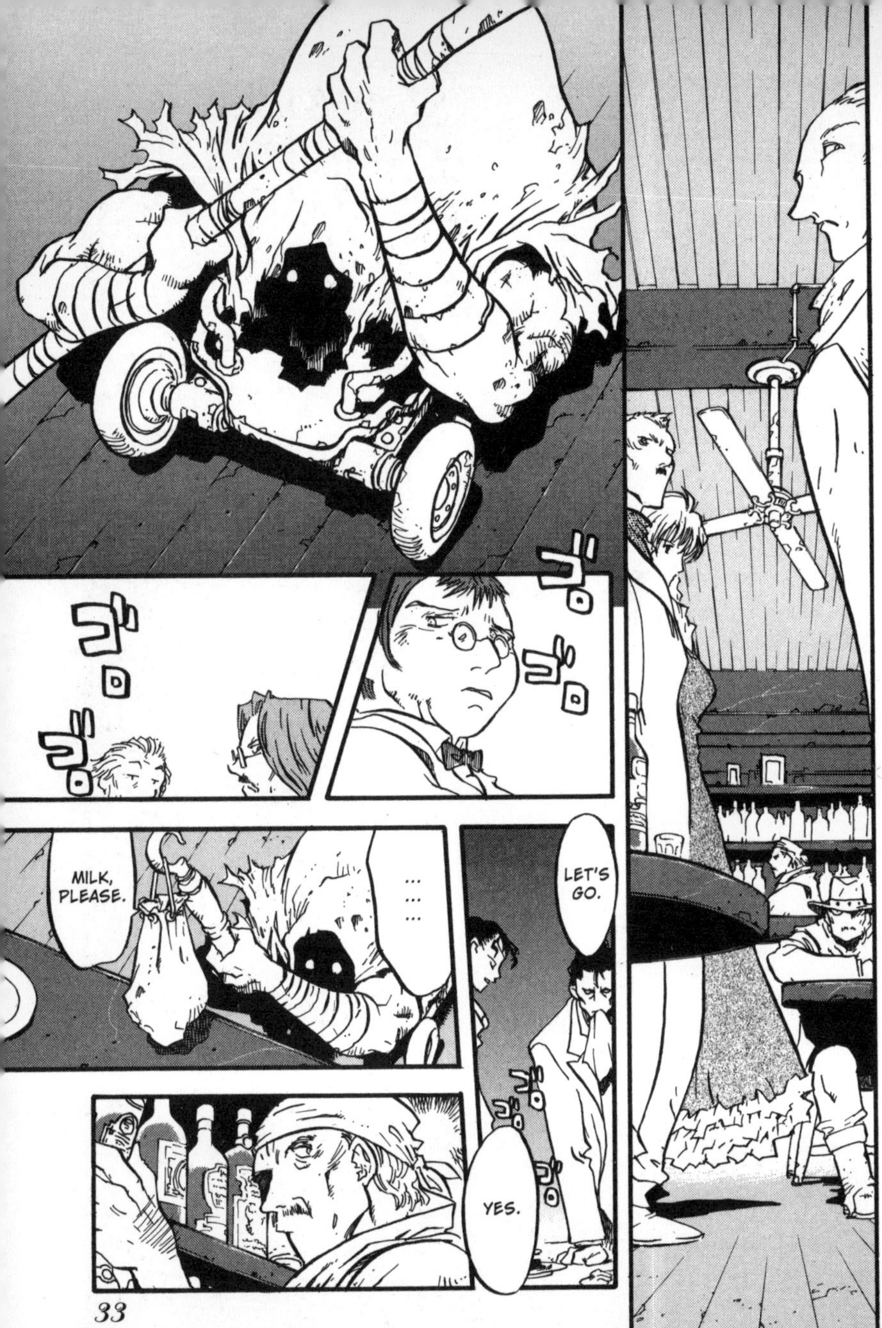
ゴロ
ゴロ
ゴロ
ゴロ
LET'S GO.
ゴロ
ゴロ
ゴロ
YES.
...
...
...
MILK, PLEASE.

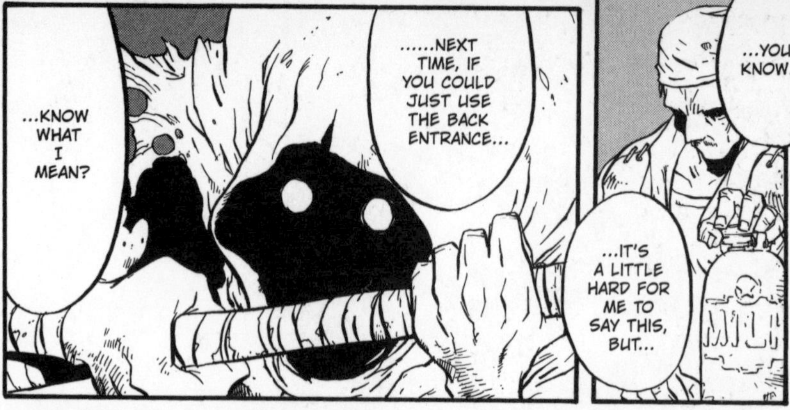
...YOU KNOW...
...IT'S A LITTLE HARD FOR ME TO SAY THIS, BUT...
......NEXT TIME, IF YOU COULD JUST USE THE BACK ENTRANCE...
...KNOW WHAT I MEAN?

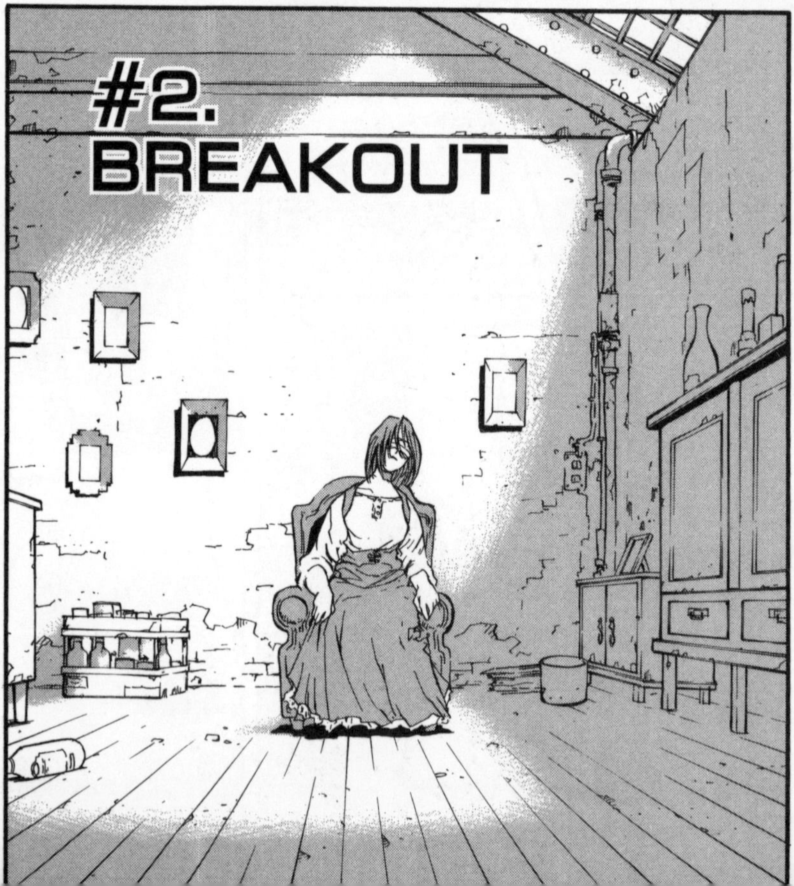
#2. BREAKOUT

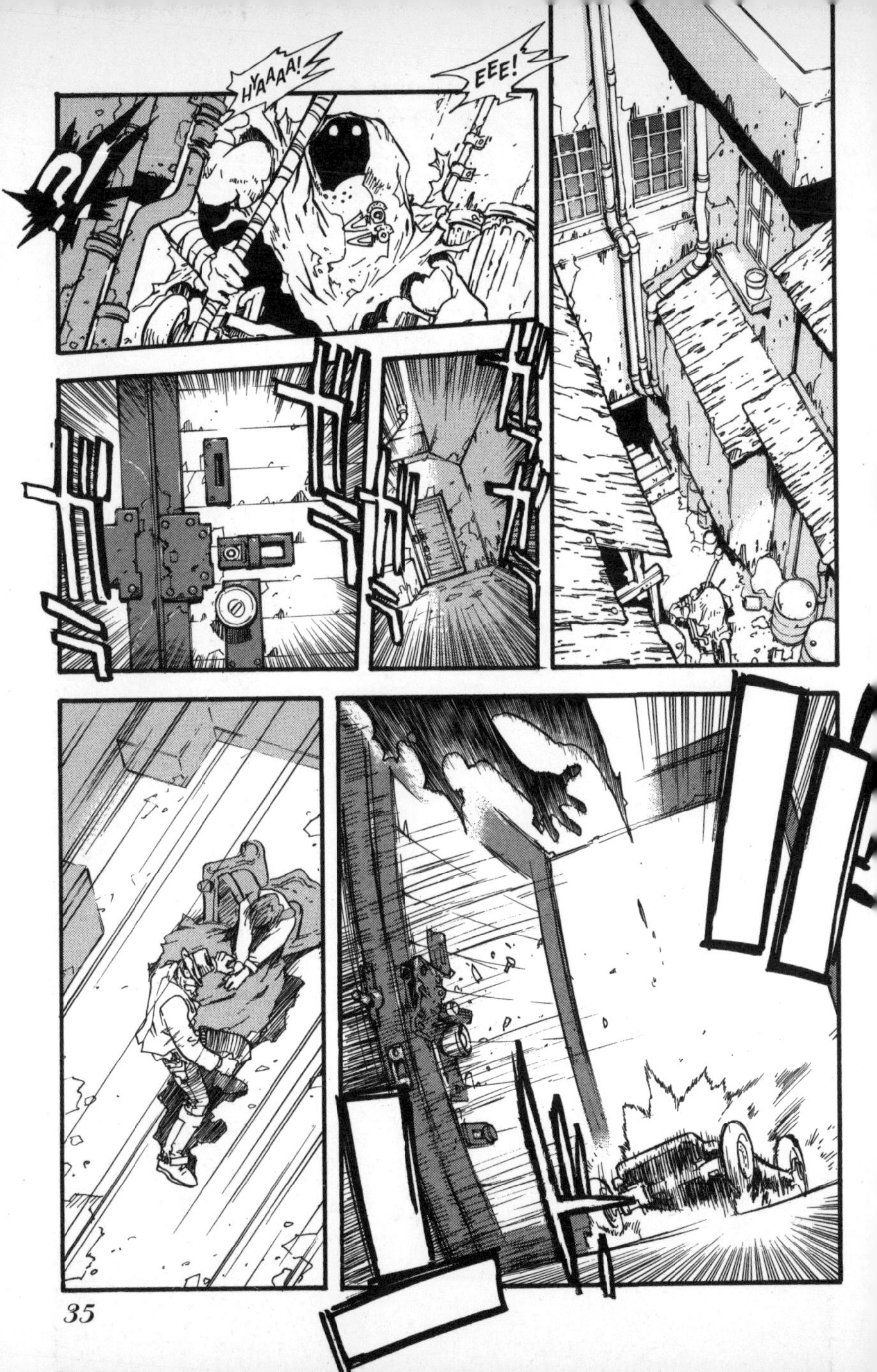
EEE!
HYAAAA!
?!

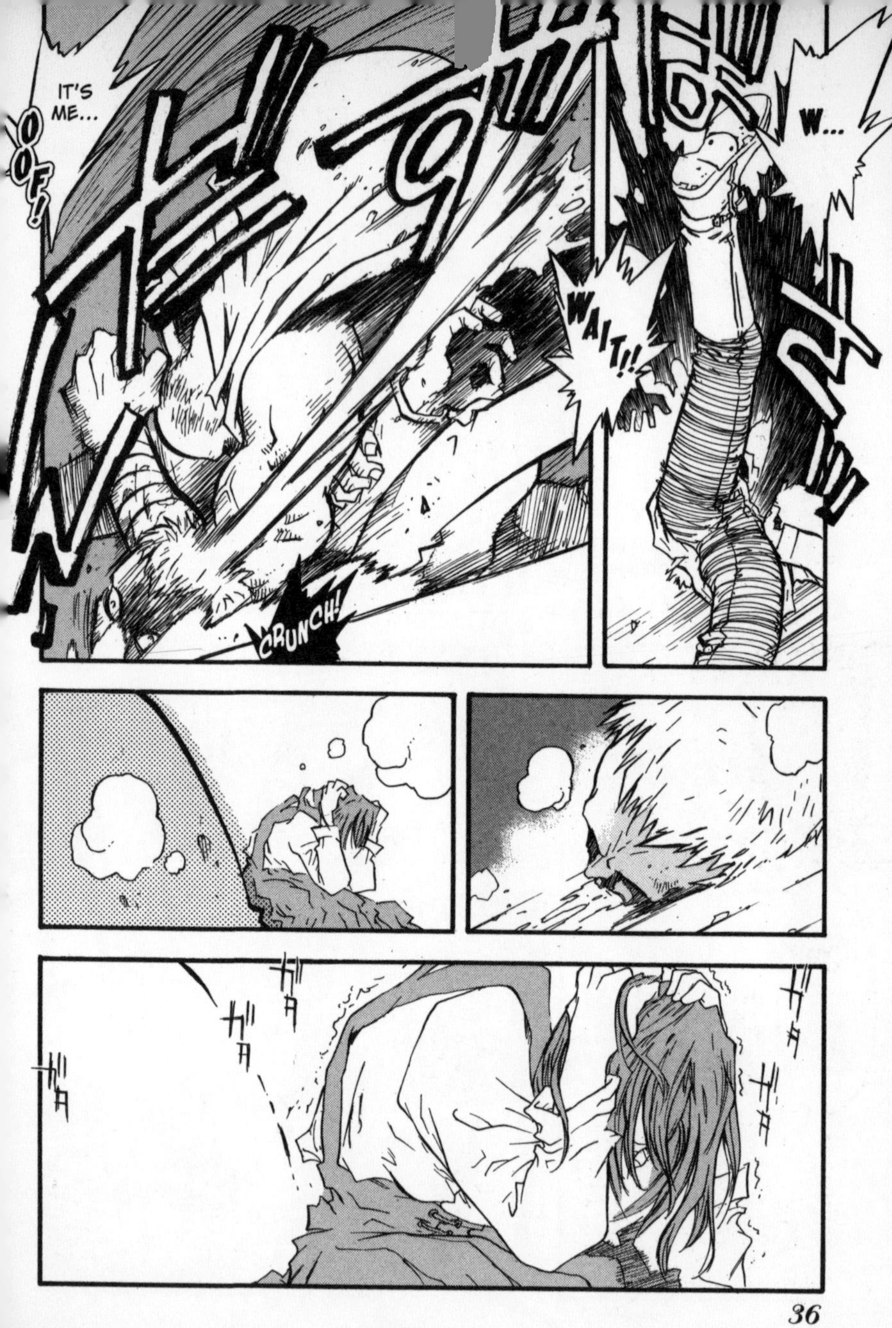
W...
WAIT!!
IT'S ME...
OOF!
CRUNCH!
ガタ
ガタ
ガタ
ガタ
ガタ
ガタ

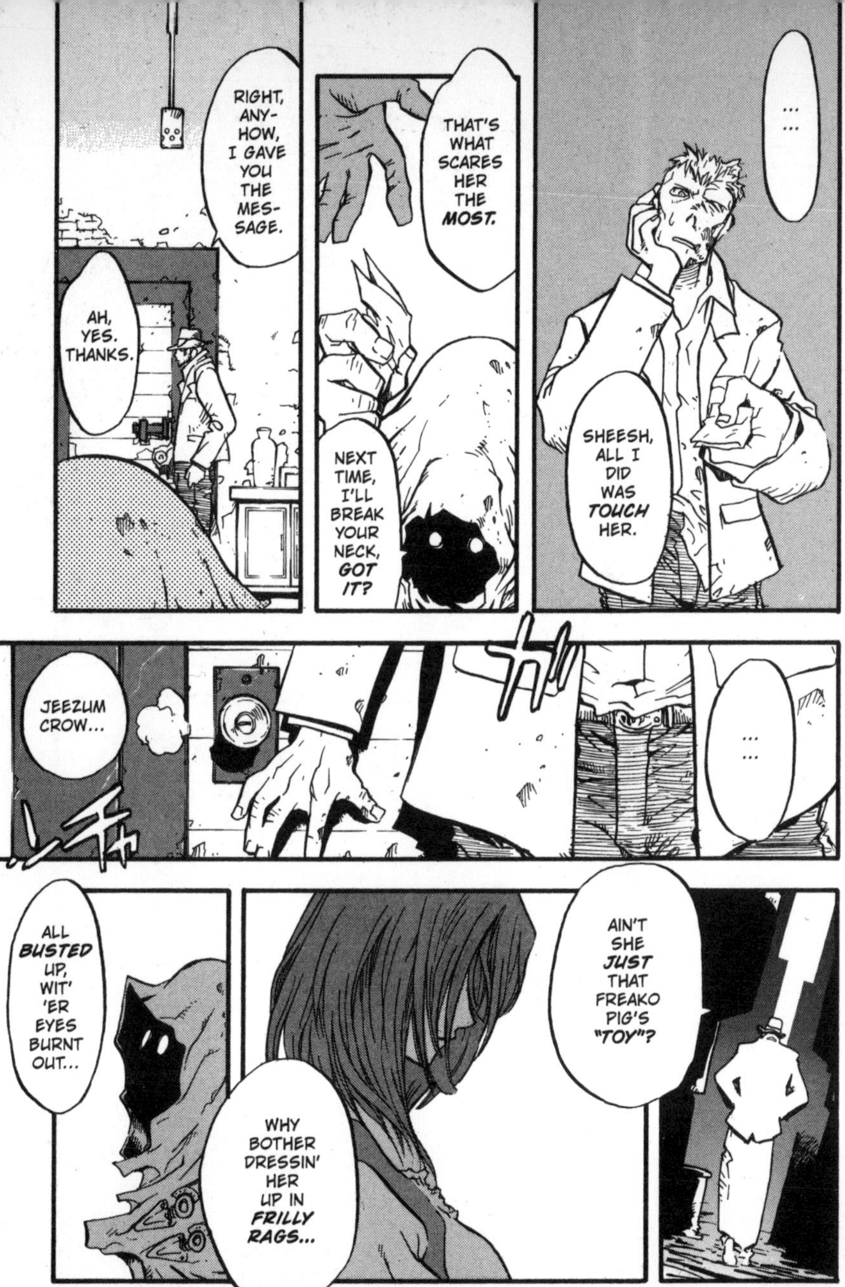
……
SHEESH, ALL I DID WAS *TOUCH* HER.
THAT'S WHAT SCARES HER THE *MOST.*
NEXT TIME, I'LL BREAK YOUR NECK, *GOT IT?*
RIGHT, ANYHOW, I GAVE YOU THE MESSAGE.
AH, YES. THANKS.
……
JEEZUM CROW...
AIN'T SHE *JUST* THAT FREAKO PIG'S *"TOY"?*
WHY BOTHER DRESSIN' HER UP IN *FRILLY RAGS...*
ALL *BUSTED* UP, WIT' 'ER EYES BURNT OUT...

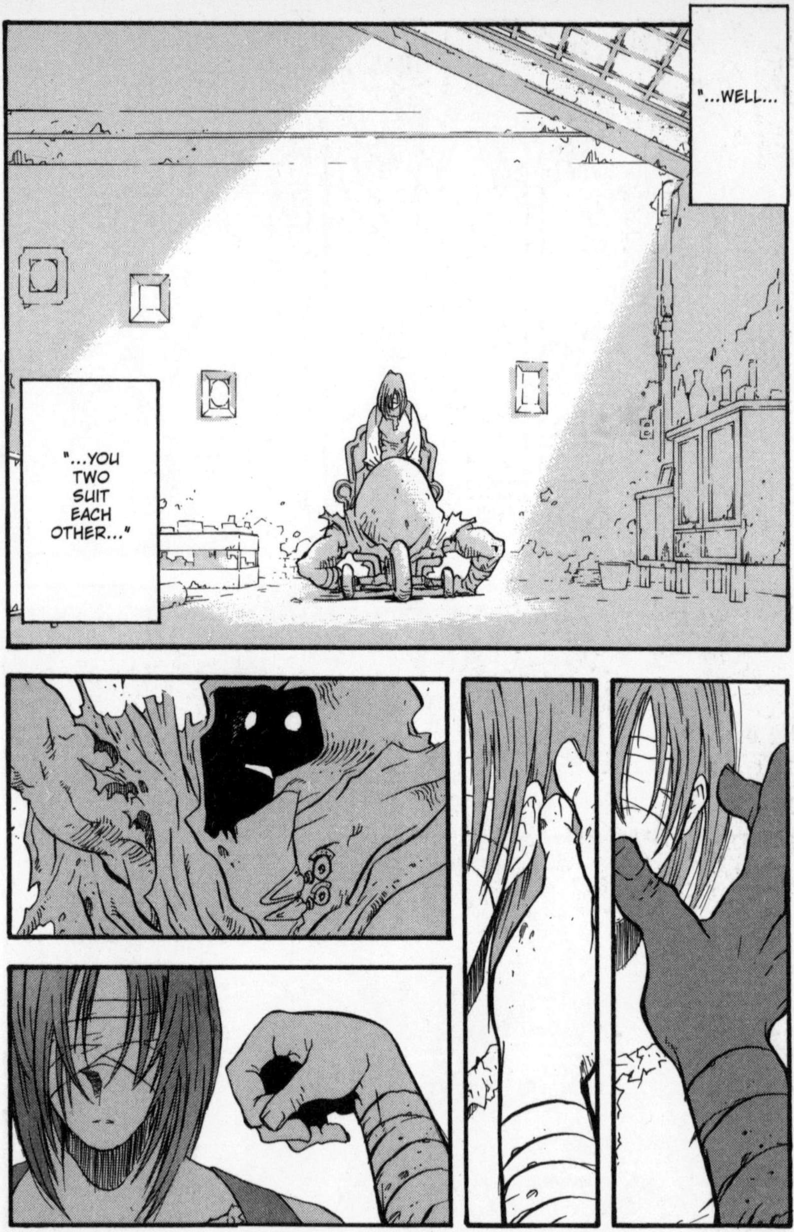
"...WELL...
"...YOU TWO SUIT EACH OTHER..."

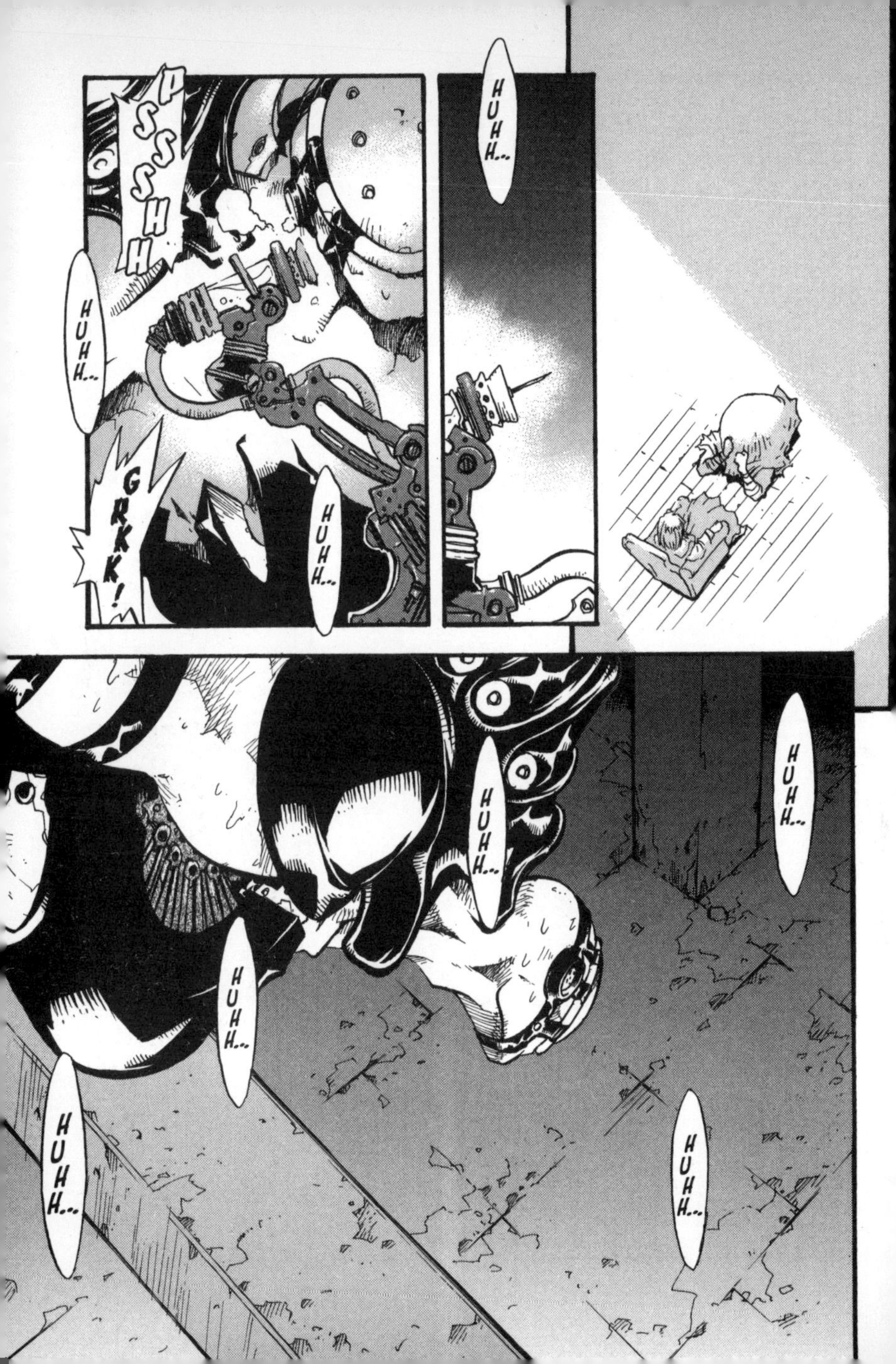
HUHH...
PSSSHH
HUHH...
GRKK!
HUHH...
HUHH...
HUHH...
HUHH...
HUHH...
HUHH...

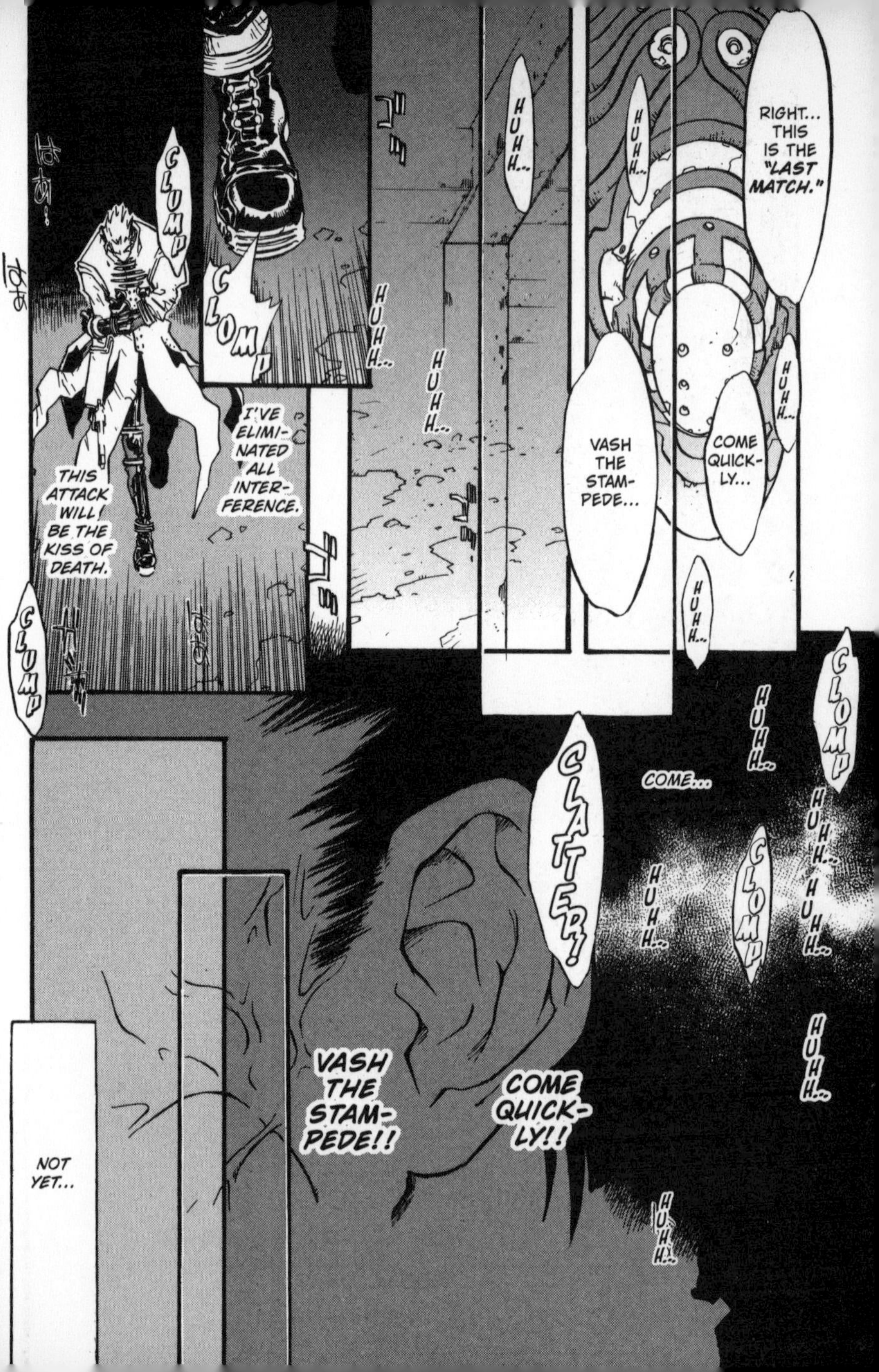

RIGHT... THIS IS THE "LAST MATCH."
HUHH...
HUHH...
COME QUICKLY...
VASH THE STAMPEDE...
HUHH...
HUHH...
HUHH...
HUHH...
HUHH...
CLOMP
CLUMP
I'VE ELIMINATED ALL INTERFERENCE.
THIS ATTACK WILL BE THE KISS OF DEATH.
CLUMP
CLOMP
HUHH...
COME...
HUHH... HUHH... HUHH...
CLOMP
HUHH...
HUHH...
CLATTER!
HUHH...
COME QUICKLY!!
VASH THE STAMPEDE!!
NOT YET...

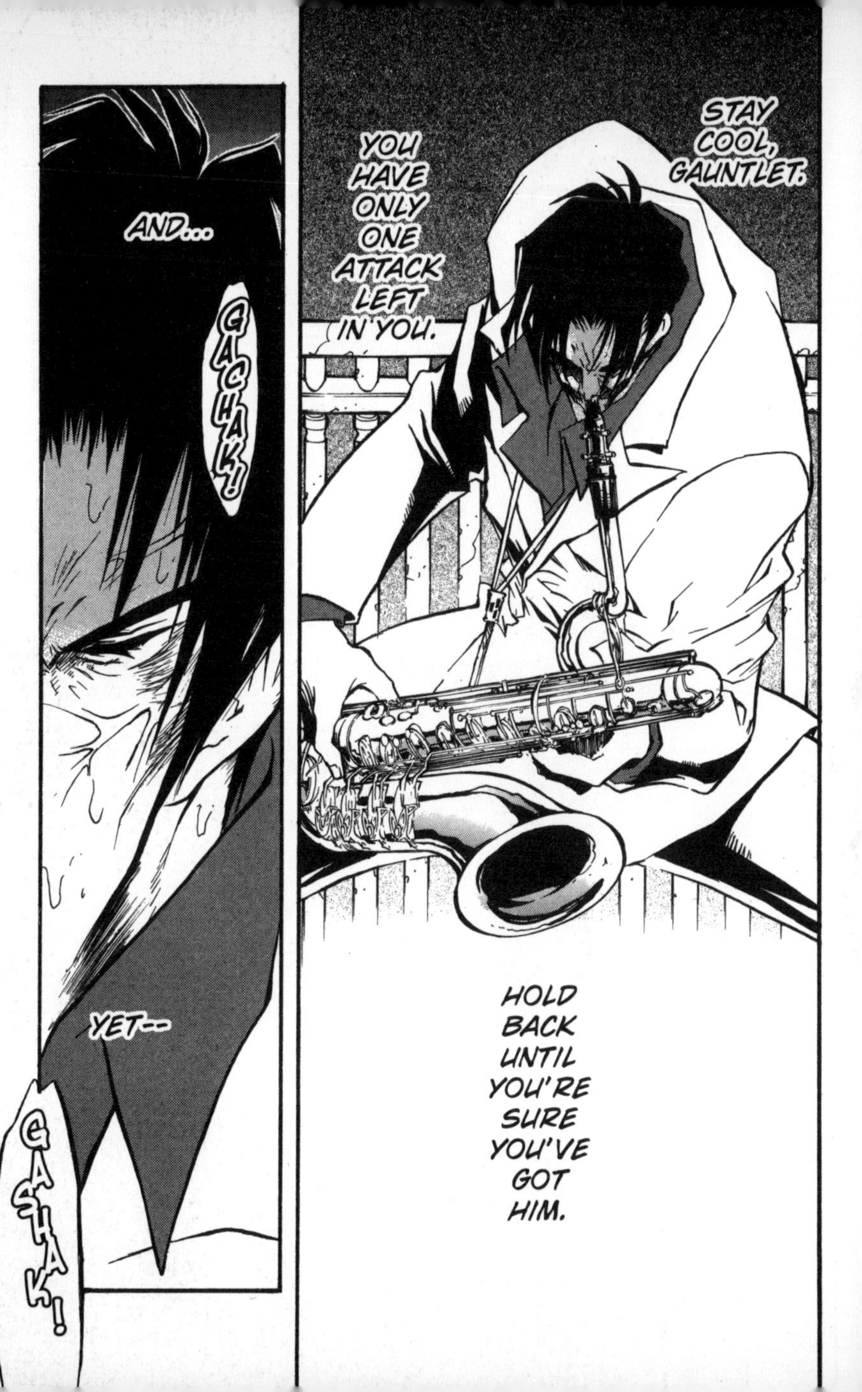
STAY COOL, GAUNTLET.
YOU HAVE ONLY ONE ATTACK LEFT IN YOU.
HOLD BACK UNTIL YOU'RE SURE YOU'VE GOT HIM.
AND...
GACHAK!
YET--
GASHAK!

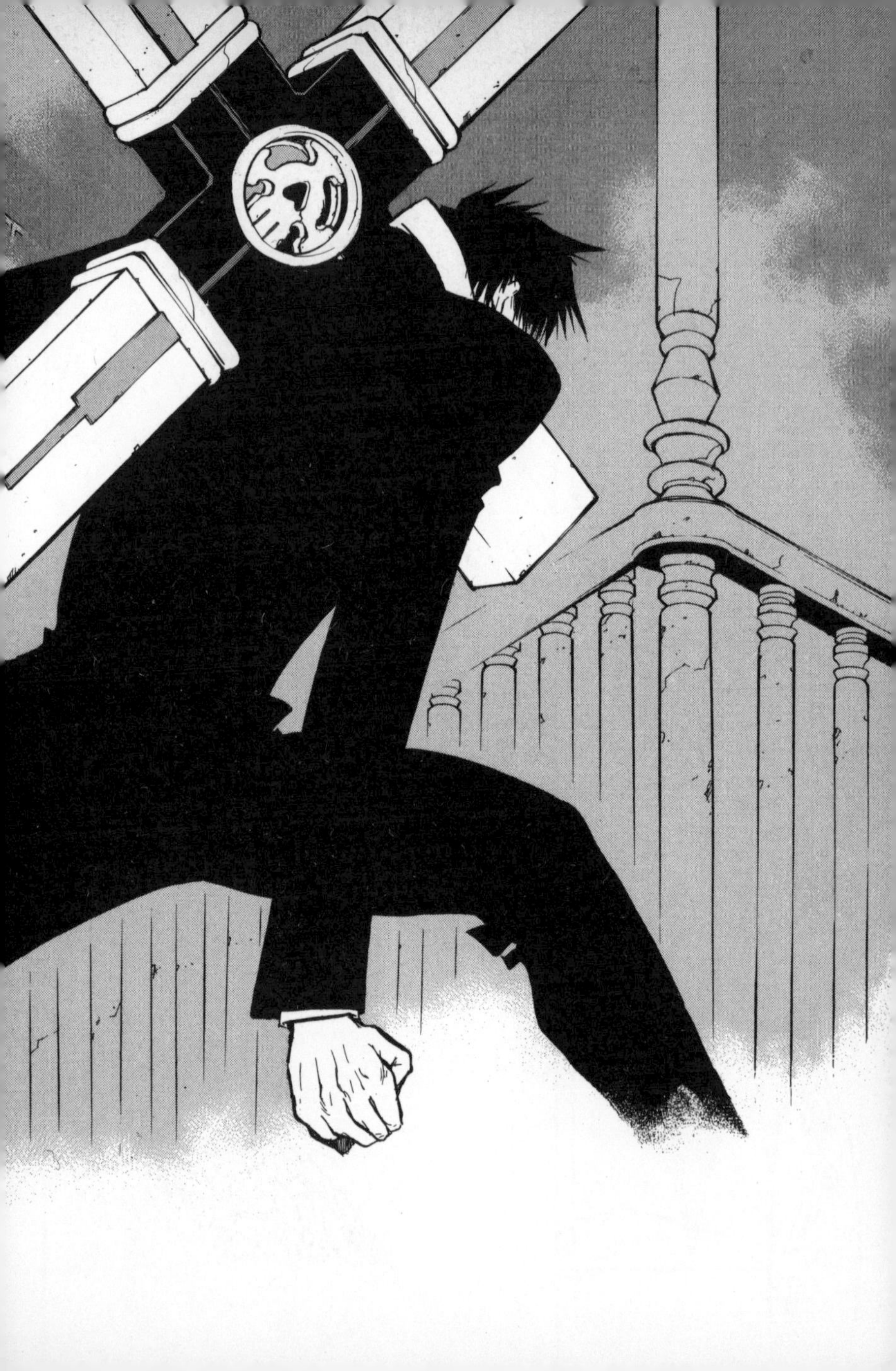

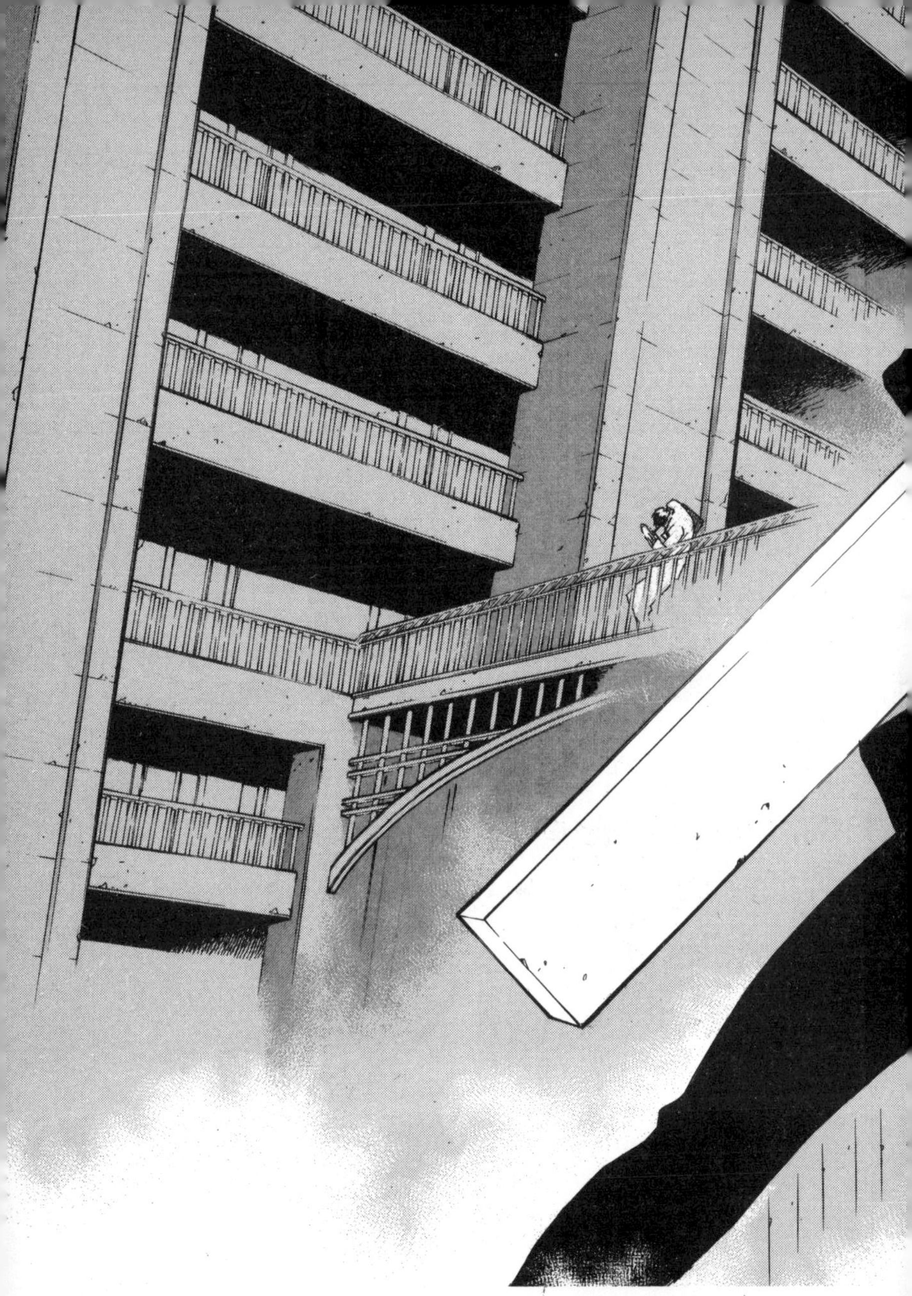

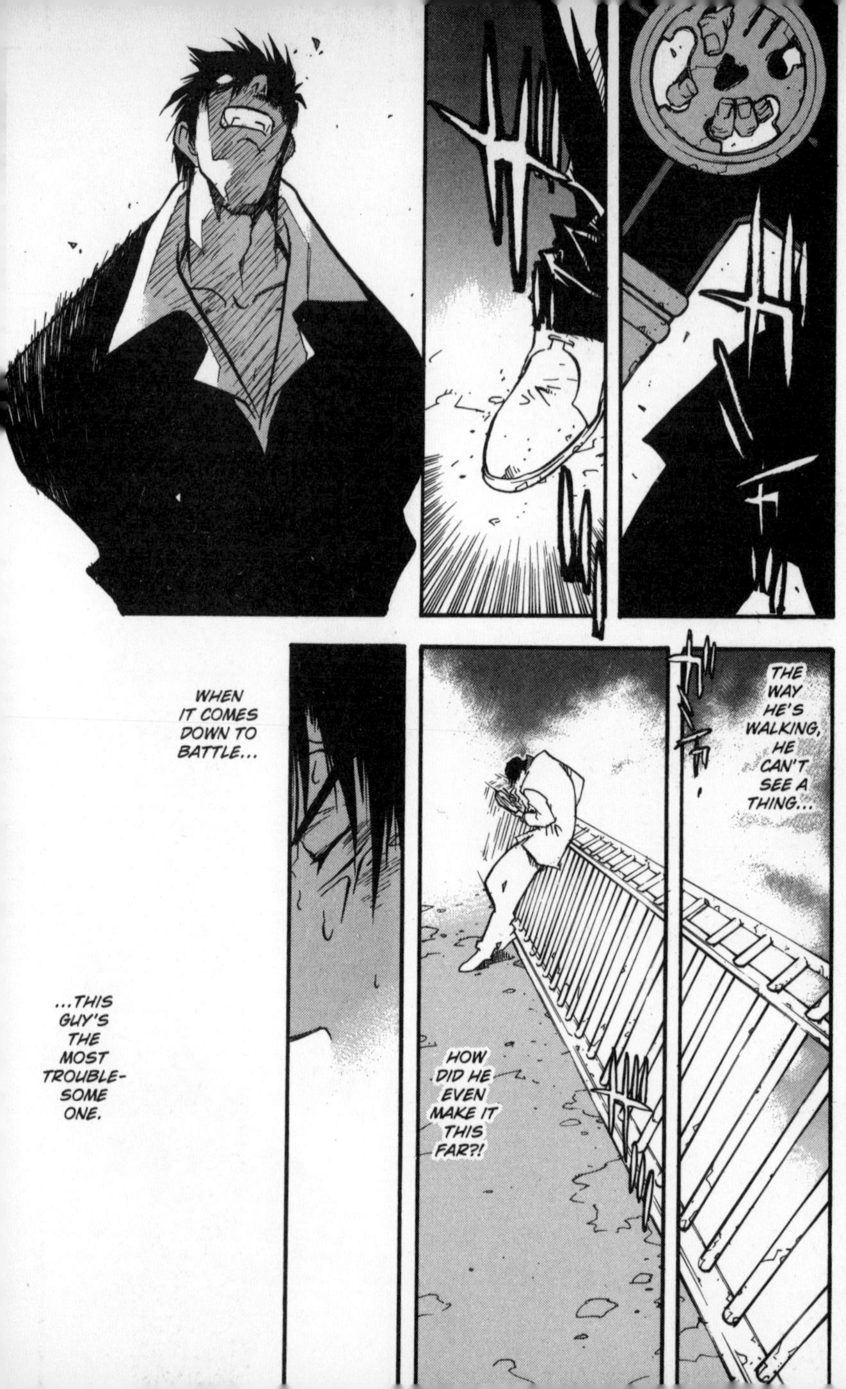
THE WAY HE'S WALKING, HE CAN'T SEE A THING...
HOW DID HE EVEN MAKE IT THIS FAR?!
WHEN IT COMES DOWN TO BATTLE...
...THIS GUY'S THE MOST TROUBLE-SOME ONE.

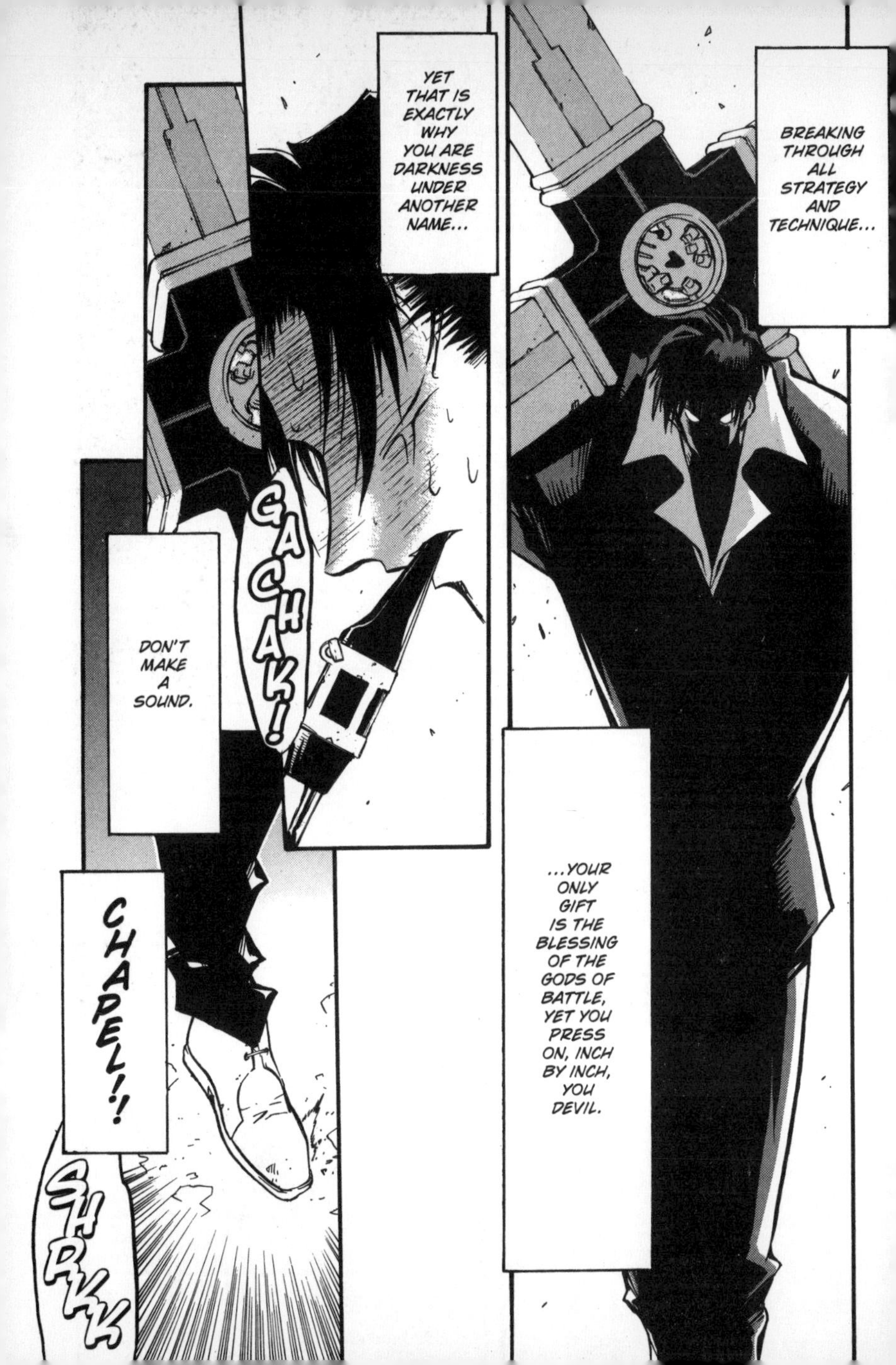
BREAKING THROUGH ALL STRATEGY AND TECHNIQUE...
...YOUR ONLY GIFT IS THE BLESSING OF THE GODS OF BATTLE, YET YOU PRESS ON, INCH BY INCH, YOU DEVIL.
YET THAT IS EXACTLY WHY YOU ARE DARKNESS UNDER ANOTHER NAME...
GACHAK!
DON'T MAKE A SOUND.
CHAPEL!!
SHRKK

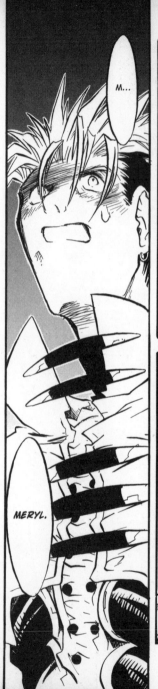

M...

MERYL.

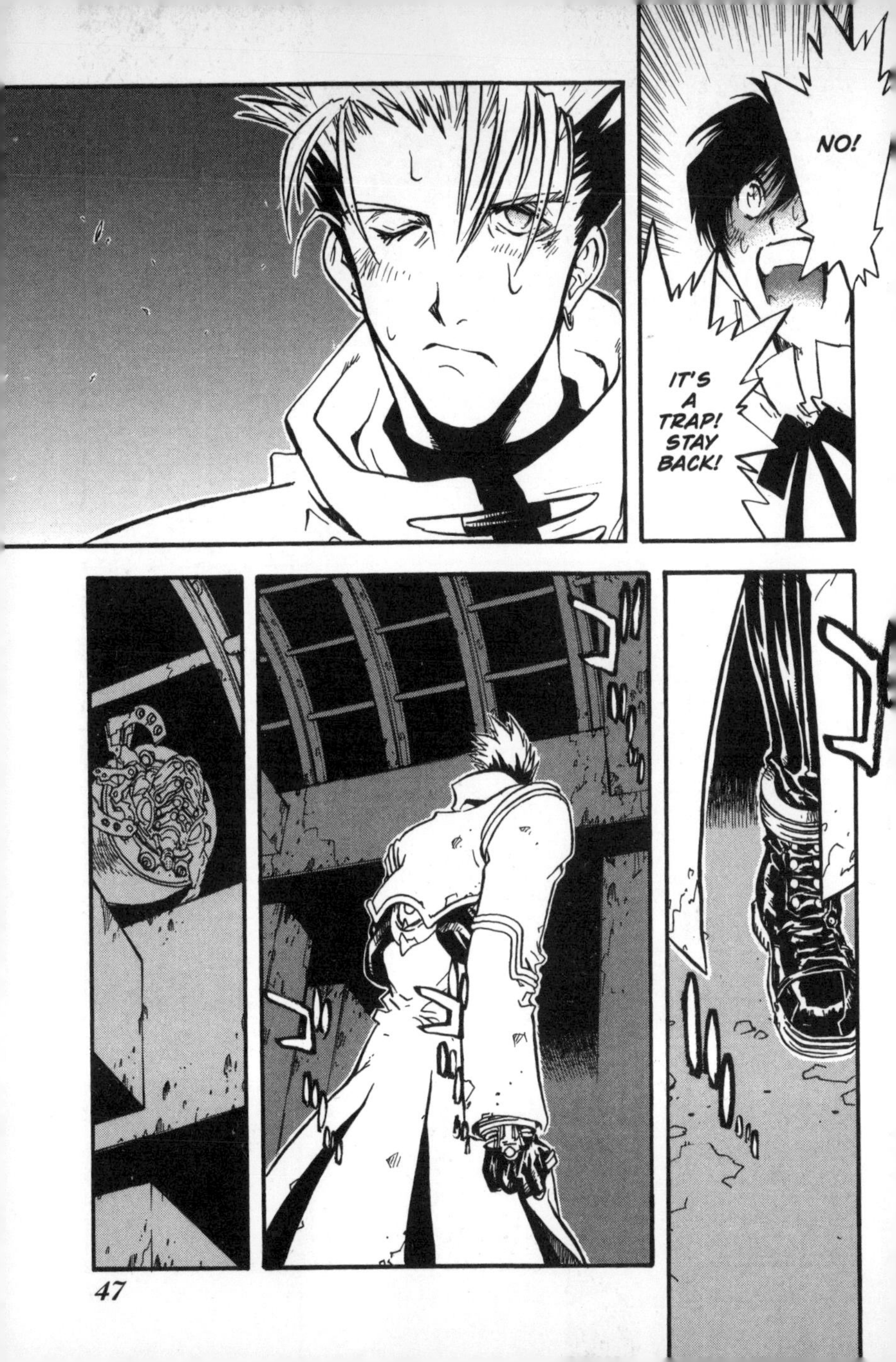
NO!
IT'S A TRAP! STAY BACK!

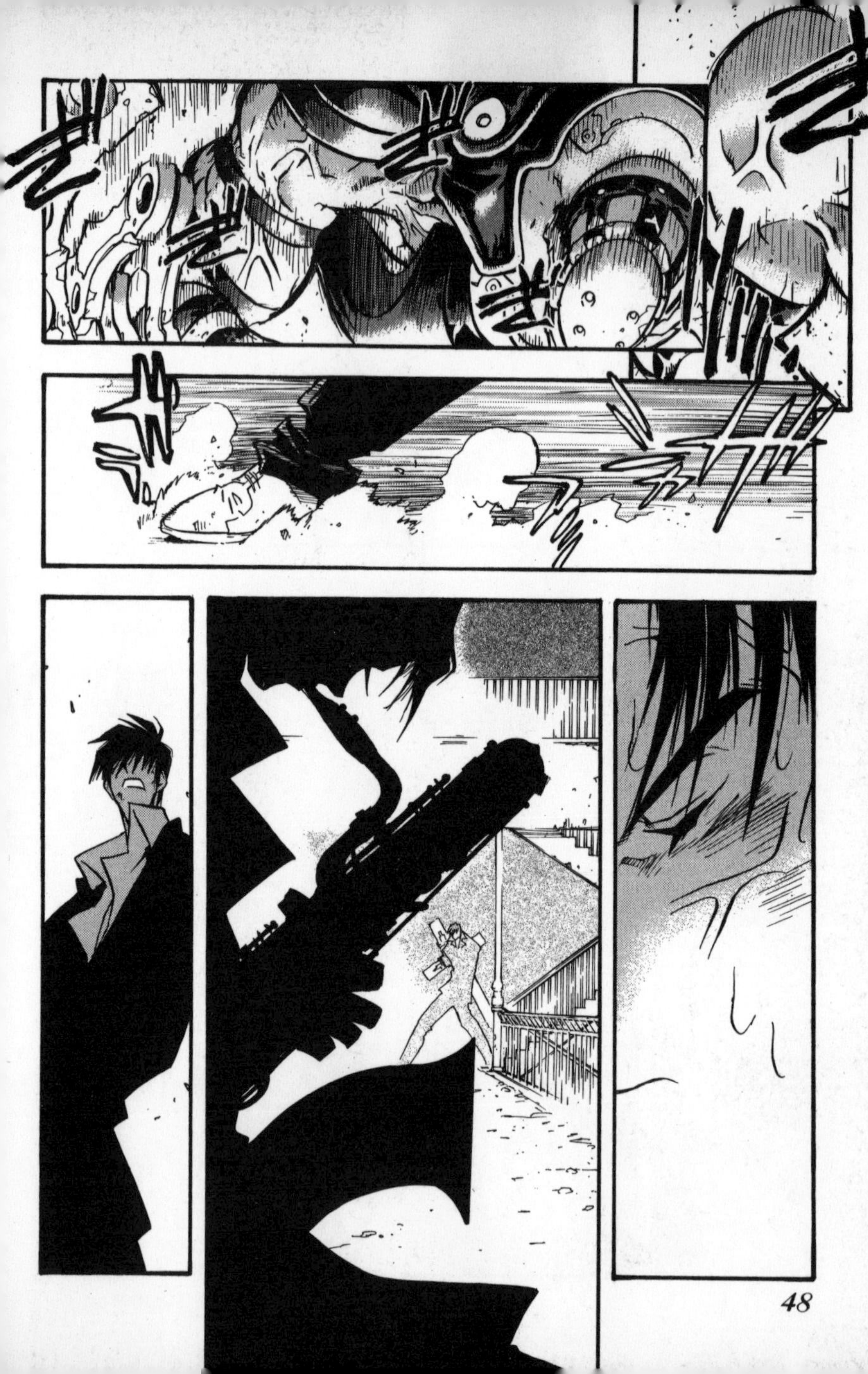

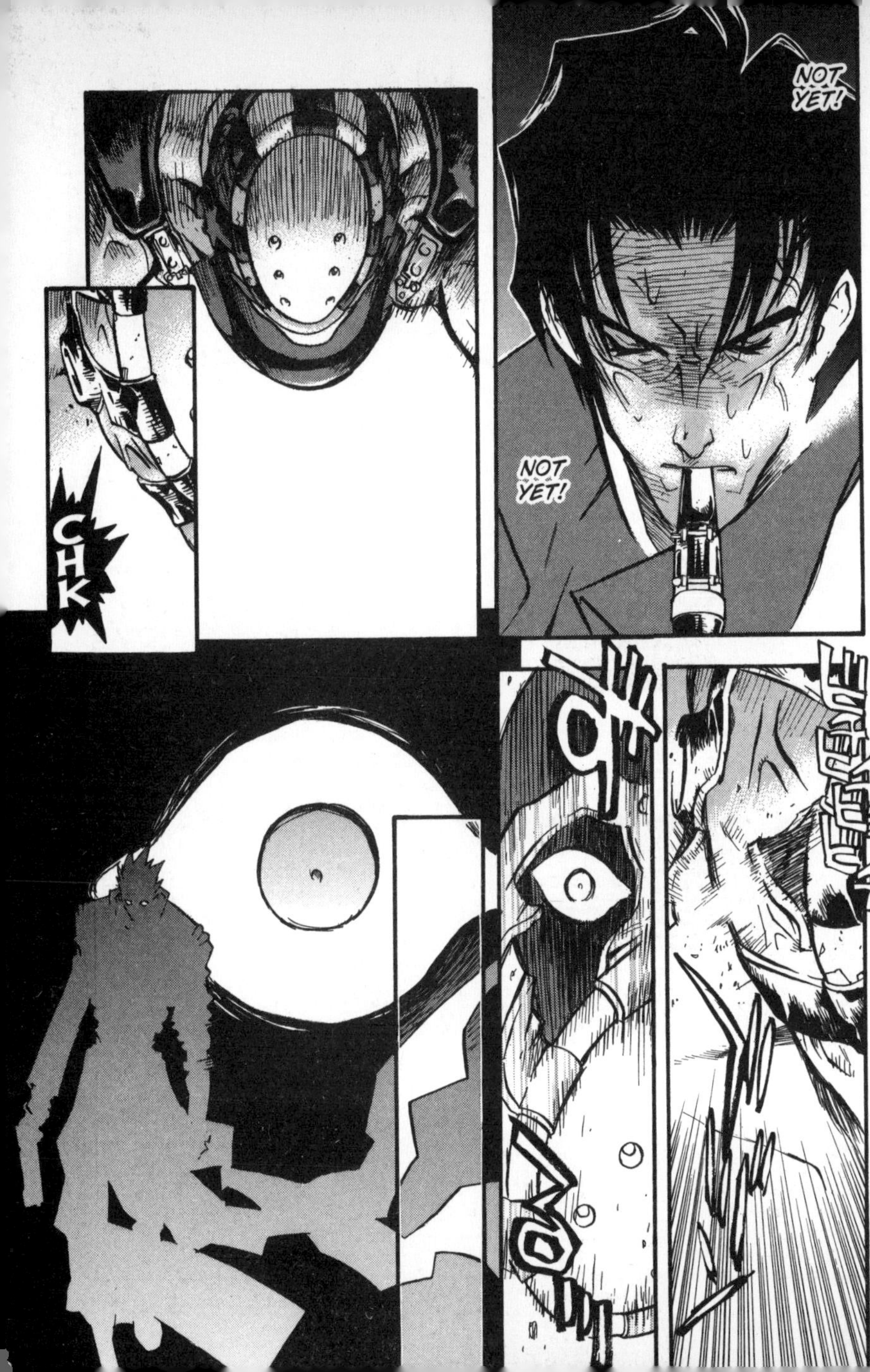
NOT YET!
NOT YET!
CHK

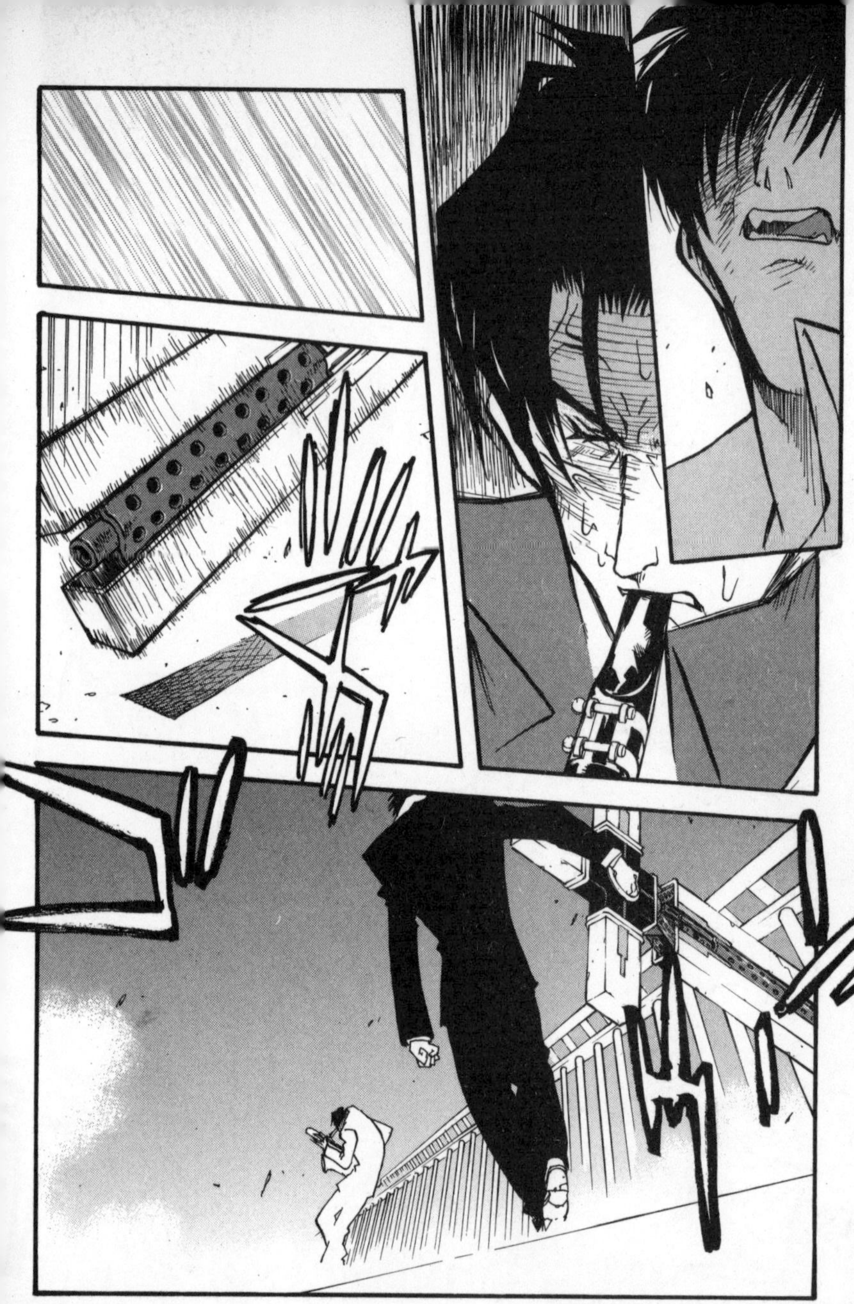

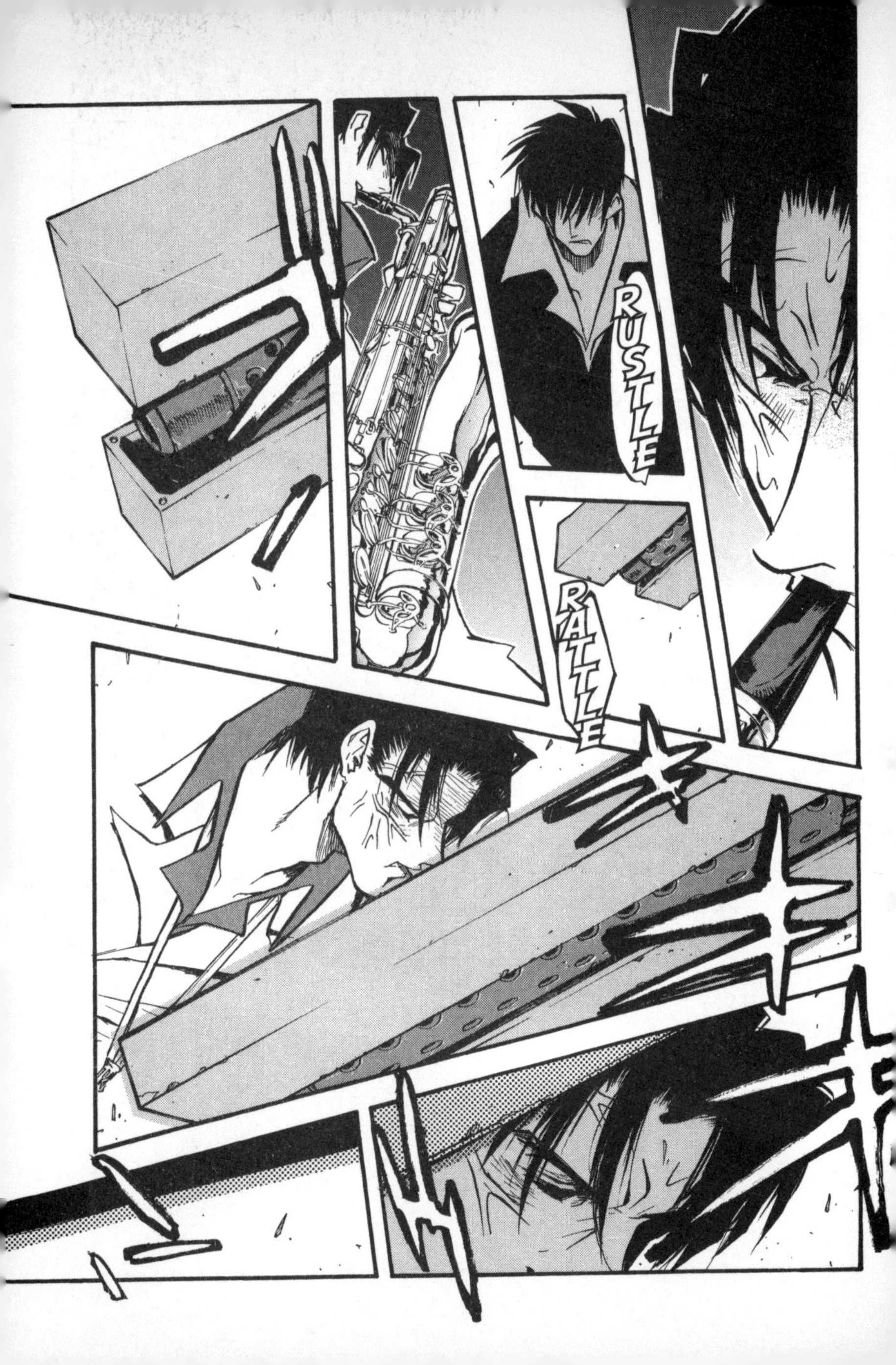
RUSTLE
RATTLE

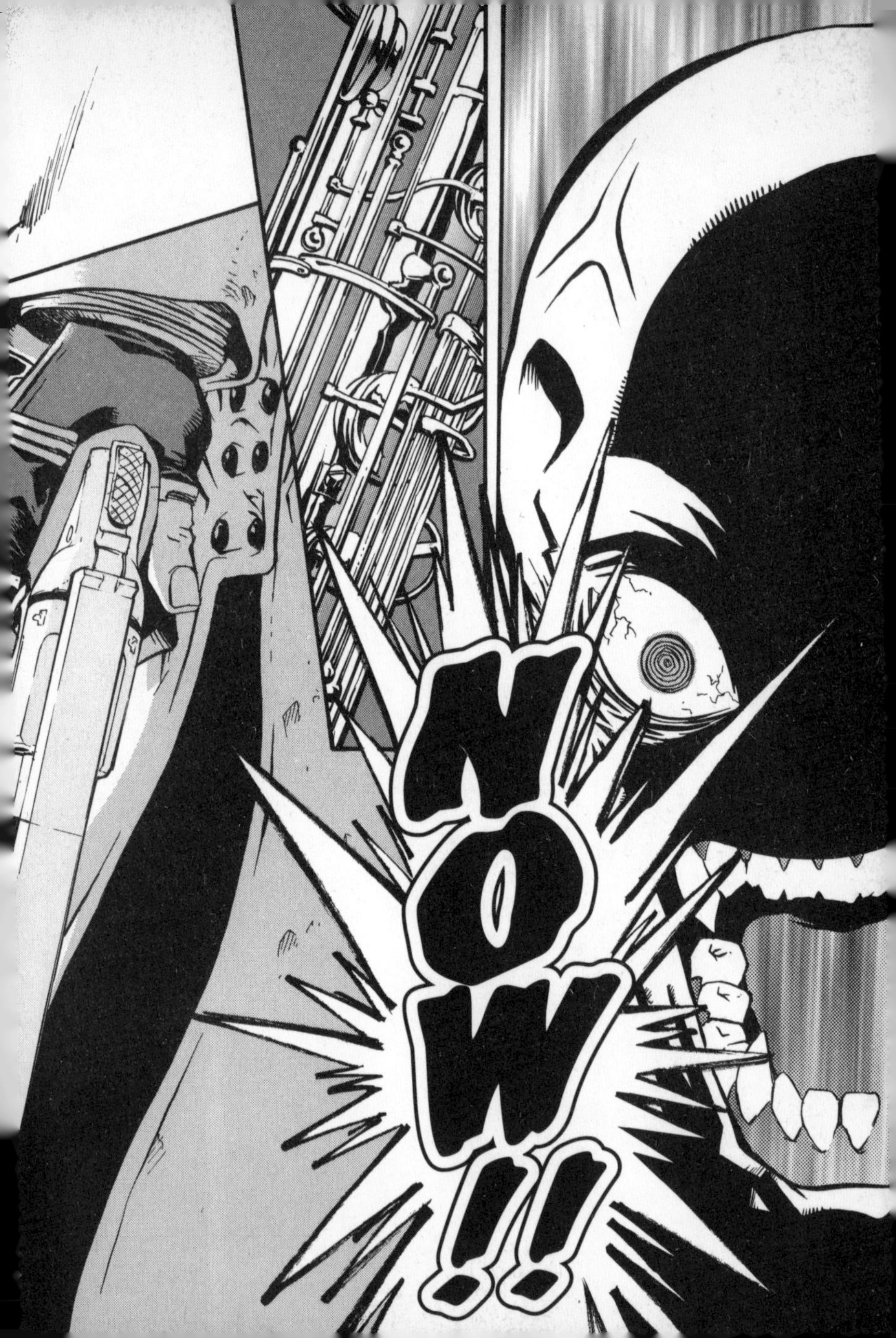
NOW!!

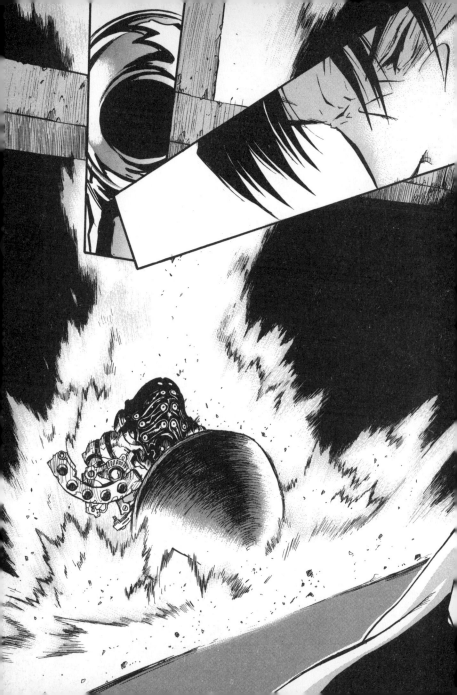

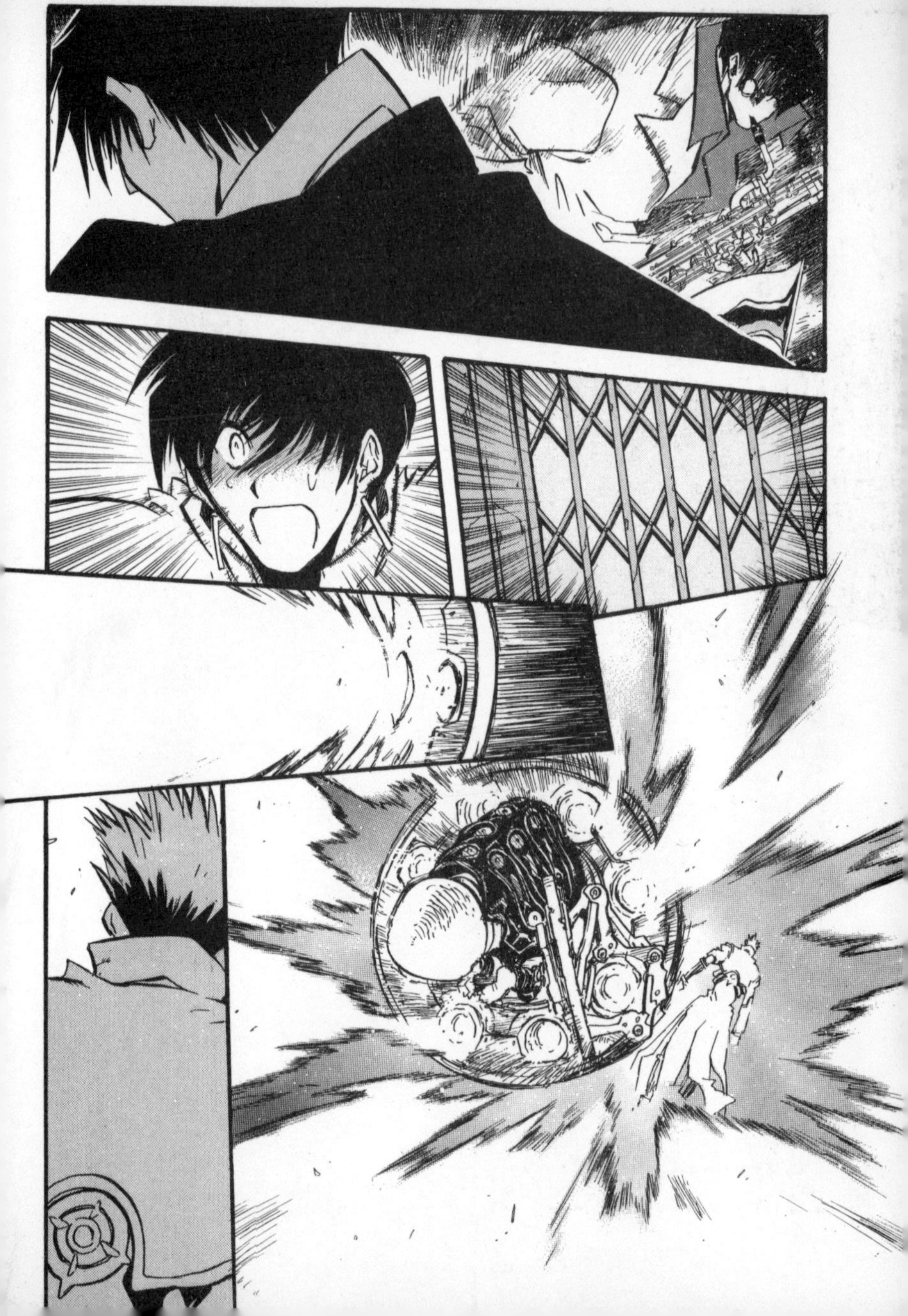

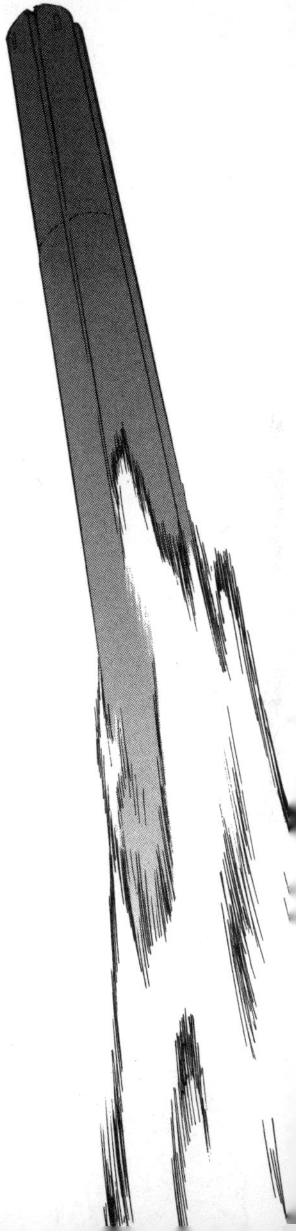
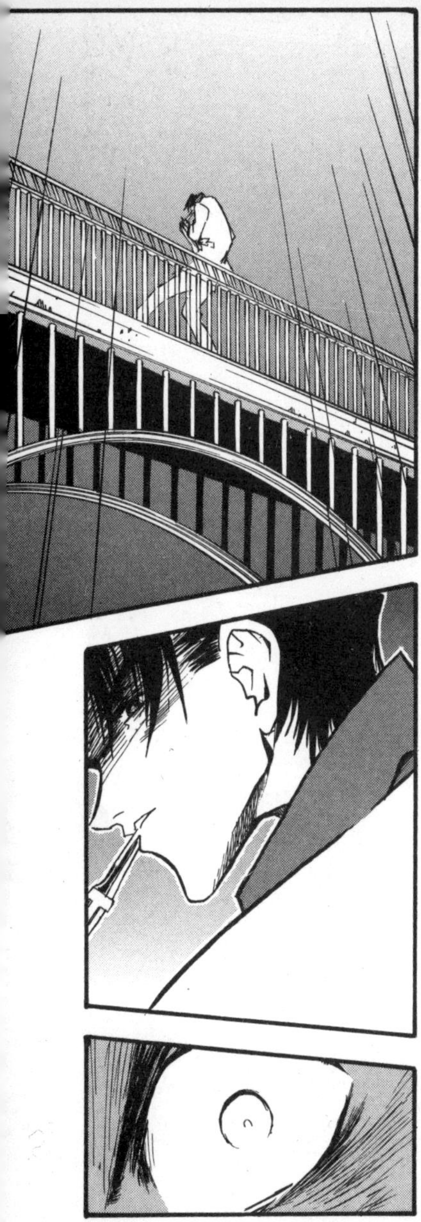

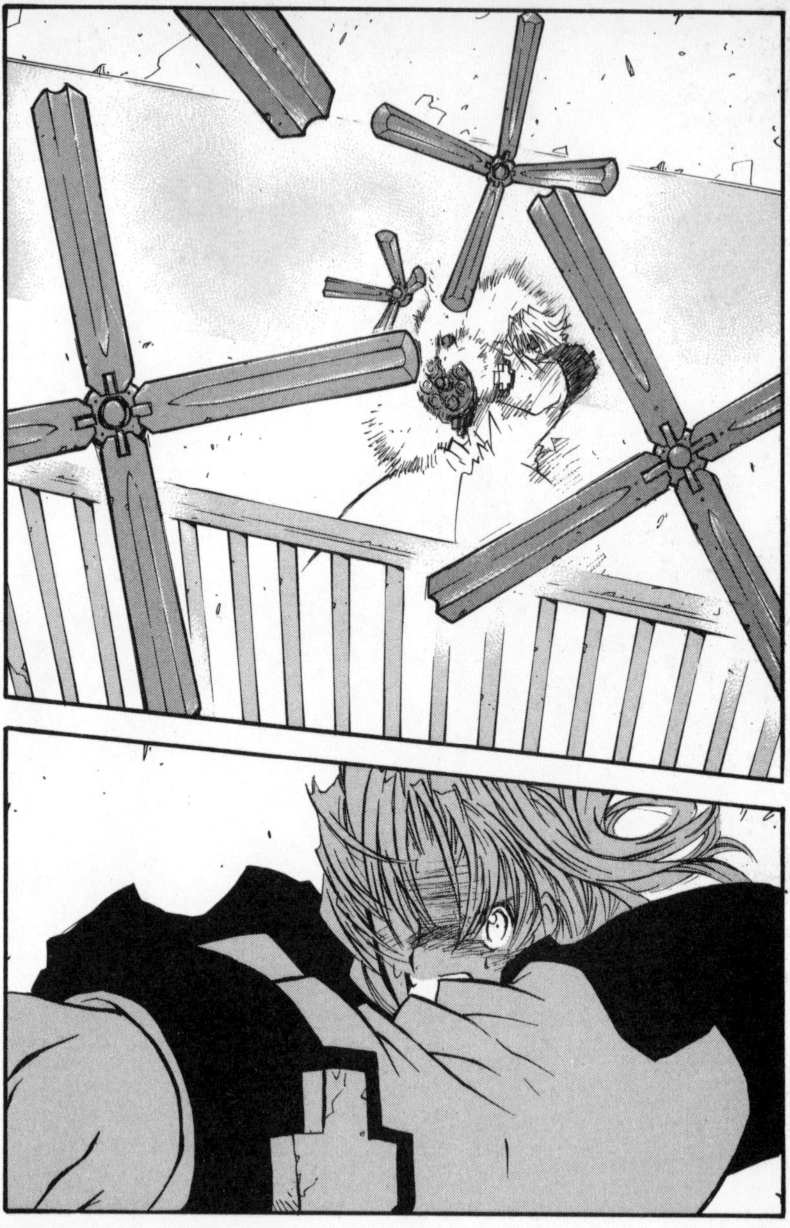

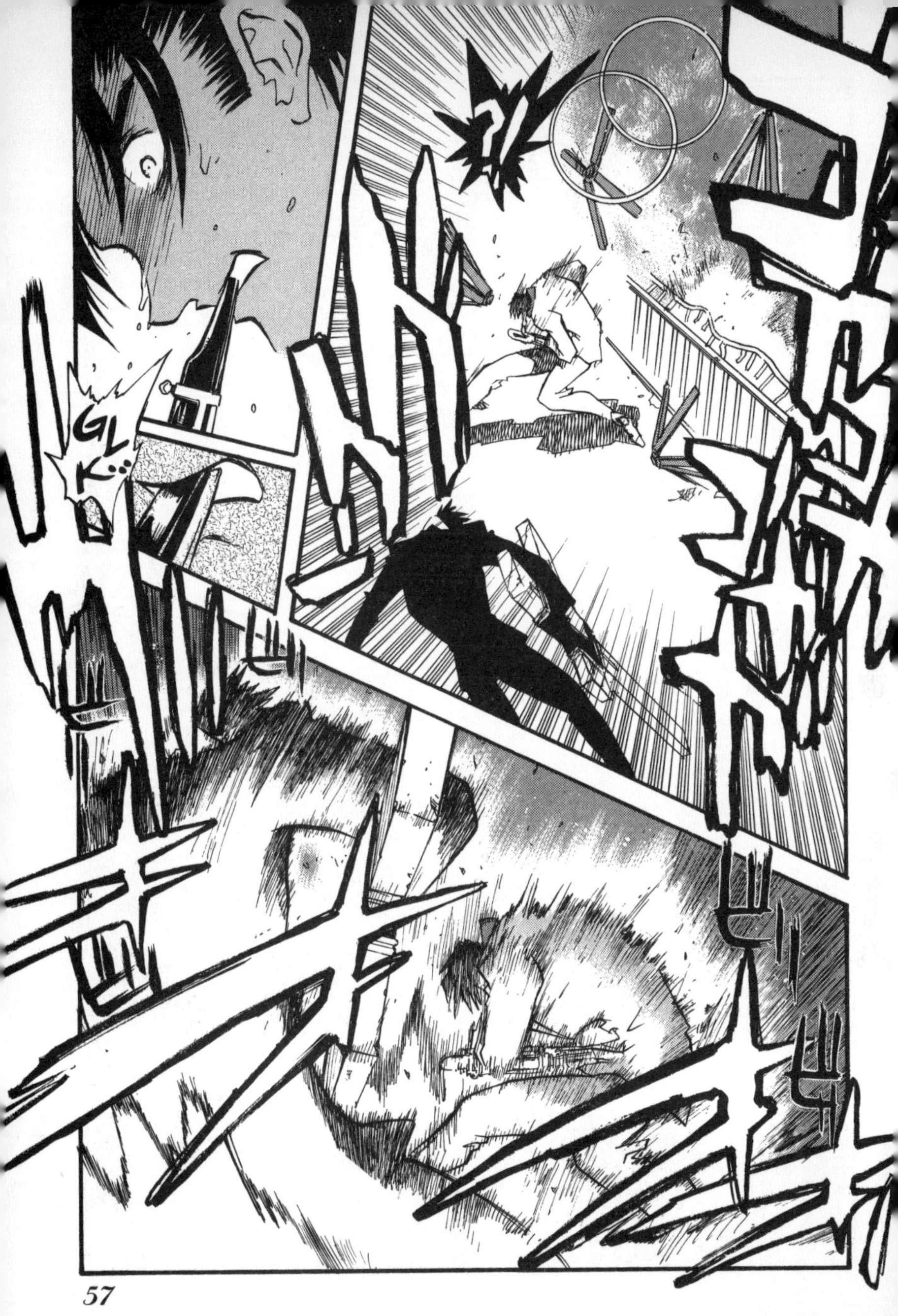
?!
GLK...

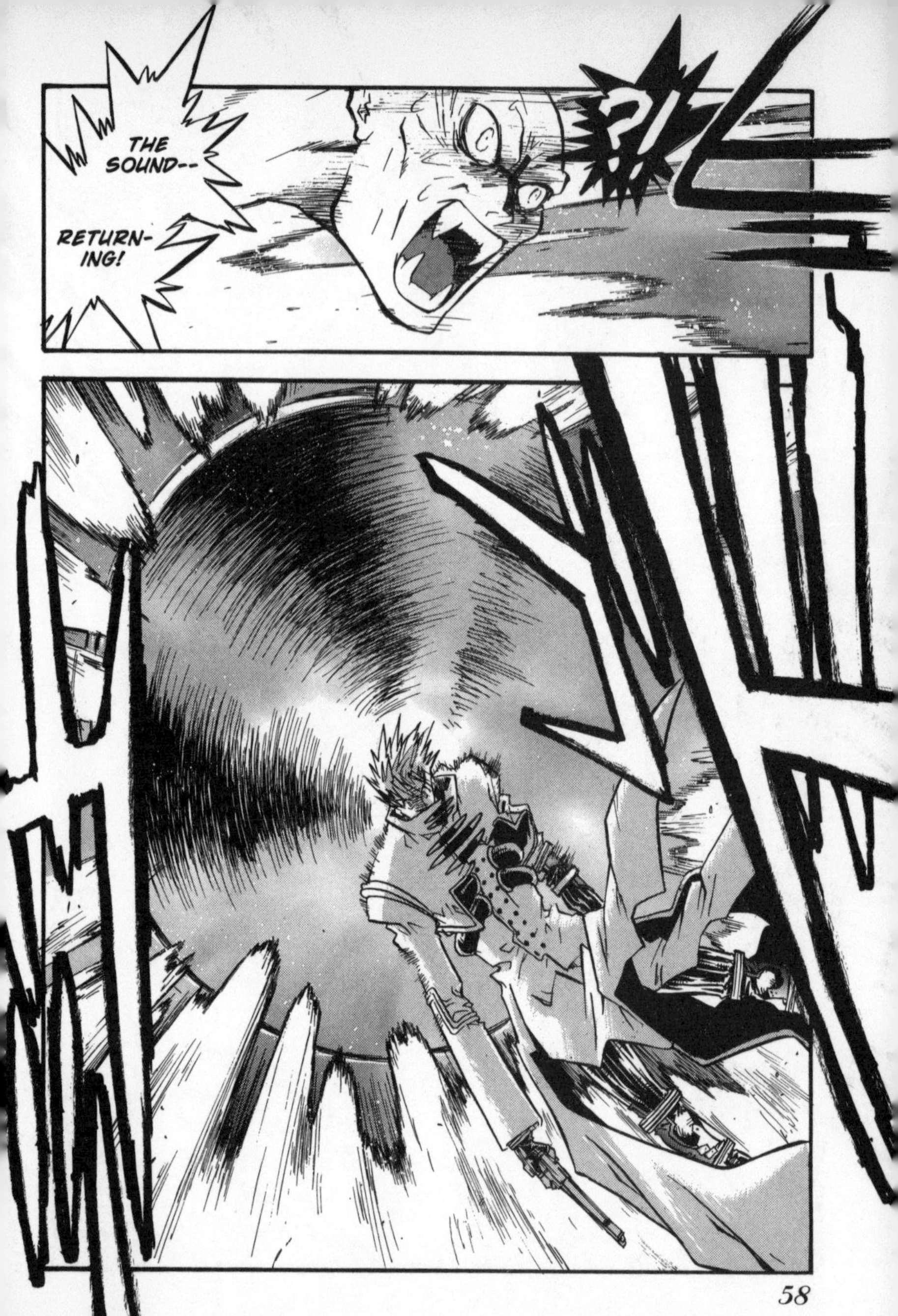
THE SOUND--
RETURNING!
?!

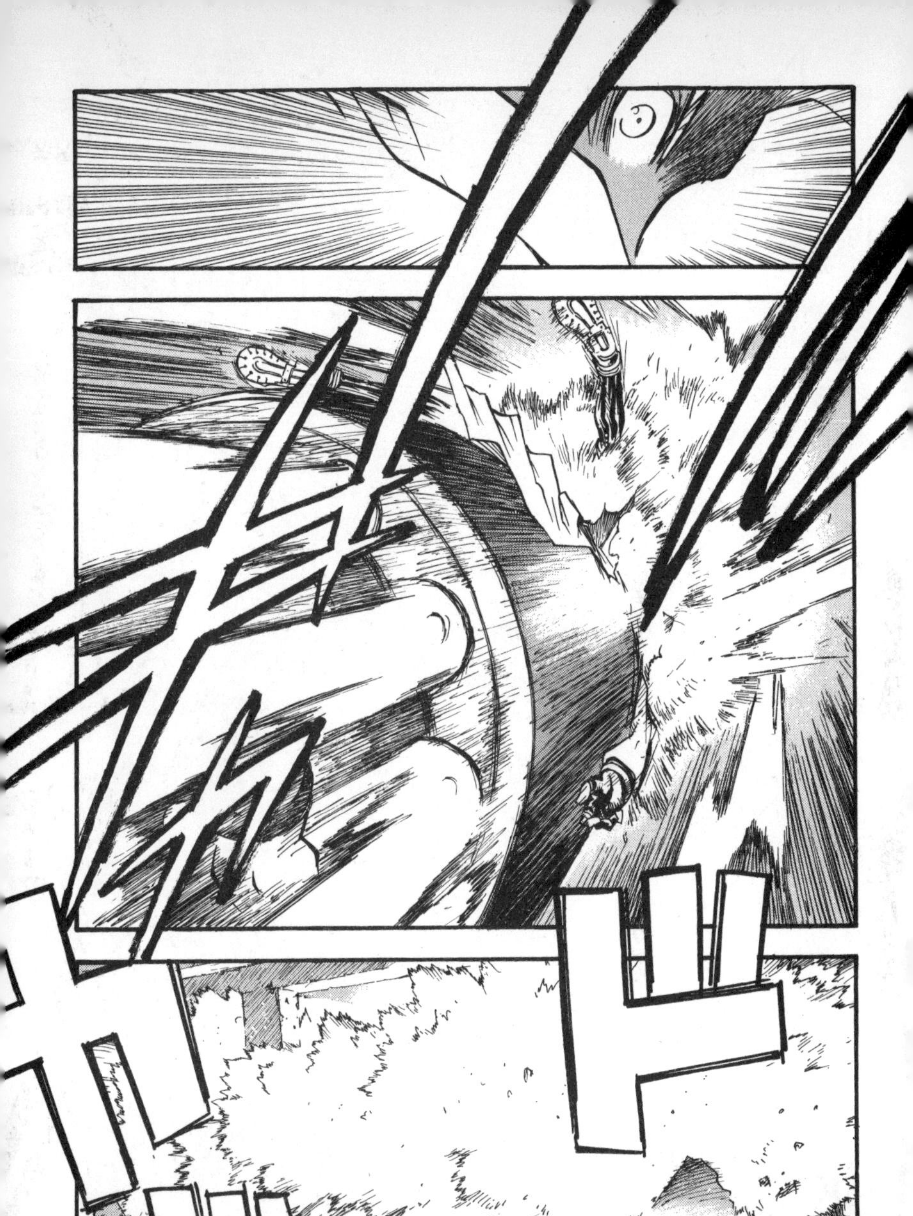

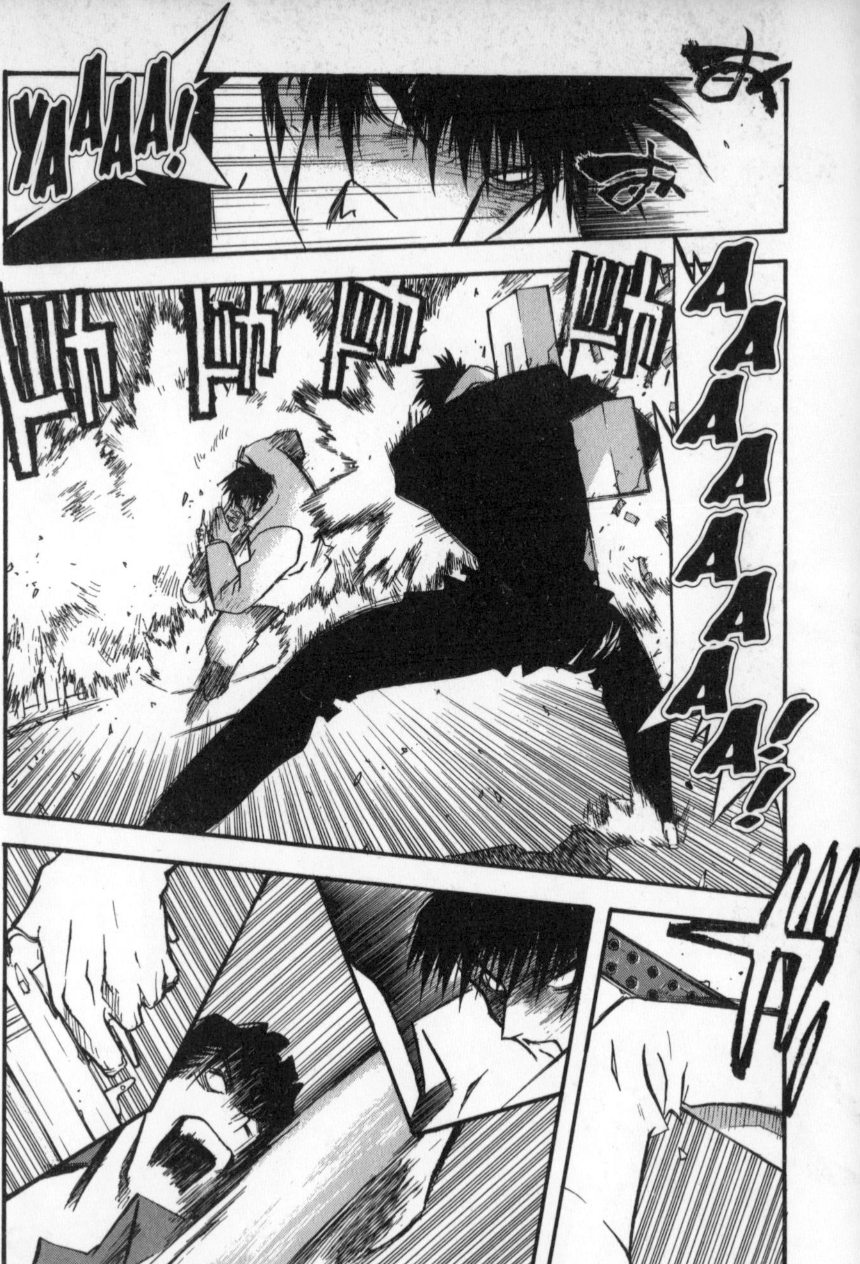

YAAAA!
AAAAAAAA!!

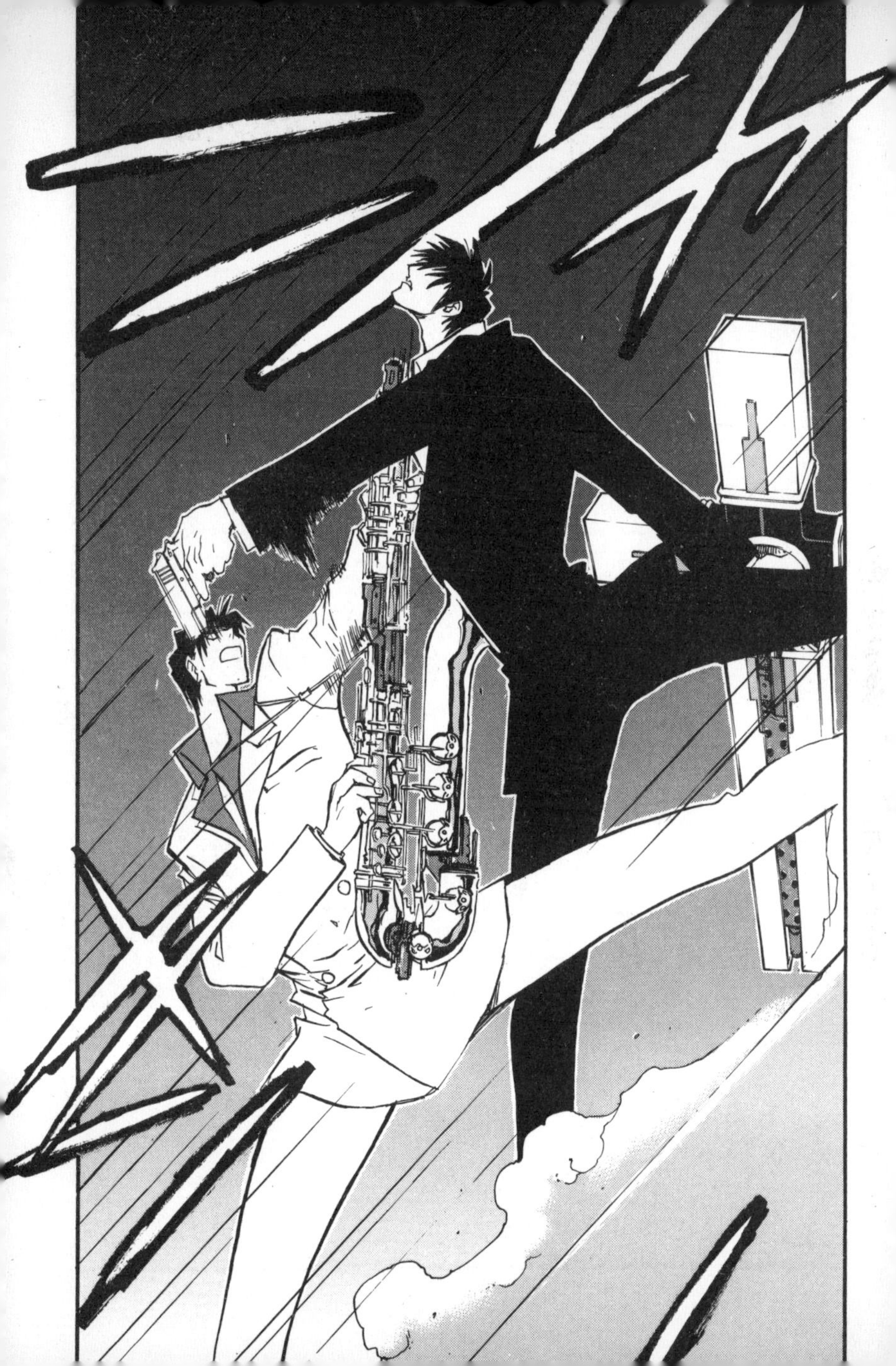

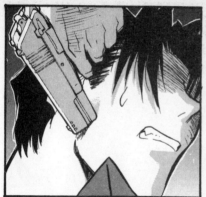

FOUND YOU, *PLAYER*--

YOU KNOW...

...THIS DISTRACTION WILL COST YOU MORE THAN JUST YOUR LIFE.

#2. BREAKOUT / END

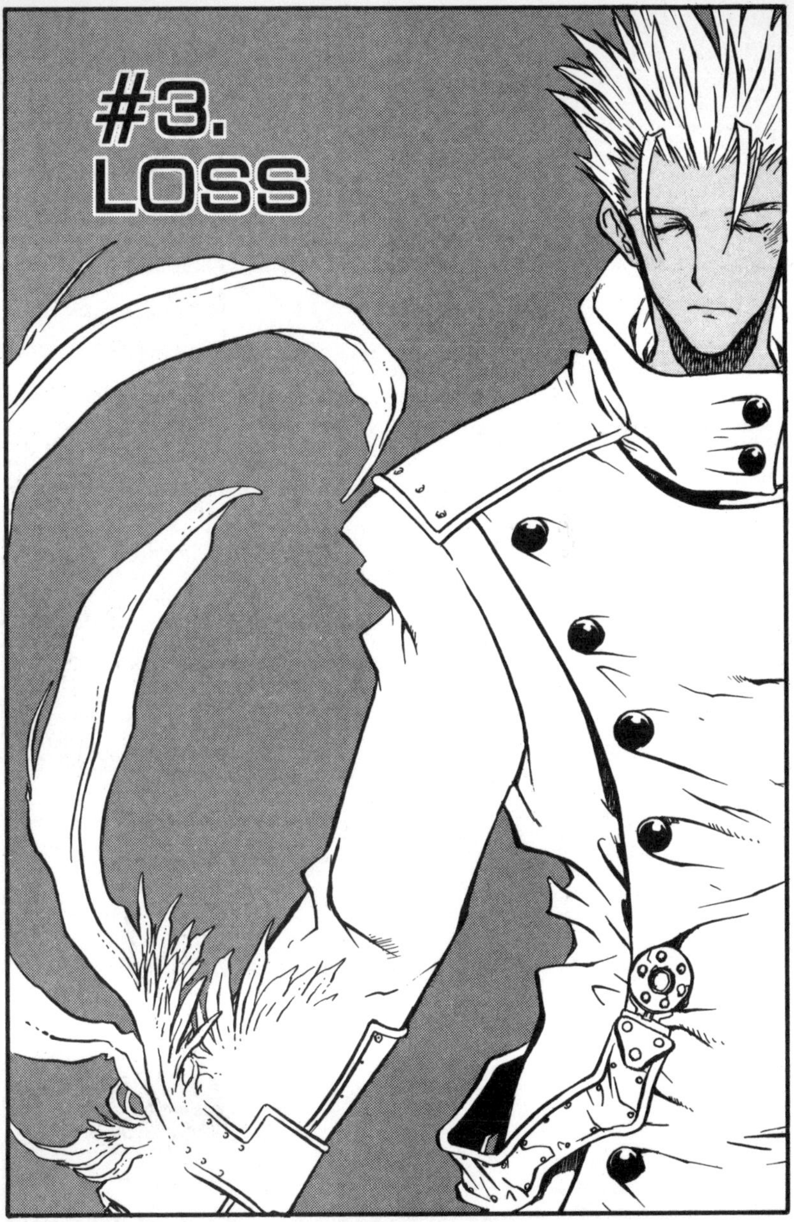
#3.
LOSS

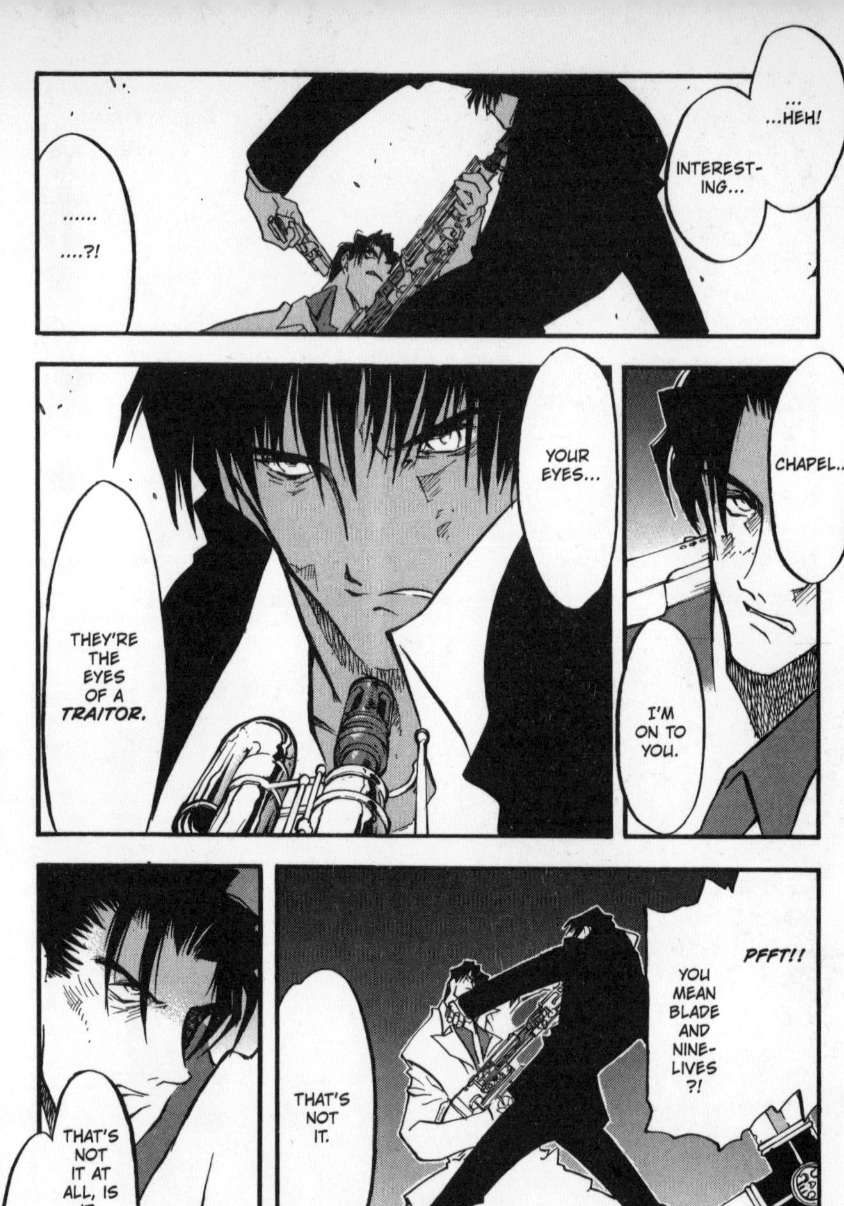
... ...HEH!
INTERESTING...
......
....?!
CHAPEL...
I'M ON TO YOU.
YOUR EYES...
THEY'RE THE EYES OF A *TRAITOR.*
PFFT!!
YOU MEAN BLADE AND NINE-LIVES ?!
THAT'S NOT IT.
THAT'S NOT IT AT ALL, IS IT...
...CHAPEL?

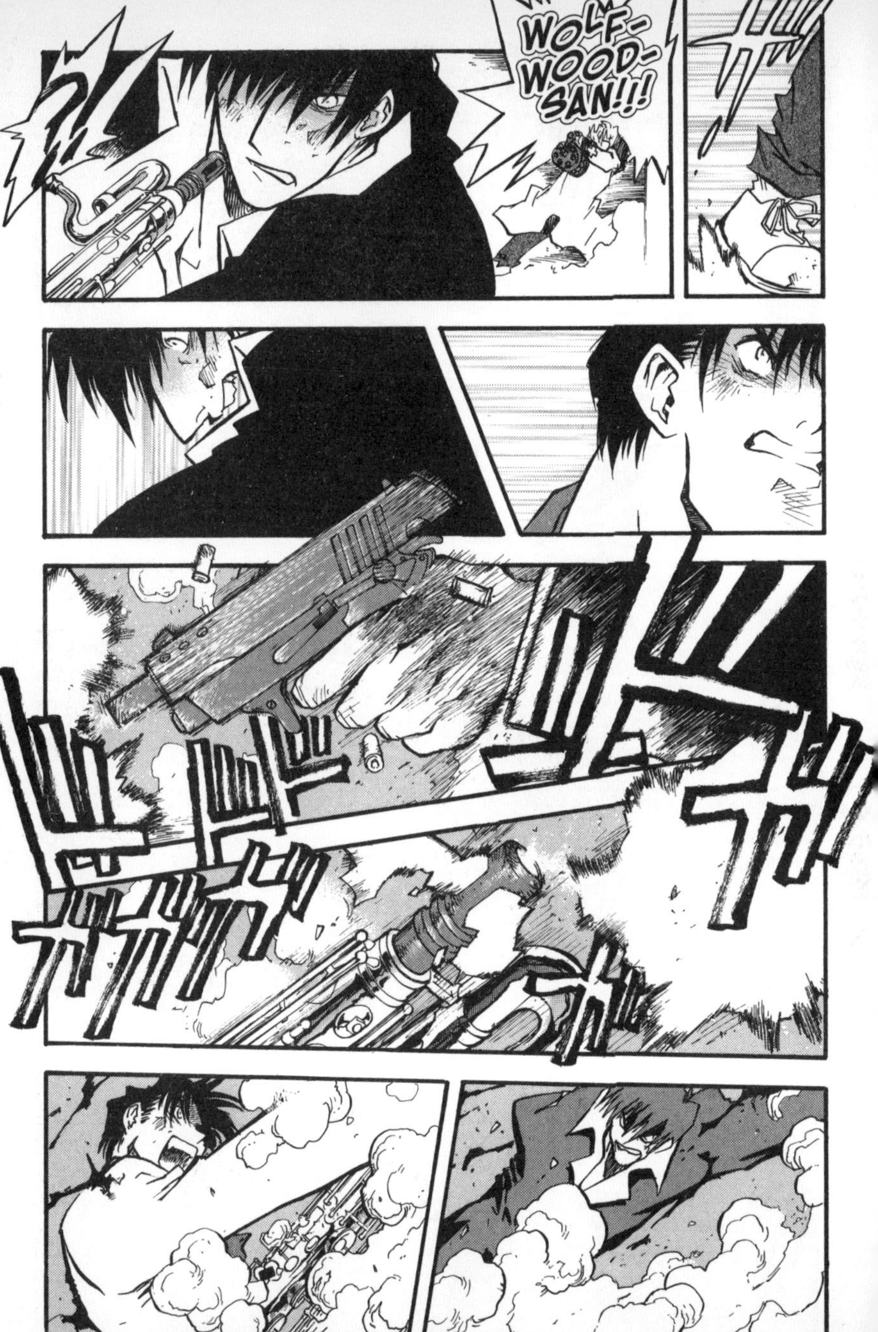
WOLF-WOOD-SAN!!!

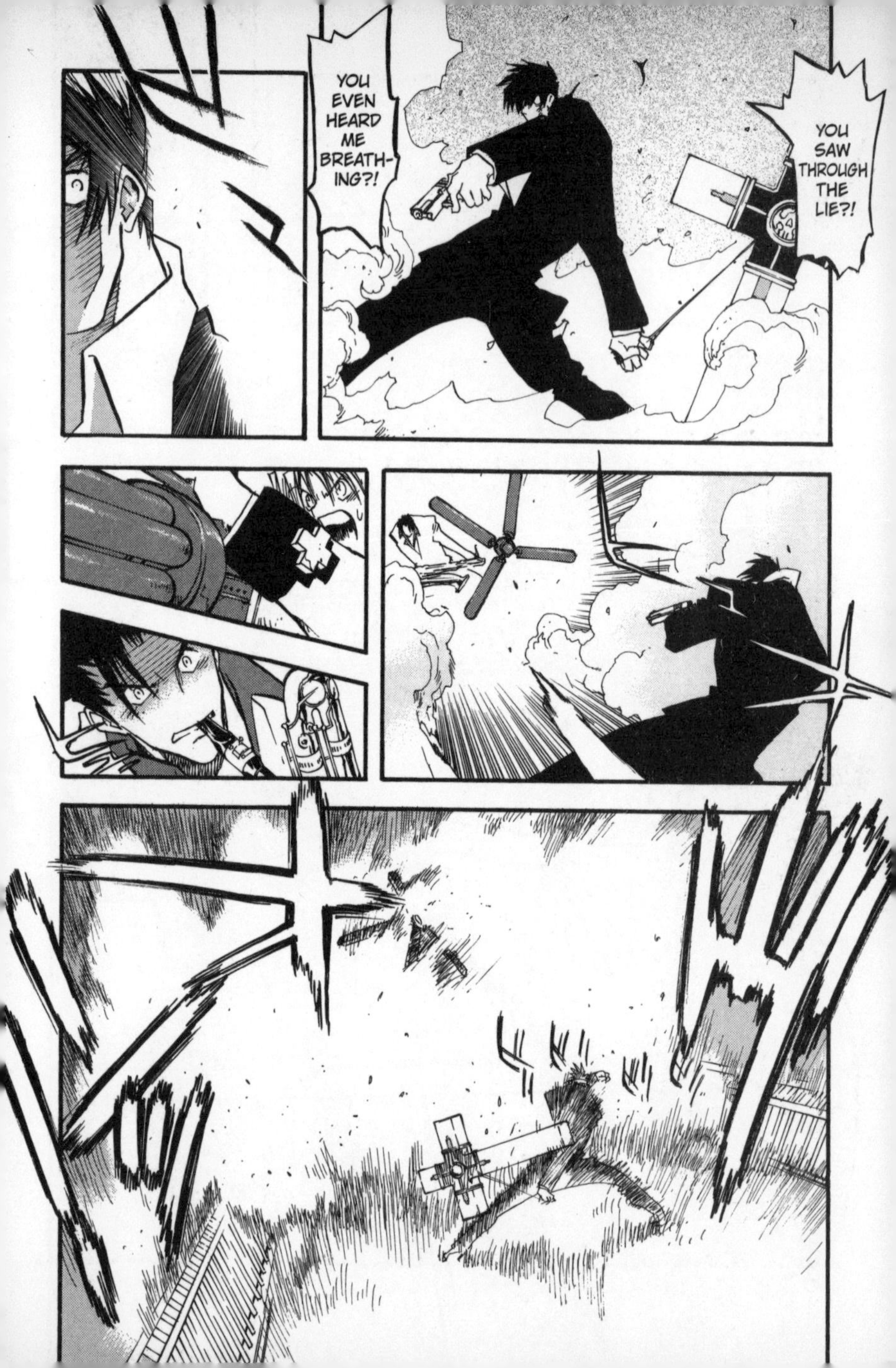
YOU SAW THROUGH THE LIE?!
YOU EVEN HEARD ME BREATHING?!

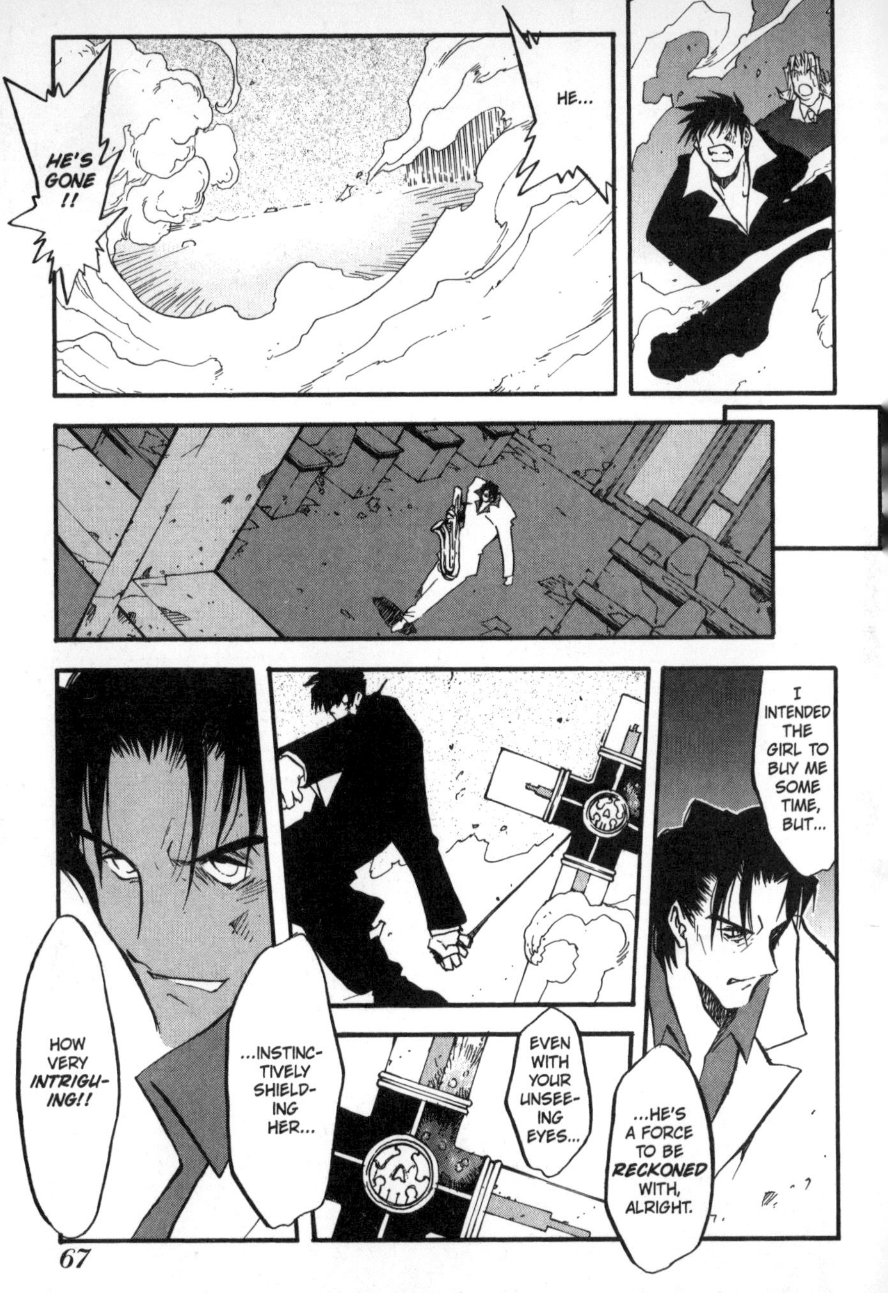
HE...
HE'S GONE!!
I INTENDED THE GIRL TO BUY ME SOME TIME, BUT...
...HE'S A FORCE TO BE RECKONED WITH, ALRIGHT.
EVEN WITH YOUR UNSEEING EYES...
...INSTINCTIVELY SHIELDING HER...
HOW VERY INTRIGUING!!

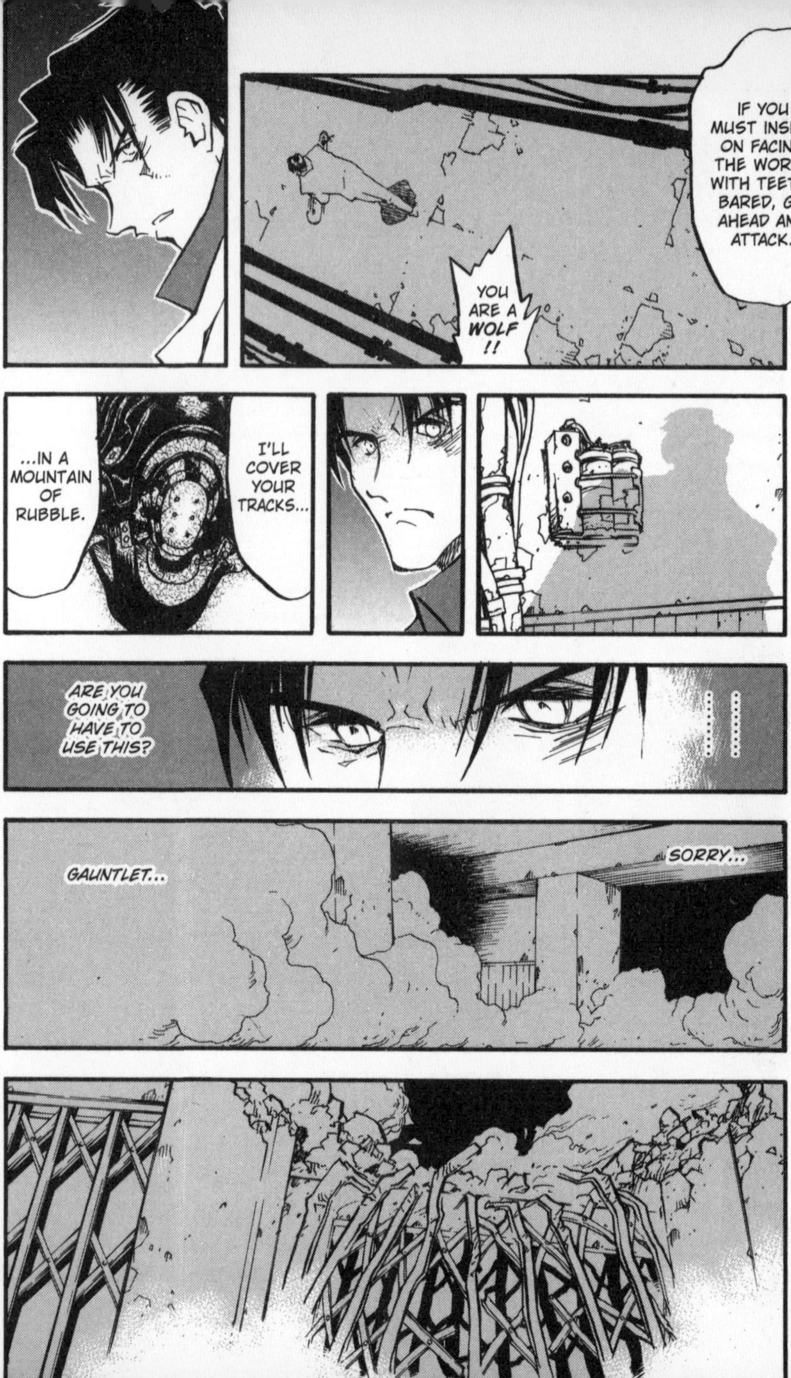
IF YOU MUST INSIST ON FACING THE WORLD WITH TEETH BARED, GO AHEAD AND ATTACK.
YOU ARE A *WOLF* !!
I'LL COVER YOUR TRACKS...
...IN A MOUNTAIN OF RUBBLE.
......
......
ARE YOU GOING TO HAVE TO USE THIS?
SORRY...
GAUNTLET...

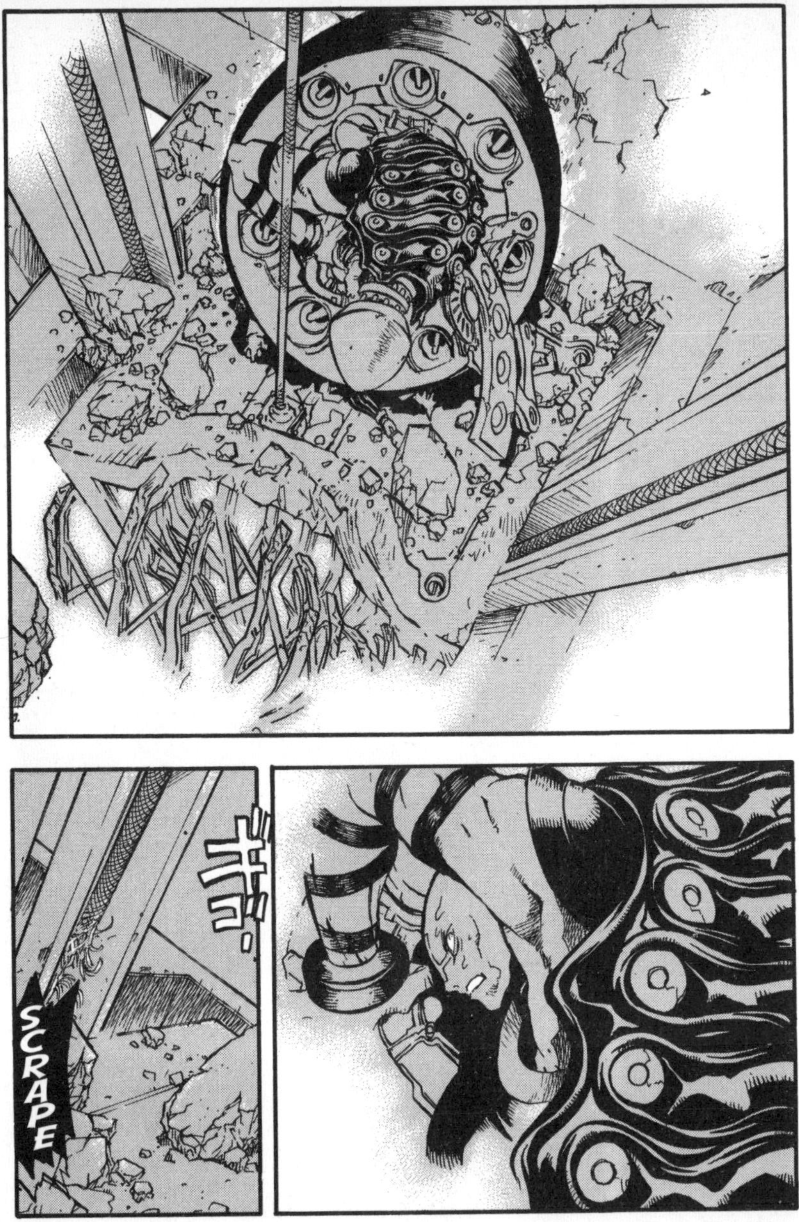
ギョ
SCRAPE

....
....

GUH...

NO...I CAN FEEL SOME-THING... THERE WAS AN UNUSUAL DECELER-ATION.

DID I DO IT?!

?!

IN THE END, DID I MISS MY LAST CHANCE ...?

I CAN'T MOVE...

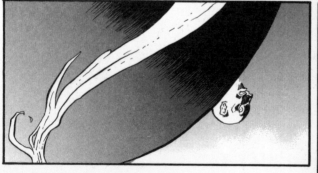

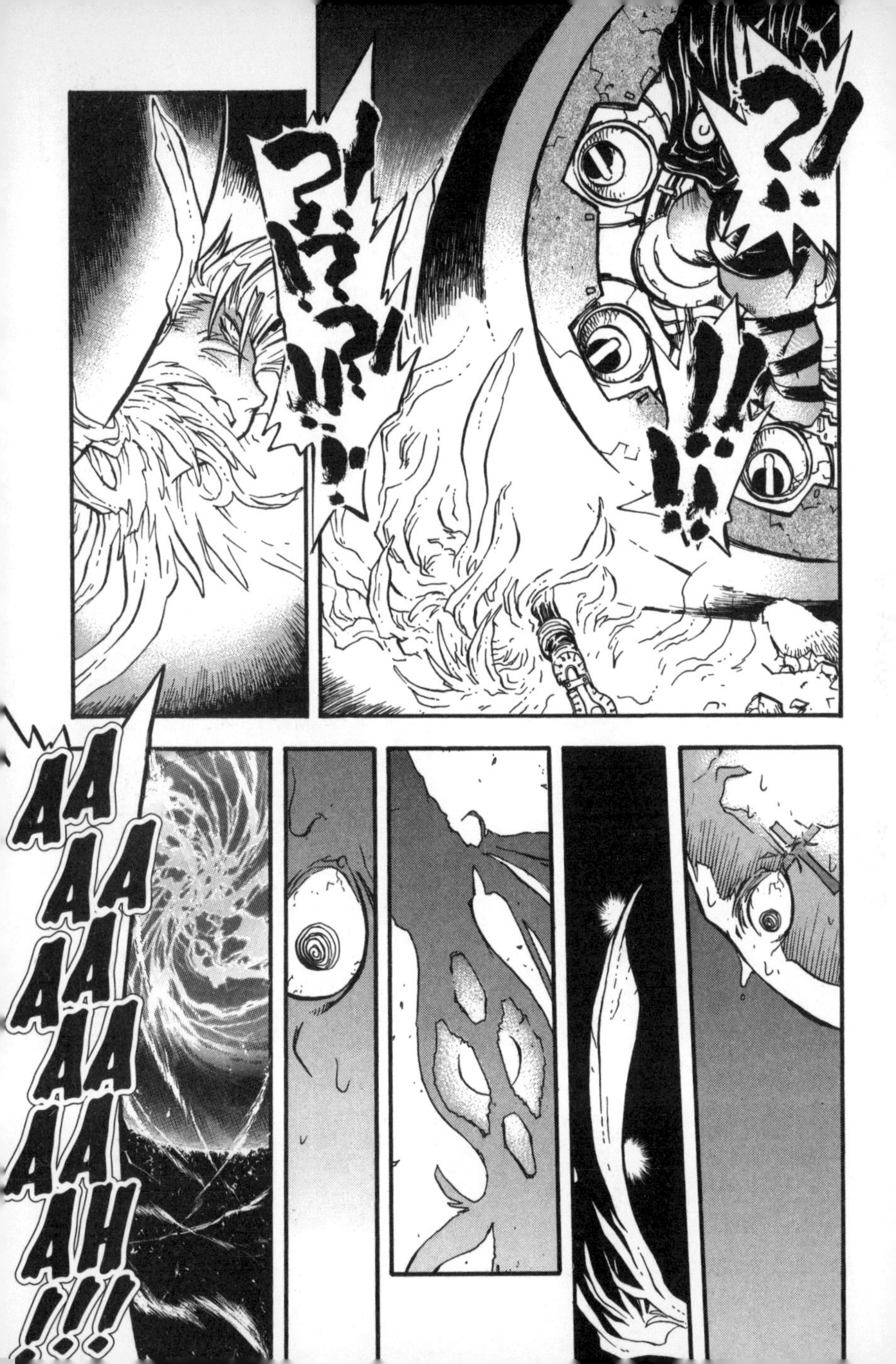

?!
!!!
?!?!?!!!
AAAAAAAAAAAAAH!!!

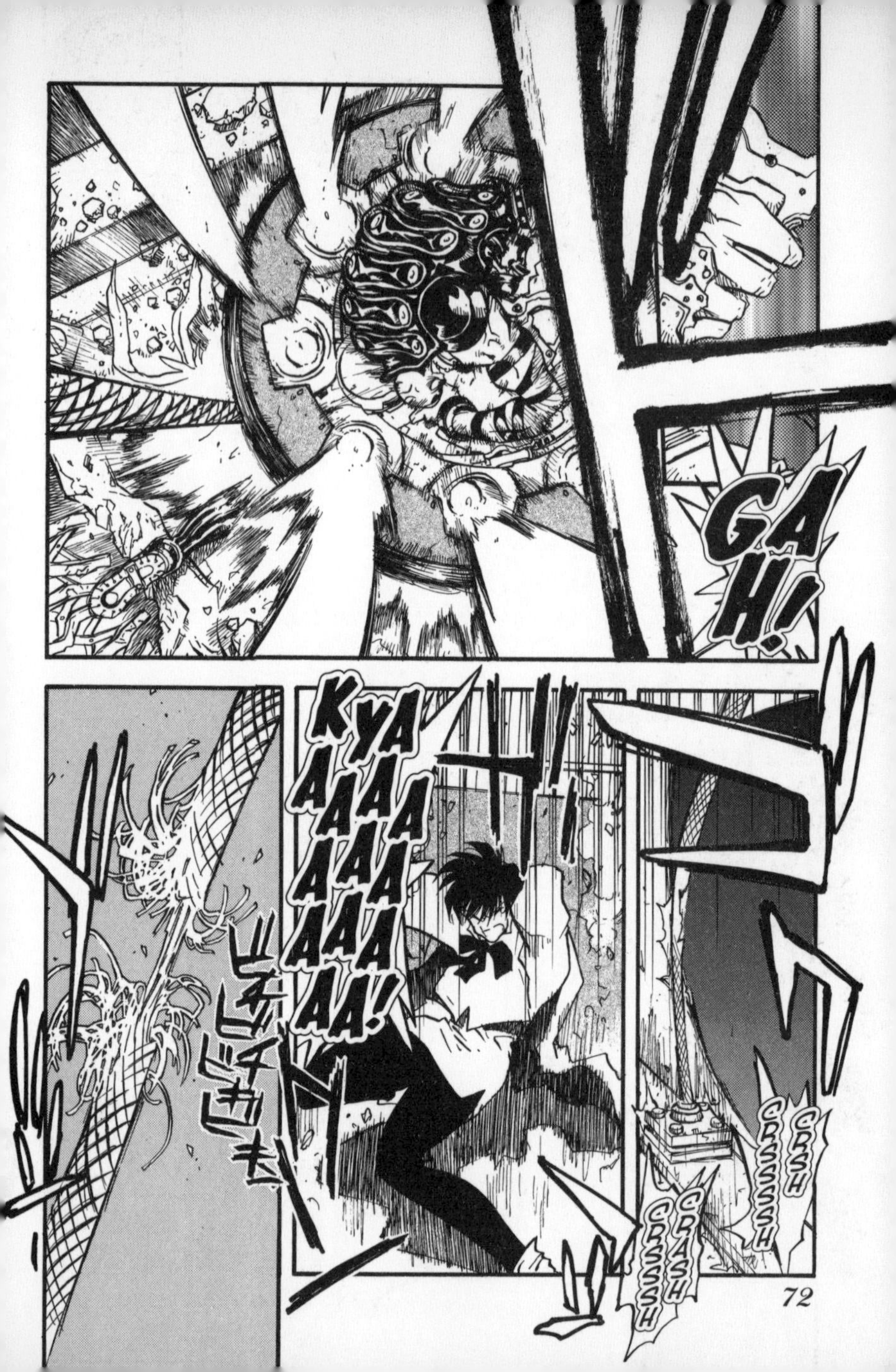
GAH!
CRSH
CRSSSSH
CRASH
CRSSSH
KYAAAAAAAAAAAAAAA!

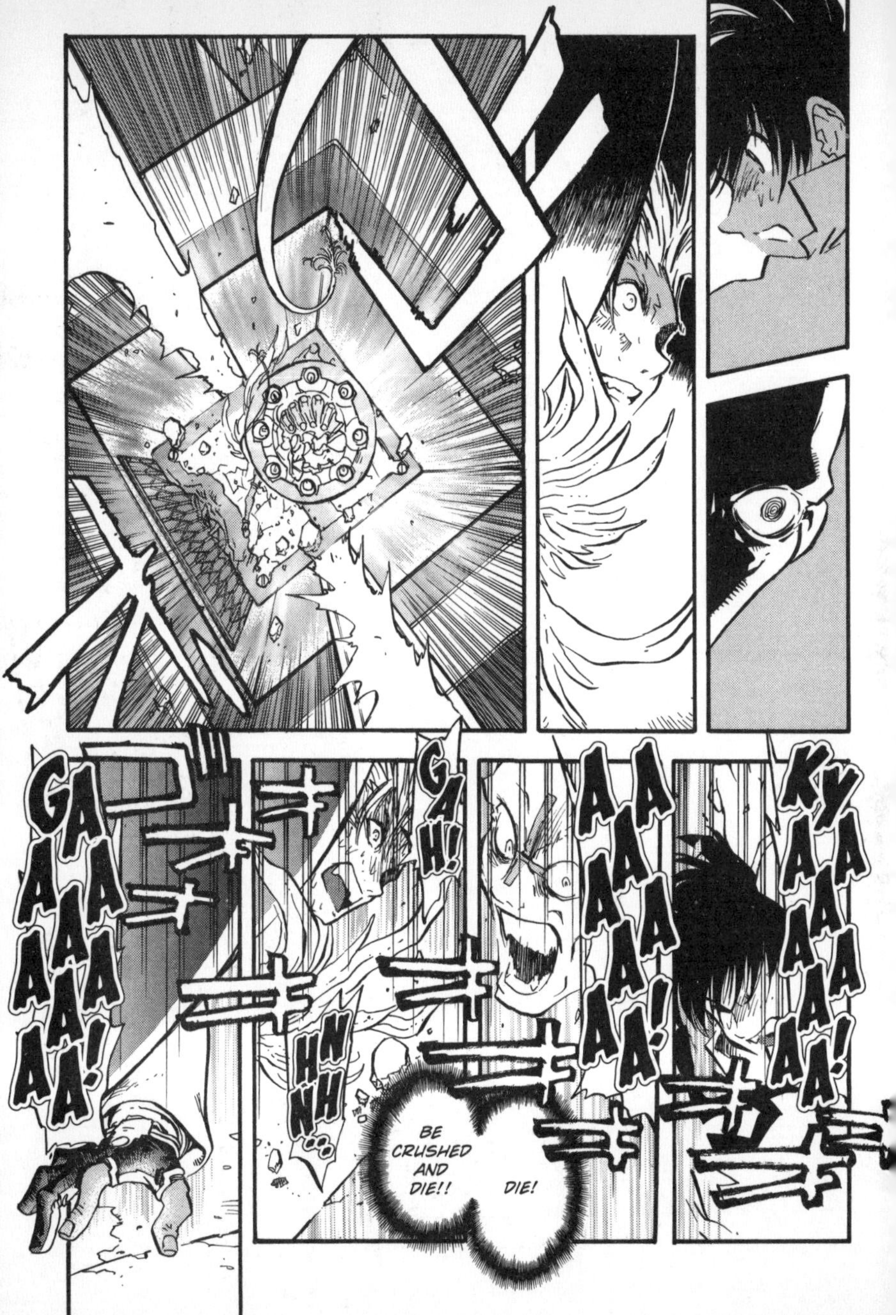
KYAAAAAAAA!
AAAAAAAAA!
GAH!
HNNNH..
BE CRUSHED AND DIE!!
DIE!
GAAAAAAAAAA!

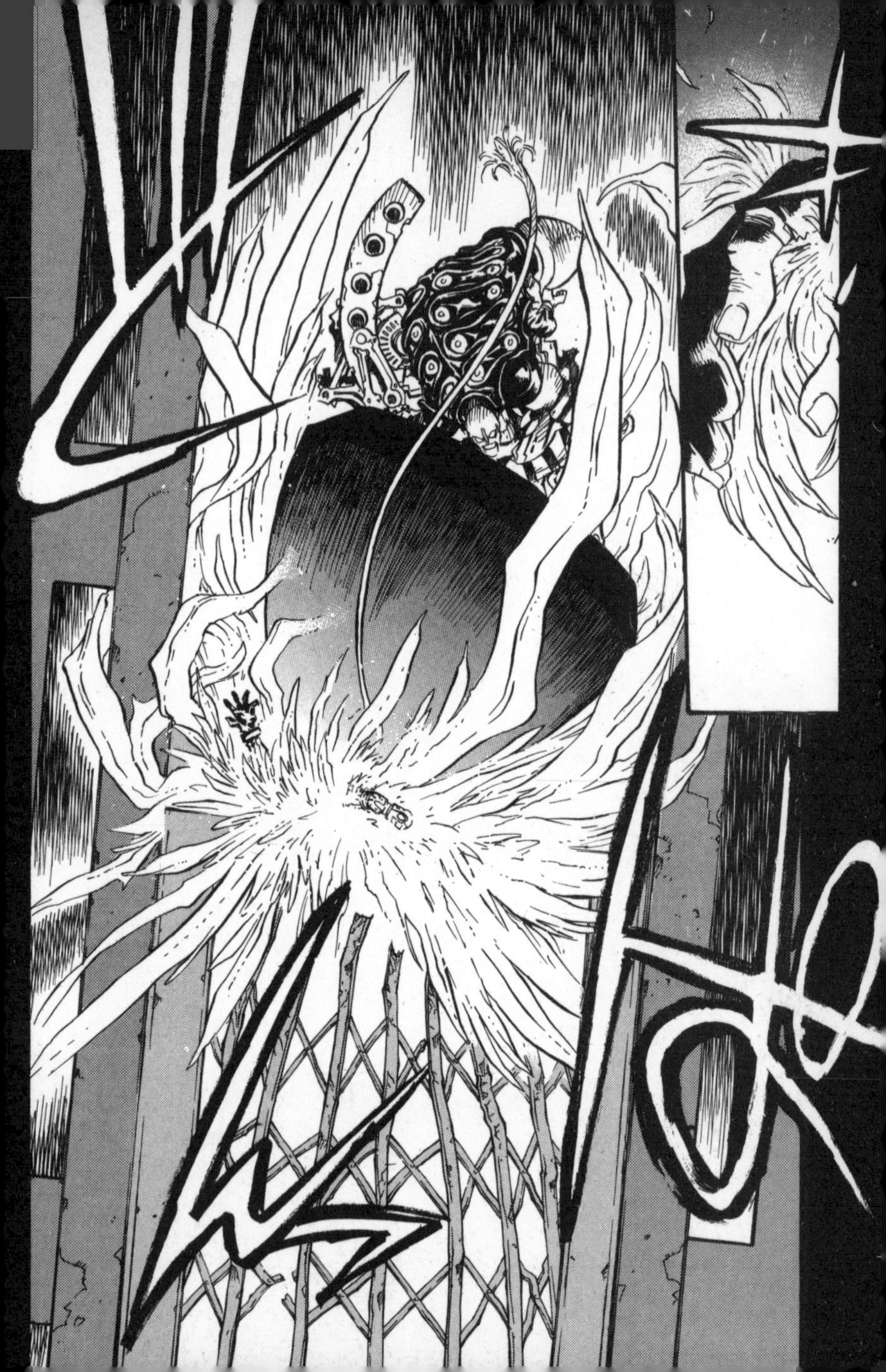

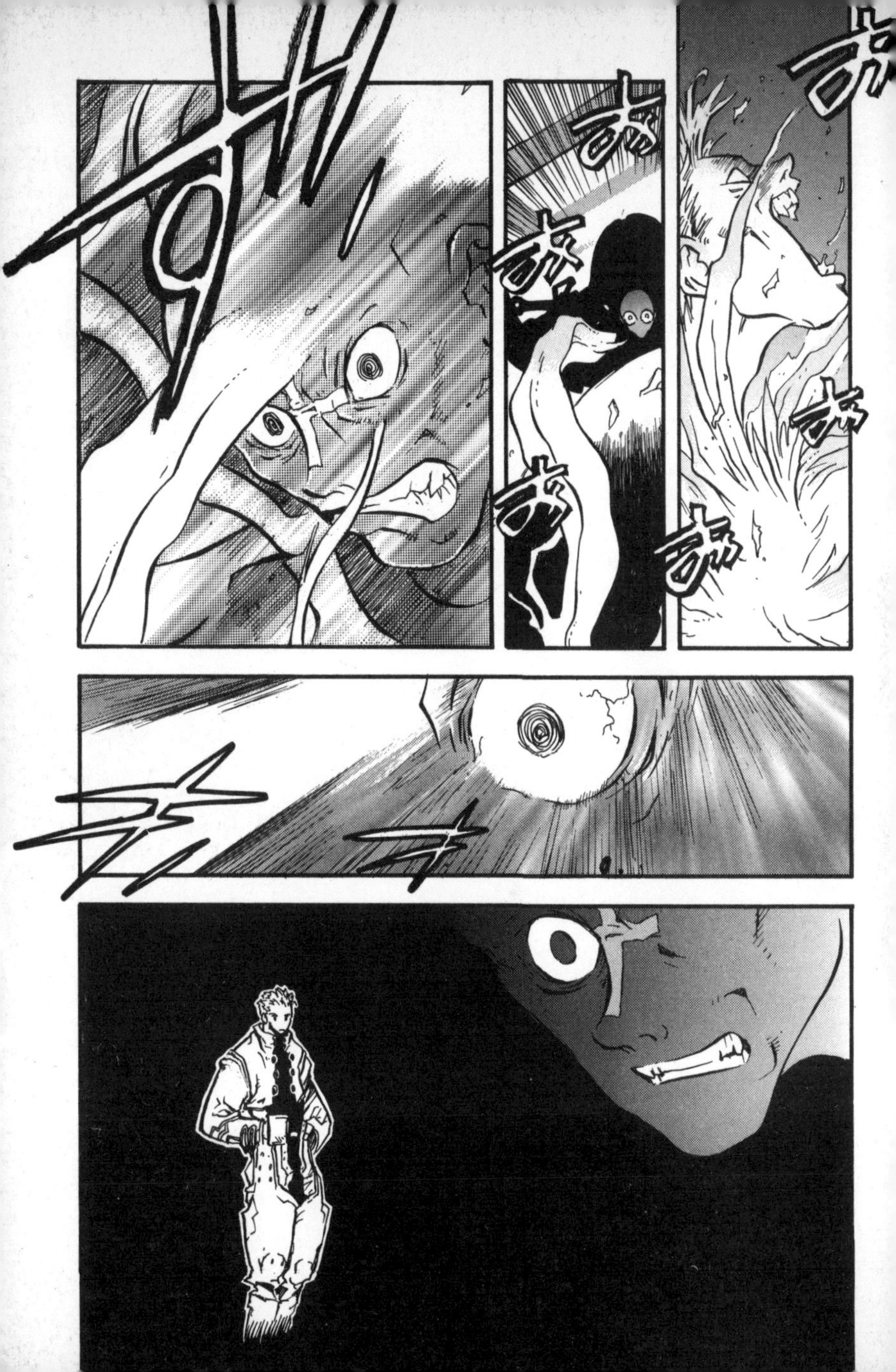

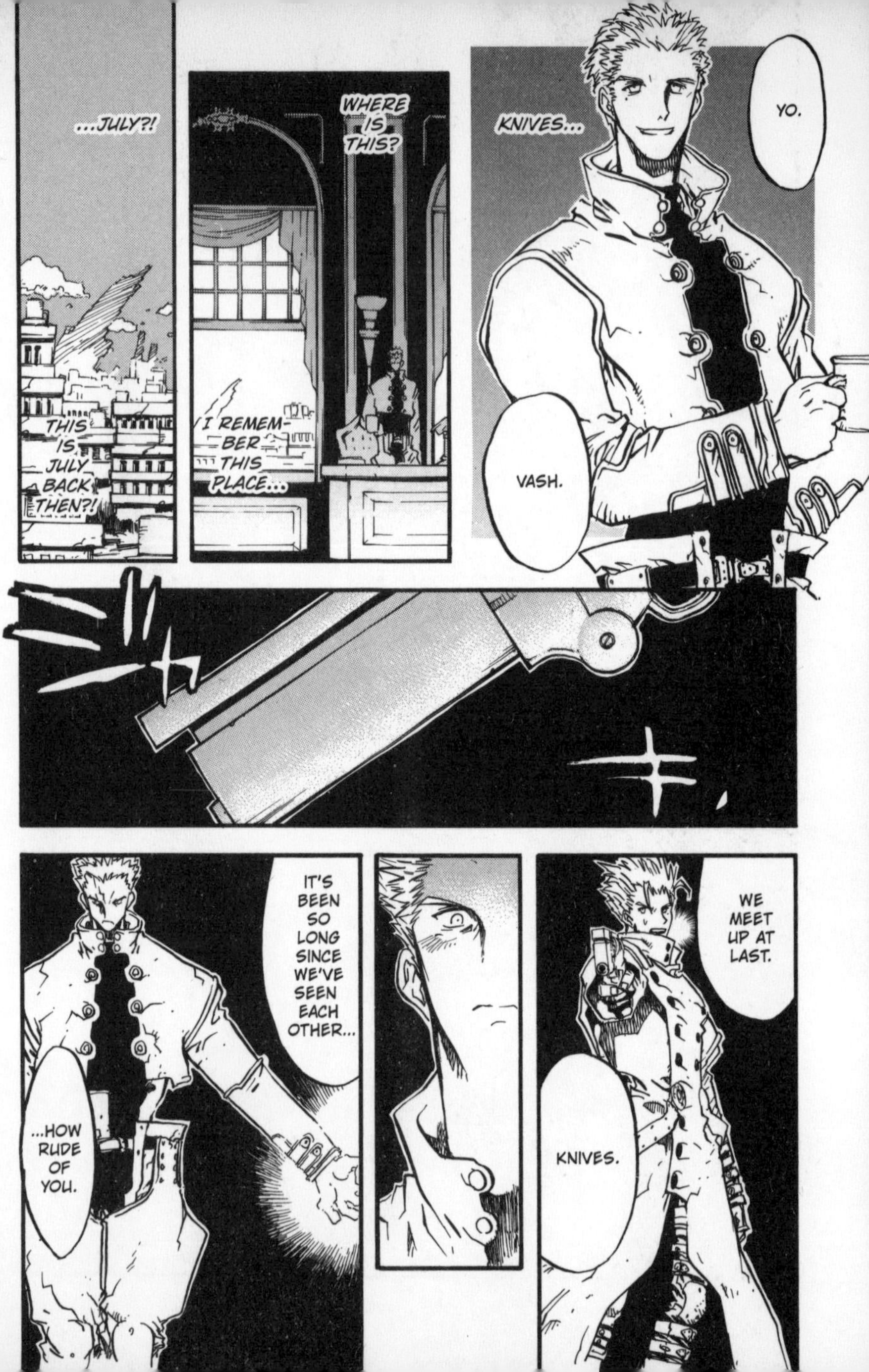
YO.
KNIVES...
VASH.
WHERE IS THIS?
I REMEMBER THIS PLACE...
...JULY?!
THIS IS JULY BACK THEN?!
WE MEET UP AT LAST.
KNIVES.
IT'S BEEN SO LONG SINCE WE'VE SEEN EACH OTHER...
...HOW RUDE OF YOU.

TAKE IT EASY...

I'VE BEEN WAITING FOR YOU, YOU KNOW.

WHA --!!

WHERE... ...IS THAT?

WHERE IS HE GOING...?

HOW'S THAT...

...DOC-TOR?

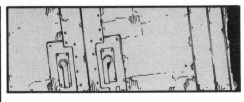

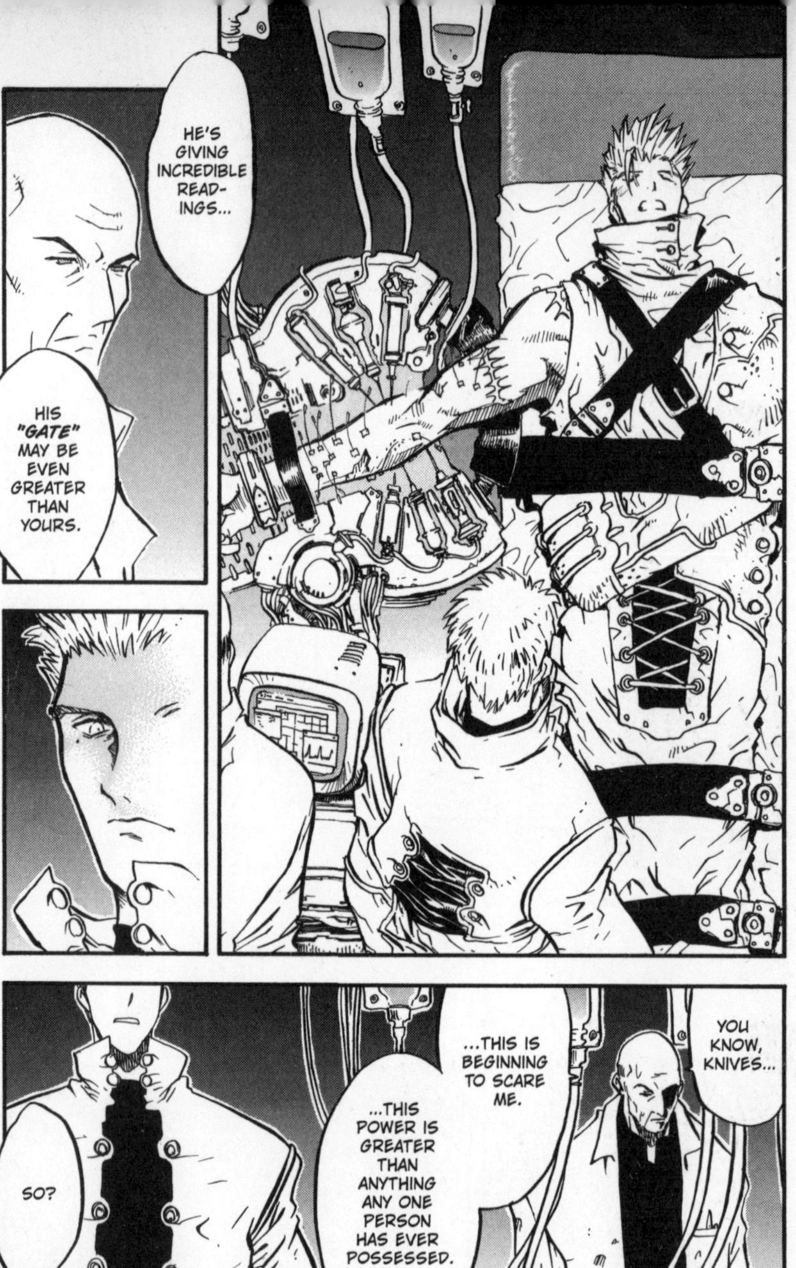
HE'S GIVING INCREDIBLE READINGS...
HIS "GATE" MAY BE EVEN GREATER THAN YOURS.
YOU KNOW, KNIVES...
...THIS IS BEGINNING TO SCARE ME.
...THIS POWER IS GREATER THAN ANYTHING ANY ONE PERSON HAS EVER POSSESSED.
SO?

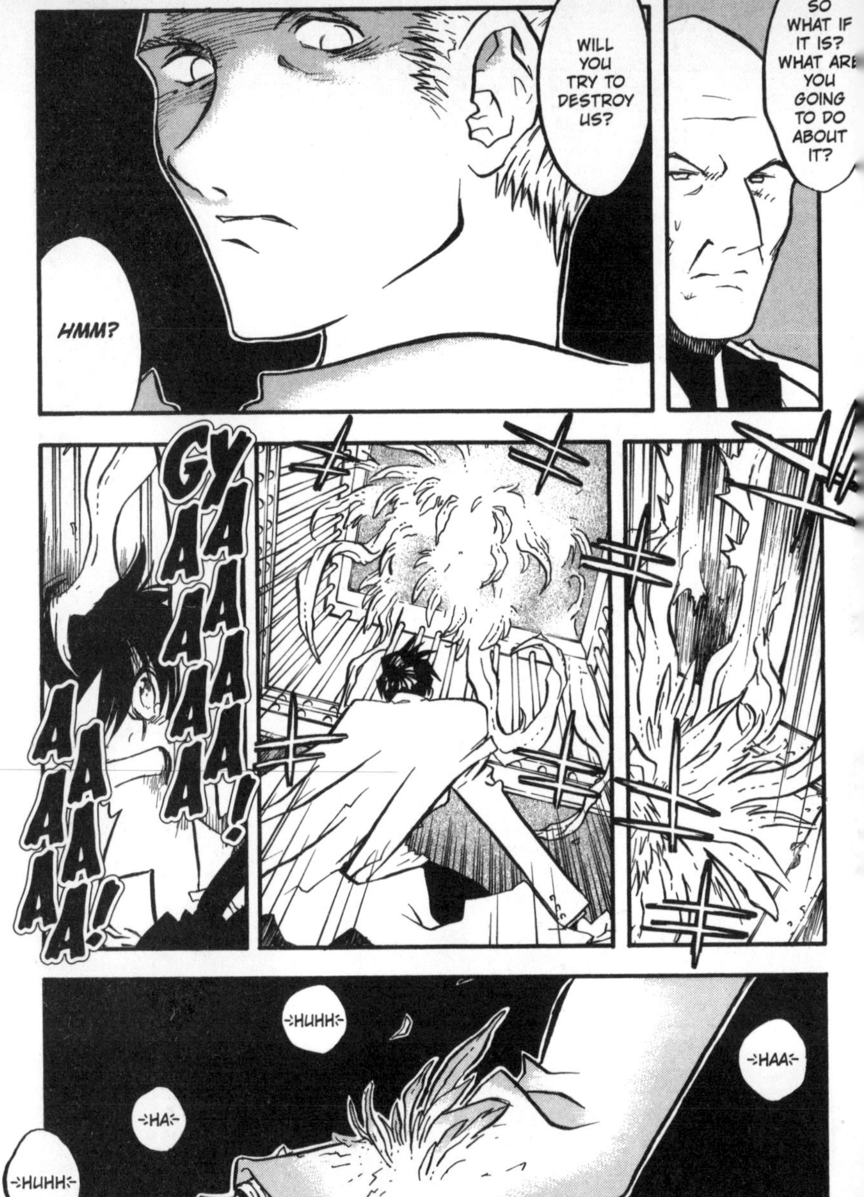
SO WHAT IF IT IS? WHAT ARE YOU GOING TO DO ABOUT IT?
WILL YOU TRY TO DESTROY US?
HMM?
GYAAAAAAAA!
AAAAAA!
HAA
HUHH
HA
HUHH

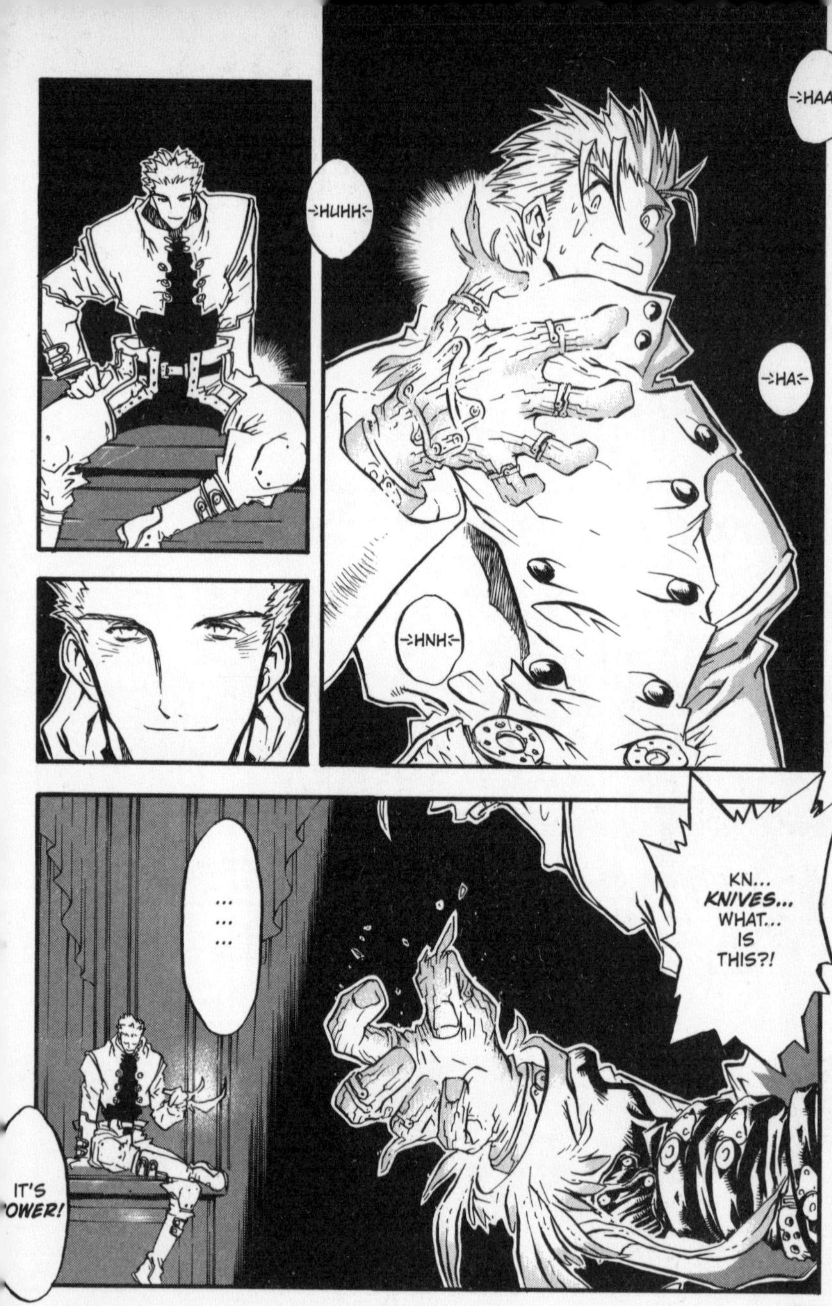

HAA
HUHH
HA
HNH
KN... KNIVES... WHAT... IS THIS?!
...
...
...
IT'S
OWER!

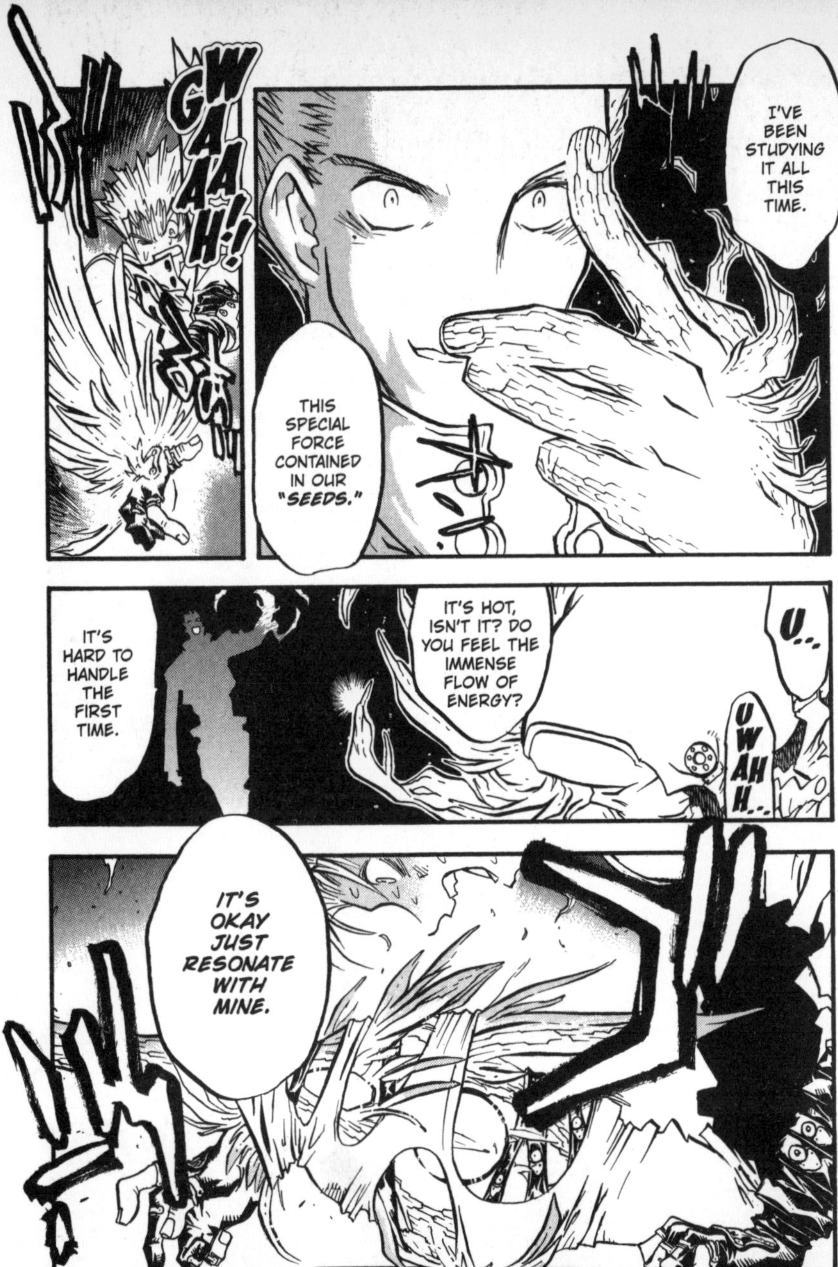
I'VE BEEN STUDYING IT ALL THIS TIME.
THIS SPECIAL FORCE CONTAINED IN OUR "SEEDS."
GWAAAH!!
U...
UWAH...
IT'S HOT, ISN'T IT? DO YOU FEEL THE IMMENSE FLOW OF ENERGY?
IT'S HARD TO HANDLE THE FIRST TIME.
IT'S OKAY JUST RESONATE WITH MINE.

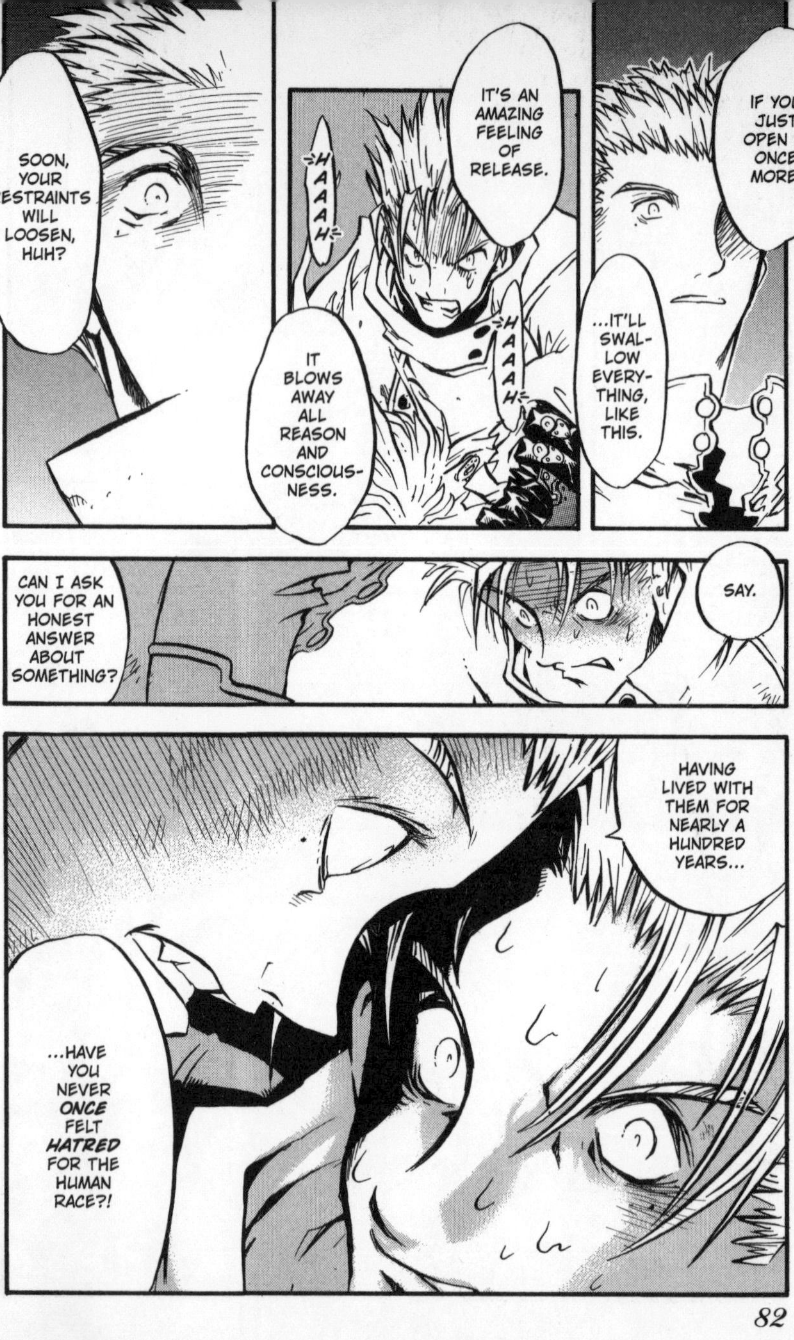
IF YOU JUST OPEN IT ONCE MORE...
...IT'LL SWALLOW EVERYTHING, LIKE THIS.
IT'S AN AMAZING FEELING OF RELEASE.
HAAAAH
HAAAAH
IT BLOWS AWAY ALL REASON AND CONSCIOUSNESS.
SOON, YOUR RESTRAINTS WILL LOOSEN, HUH?
SAY.
CAN I ASK YOU FOR AN HONEST ANSWER ABOUT SOMETHING?
HAVING LIVED WITH THEM FOR NEARLY A HUNDRED YEARS...
...HAVE YOU NEVER ONCE FELT HATRED FOR THE HUMAN RACE?!

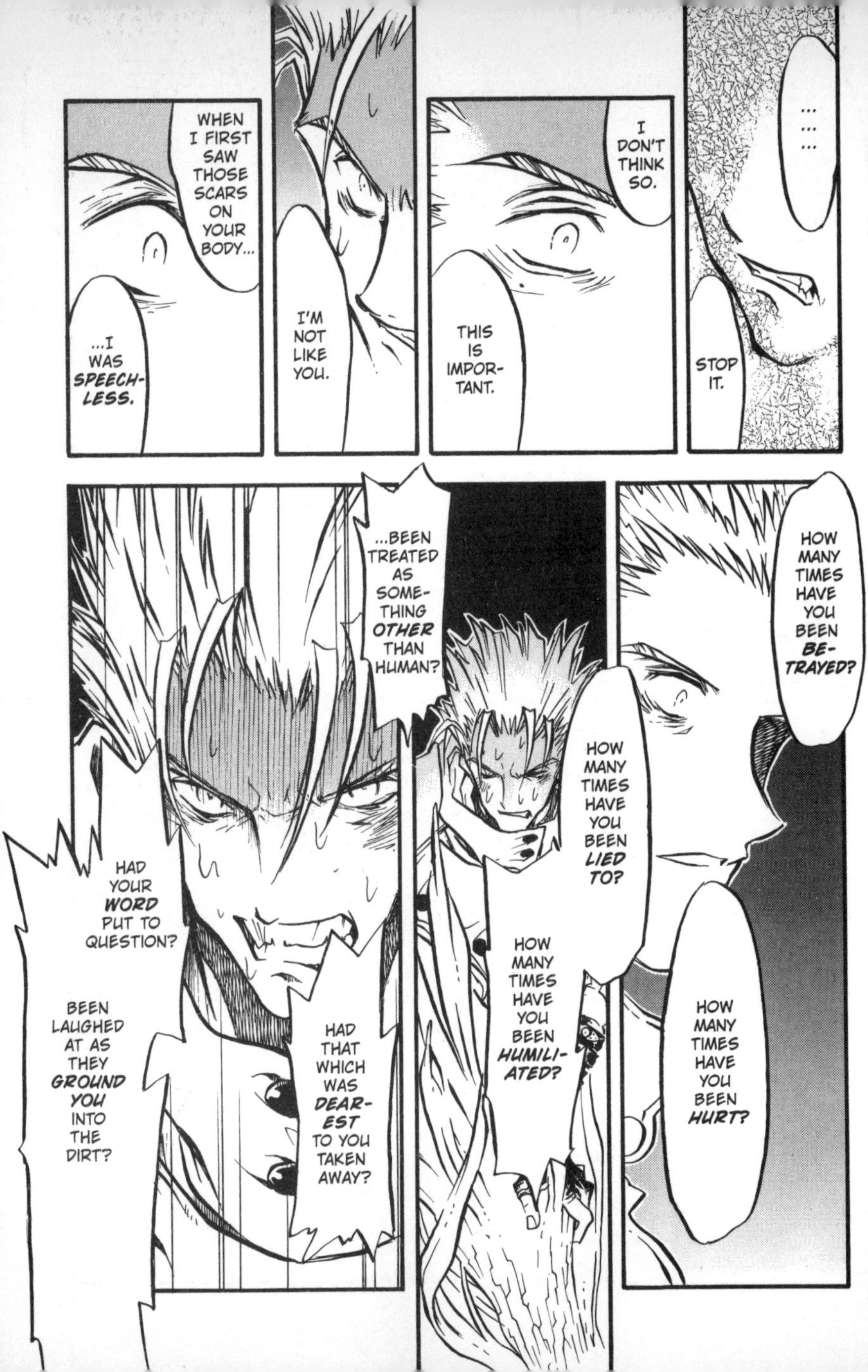
... ... ...
STOP IT.
I DON'T THINK SO.
THIS IS IMPORTANT.
I'M NOT LIKE YOU.
WHEN I FIRST SAW THOSE SCARS ON YOUR BODY...
...I WAS *SPEECHLESS.*
HOW MANY TIMES HAVE YOU BEEN *BETRAYED?*
HOW MANY TIMES HAVE YOU BEEN *LIED TO?*
HOW MANY TIMES HAVE YOU BEEN *HURT?*
...BEEN TREATED AS SOMETHING *OTHER* THAN HUMAN?
HOW MANY TIMES HAVE YOU BEEN *HUMILIATED?*
HAD YOUR *WORD* PUT TO QUESTION?
HAD THAT WHICH WAS *DEAREST* TO YOU TAKEN AWAY?
BEEN LAUGHED AT AS THEY *GROUND YOU* INTO THE DIRT?

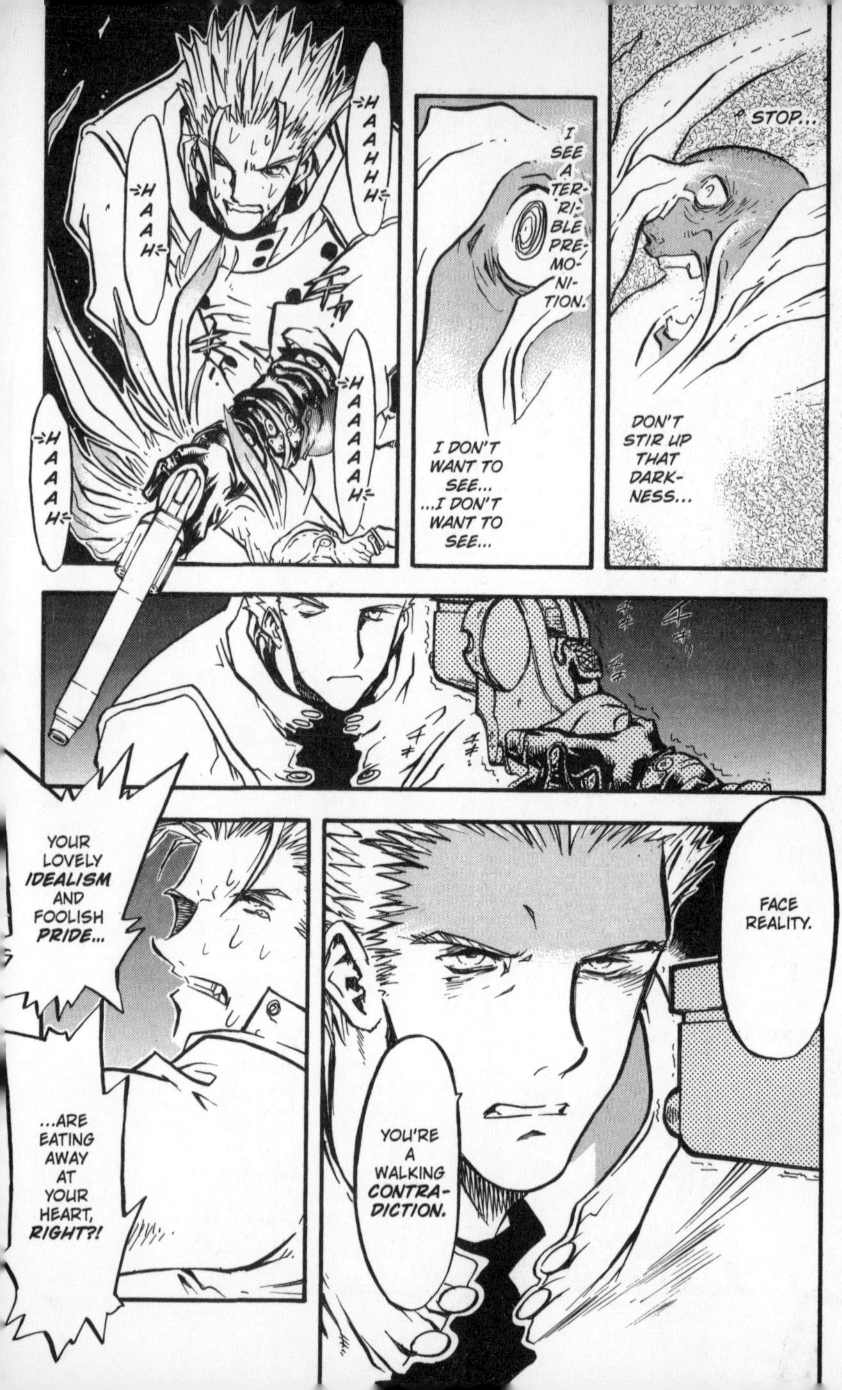

STOP...
DON'T STIR UP THAT DARKNESS...
I SEE A TERRIBLE PREMONITION.
I DON'T WANT TO SEE... ...I DON'T WANT TO SEE...
HAAHHH
HAAAH
HAAAAAAH
HAAAAH
FACE REALITY.
YOU'RE A WALKING CONTRADICTION.
YOUR LOVELY IDEALISM AND FOOLISH PRIDE...
...ARE EATING AWAY AT YOUR HEART, RIGHT?!

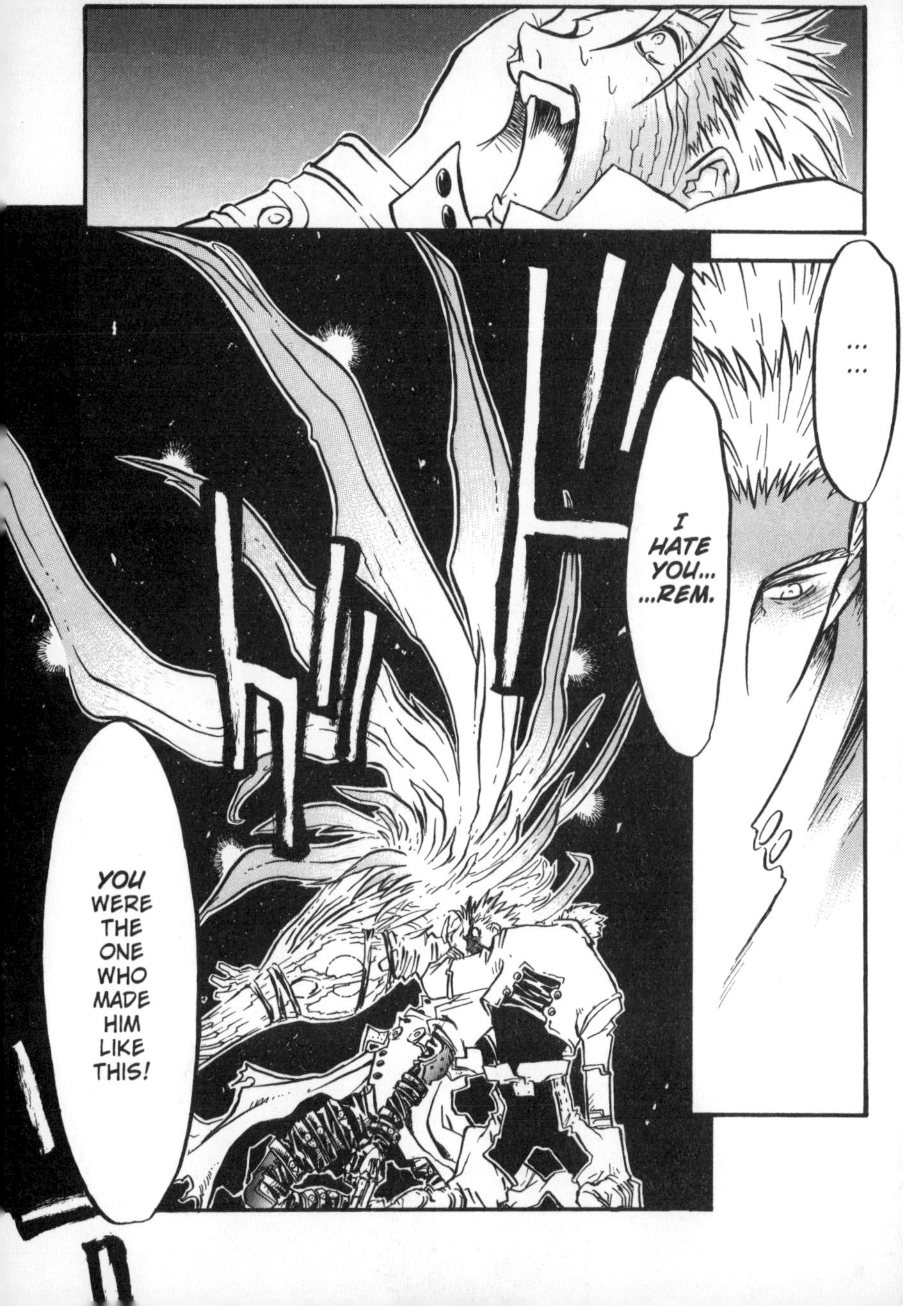
......
I HATE YOU... ...REM.
YOU WERE THE ONE WHO MADE HIM LIKE THIS!

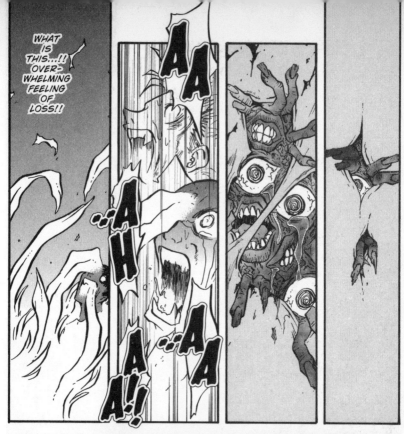

WHAT IS THIS...!! OVER-WHELMING FEELING OF LOSS!!

AAAH AH AAA!!

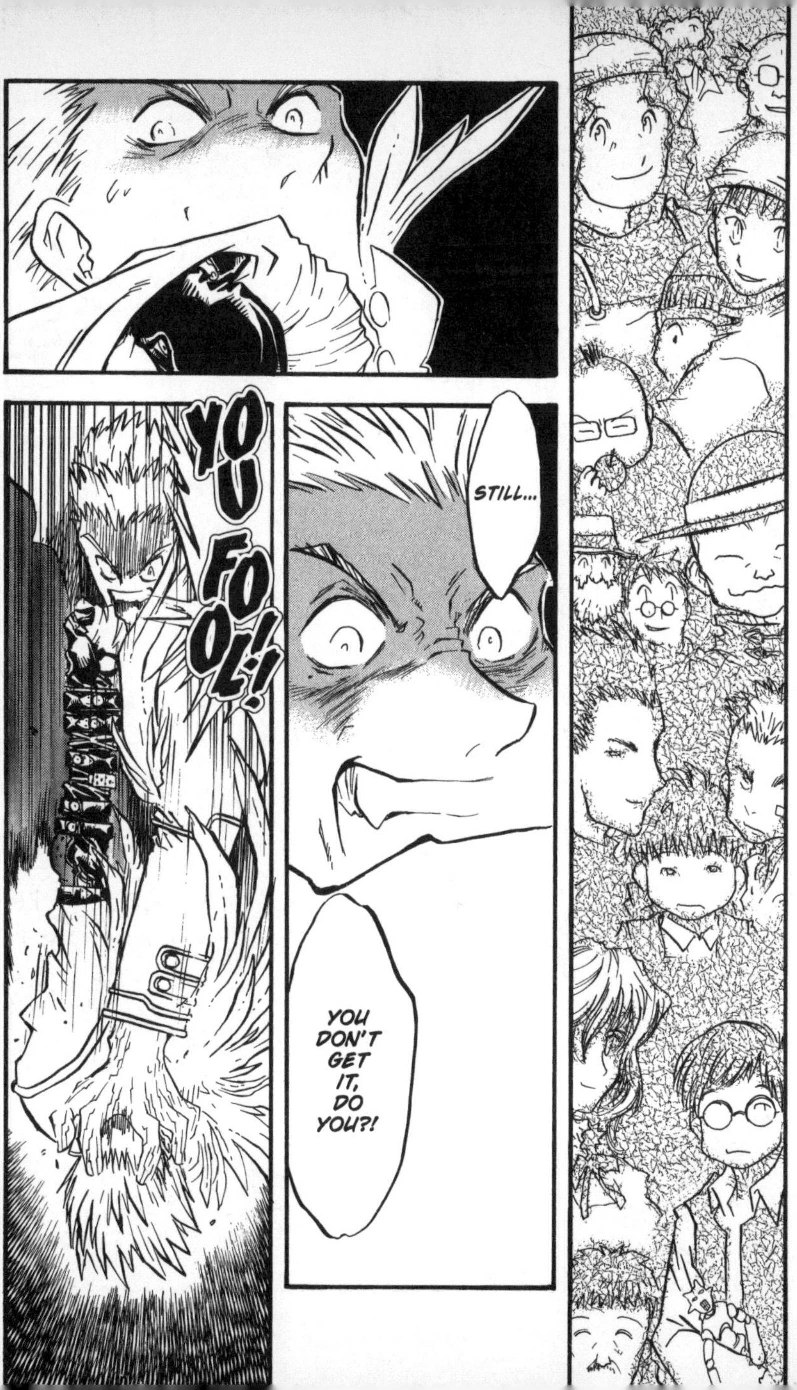
STILL...
YOU DON'T GET IT, DO YOU?!
YOU FOOL!

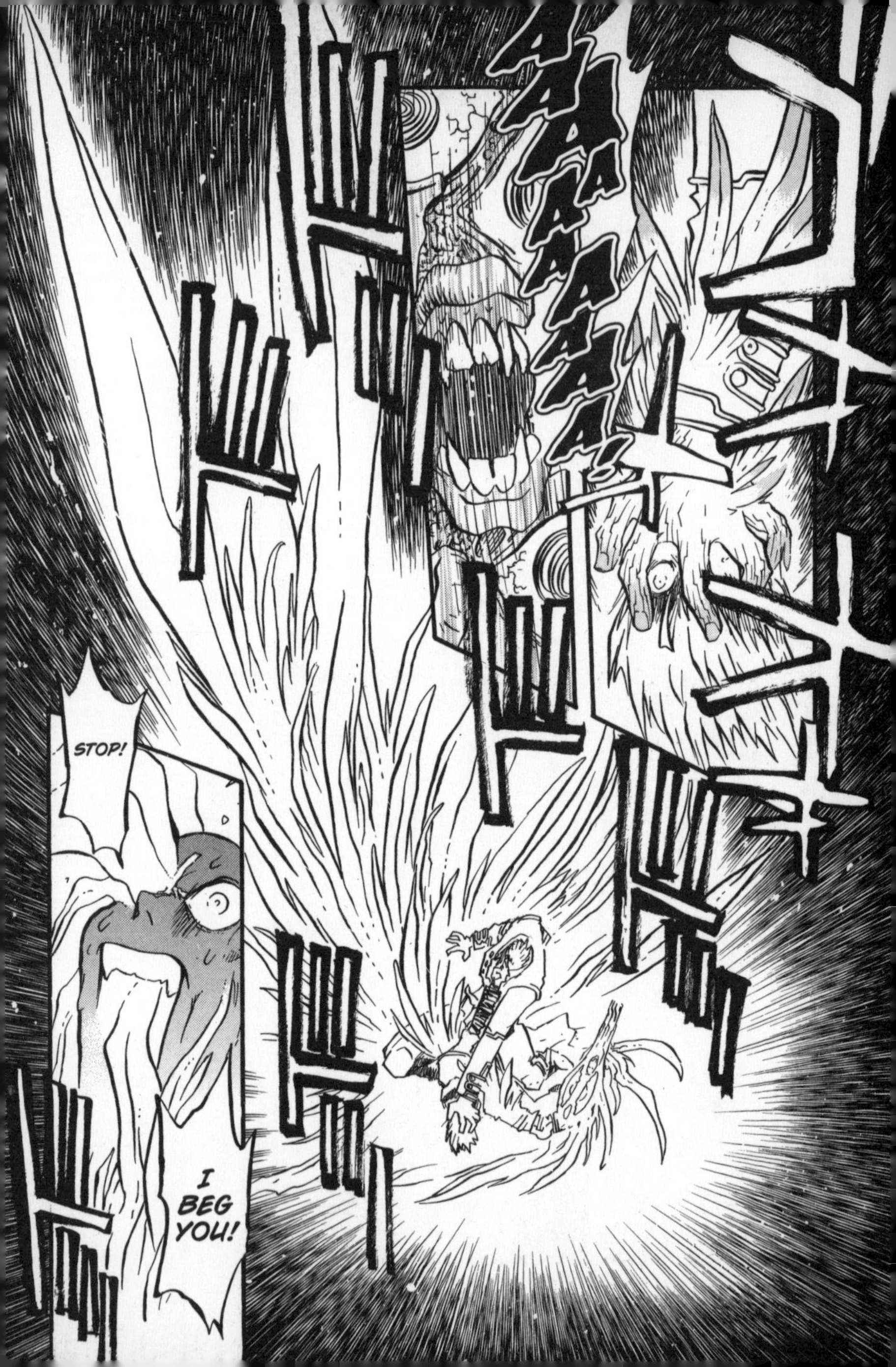
AAAAAAAAA!
STOP!
I BEG YOU!

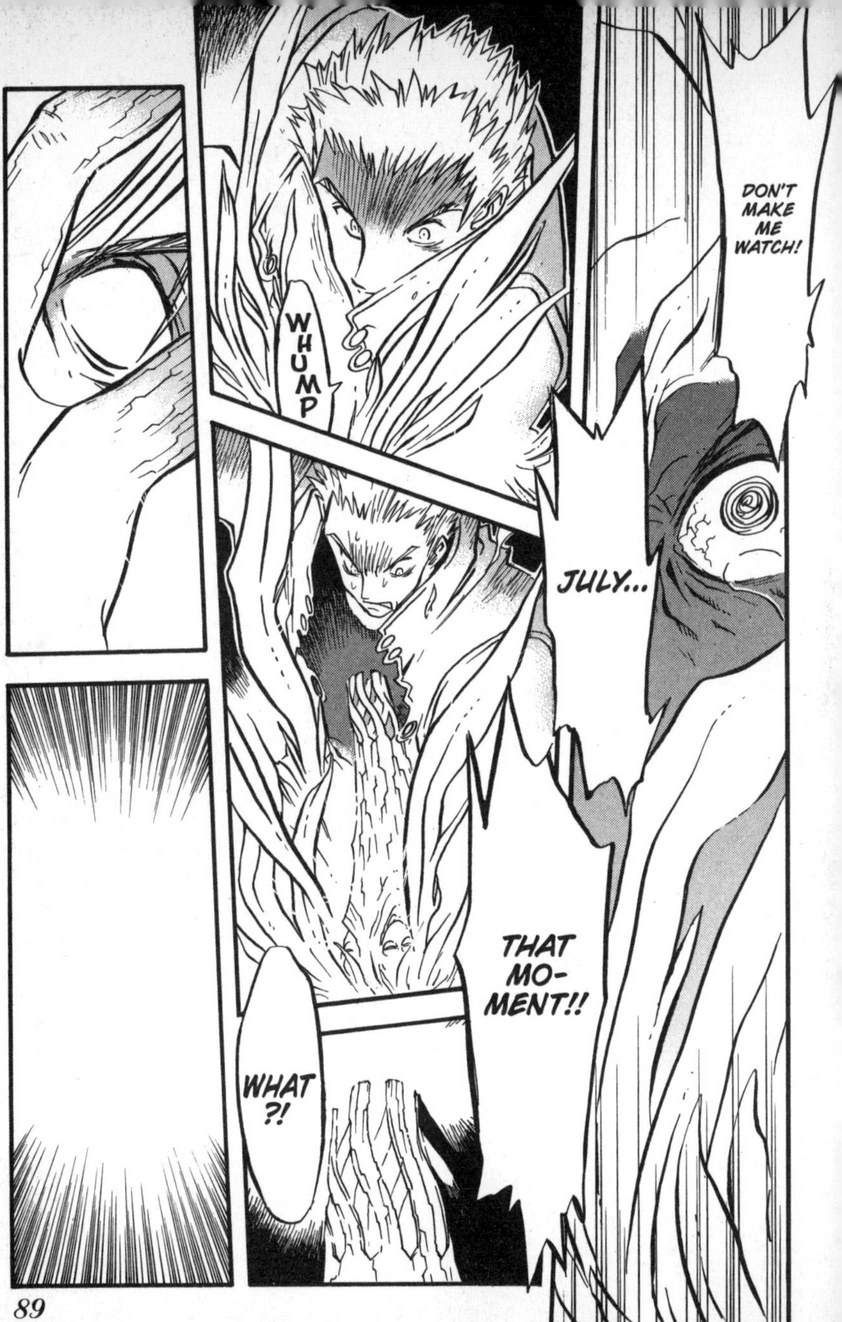
DON'T MAKE ME WATCH!
JULY...
THAT MO-MENT!!
WHUMP
WHAT?!

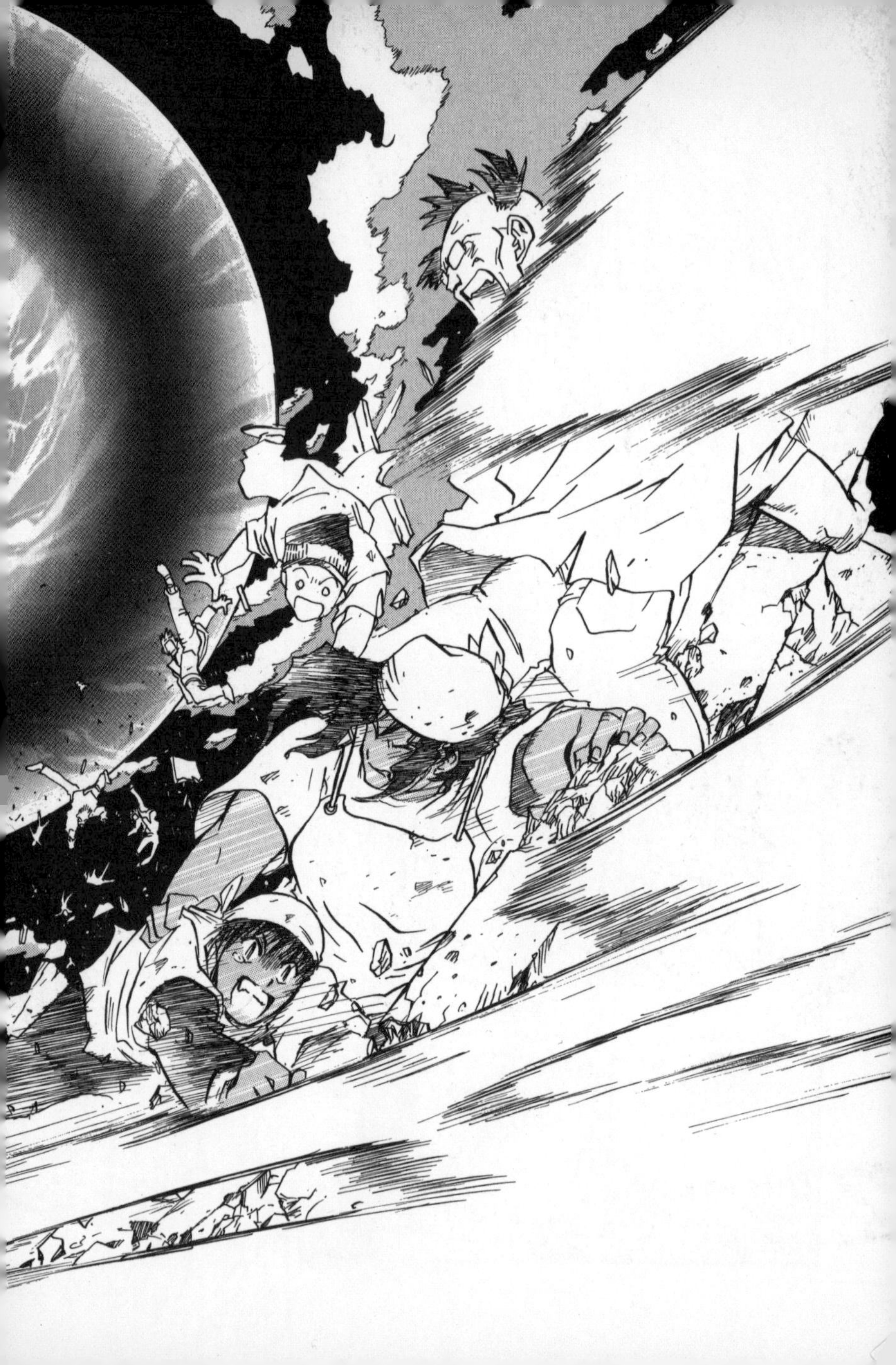

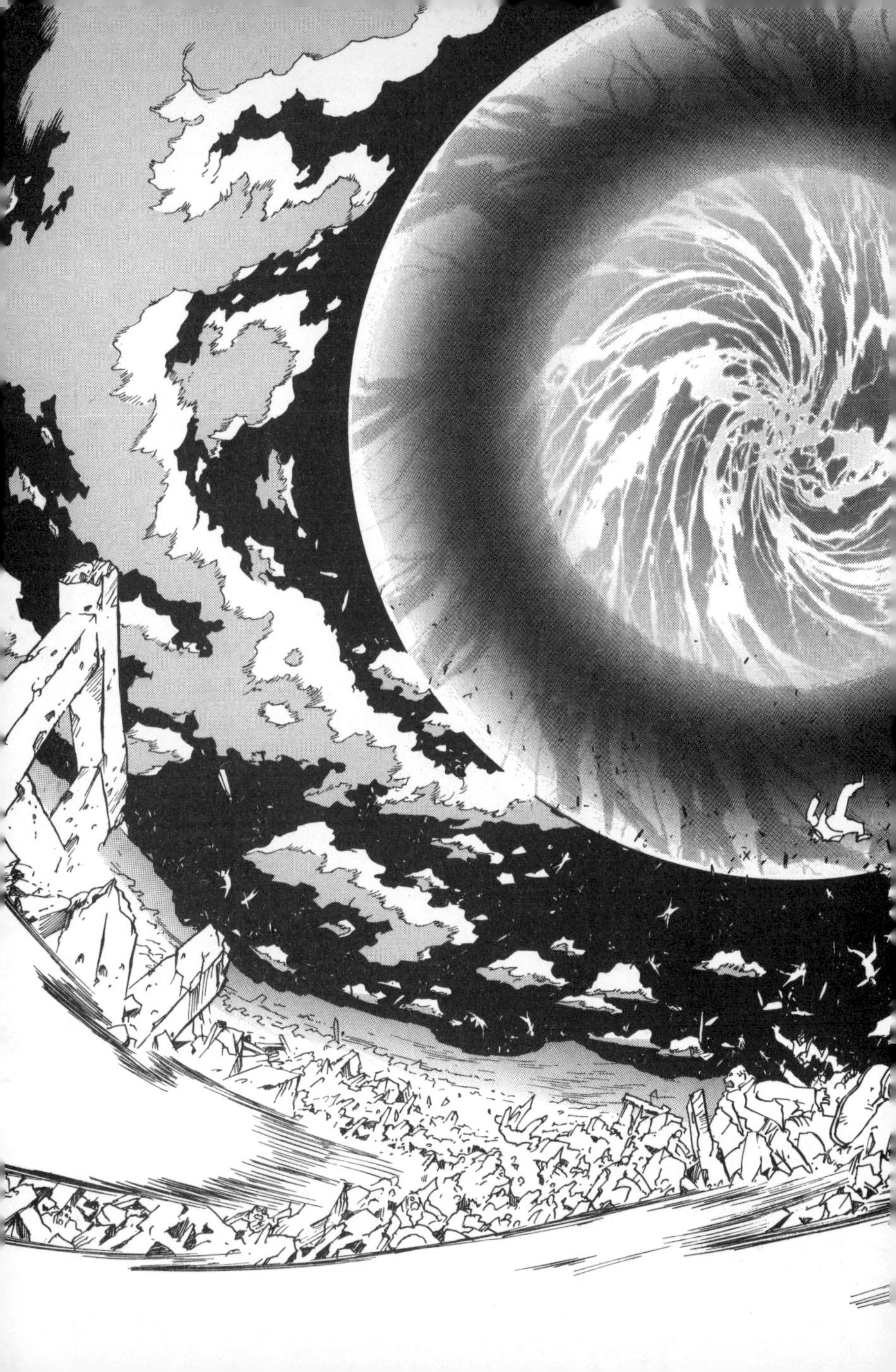

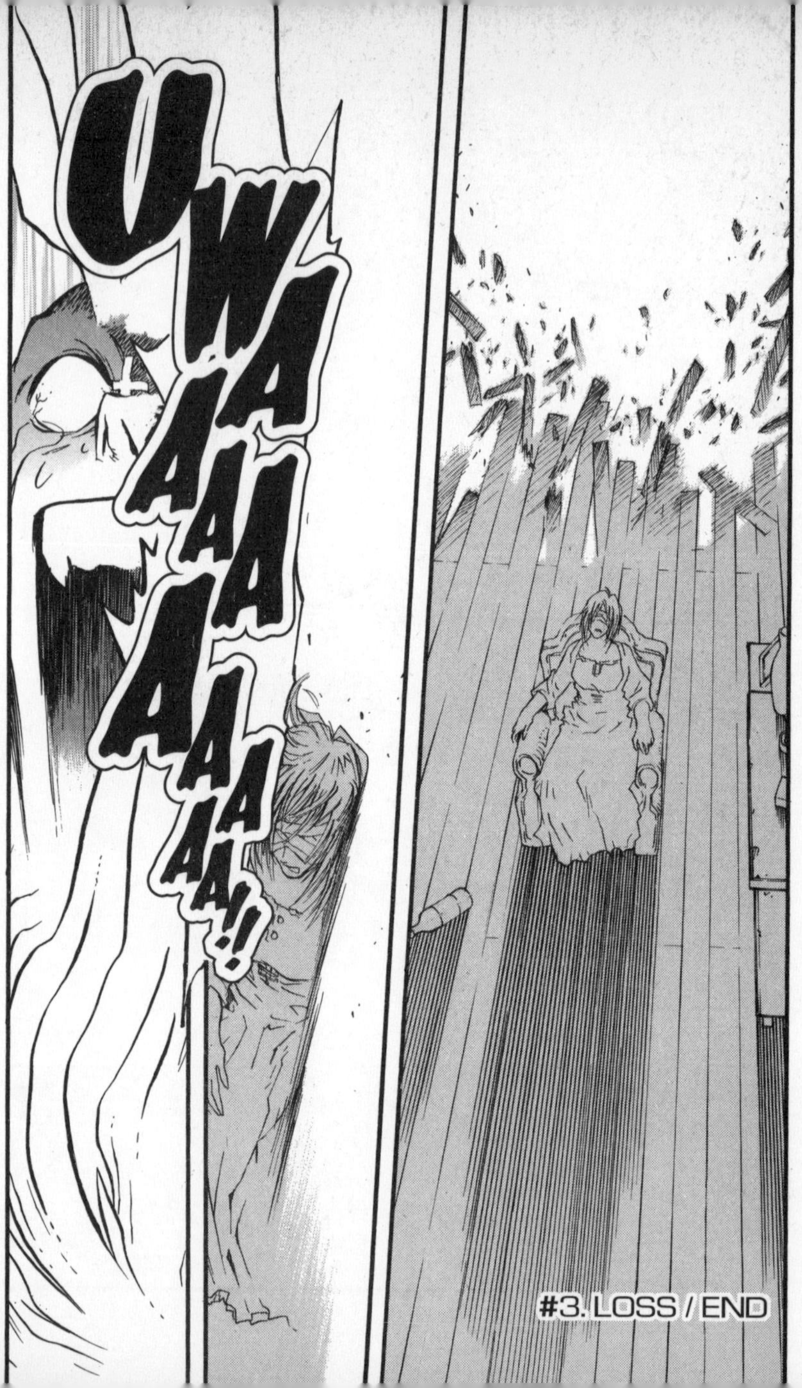
OWAAAAAAAAA!!
#3. LOSS / END

# #4 VILLAIN

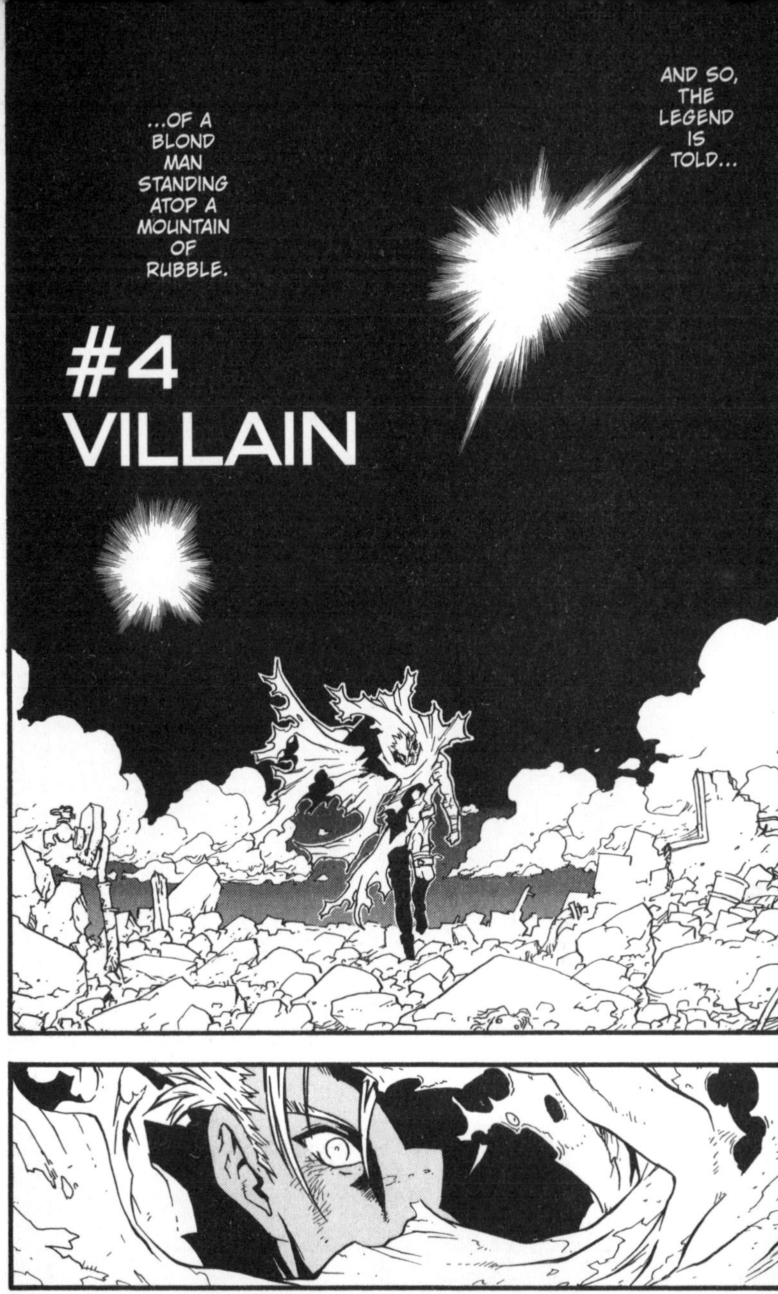
AND SO, THE LEGEND IS TOLD...
...OF A BLOND MAN STANDING ATOP A MOUNTAIN OF RUBBLE.

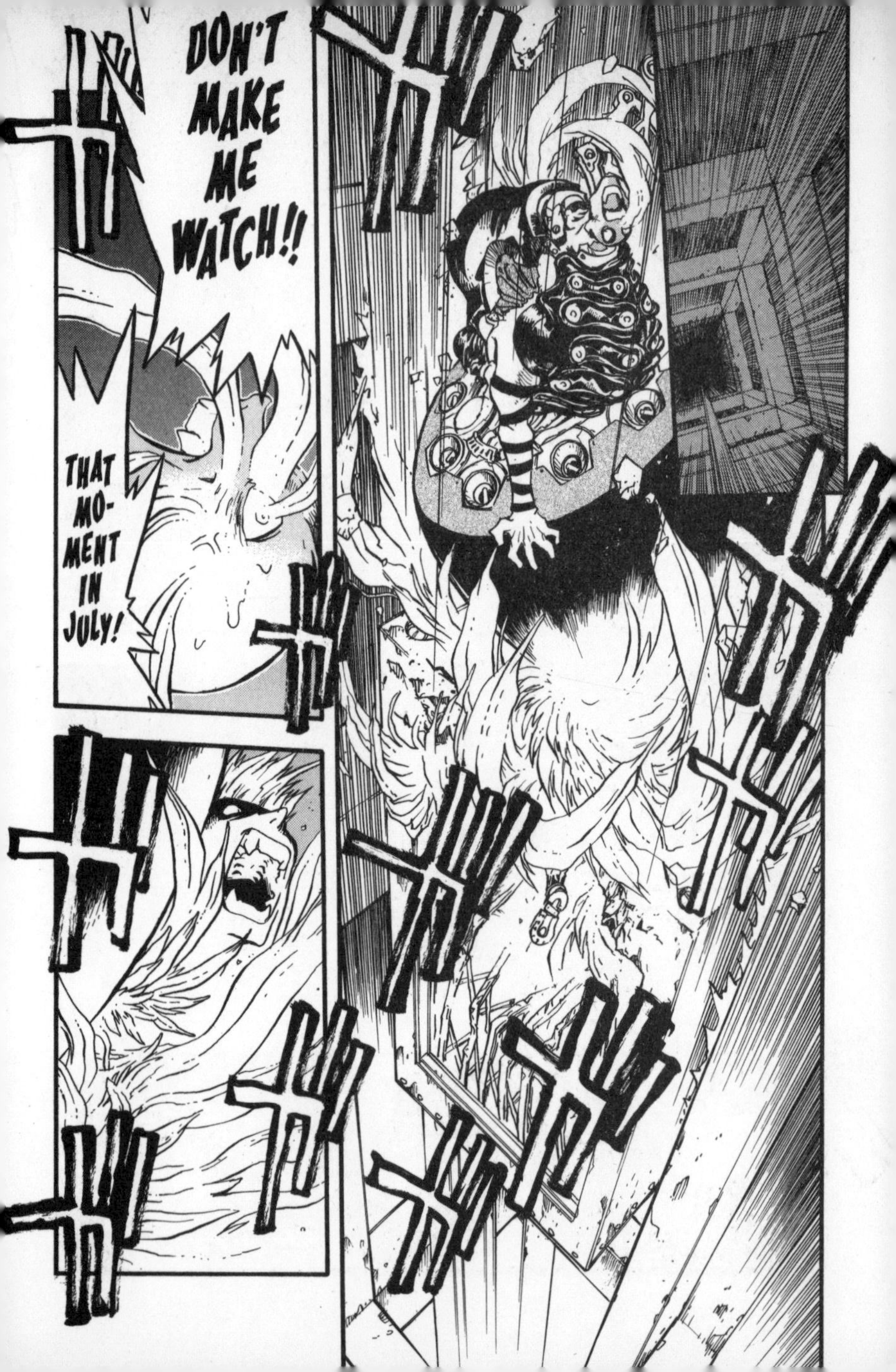
DON'T MAKE ME WATCH!!
THAT MOMENT IN JULY!

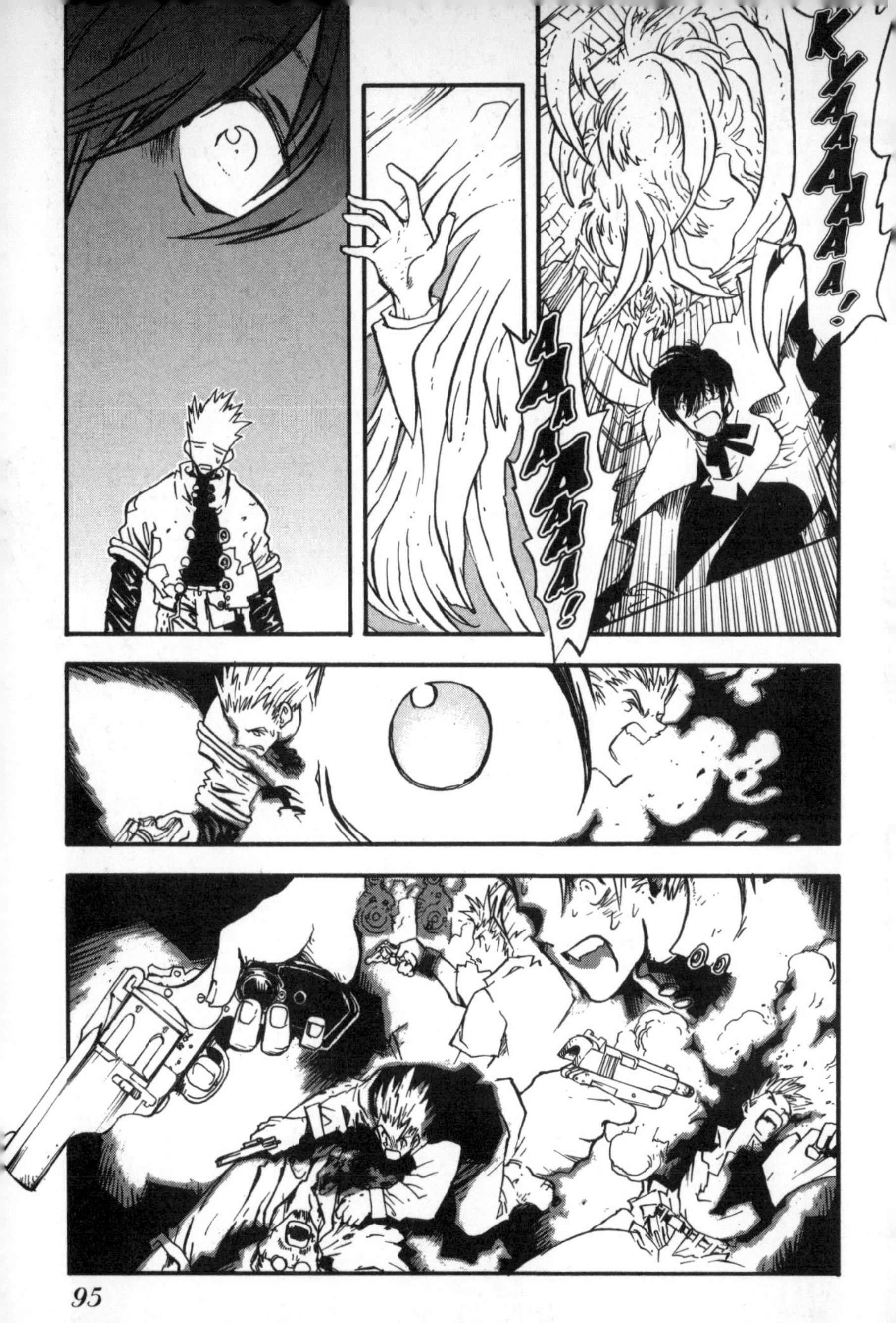
KYAAAAAAAA!
AAAAAAAAAA!

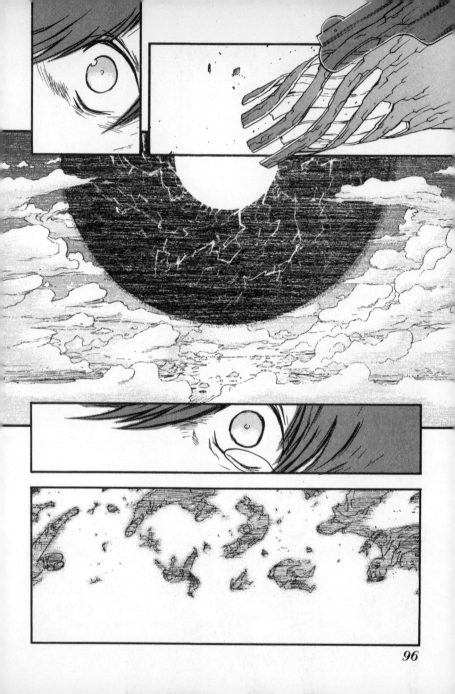

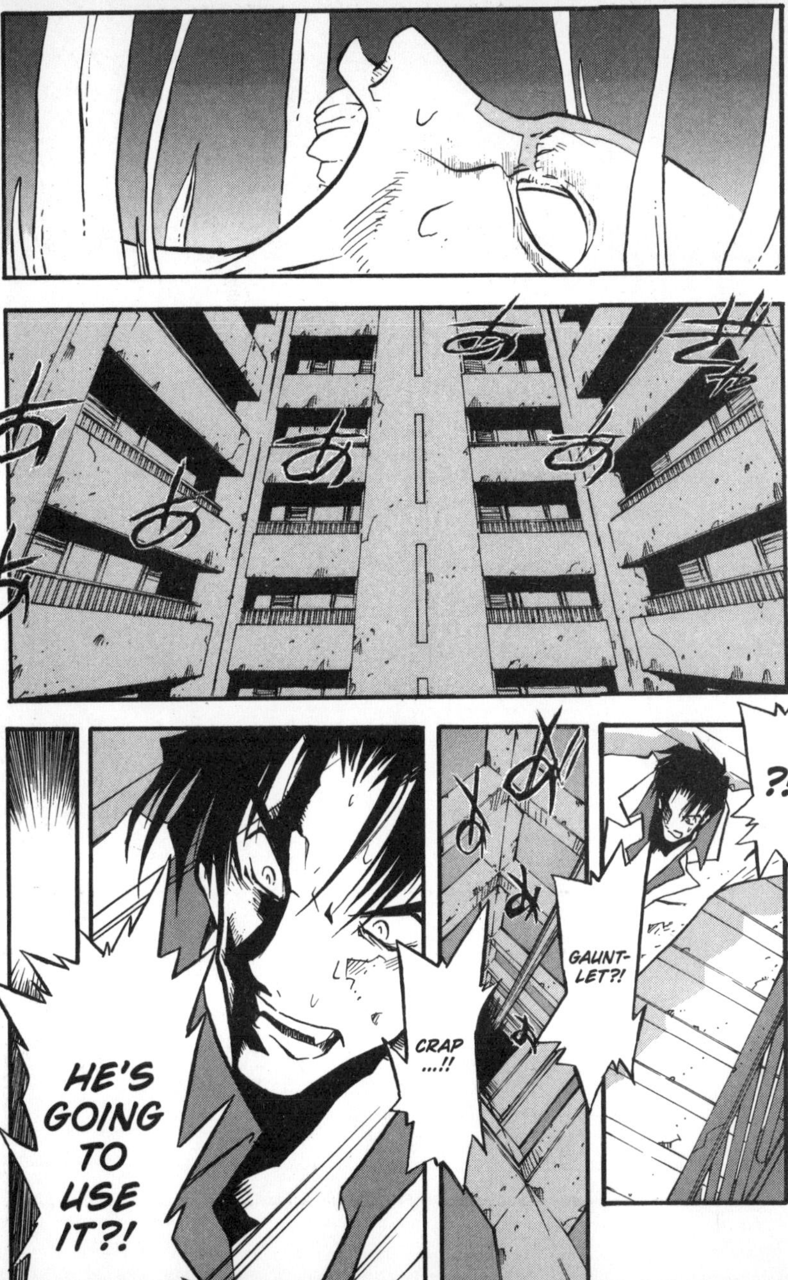
?!
GAUNT-LET?!
CRAP ...!!
HE'S GOING TO USE IT?!

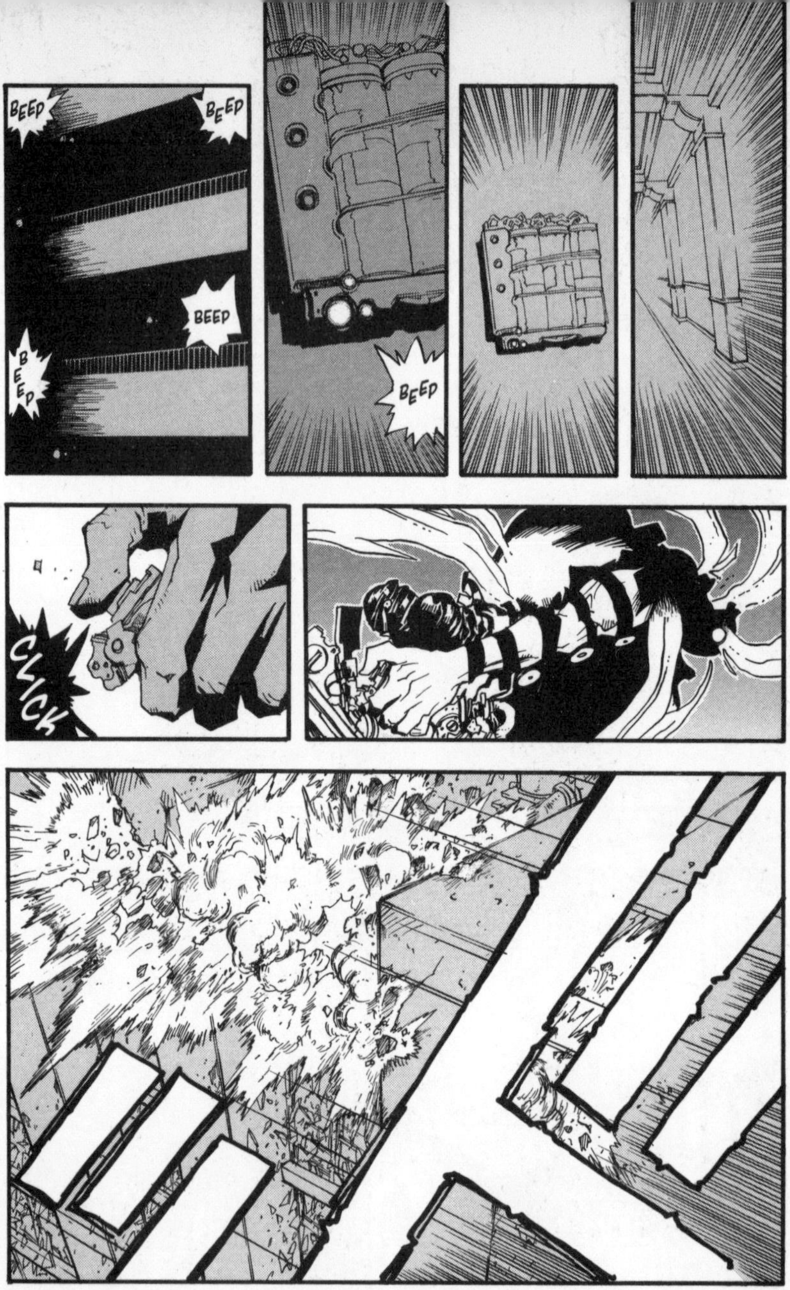
BEEP
BEEP
BEEP
BEEP
BEEP
CLICK

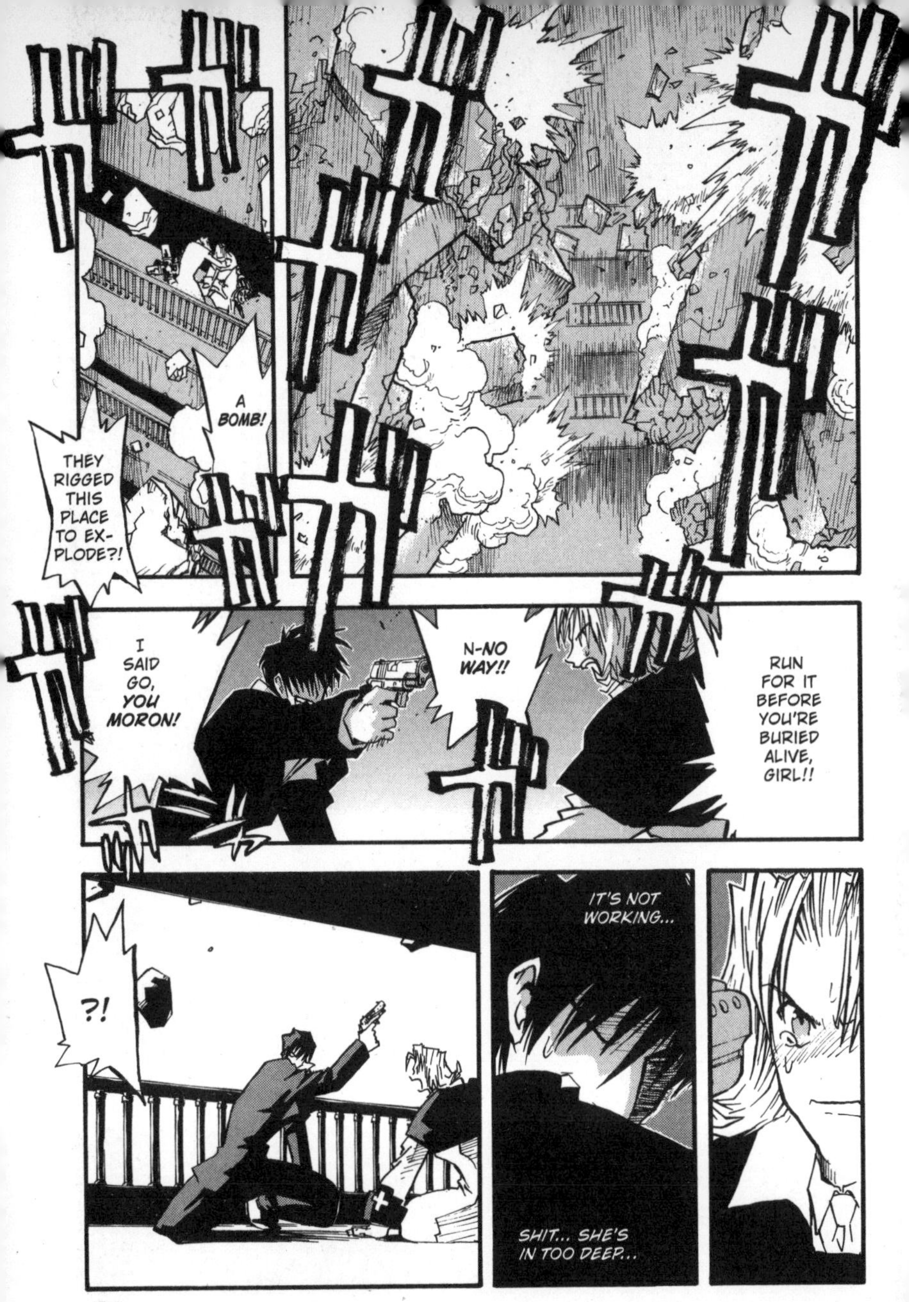
A BOMB!
THEY RIGGED THIS PLACE TO EX-PLODE?!
RUN FOR IT BEFORE YOU'RE BURIED ALIVE, GIRL!!
N-NO WAY!!
I SAID GO, YOU MORON!
IT'S NOT WORKING...
SHIT... SHE'S IN TOO DEEP...
?!

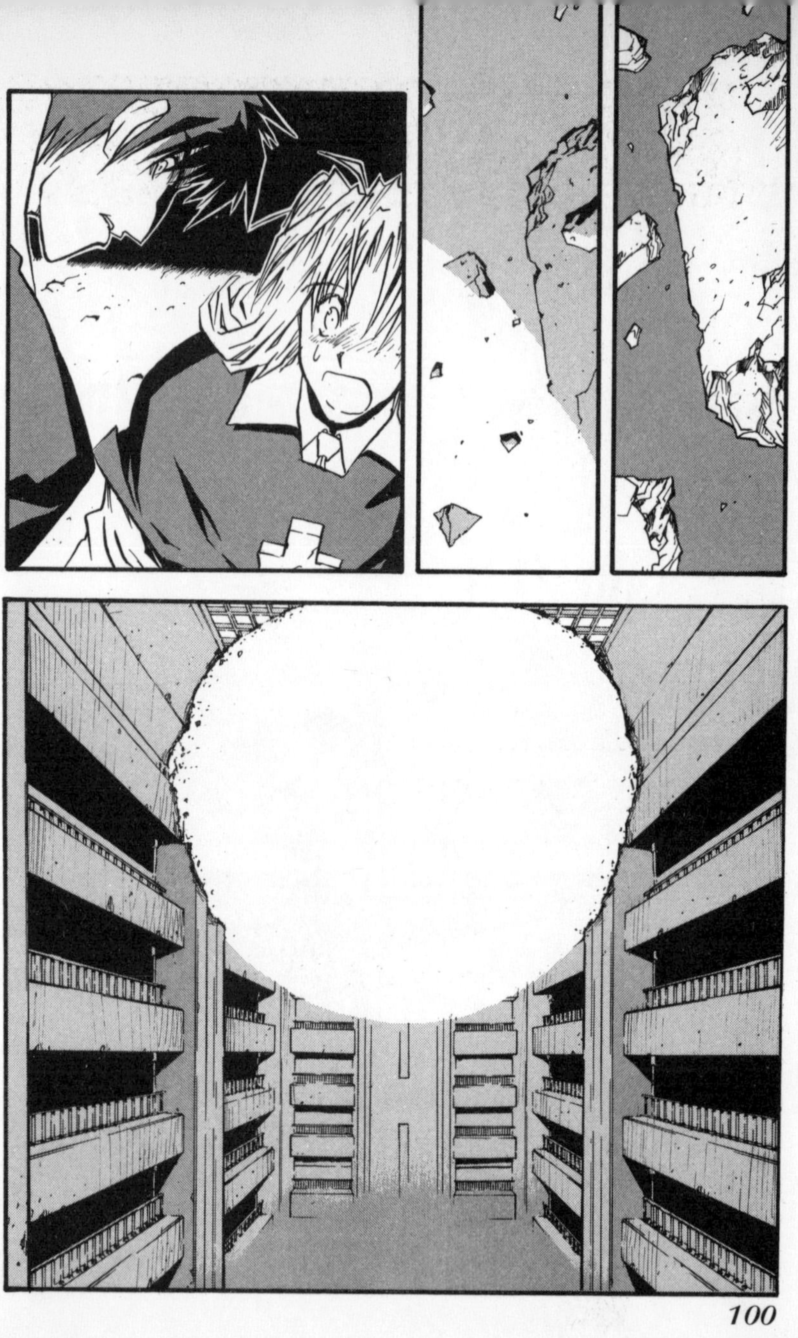

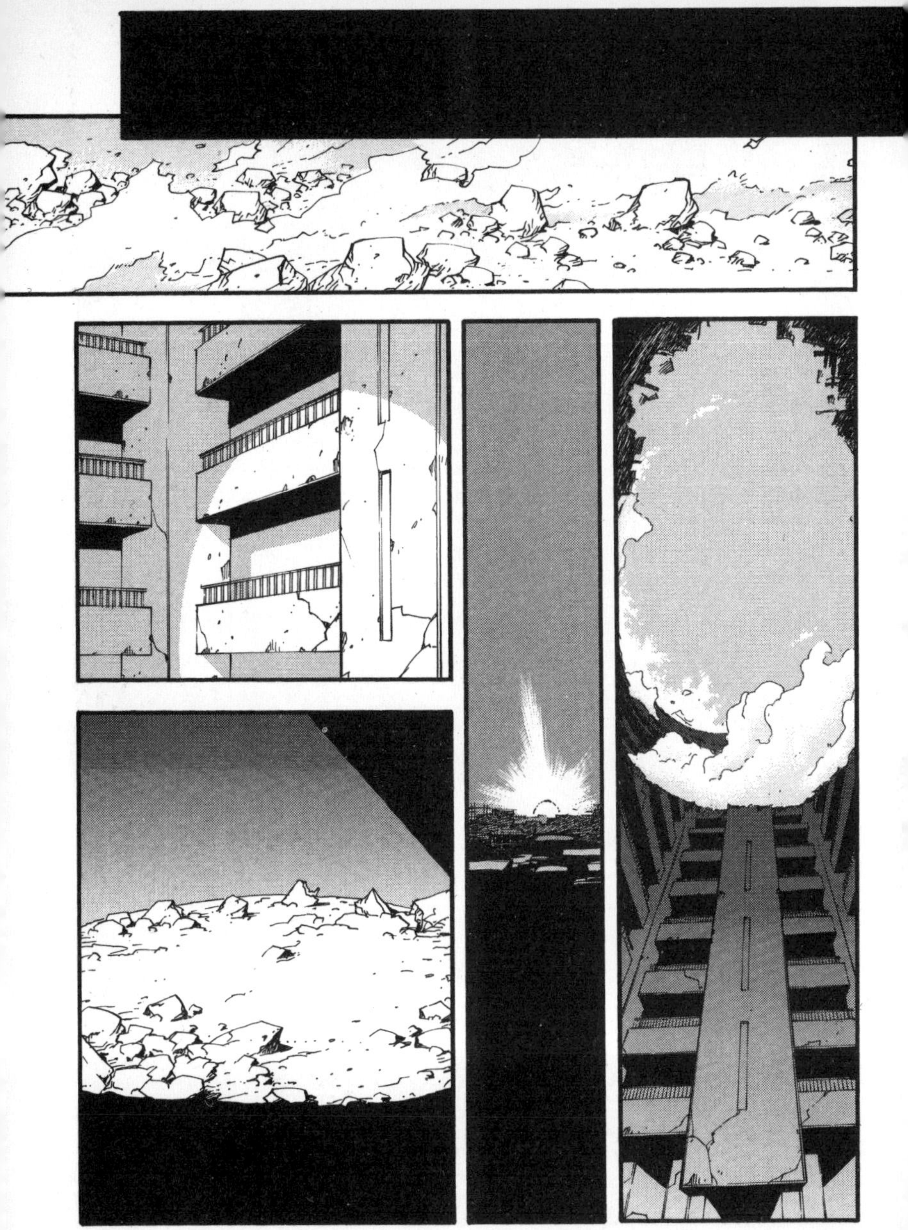

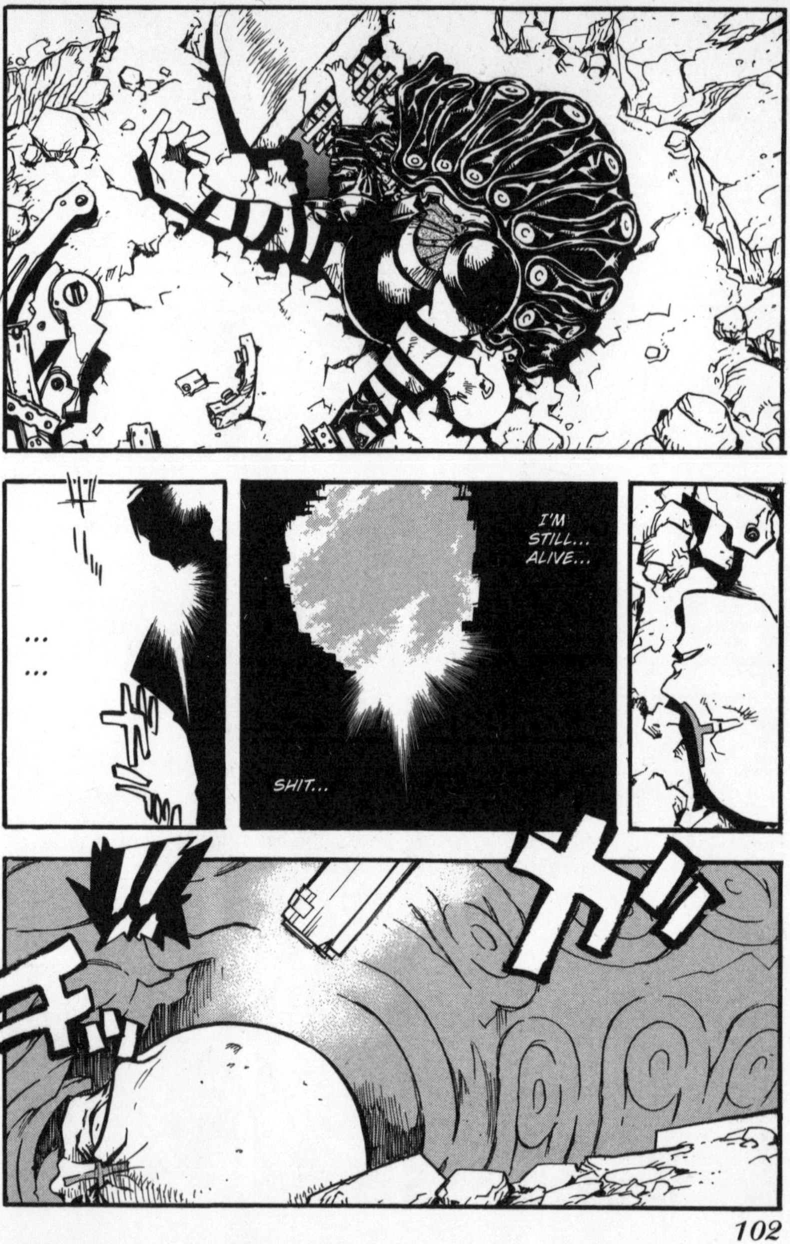
I'M STILL... ALIVE...
SHIT...
...
...

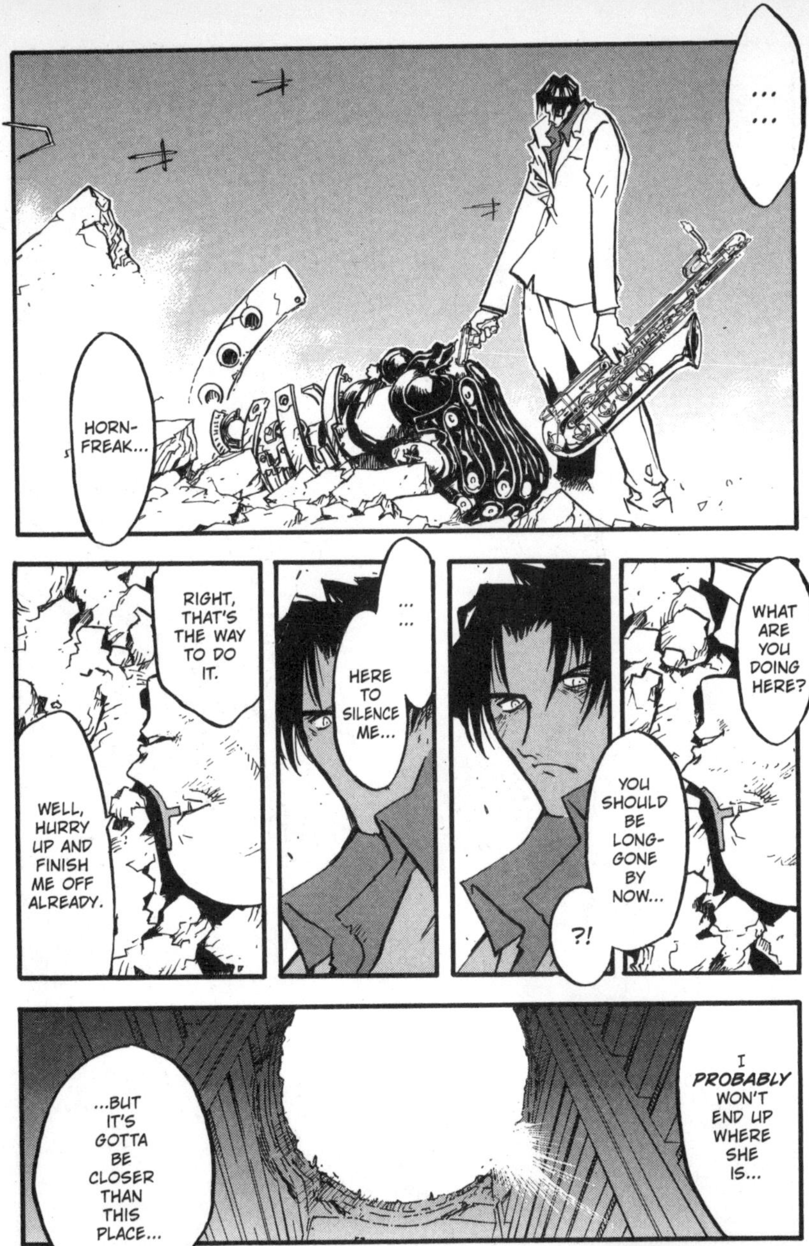
……
HORN-FREAK...
WHAT ARE YOU DOING HERE?
YOU SHOULD BE LONG-GONE BY NOW...
?!
……
HERE TO SILENCE ME...
RIGHT, THAT'S THE WAY TO DO IT.
WELL, HURRY UP AND FINISH ME OFF ALREADY.
I *PROBABLY* WON'T END UP WHERE SHE IS...
...BUT IT'S GOTTA BE CLOSER THAN THIS PLACE...

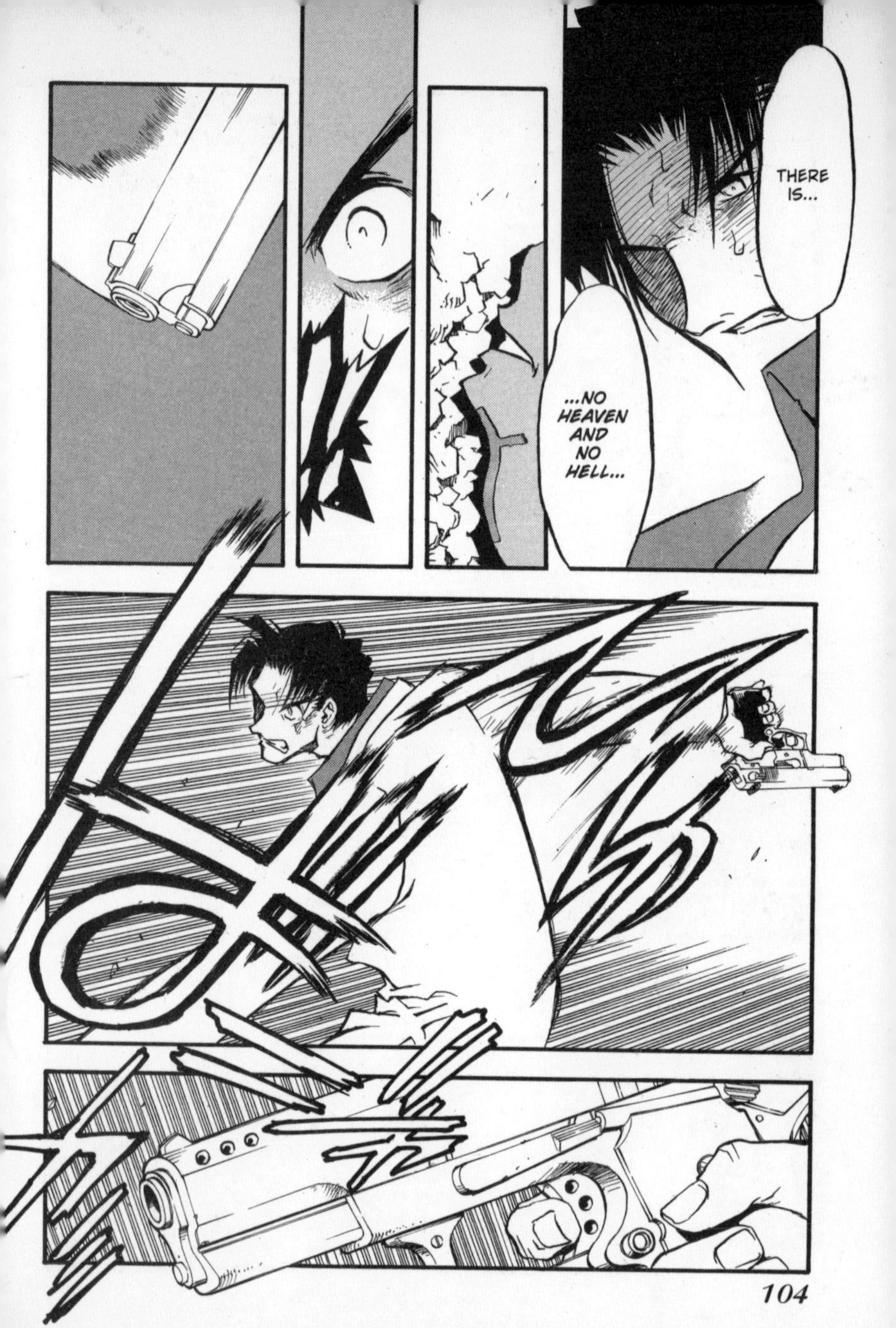
THERE IS...
...NO HEAVEN AND NO HELL...

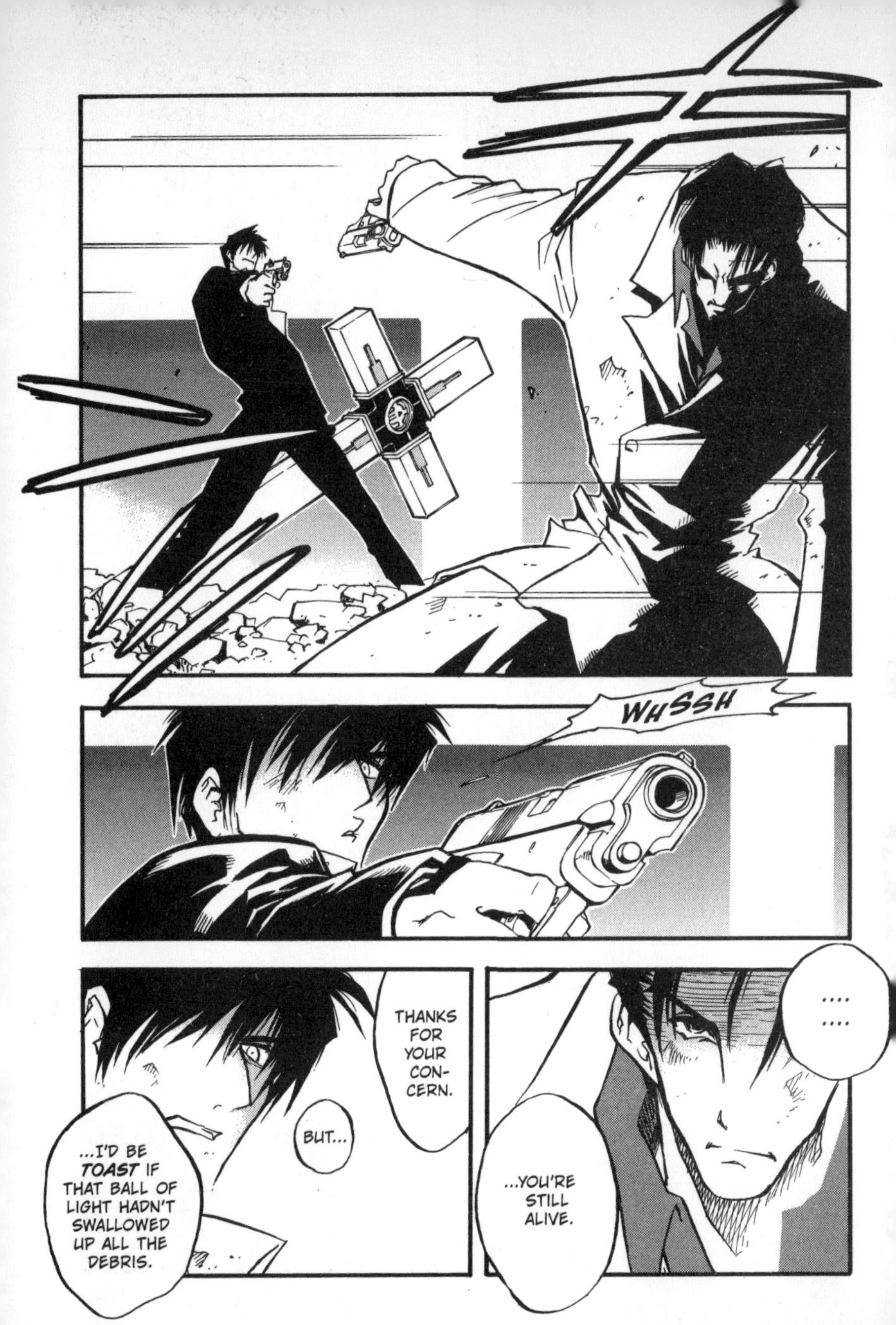
WHSSH
....
....
...YOU'RE STILL ALIVE.
THANKS FOR YOUR CON-CERN.
BUT...
...I'D BE TOAST IF THAT BALL OF LIGHT HADN'T SWALLOWED UP ALL THE DEBRIS.

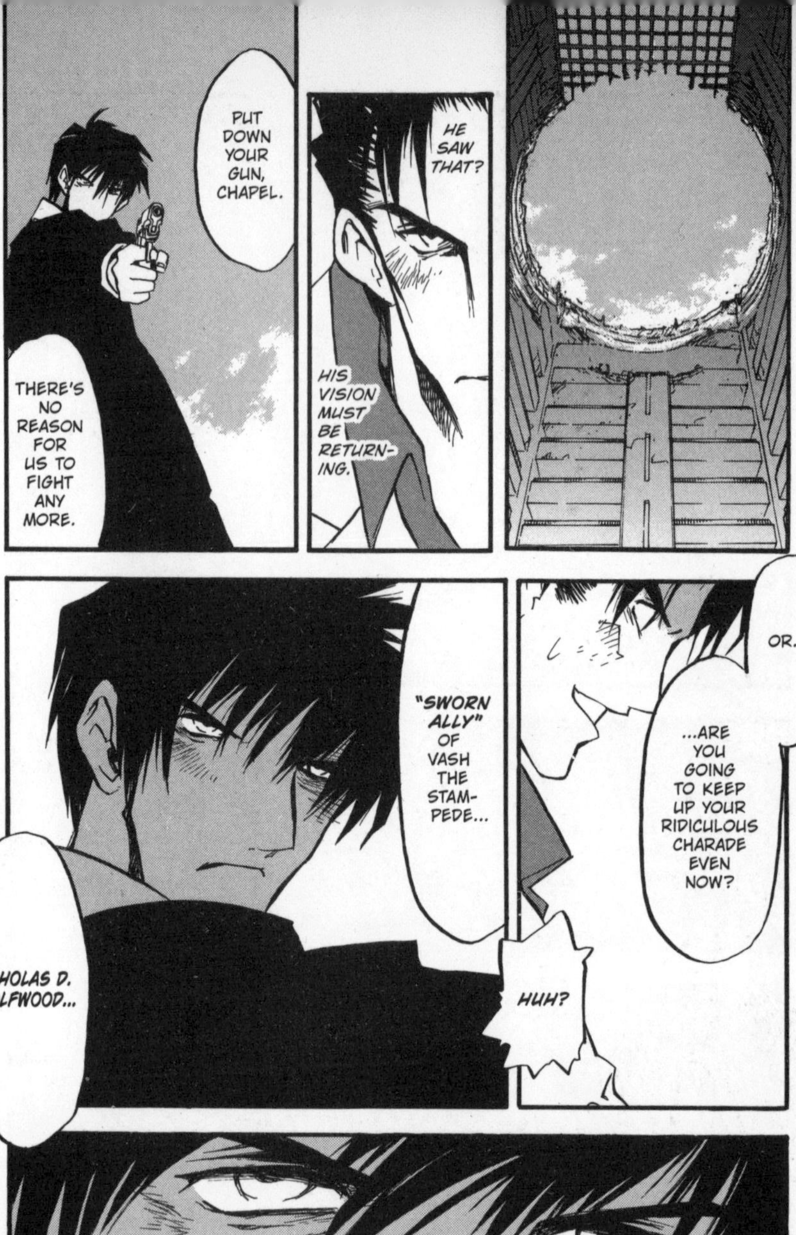
PUT DOWN YOUR GUN, CHAPEL.
THERE'S NO REASON FOR US TO FIGHT ANY MORE.
HE SAW THAT?
HIS VISION MUST BE RETURNING.
NICHOLAS D. WOLFWOOD...
"SWORN ALLY" OF VASH THE STAMPEDE...
OR...
...ARE YOU GOING TO KEEP UP YOUR RIDICULOUS CHARADE EVEN NOW?
HUH?

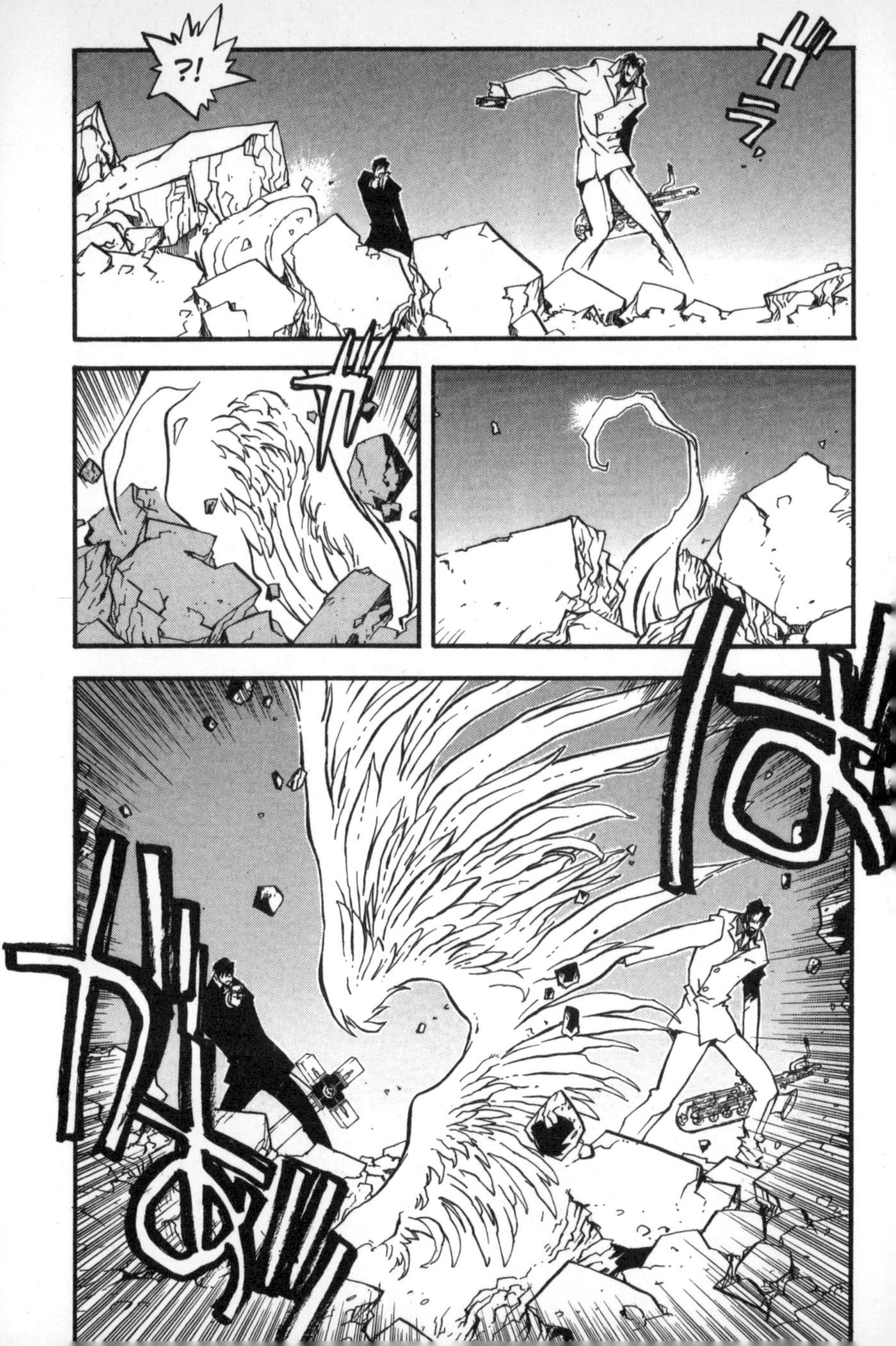

ガラ
?!

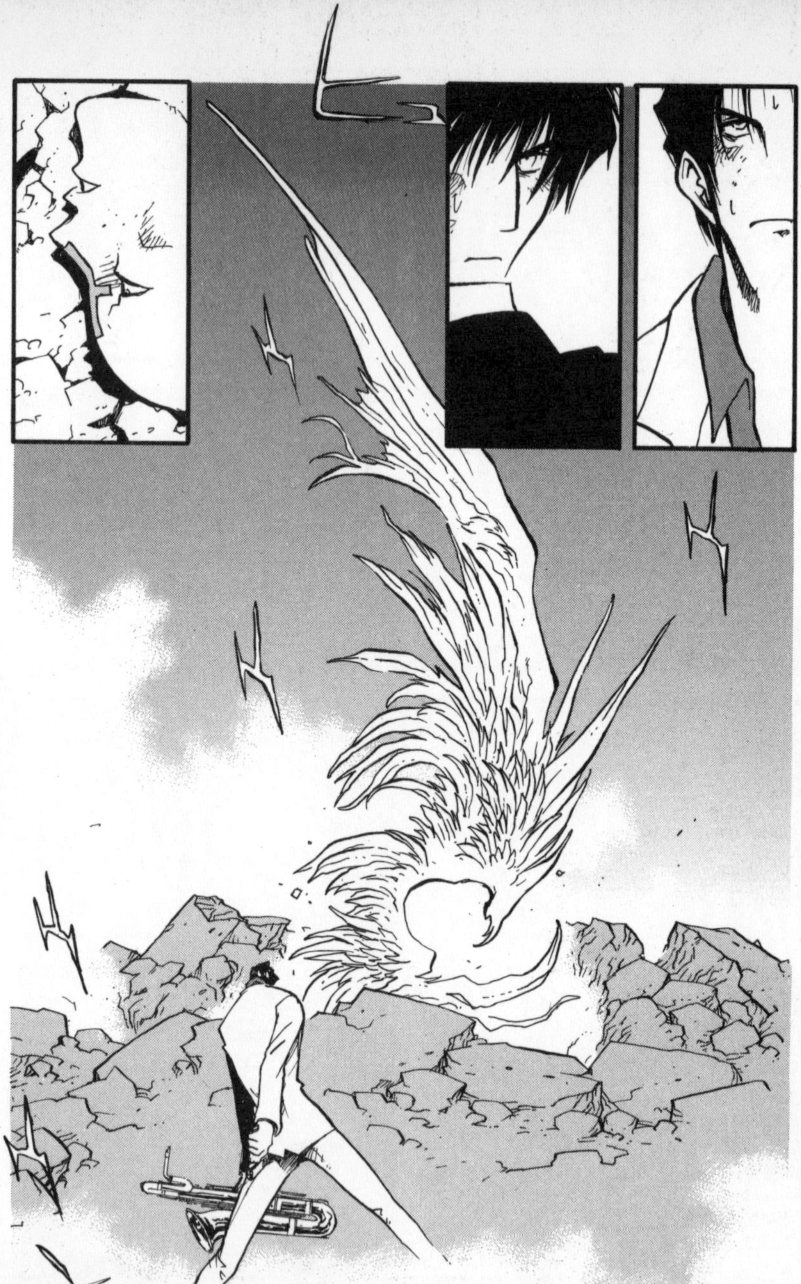

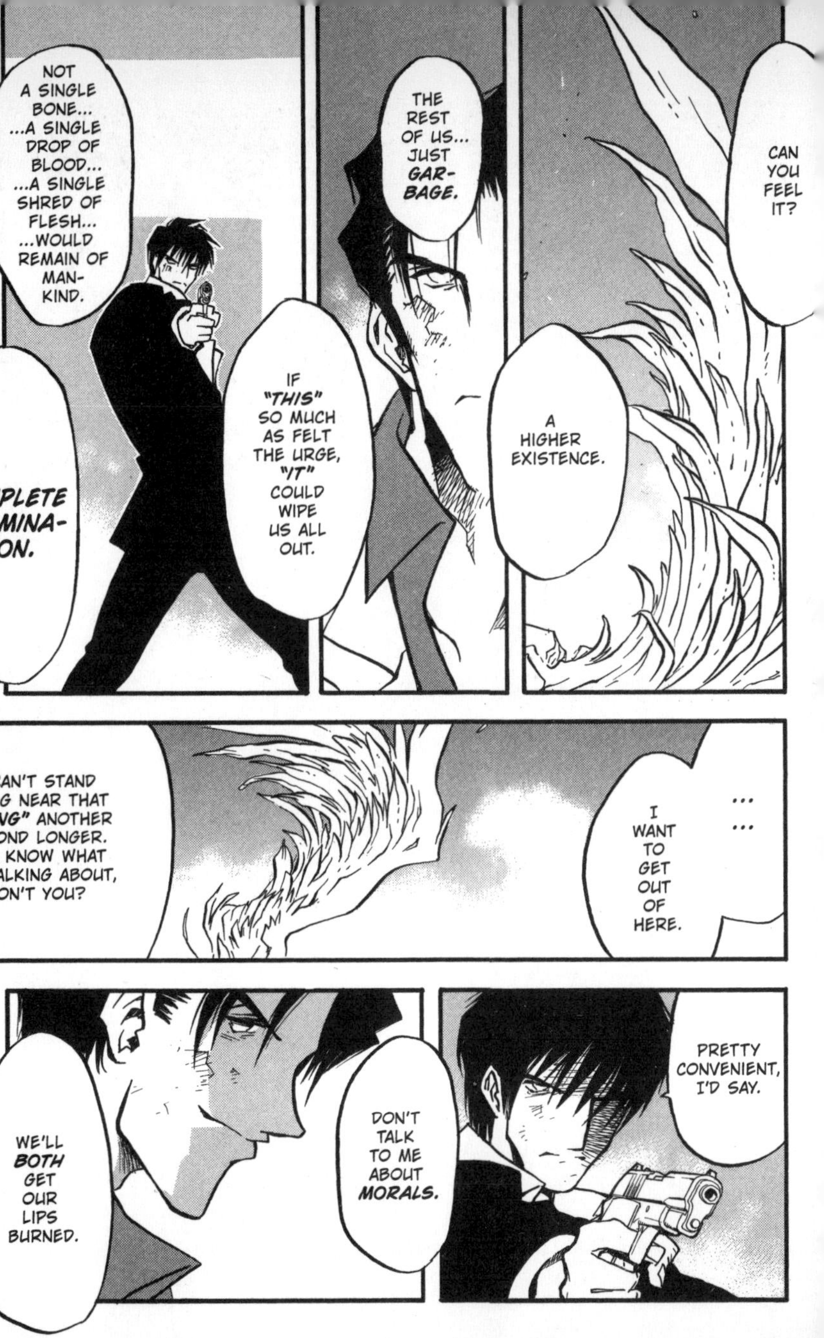
CAN YOU FEEL IT?
A HIGHER EXISTENCE.
THE REST OF US... JUST GARBAGE.
IF "THIS" SO MUCH AS FELT THE URGE, "IT" COULD WIPE US ALL OUT.
NOT A SINGLE BONE... ...A SINGLE DROP OF BLOOD... ...A SINGLE SHRED OF FLESH... ...WOULD REMAIN OF MANKIND.
COMPLETE ELIMINATION.
......
I WANT TO GET OUT OF HERE.
I CAN'T STAND BEING NEAR THAT "THING" ANOTHER SECOND LONGER. YOU KNOW WHAT I'M TALKING ABOUT, DON'T YOU?
PRETTY CONVENIENT, I'D SAY.
DON'T TALK TO ME ABOUT MORALS.
WE'LL BOTH GET OUR LIPS BURNED.

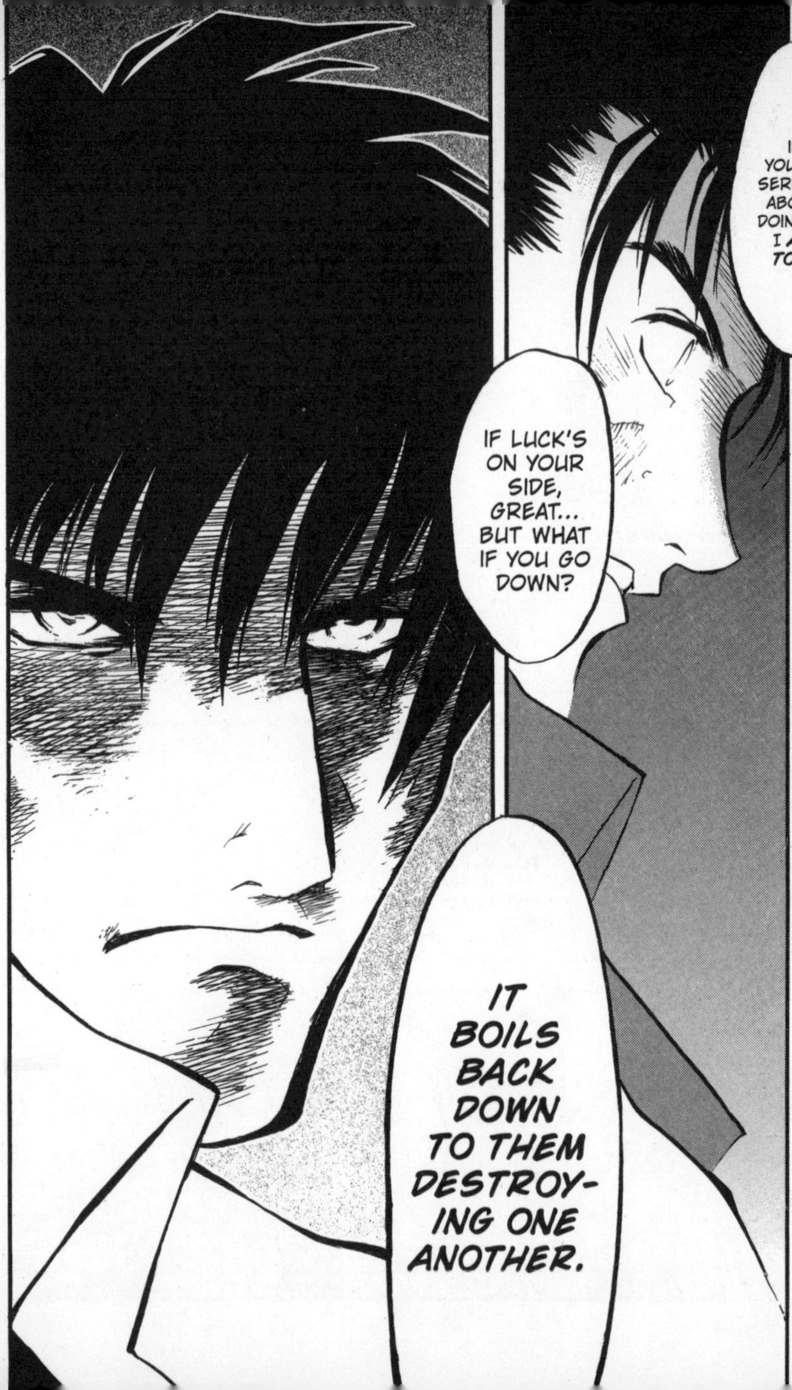
IF YOU'RE SERIOUS ABOUT DOING IT, I *AM* TOO.
IF LUCK'S ON YOUR SIDE, GREAT... BUT WHAT IF YOU GO DOWN?
IT BOILS BACK DOWN TO THEM DESTROY-ING ONE ANOTHER.

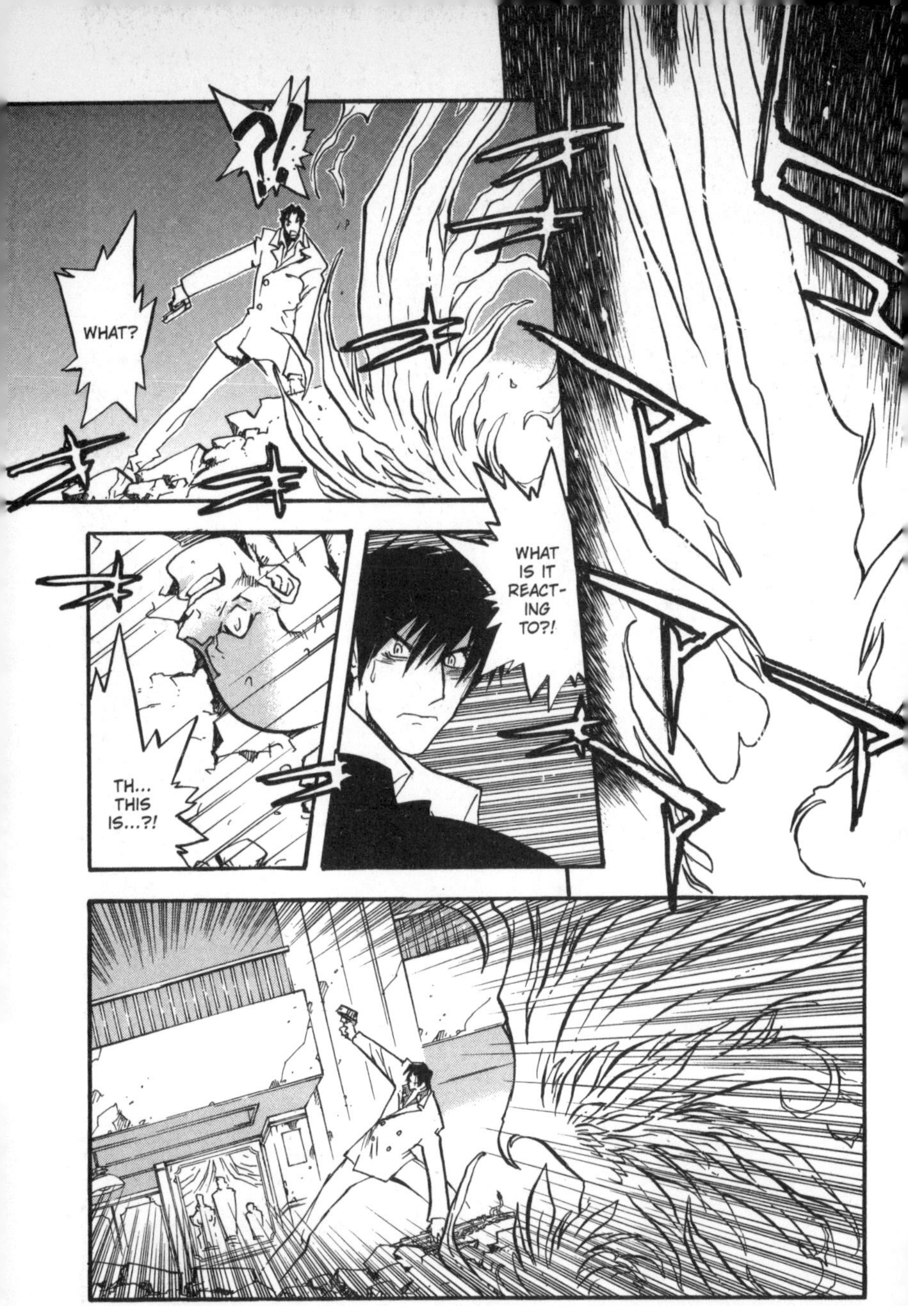
?!
WHAT?
WHAT IS IT REACTING TO?!
TH... THIS IS...?!

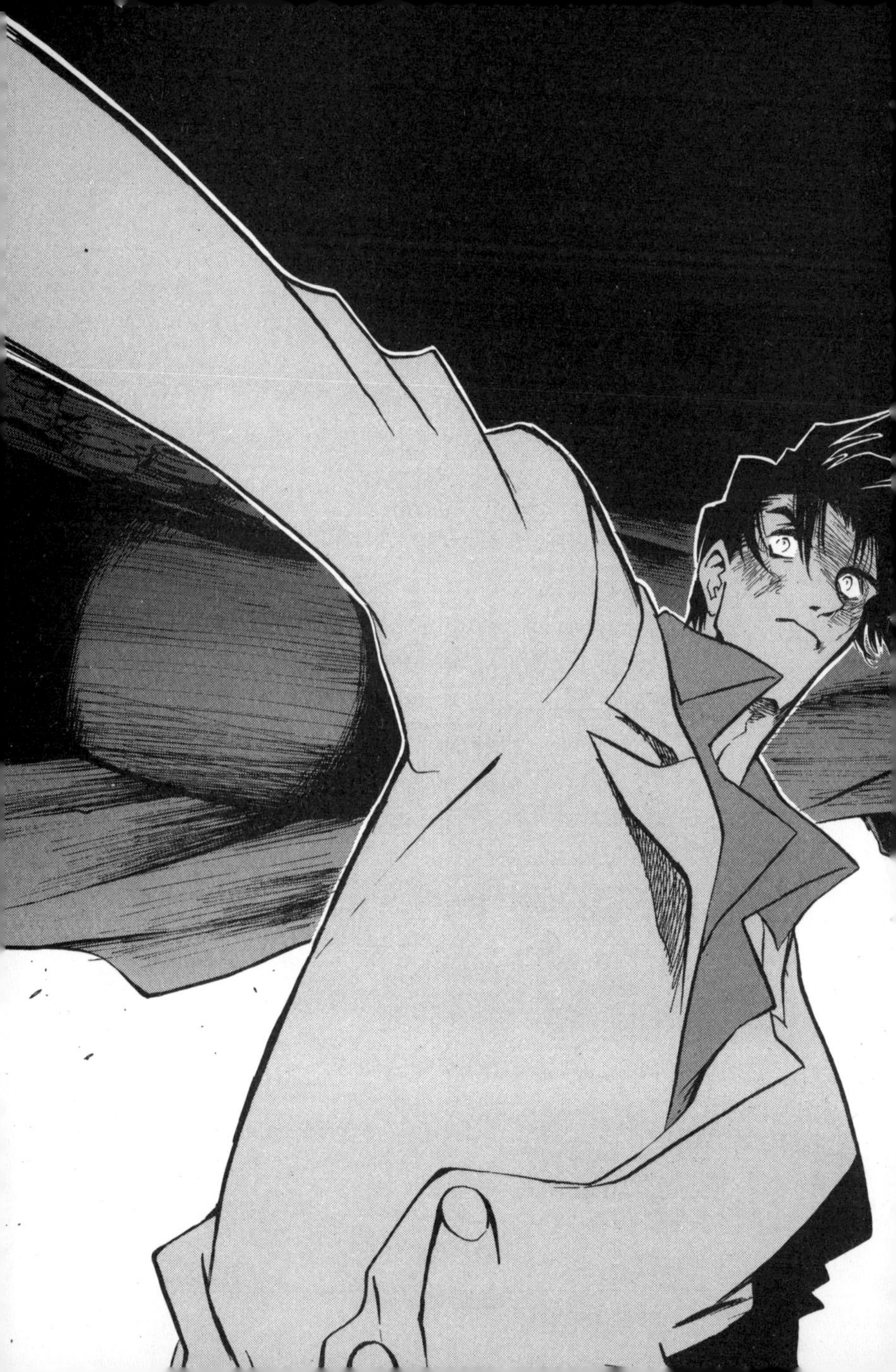

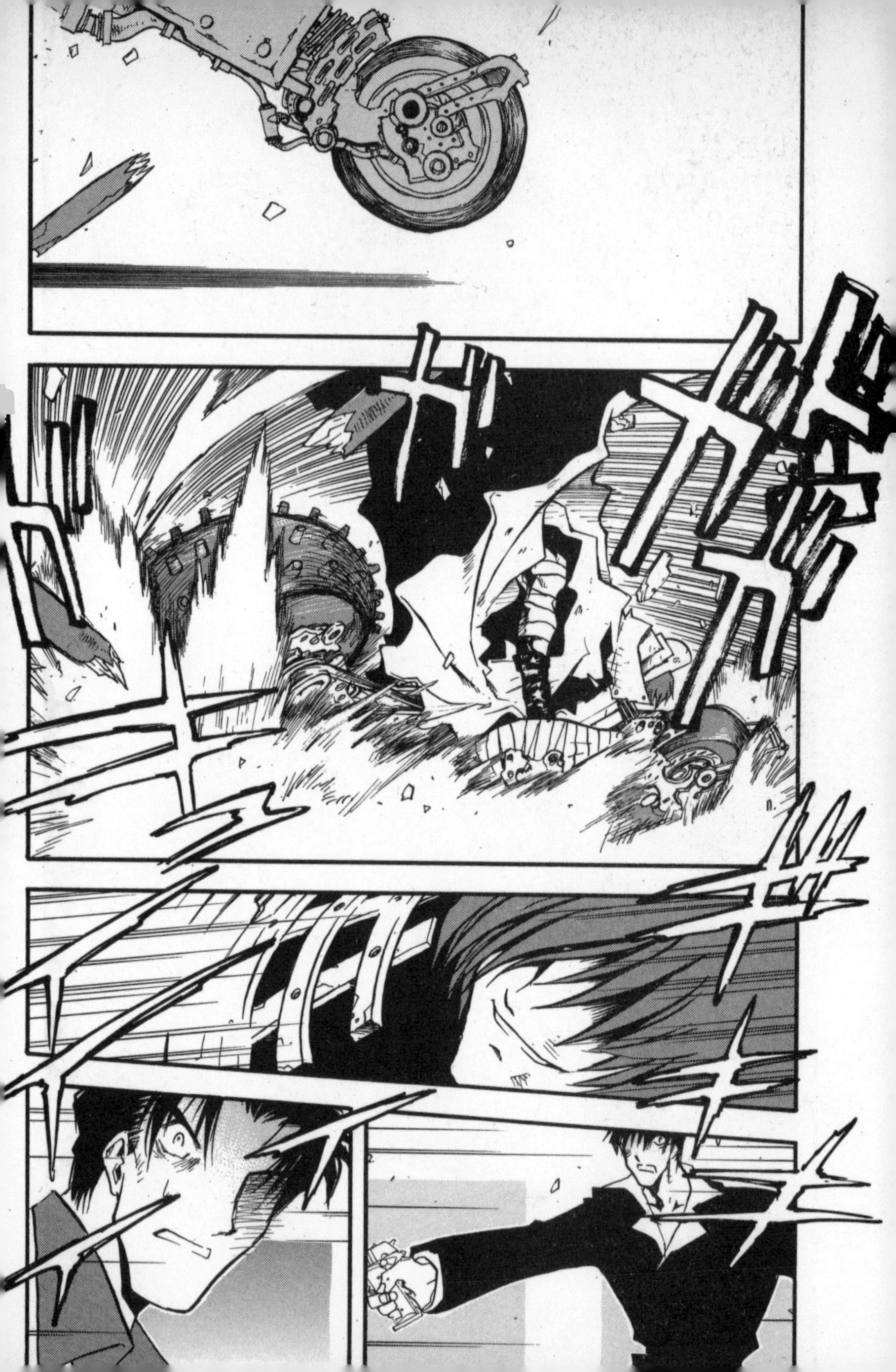

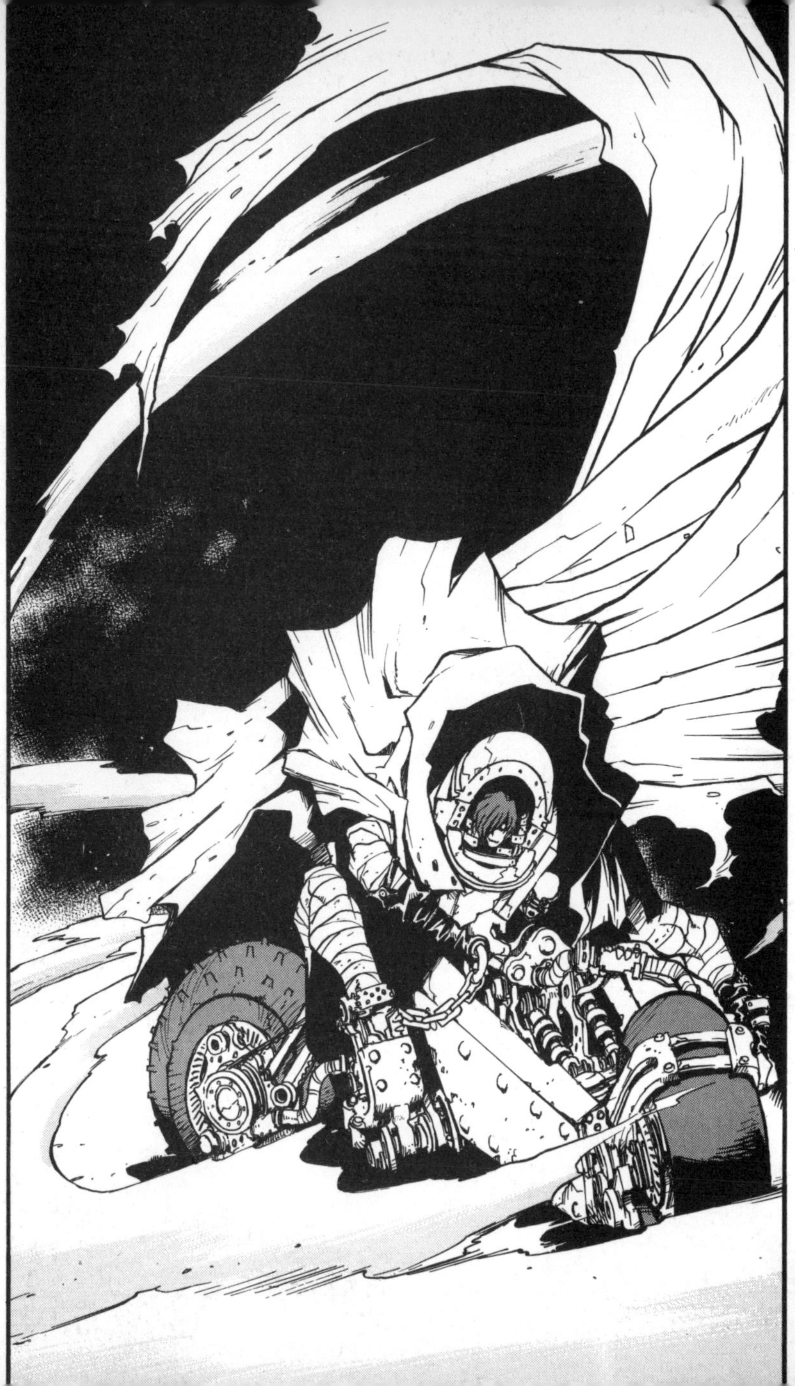

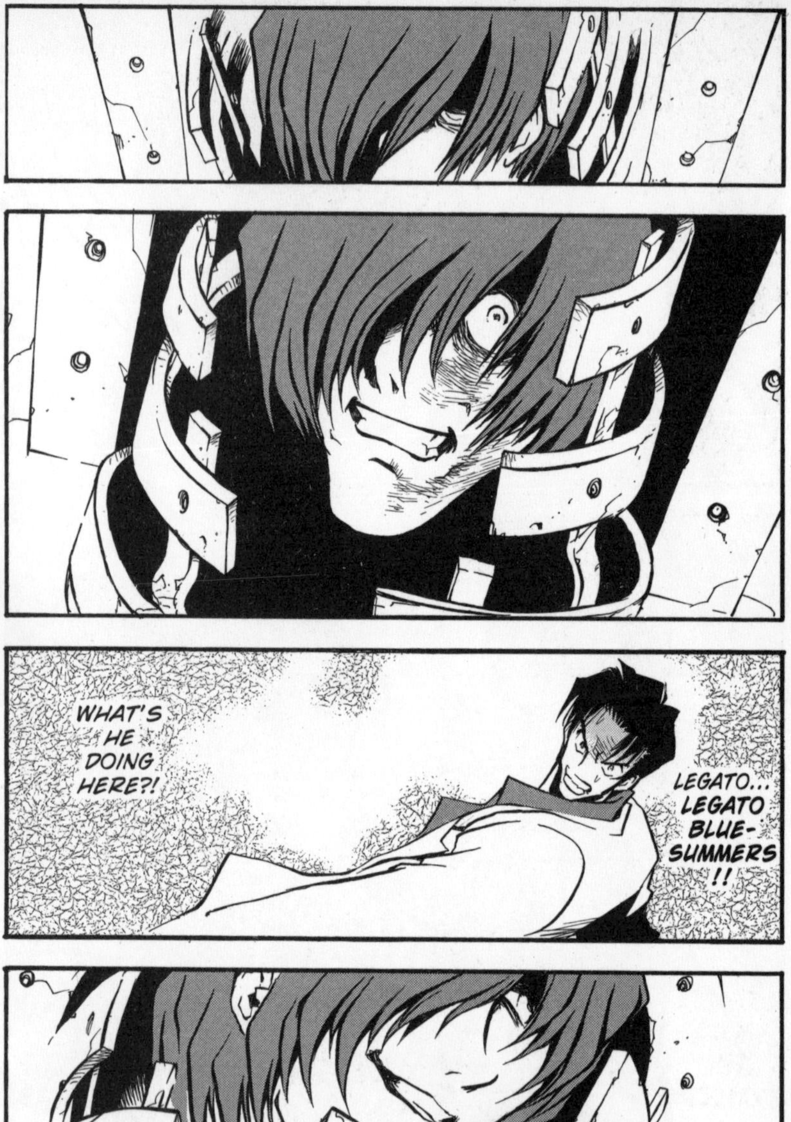
LEGATO... LEGATO BLUE-SUMMERS!!
WHAT'S HE DOING HERE?!

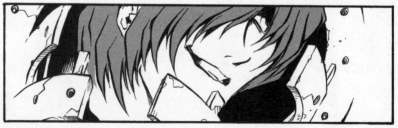

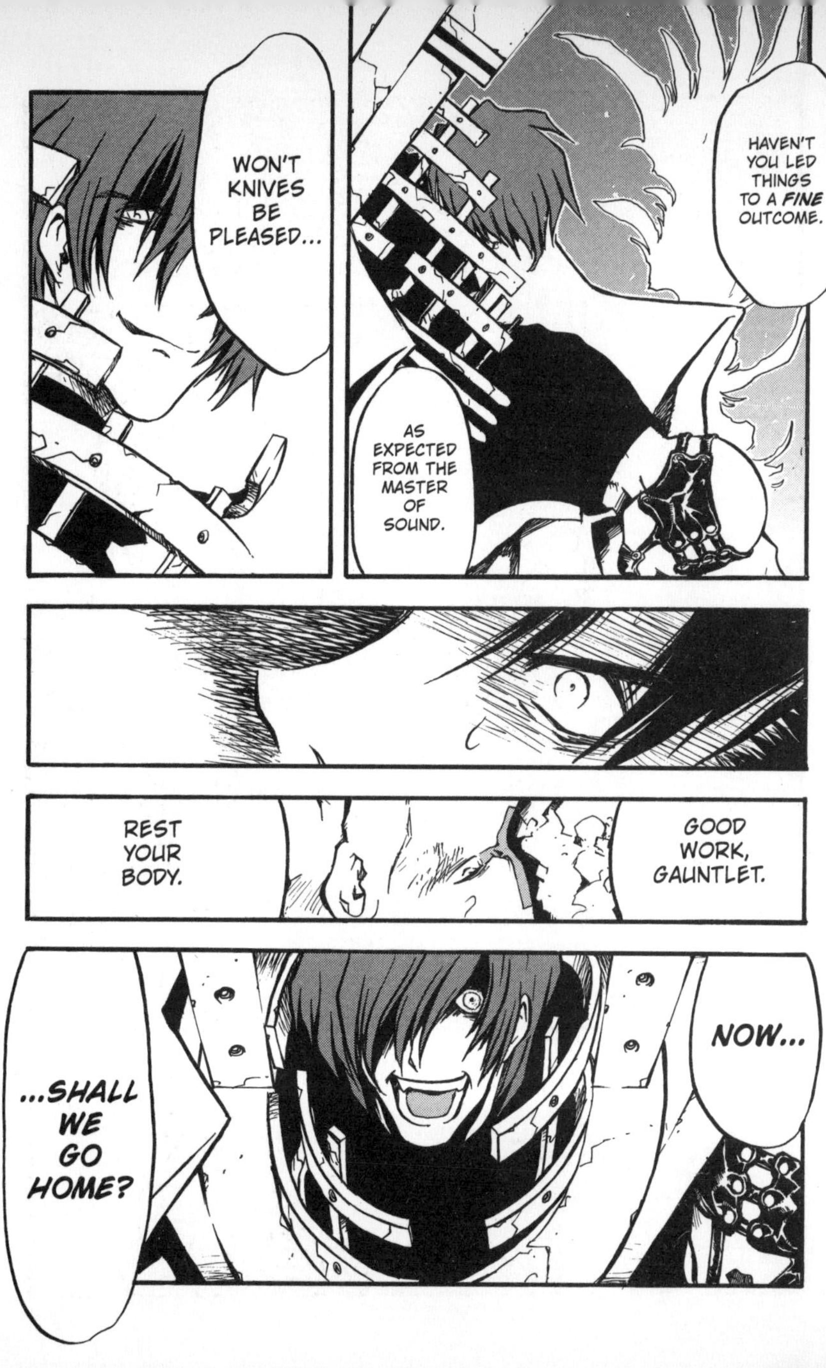
HAVEN'T YOU LED THINGS TO A *FINE* OUTCOME.
AS EXPECTED FROM THE MASTER OF SOUND.
WON'T KNIVES BE PLEASED...
GOOD WORK, GAUNTLET.
REST YOUR BODY.
*NOW...*
*...SHALL WE GO HOME?*

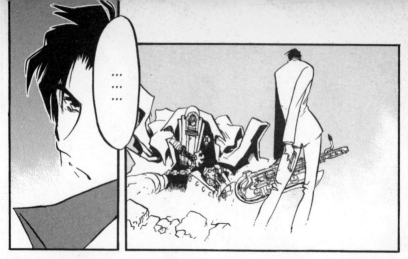

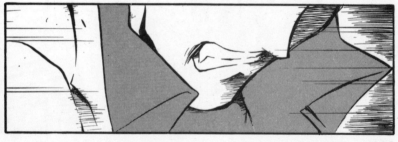

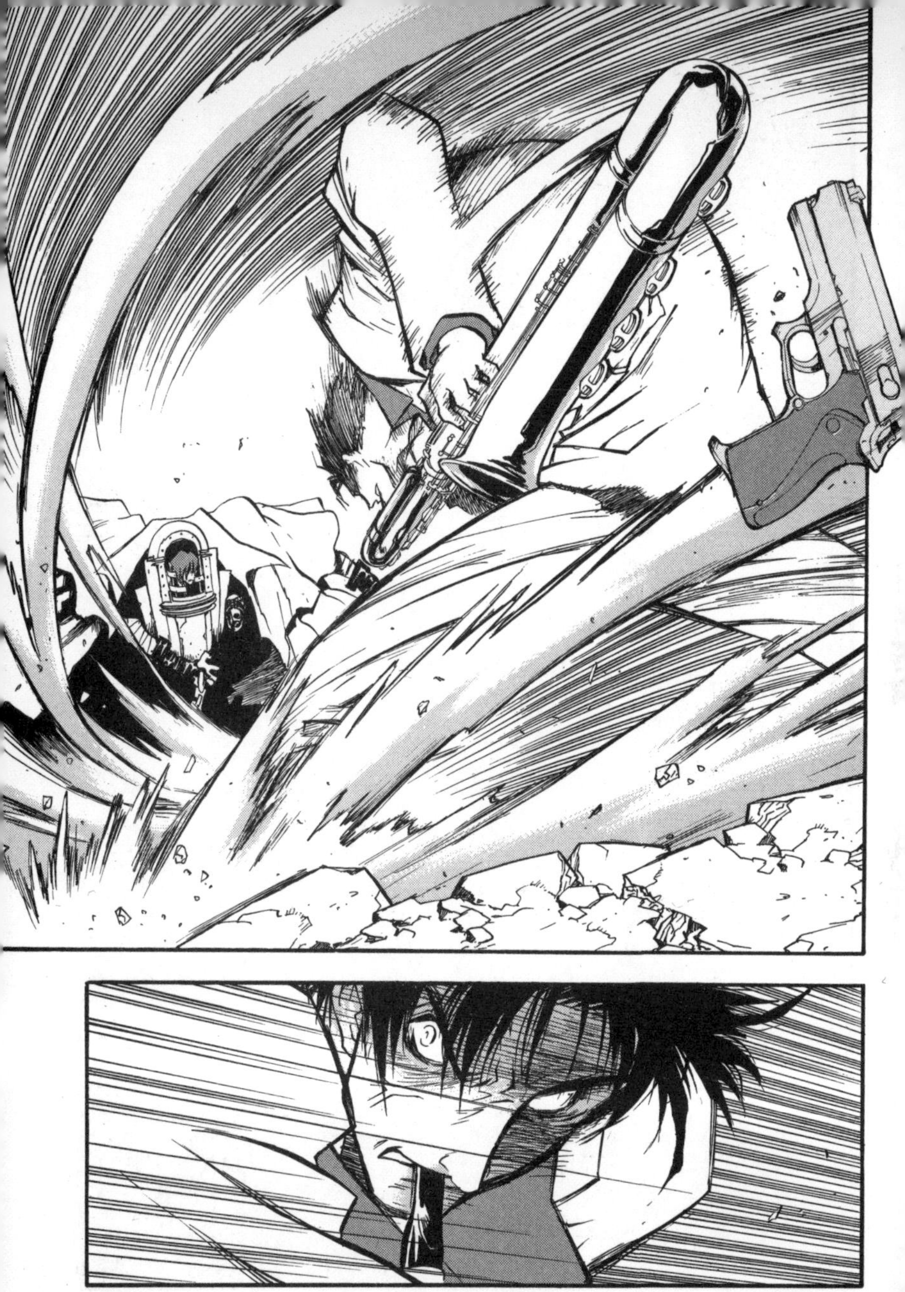

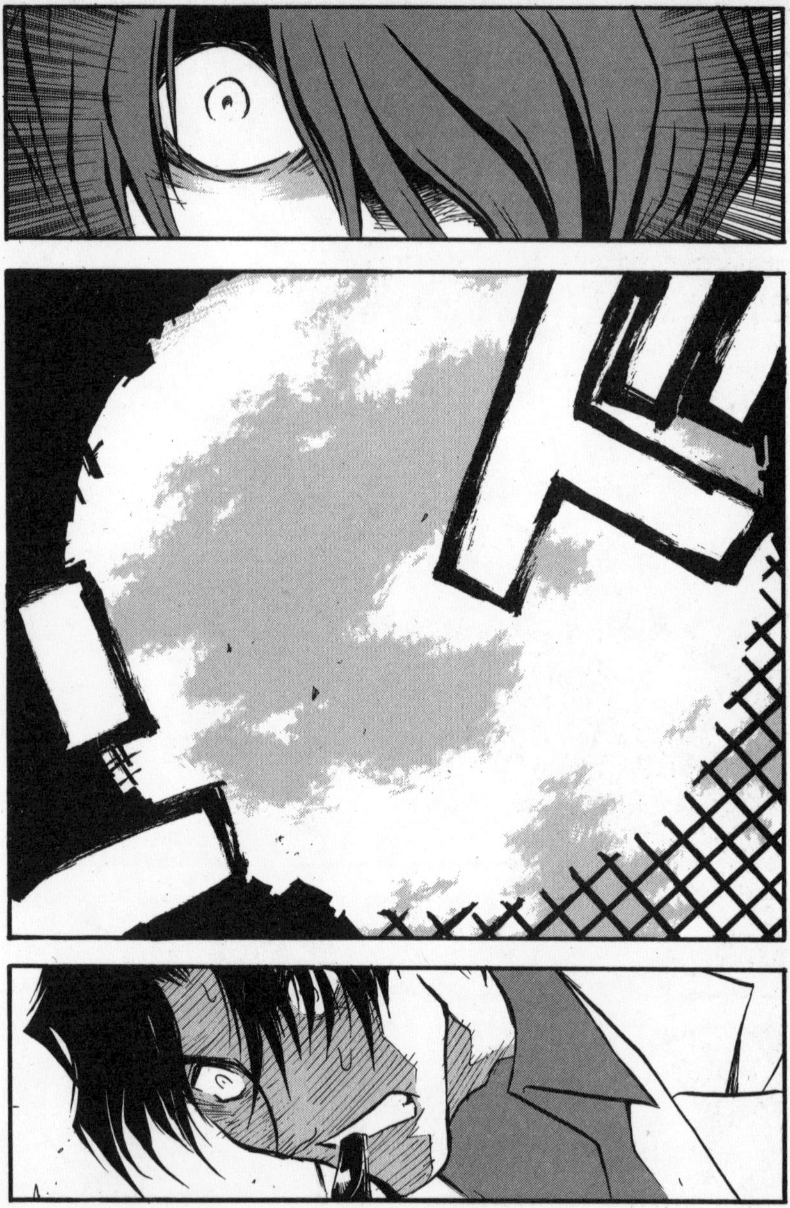

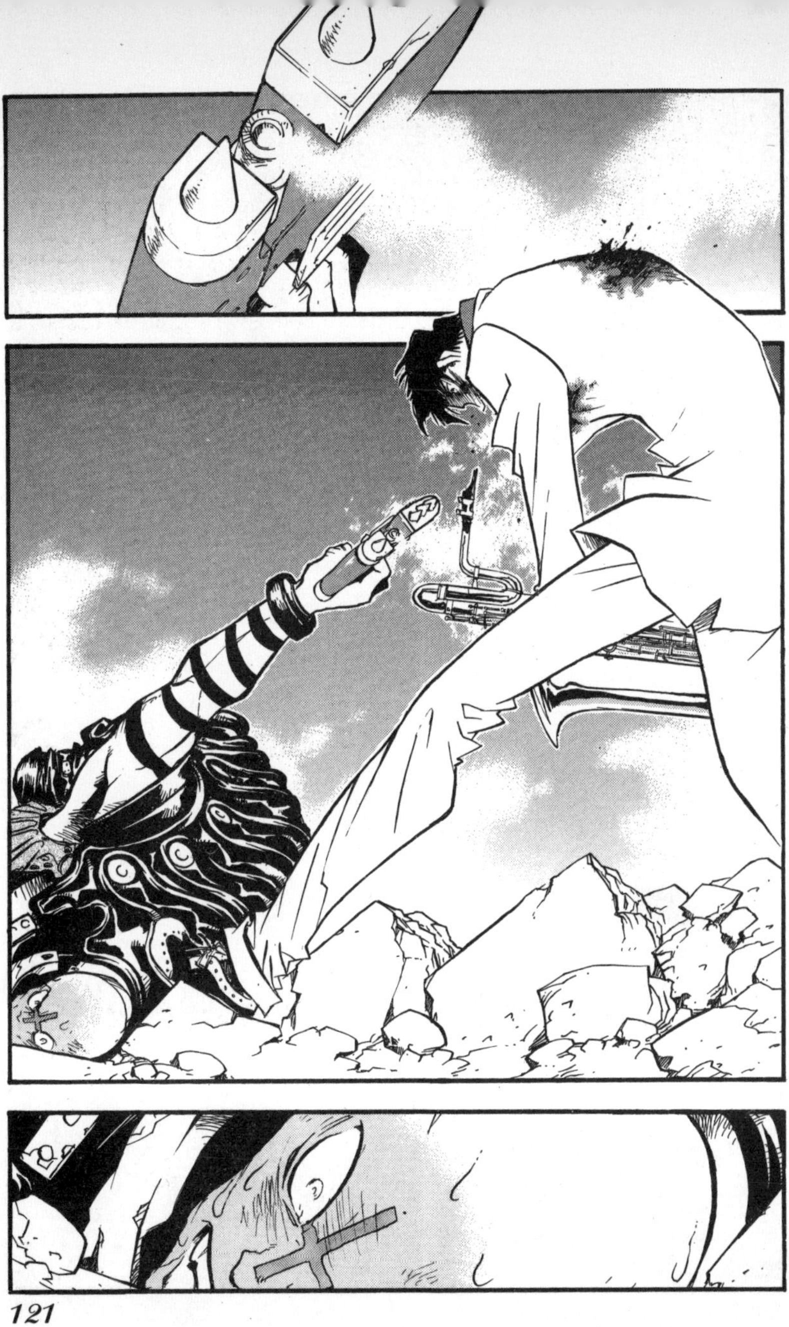

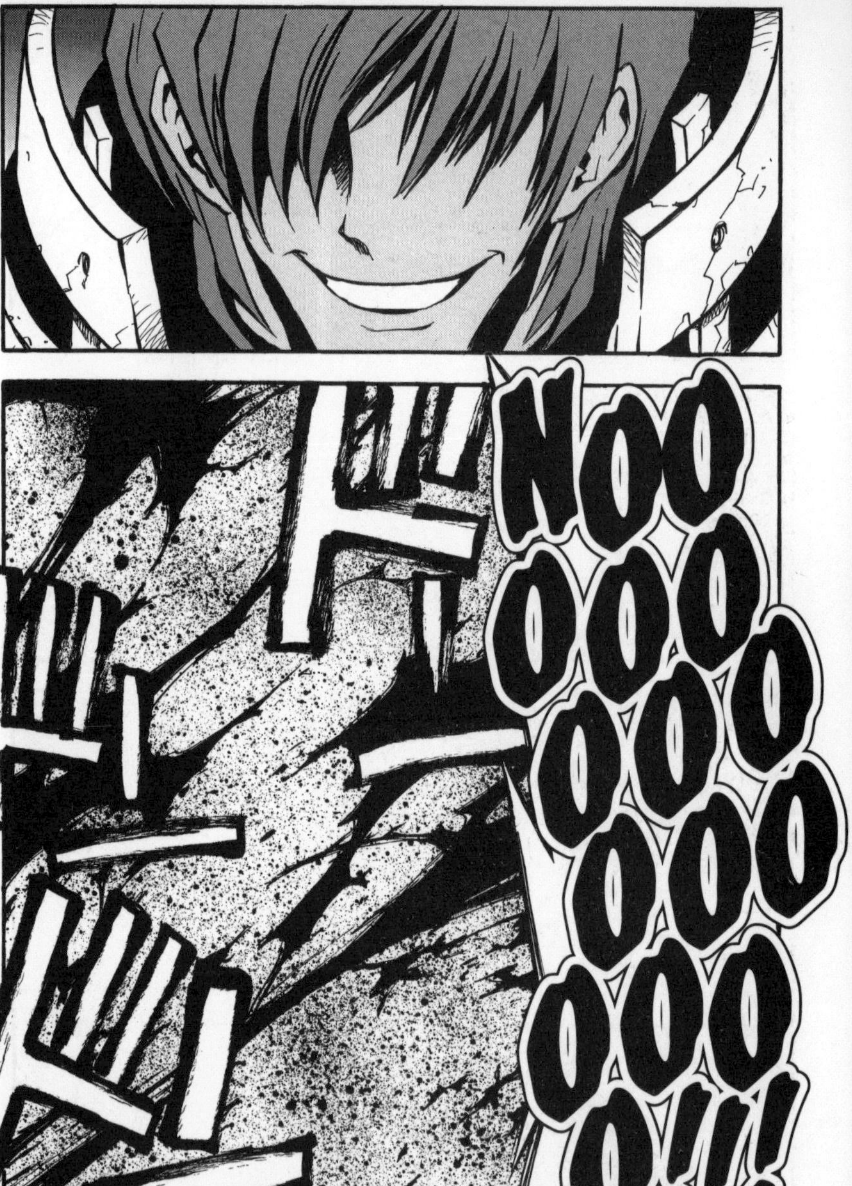
NOOOOOOOOOOOOOOOOOO!!!

#4. VILLAIN / END

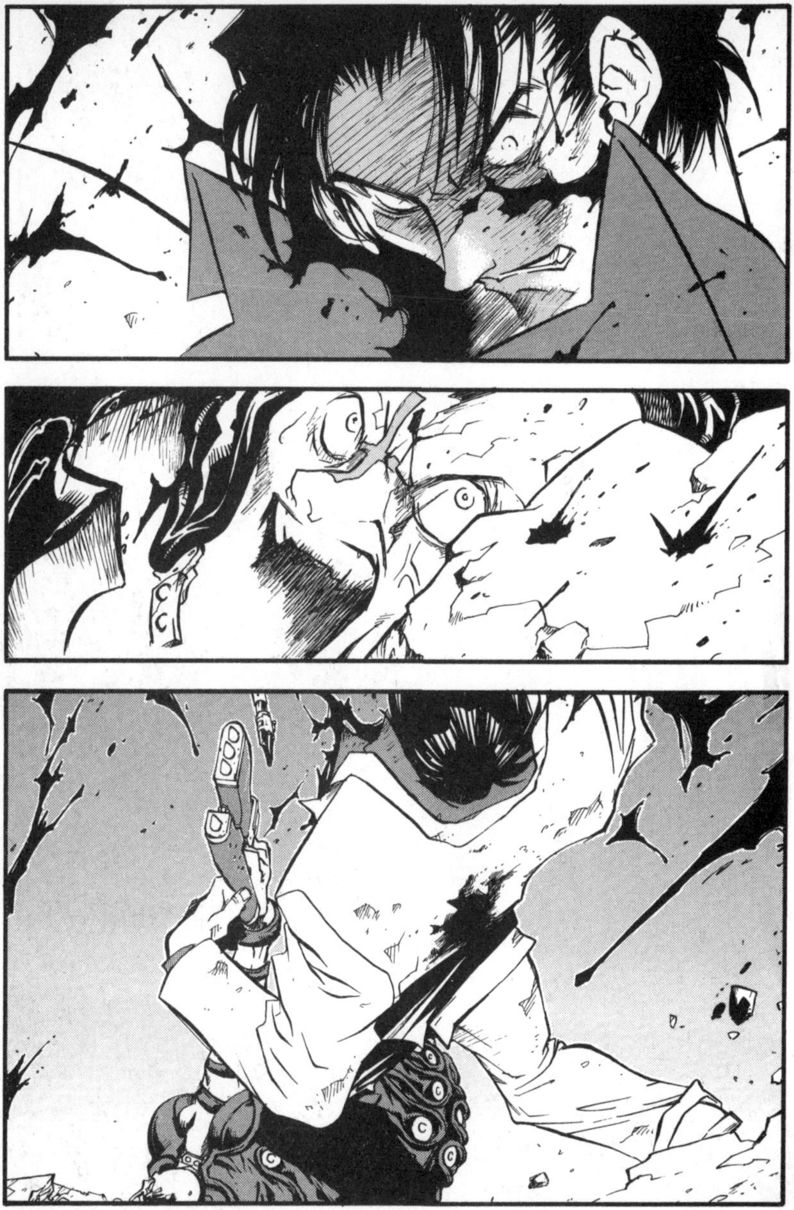

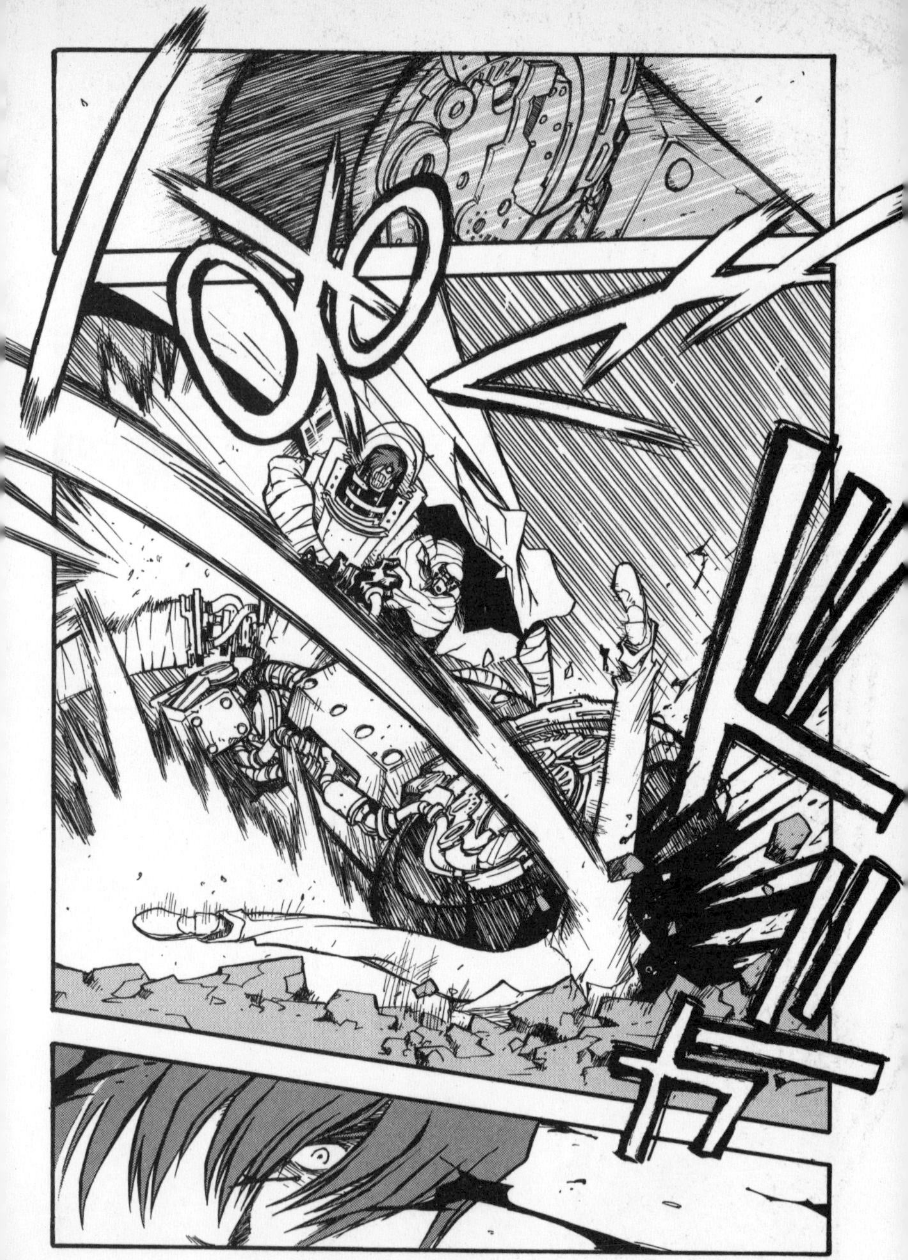

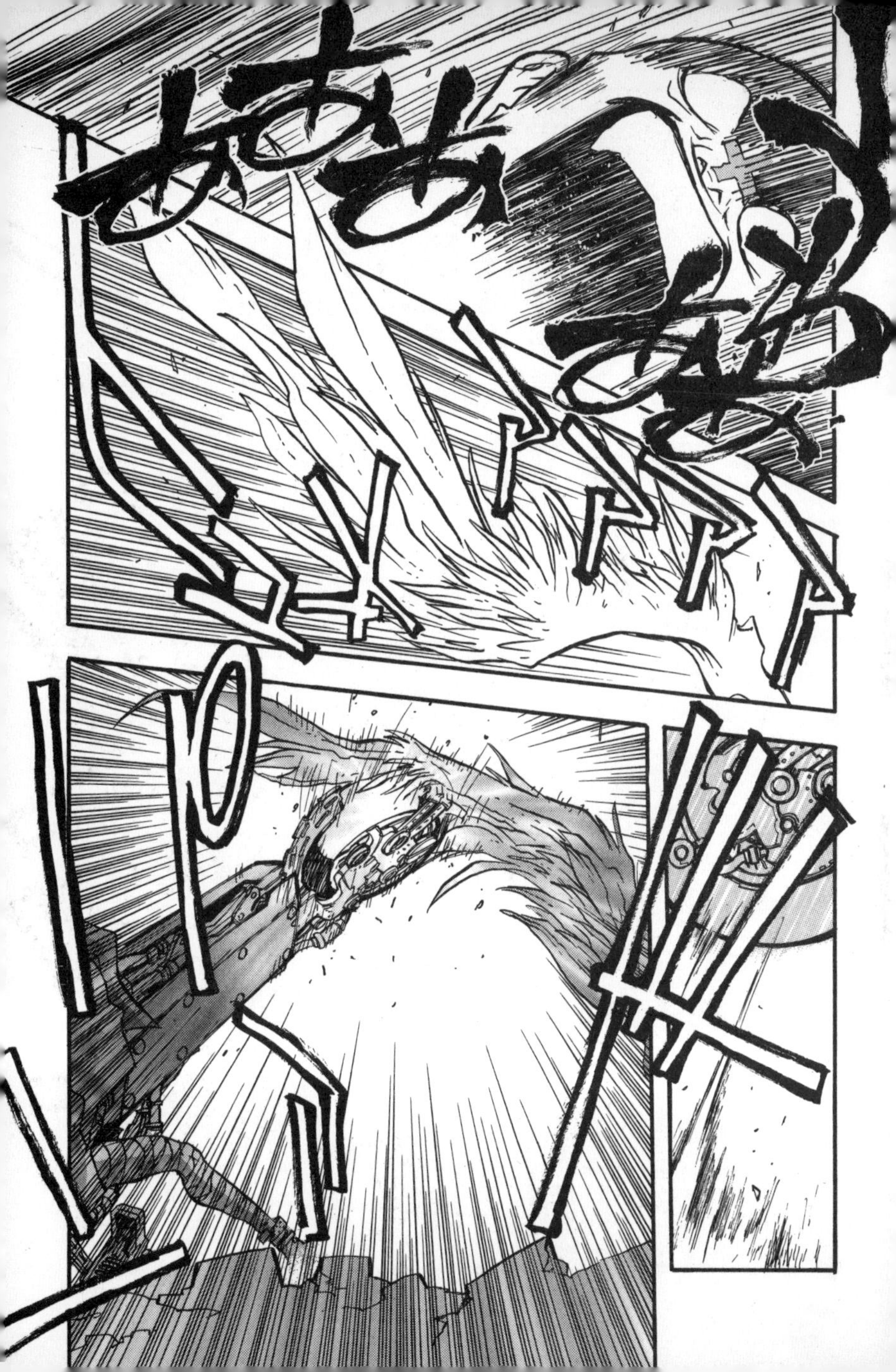

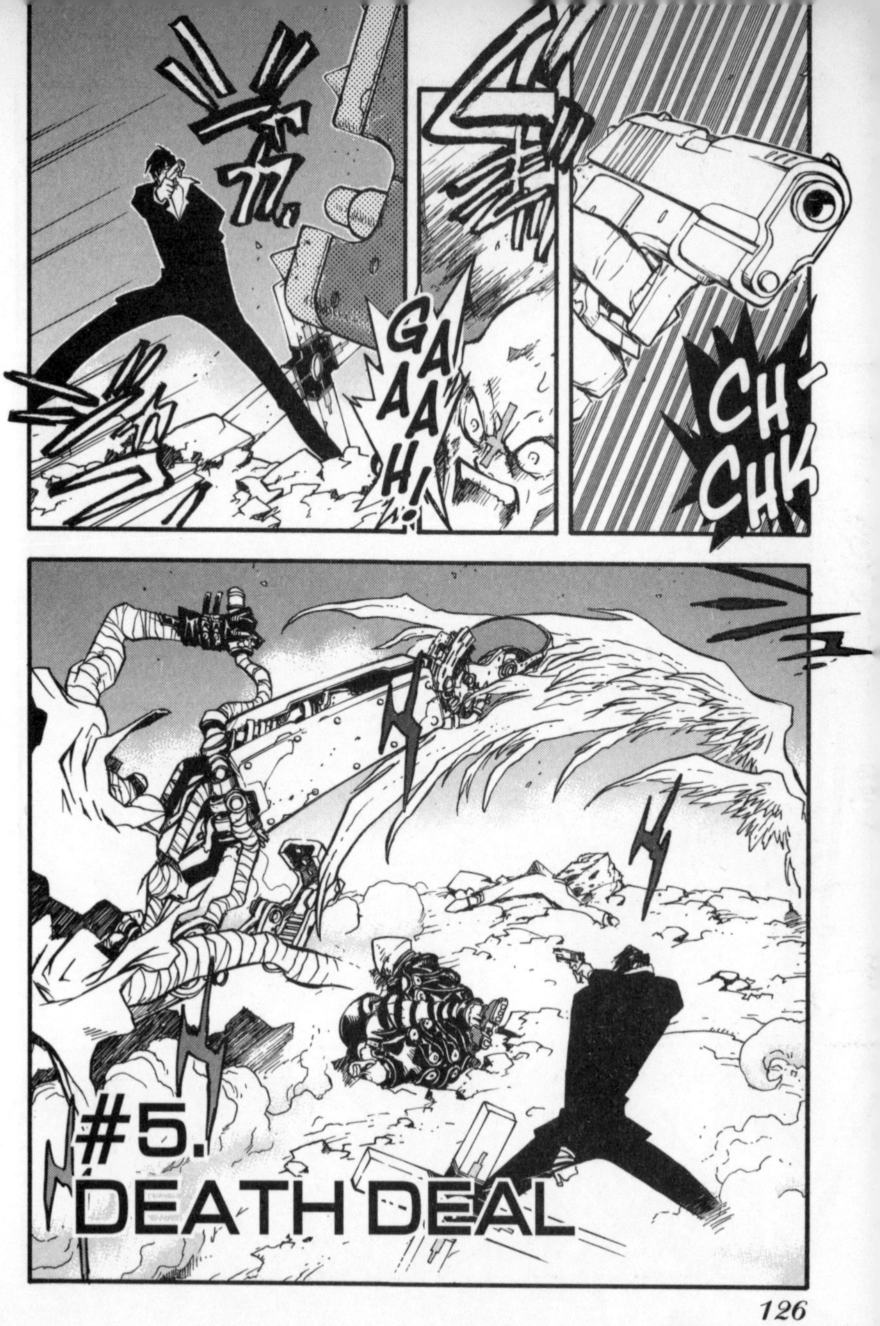
CH-CHK
GAAAH!
#5. DEATH DEAL

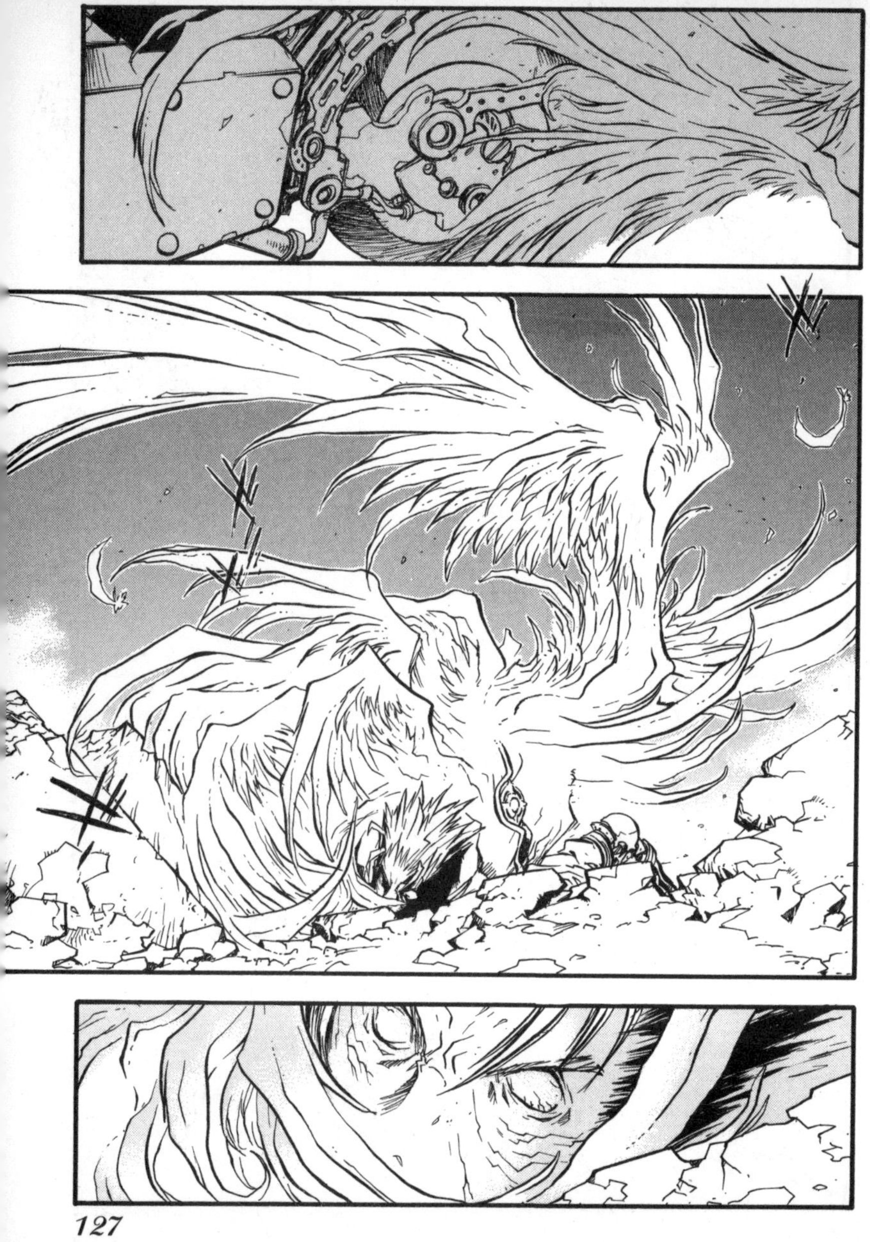

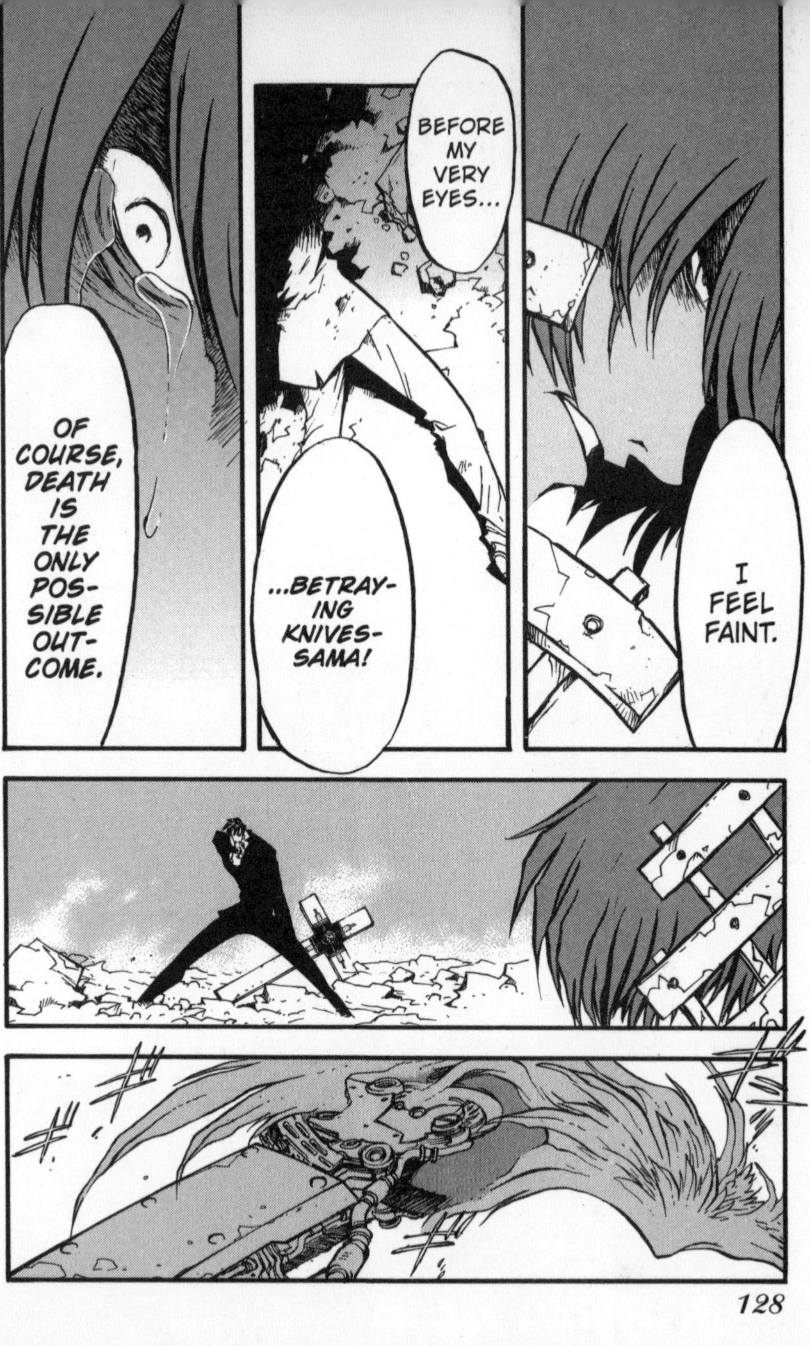
I FEEL FAINT.
BEFORE MY VERY EYES...
...BETRAY-ING KNIVES-SAMA!
OF COURSE, DEATH IS THE ONLY POS-SIBLE OUT-COME.

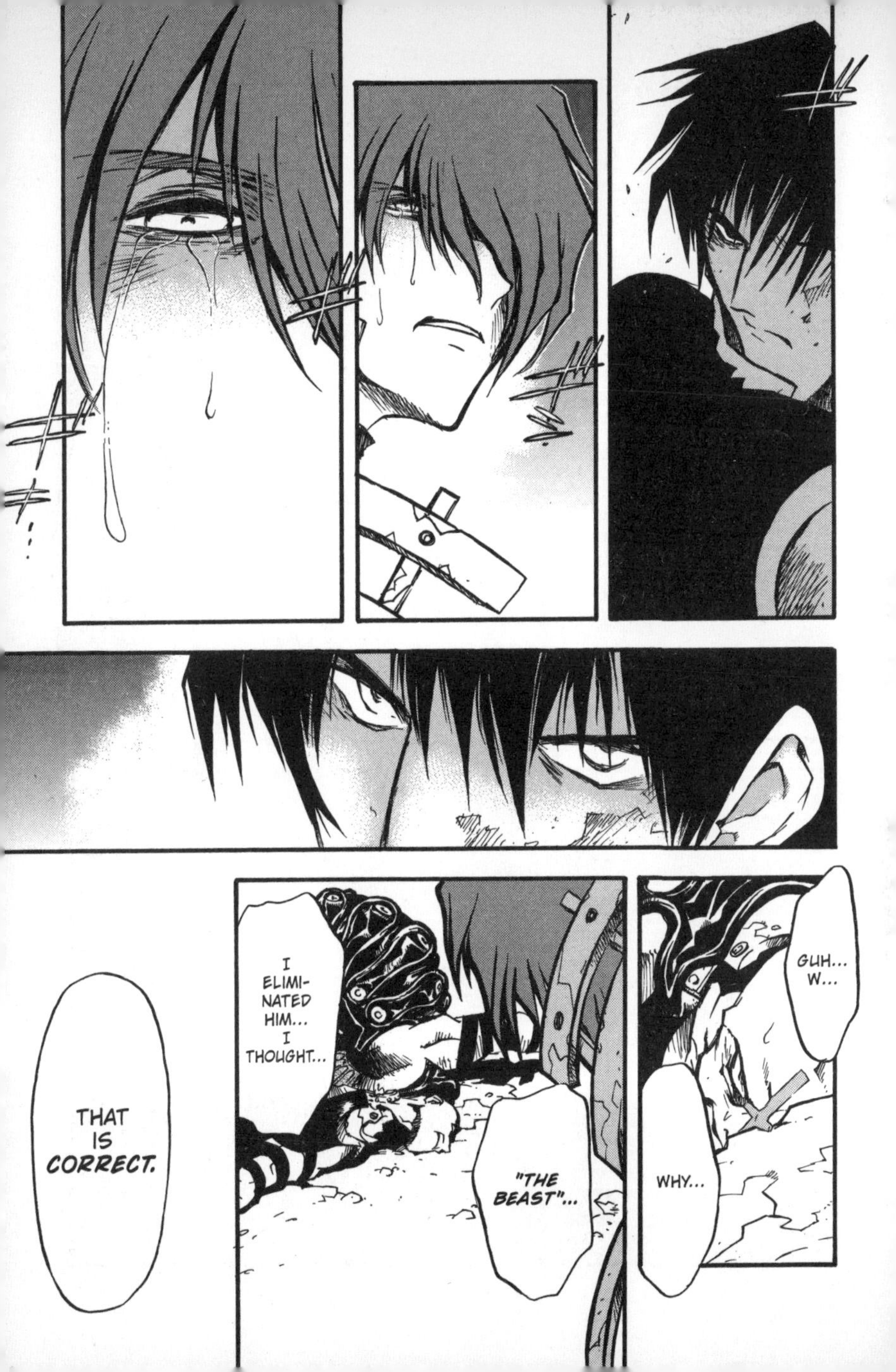
GUH... W...
WHY...
"THE BEAST"...
I ELIMINATED HIM... I THOUGHT...
THAT IS CORRECT.

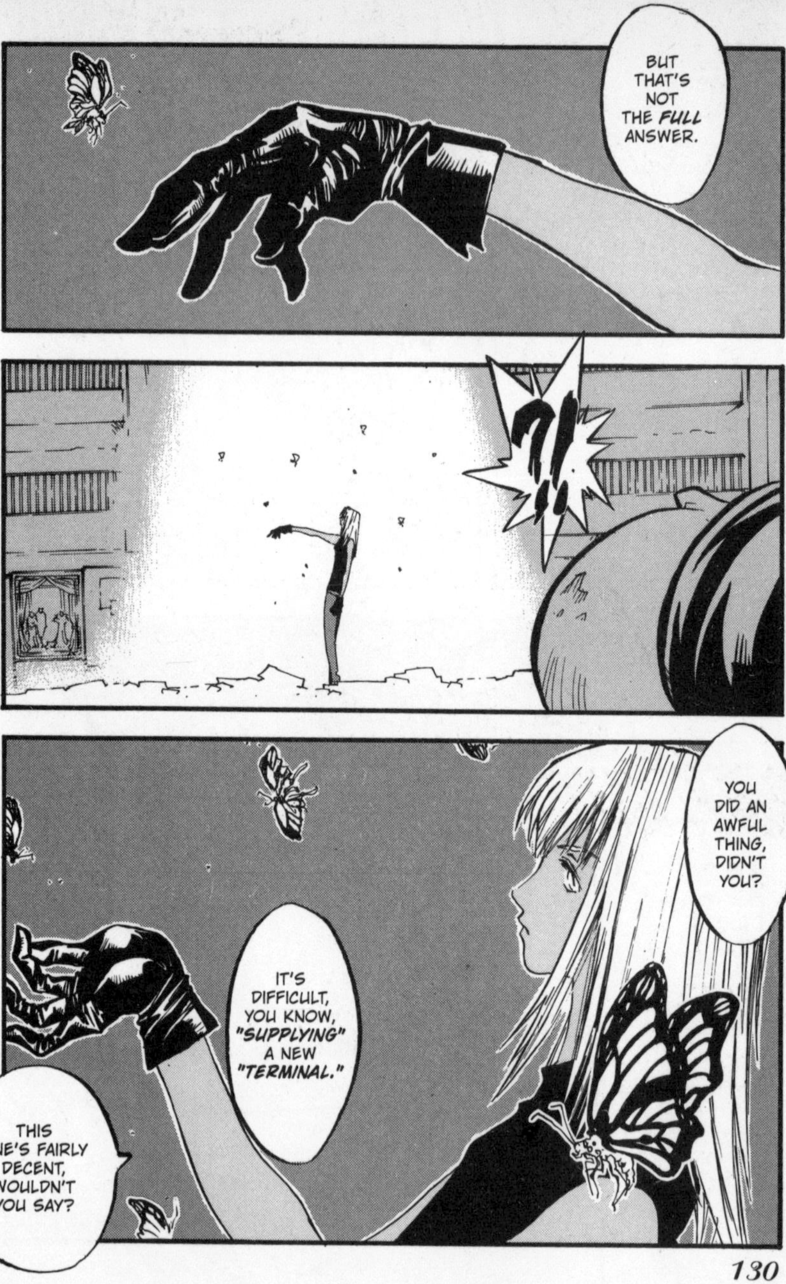
BUT THAT'S NOT THE *FULL* ANSWER.
?!
YOU DID AN AWFUL THING, DIDN'T YOU?
IT'S DIFFICULT, YOU KNOW, *"SUPPLYING"* A NEW *"TERMINAL."*
THIS ONE'S FAIRLY DECENT, WOULDN'T YOU SAY?

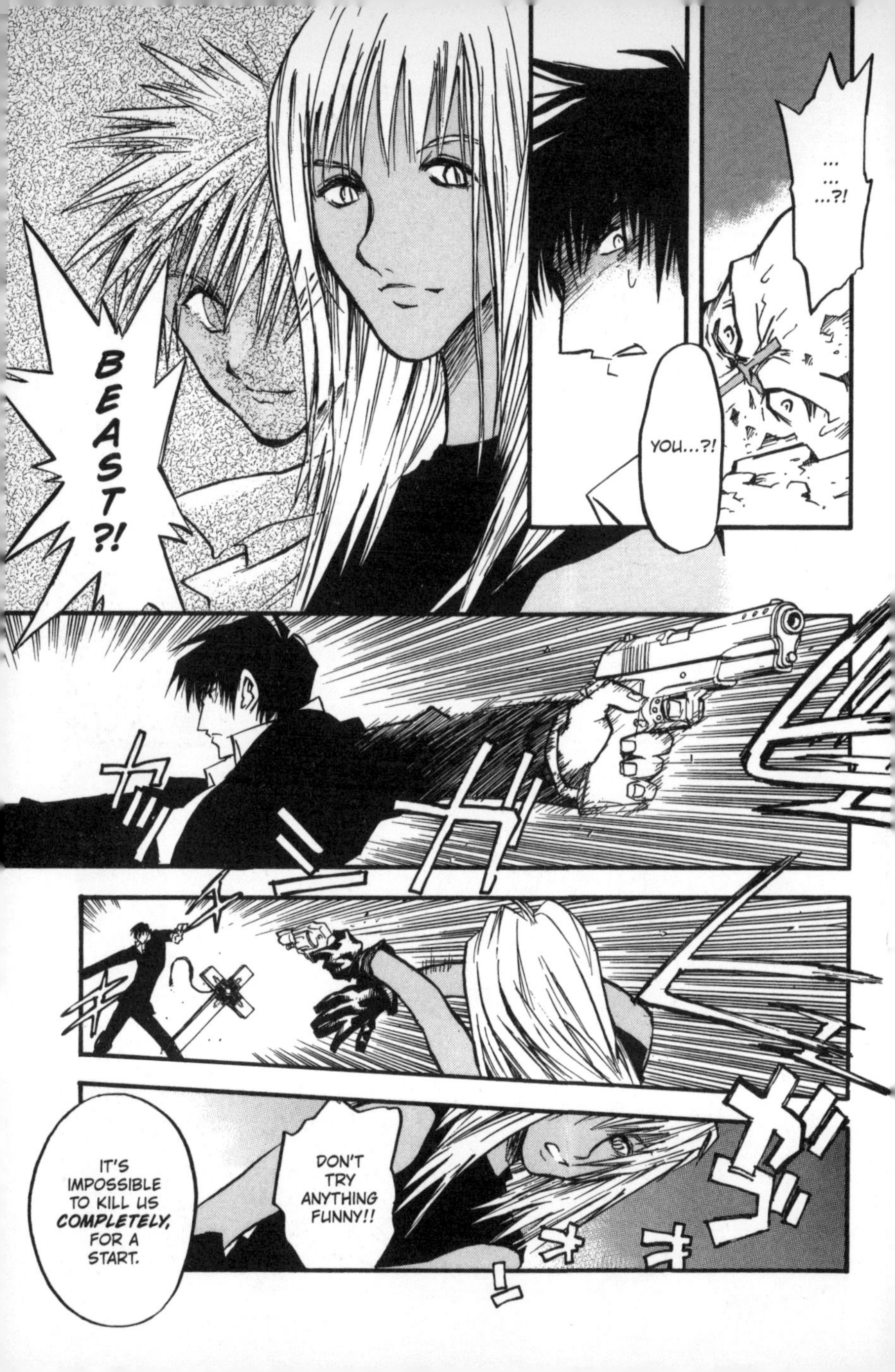

...
...
...?!
YOU...?!
BEAST?!
DON'T TRY ANYTHING FUNNY!!
IT'S IMPOSSIBLE TO KILL US COMPLETELY, FOR A START.

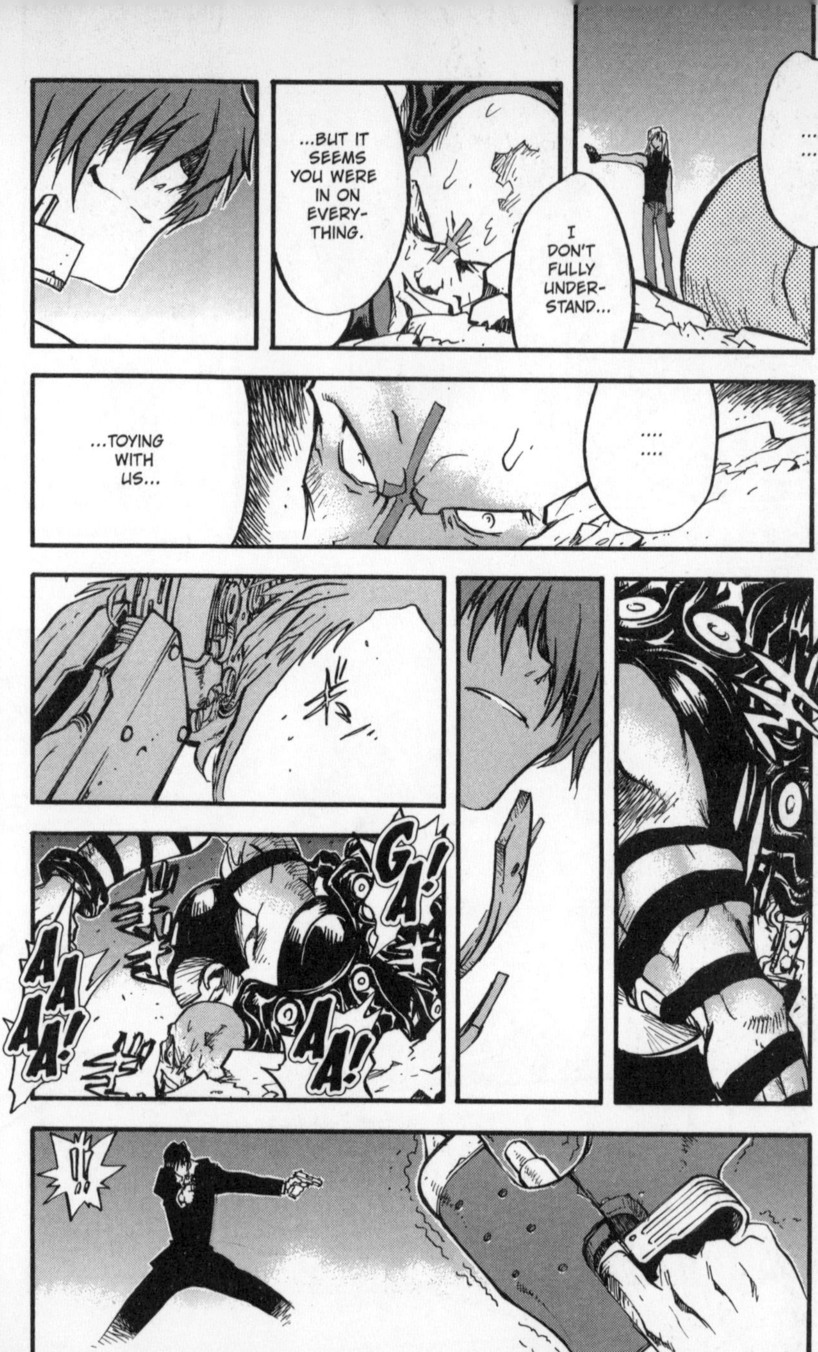
...
...
I DON'T FULLY UNDERSTAND...
...BUT IT SEEMS YOU WERE IN ON EVERYTHING.
....
....
...TOYING WITH US...
GA!
AA!
AAAA!
!!

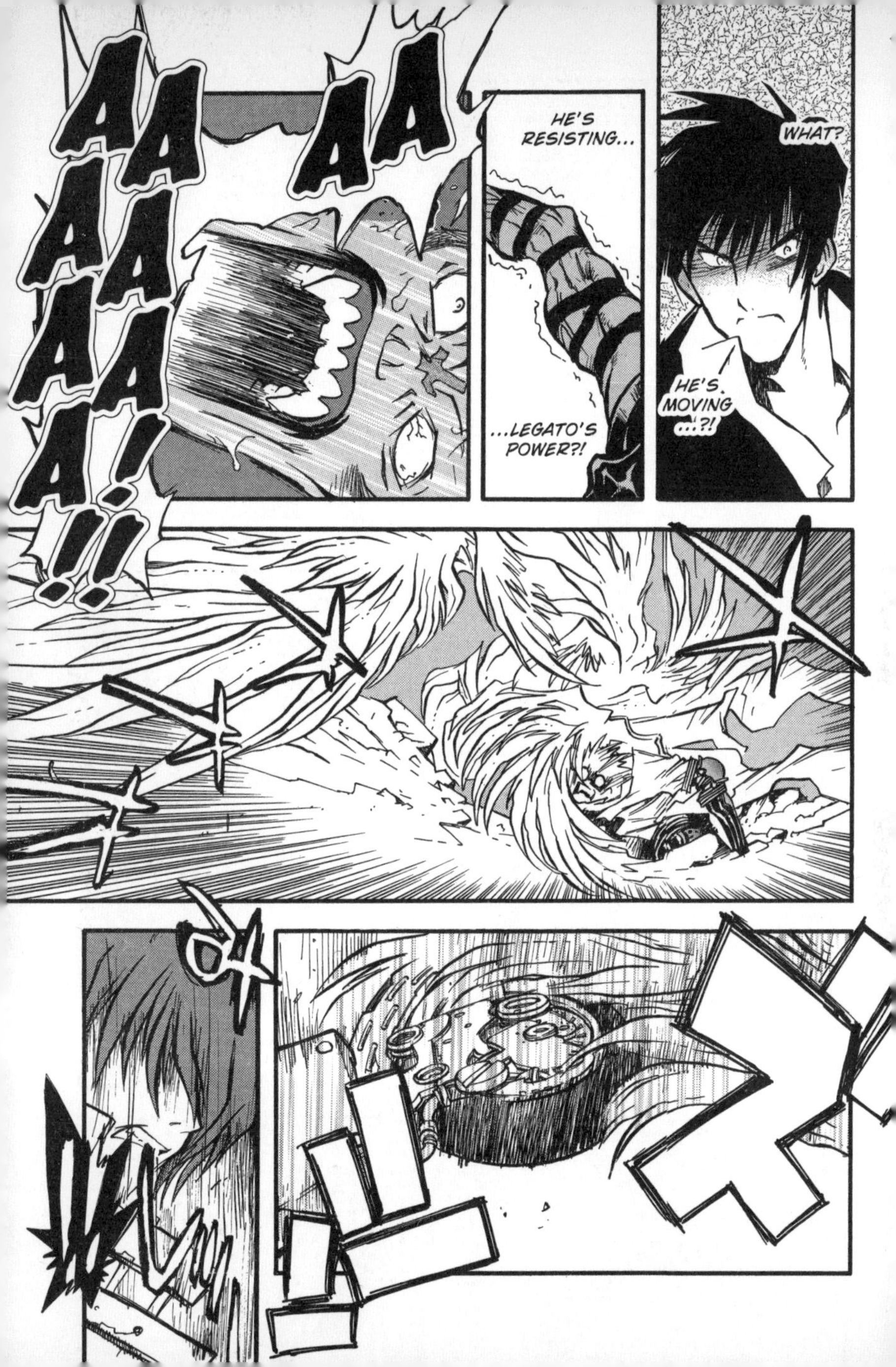
WHAT?
HE'S... MOVING ...?!
HE'S RESISTING...
...LEGATO'S POWER?!
AAAAAAAAAAA!!

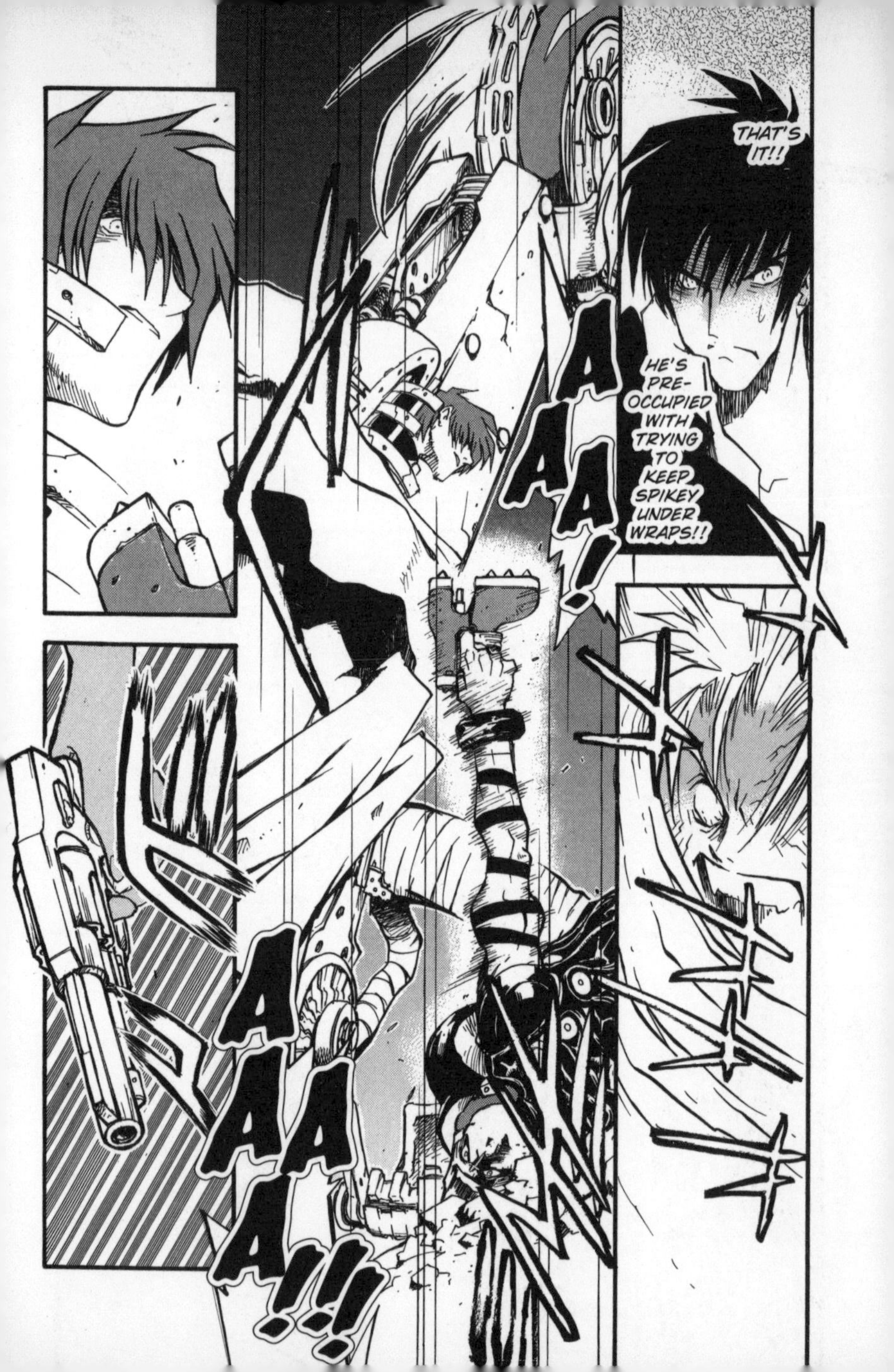
THAT'S IT!!
HE'S PRE-OCCUPIED WITH TRYING TO KEEP SPIKEY UNDER WRAPS!!
AAA!
AAAA!!!

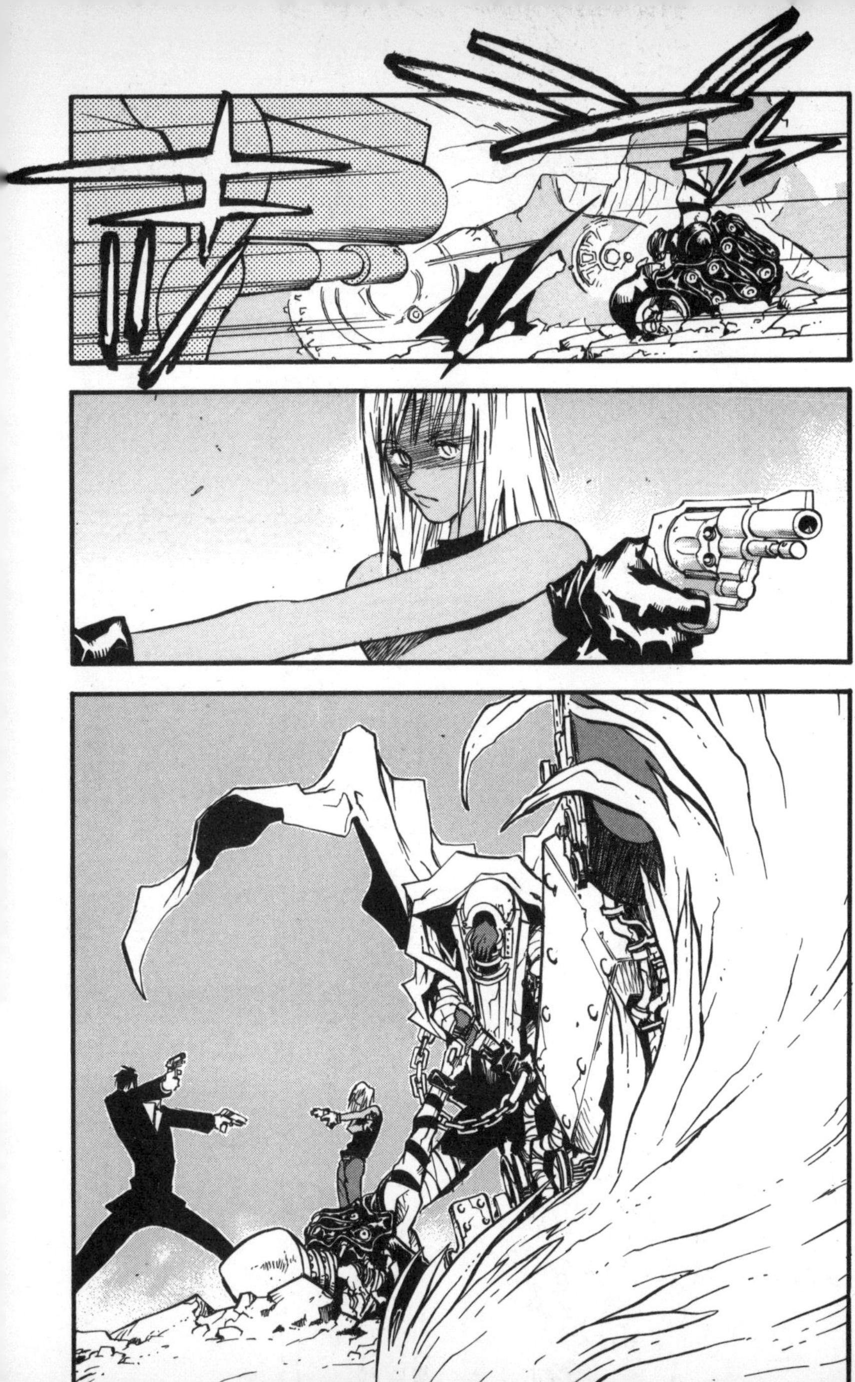

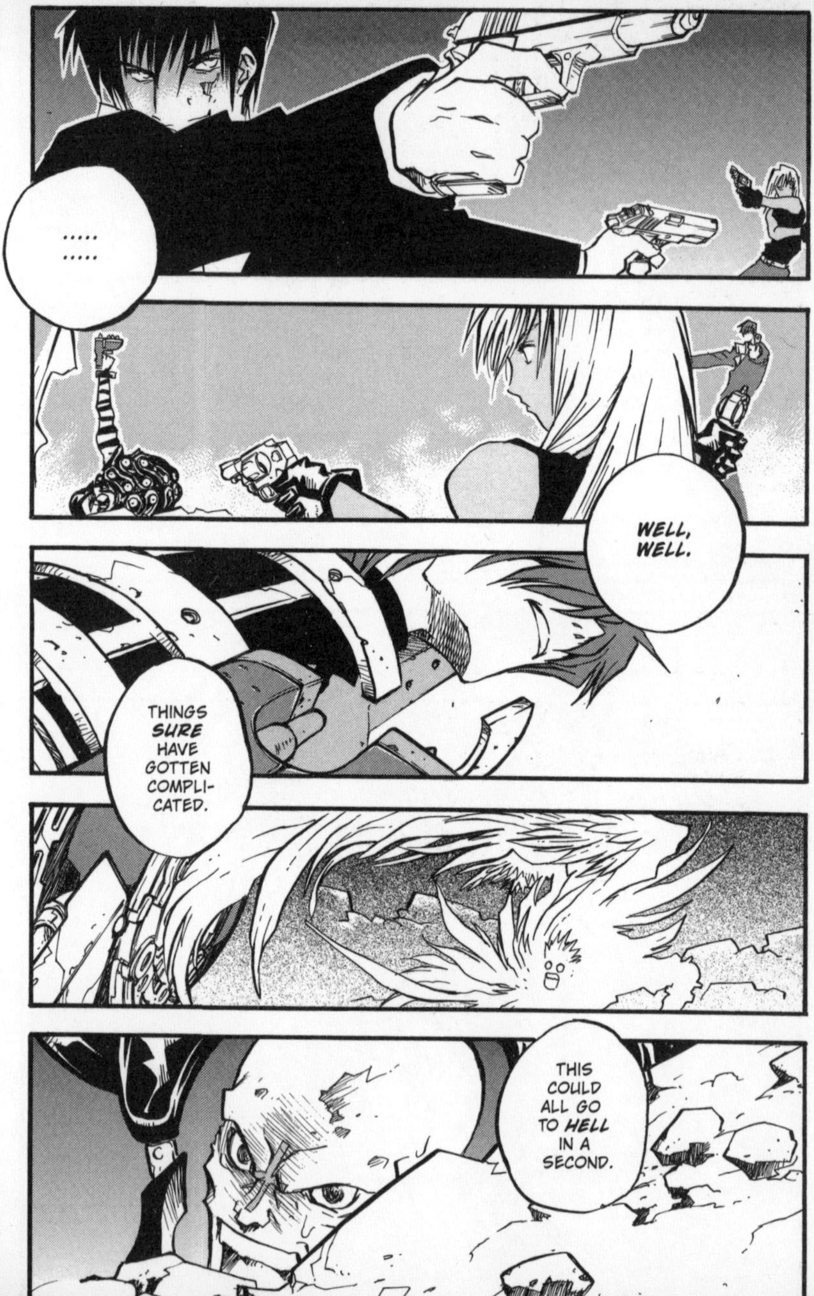
.....
.....
WELL, WELL.
THINGS SURE HAVE GOTTEN COMPLICATED.
THIS COULD ALL GO TO HELL IN A SECOND.

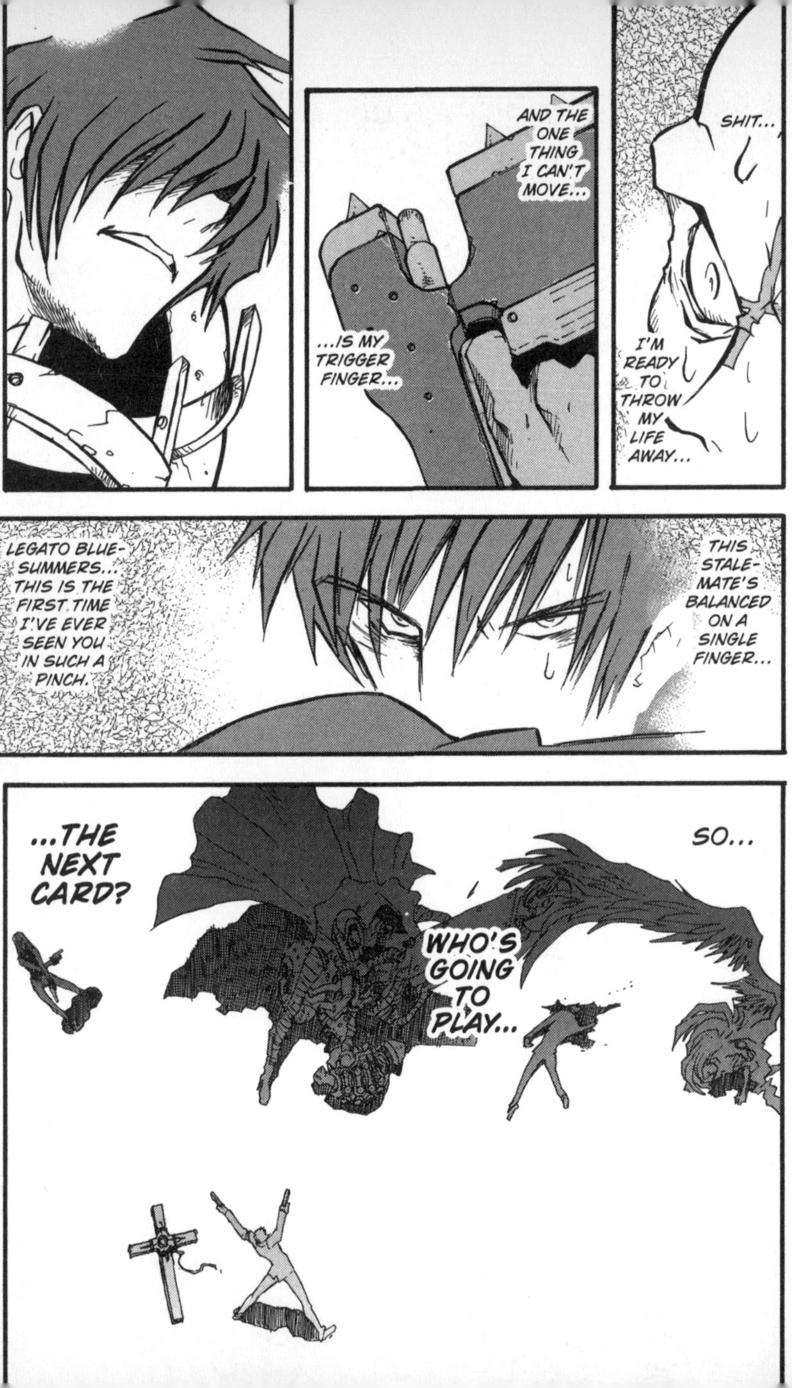
SHIT...
I'M READY TO THROW MY LIFE AWAY...
AND THE ONE THING I CAN'T MOVE...
...IS MY TRIGGER FINGER...
THIS STALE-MATE'S BALANCED ON A SINGLE FINGER...
LEGATO BLUE-SUMMERS... THIS IS THE FIRST TIME I'VE EVER SEEN YOU IN SUCH A PINCH.
SO...
WHO'S GOING TO PLAY...
...THE NEXT CARD?

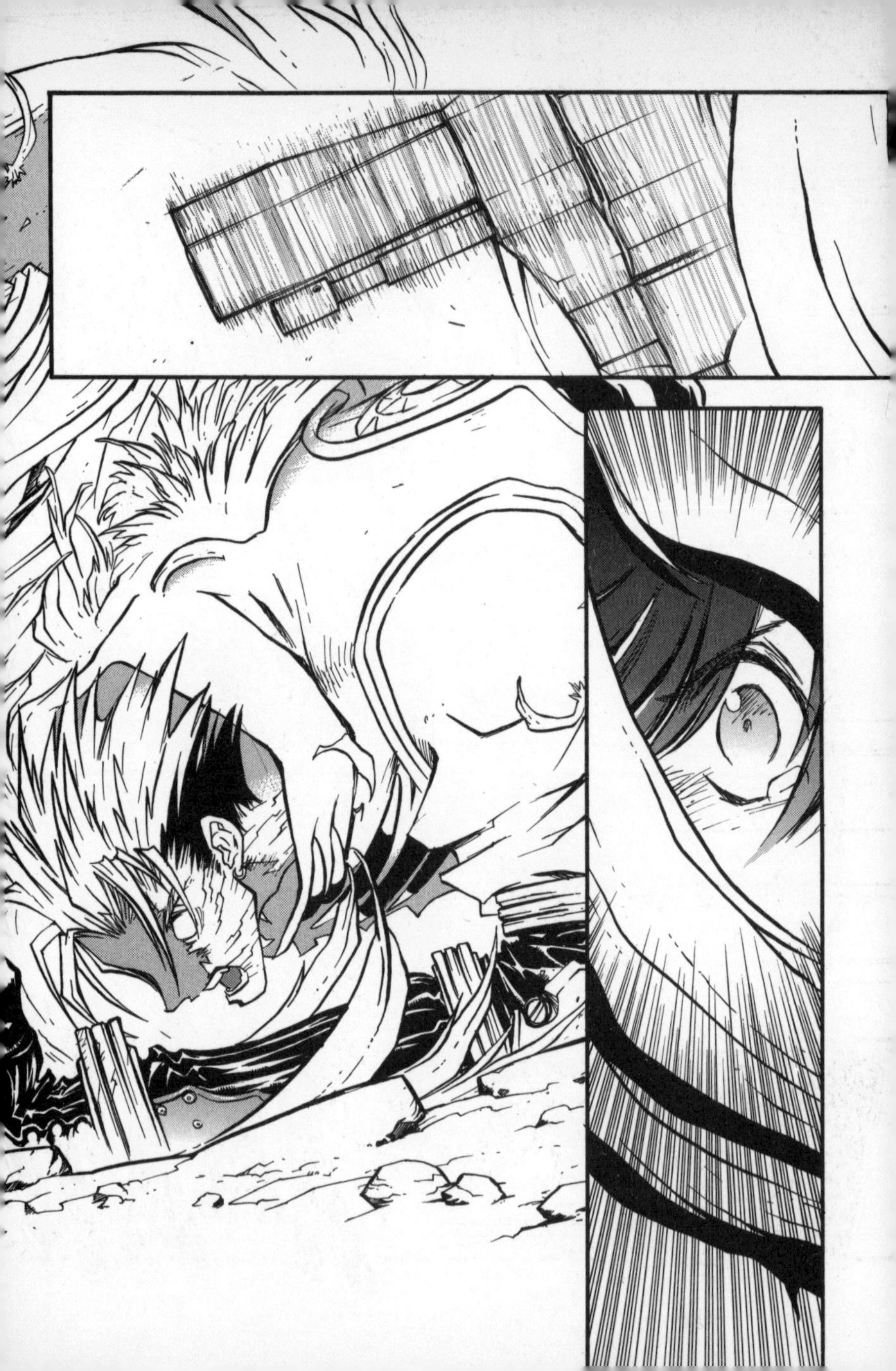

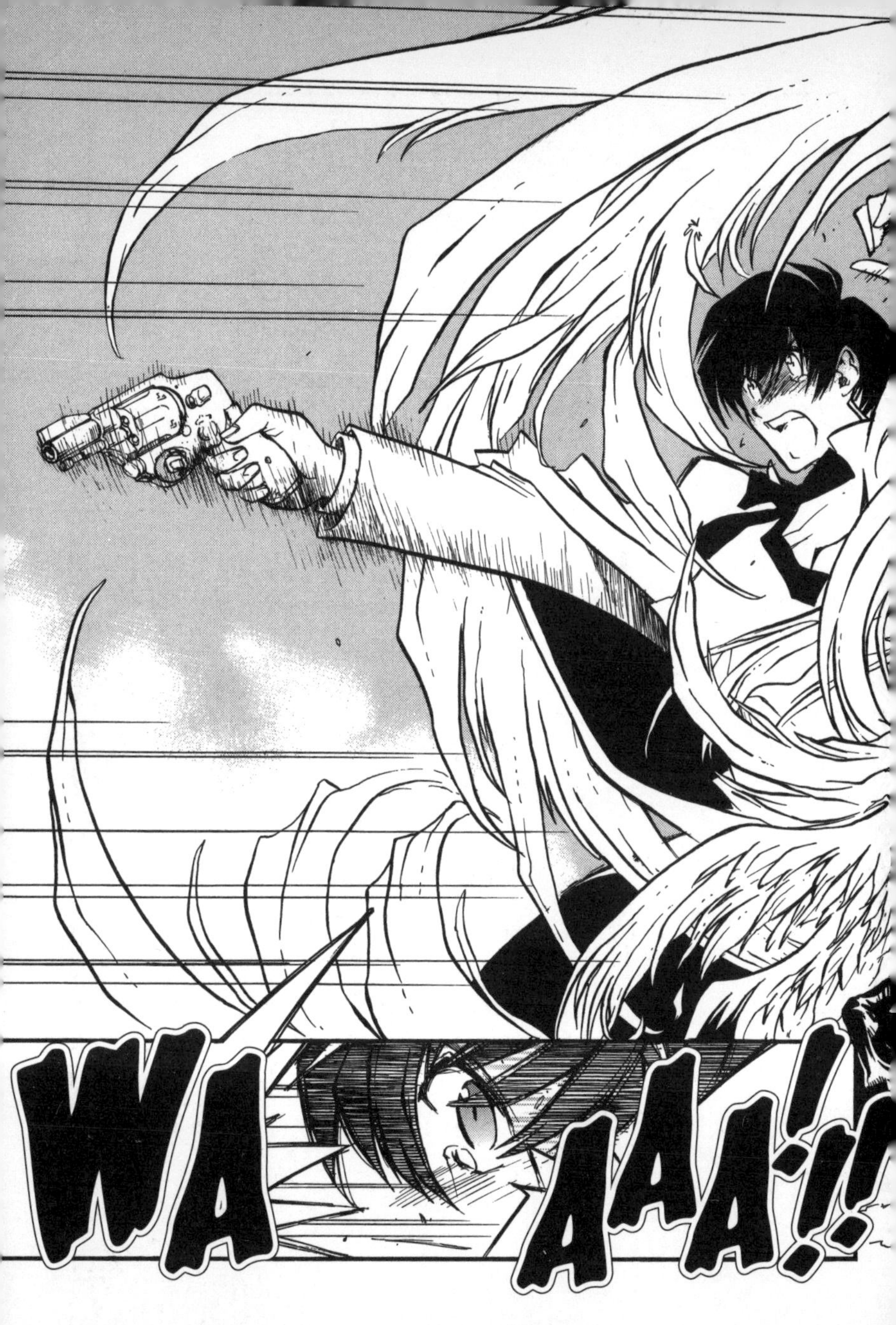
WAAAA!!

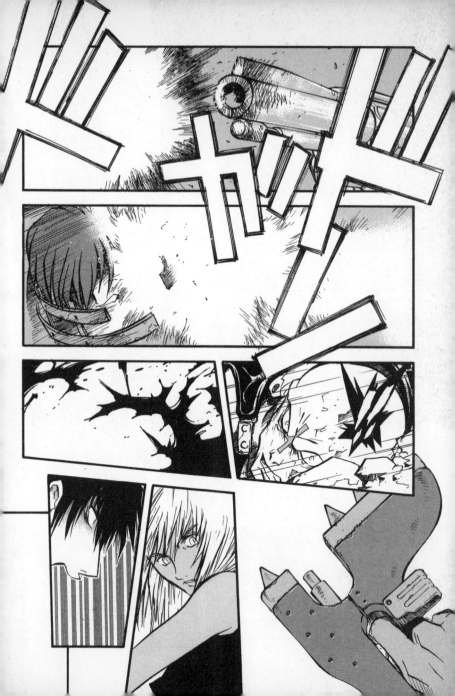

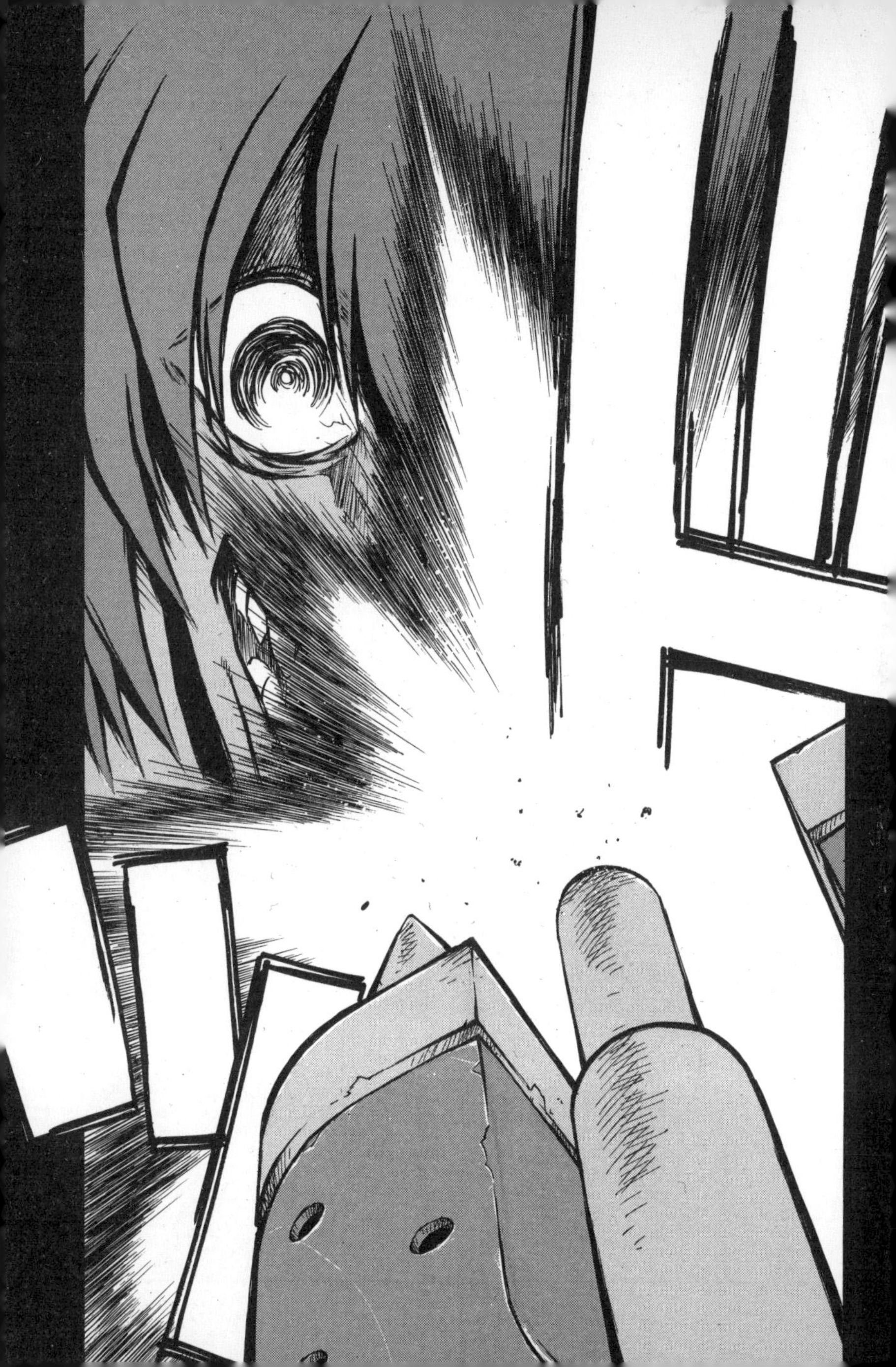

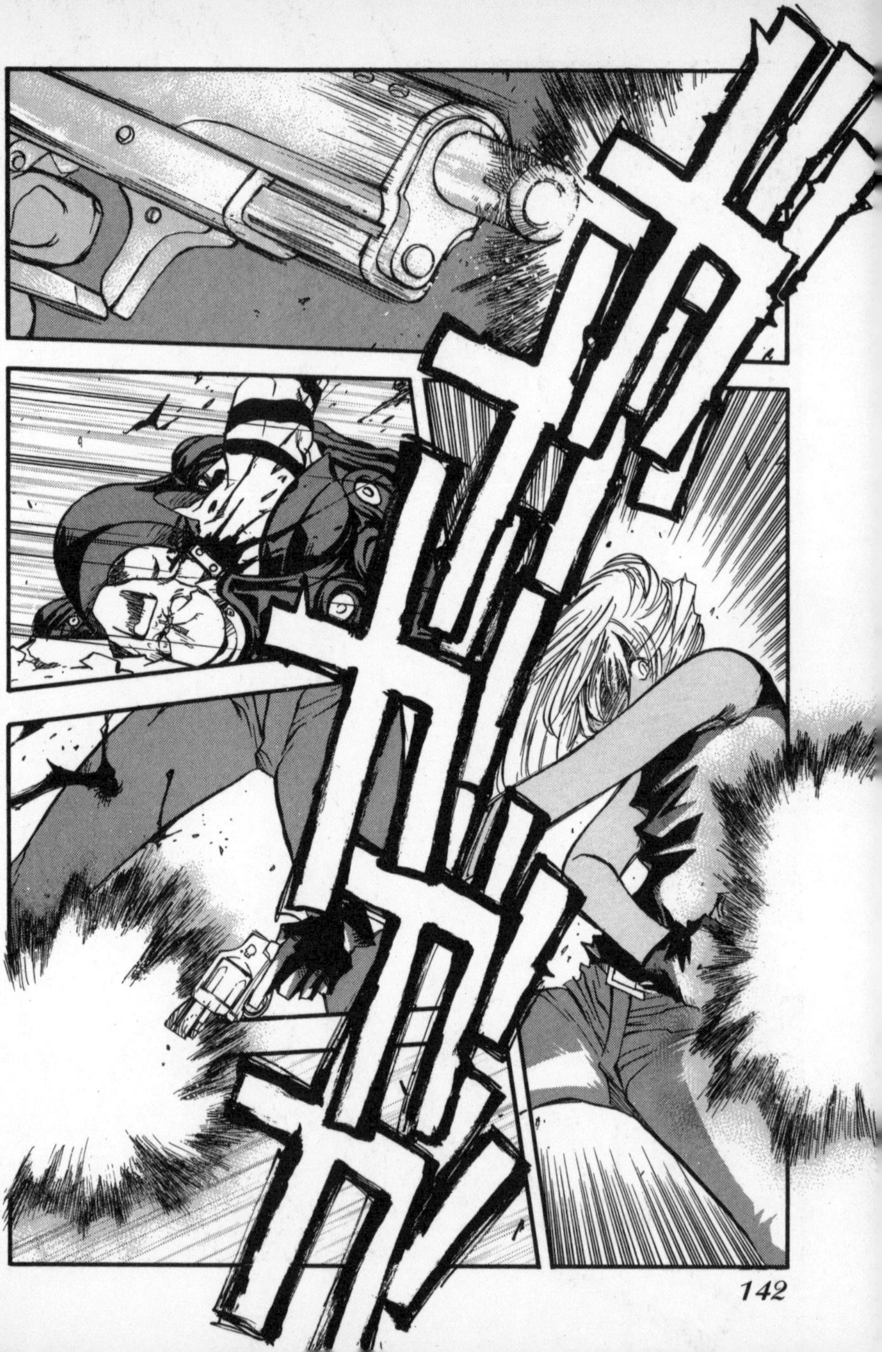

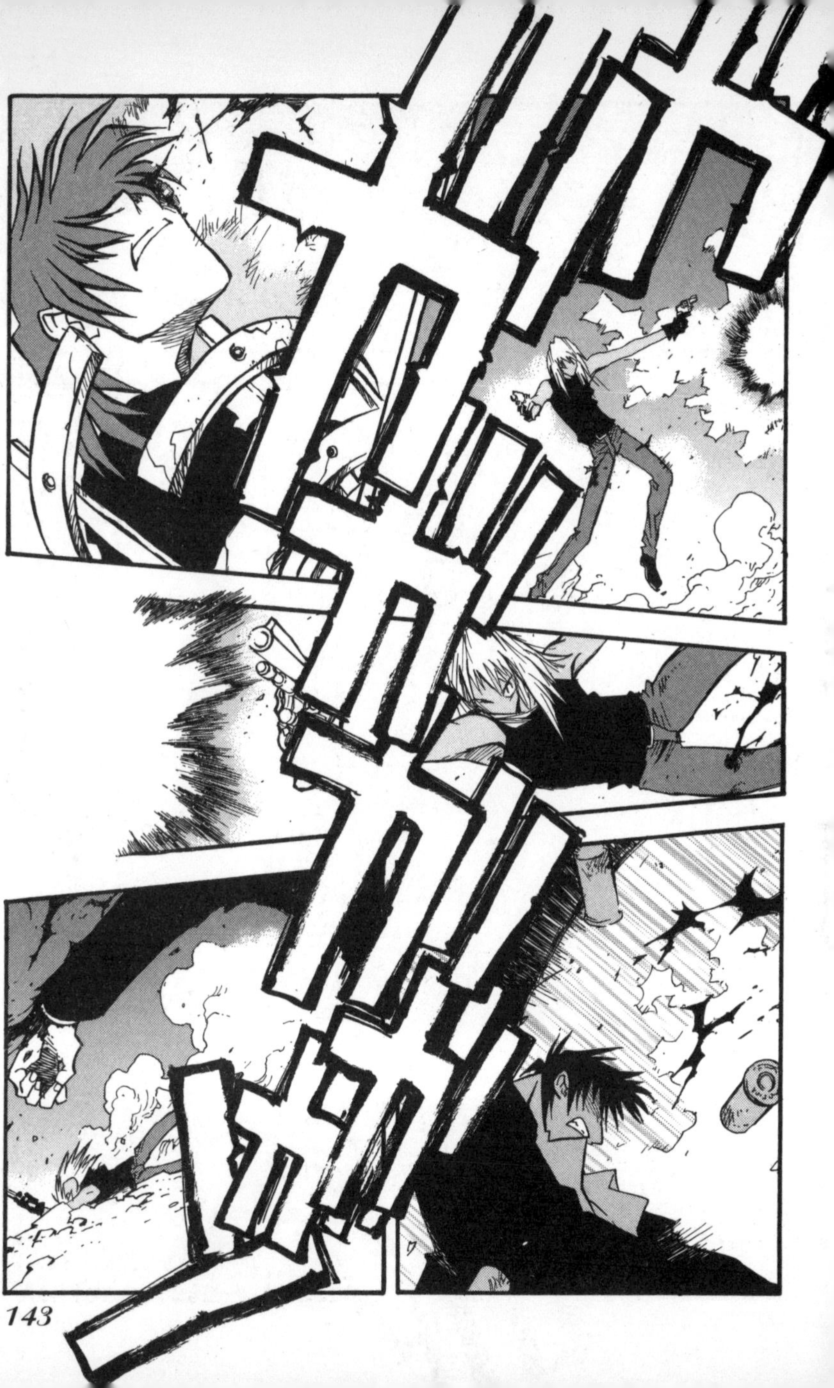

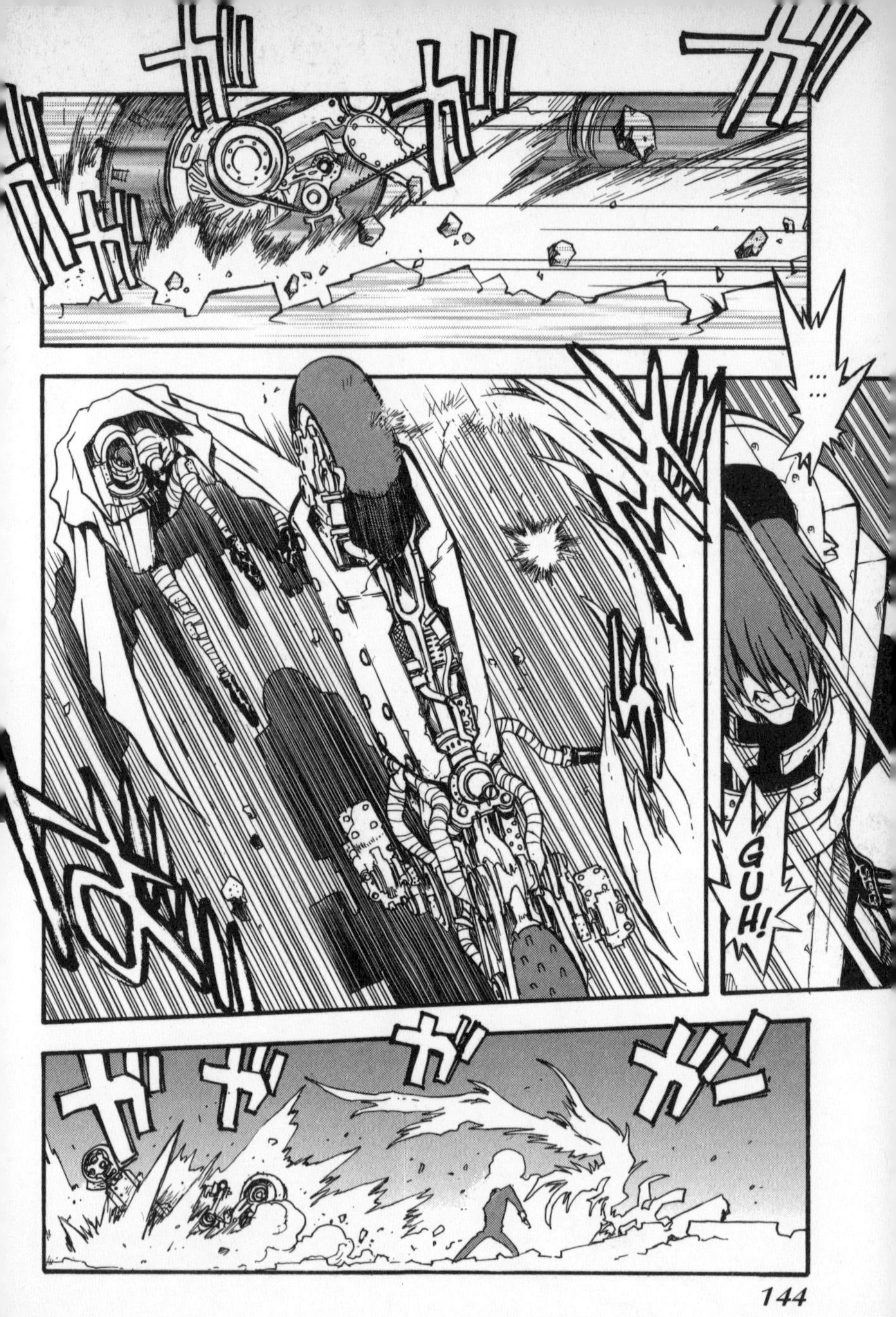
...
...
GUH!

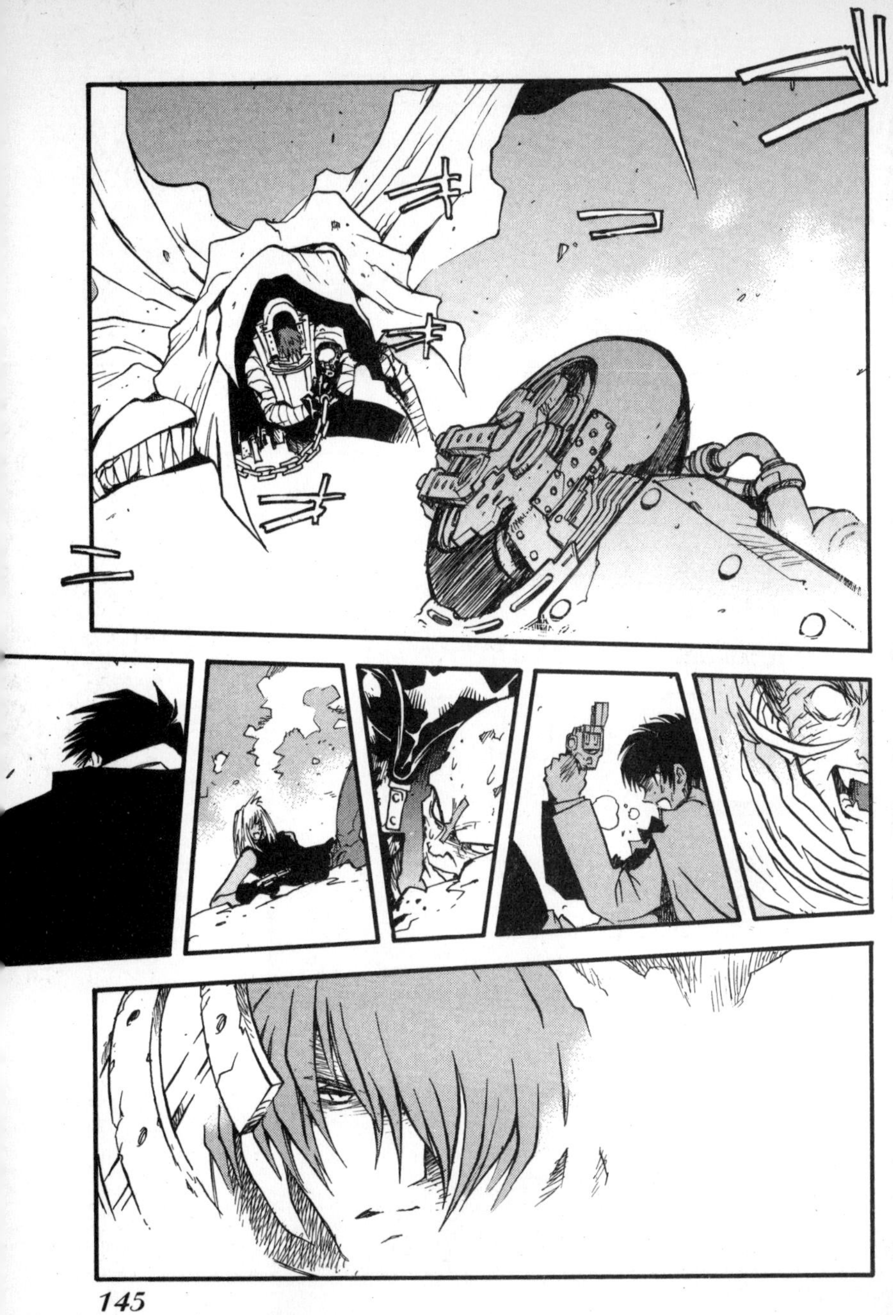

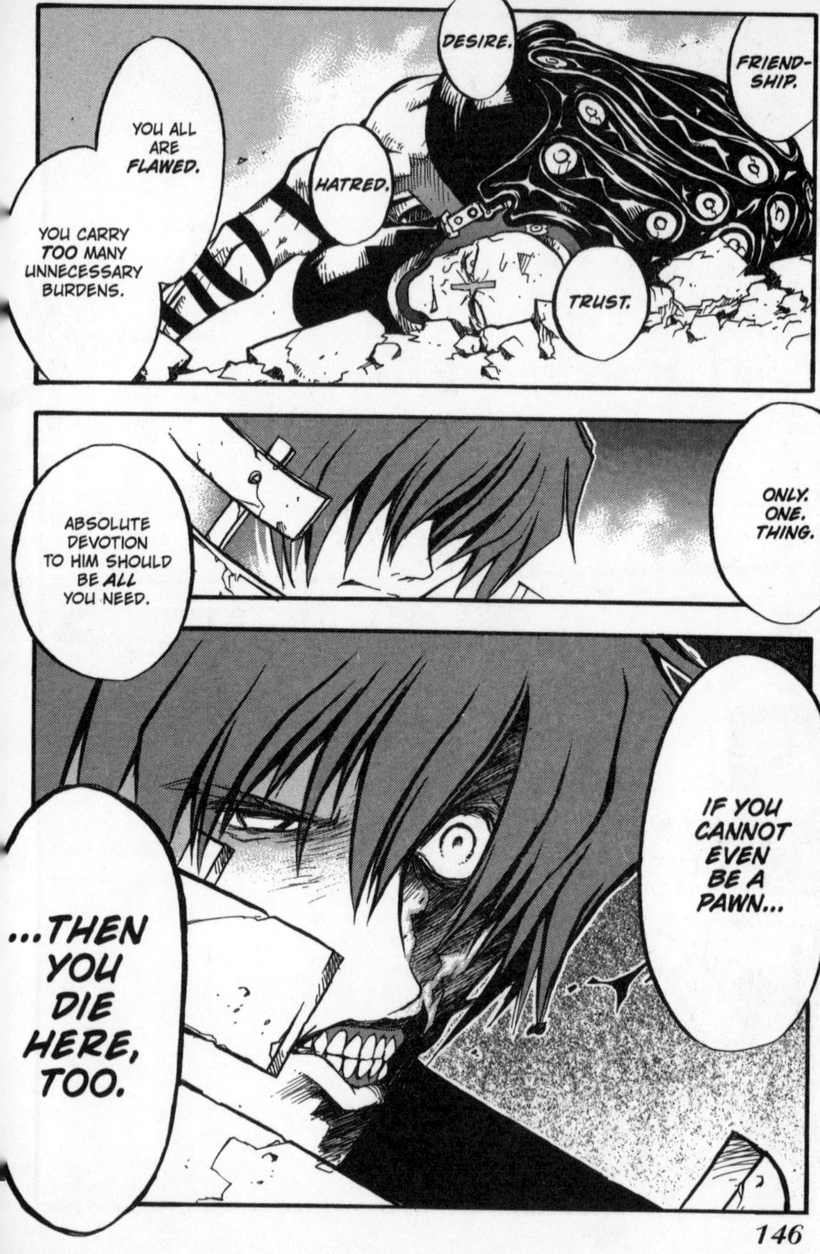
FRIEND-SHIP.
DESIRE.
TRUST.
HATRED.
YOU ALL ARE FLAWED.
YOU CARRY TOO MANY UNNECESSARY BURDENS.
ONLY. ONE. THING.
ABSOLUTE DEVOTION TO HIM SHOULD BE ALL YOU NEED.
IF YOU CANNOT EVEN BE A PAWN...
...THEN YOU DIE HERE, TOO.

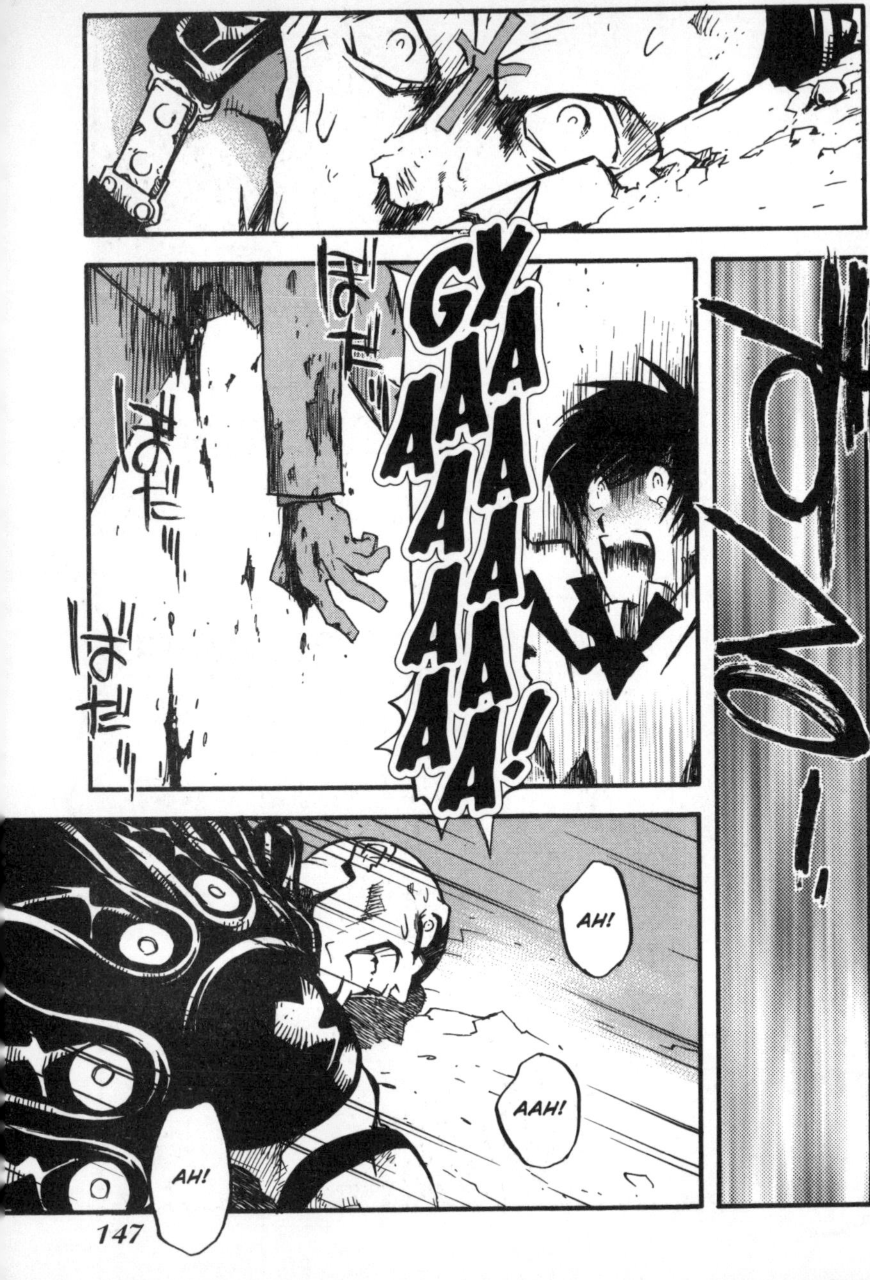
GYAAAAAAAAAAA!
AH!
AAH!
AH!

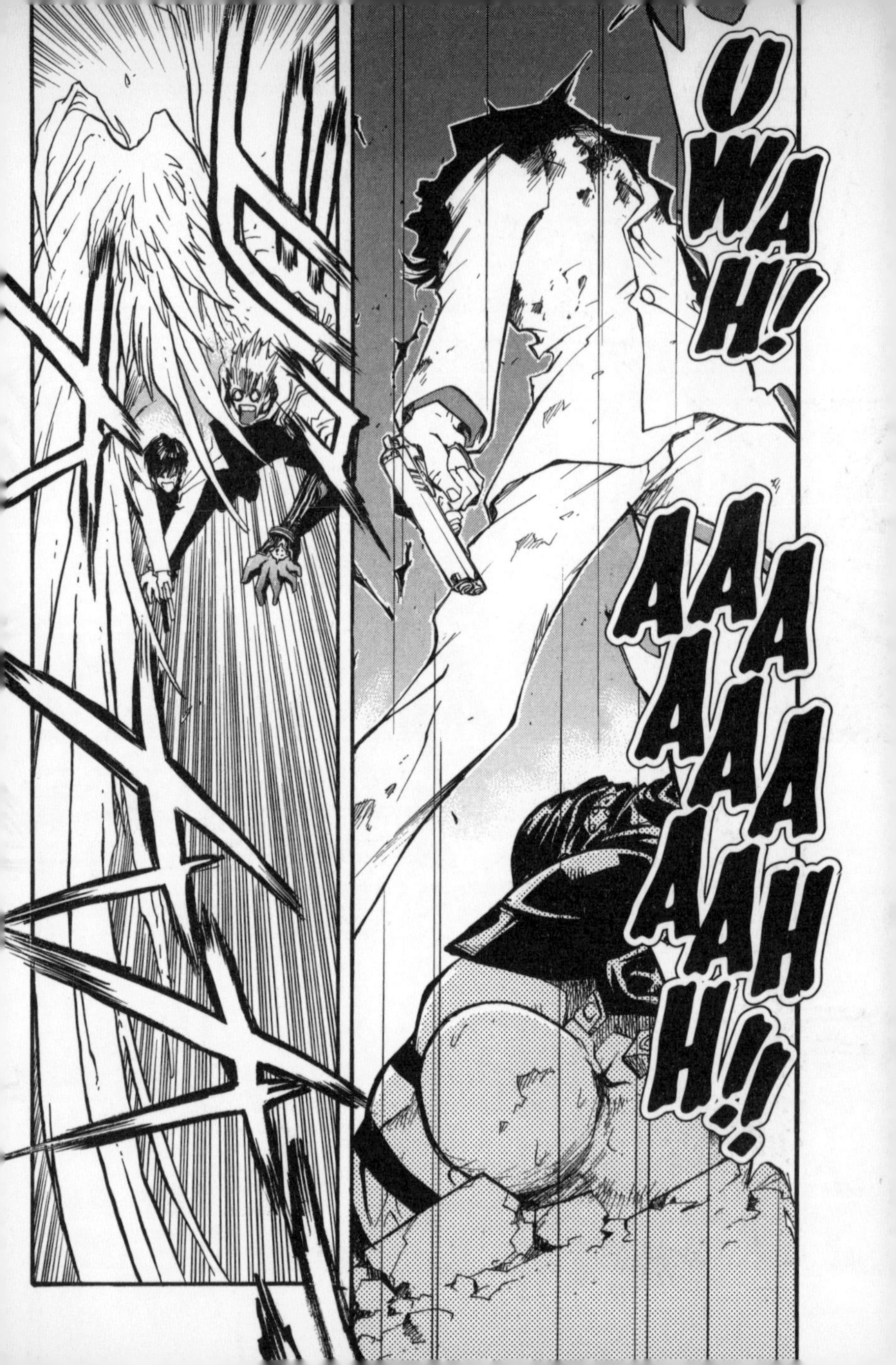

OWAAH!!
AAAAAAAAAAAH!!

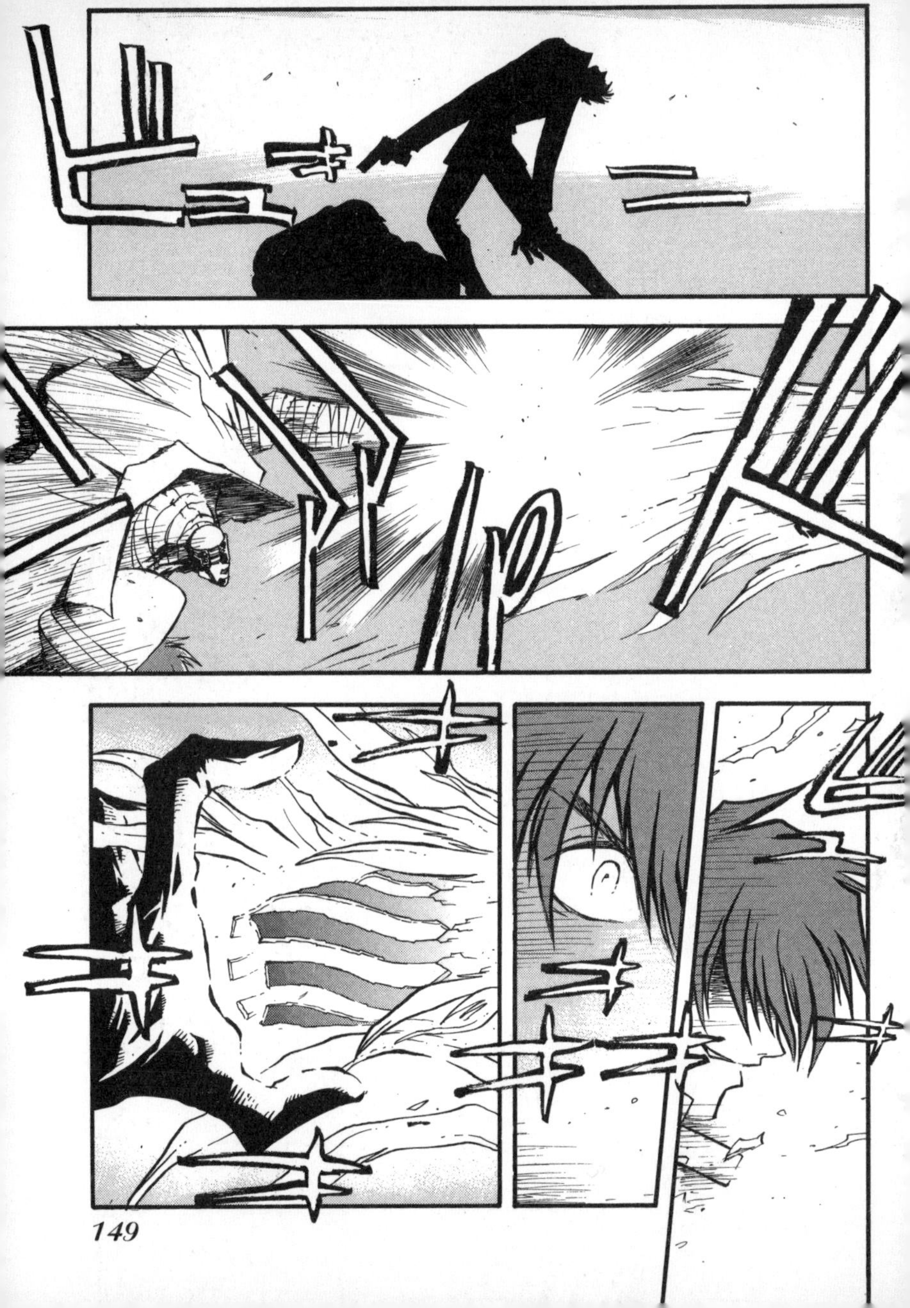

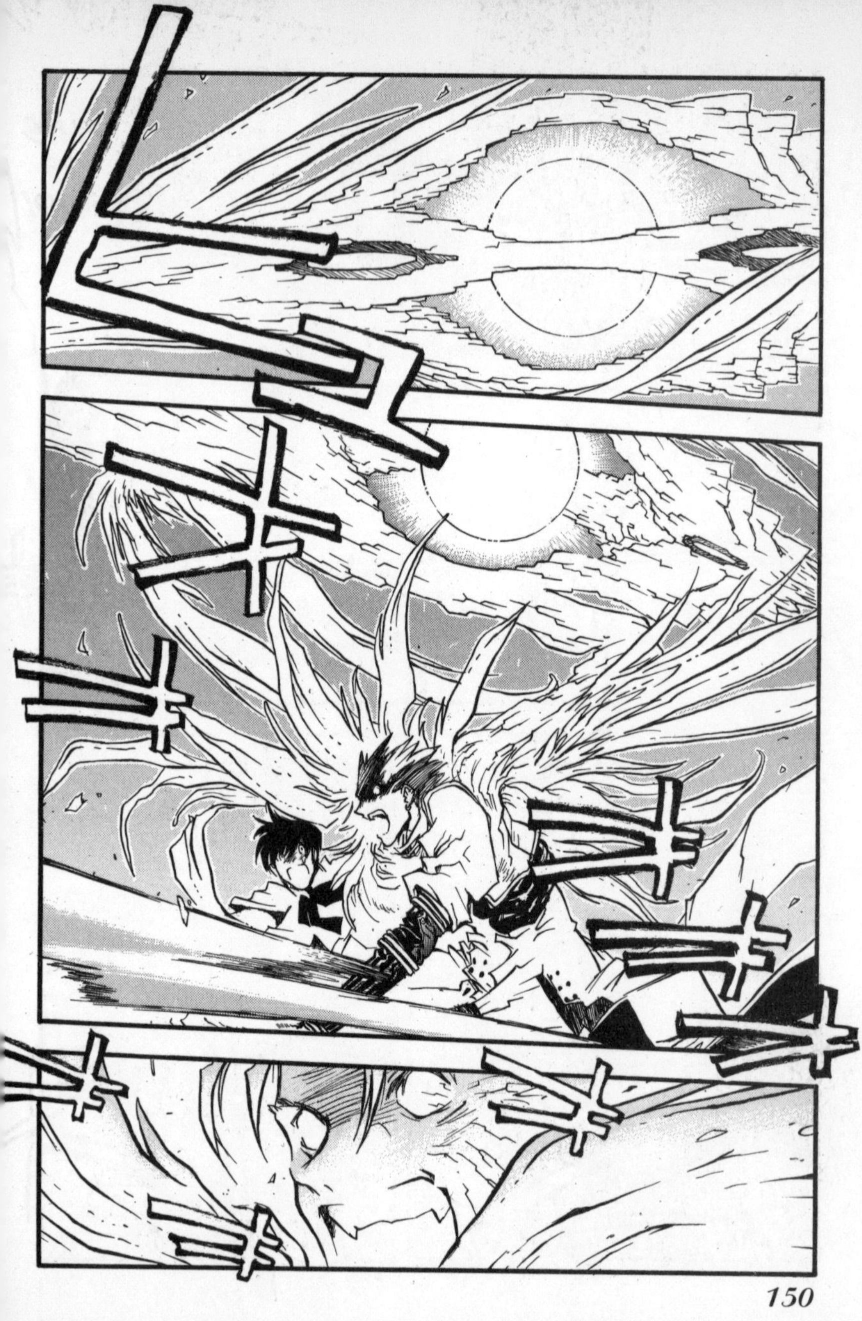

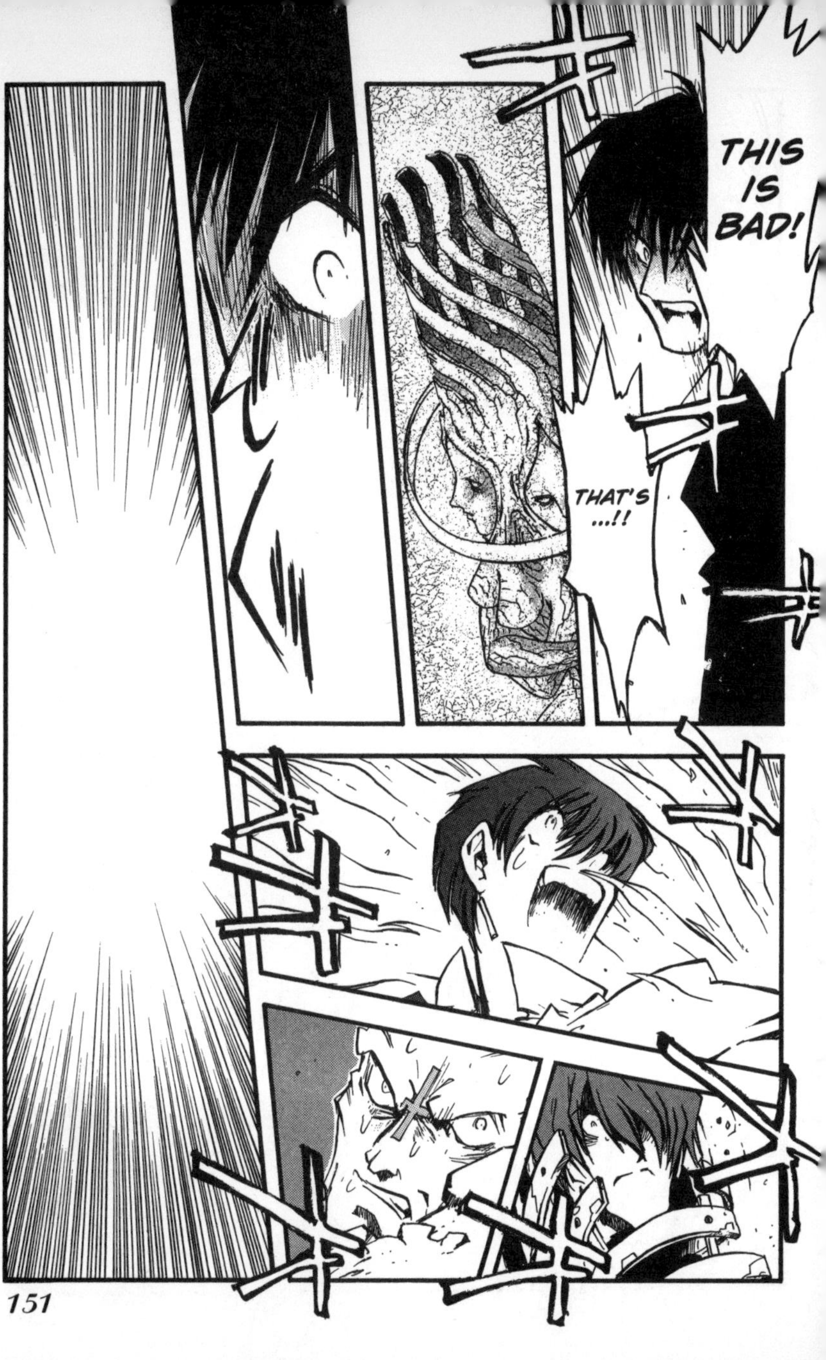
THIS IS BAD!
THAT'S ...!!

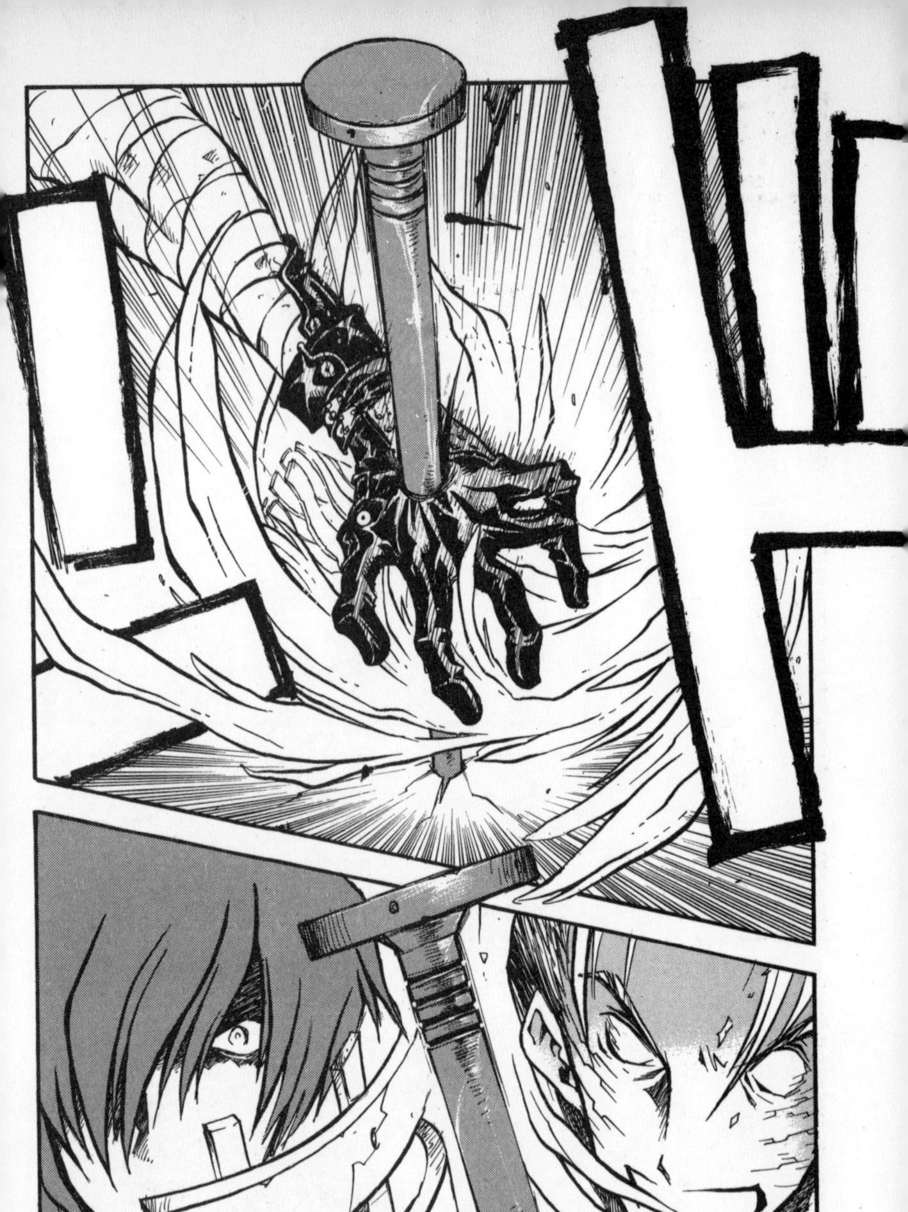

#5. DEATH DEAL / END

# #6. LET US WALK THE PATH TO REDEMPTION.

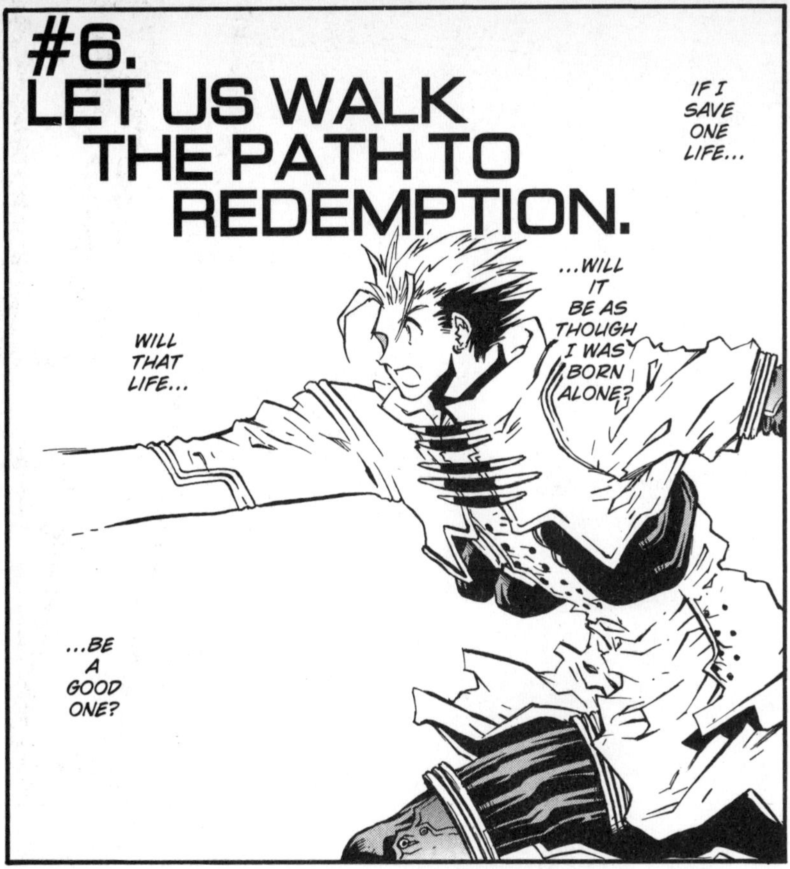
IF I SAVE ONE LIFE...
...WILL IT BE AS THOUGH I WAS BORN ALONE?
WILL THAT LIFE...
...BE A GOOD ONE?

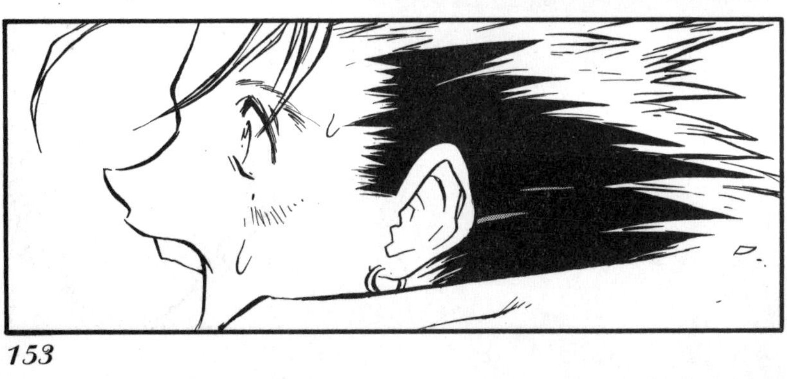

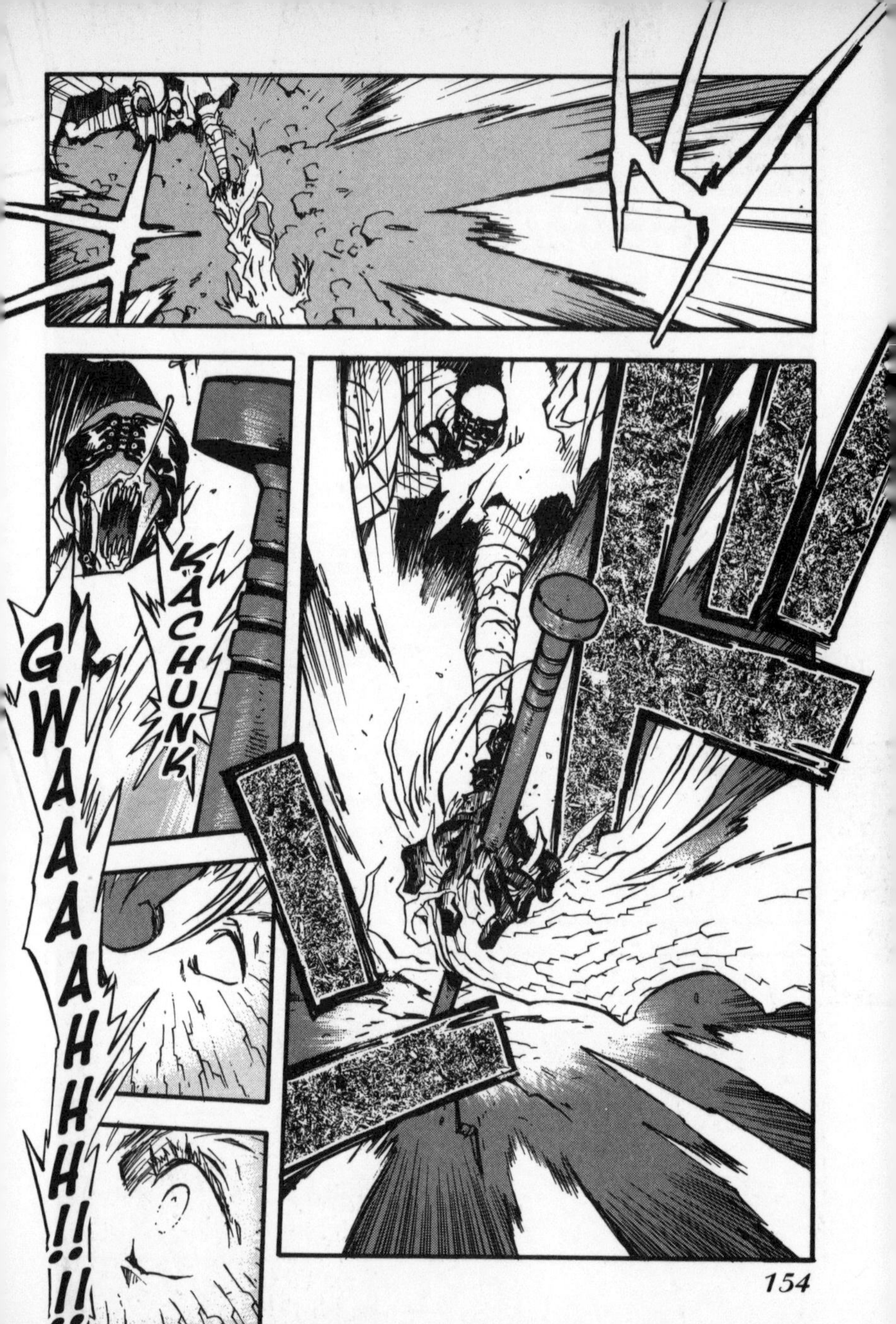
KÄCHUNK
GWAAAAHHH!!!!

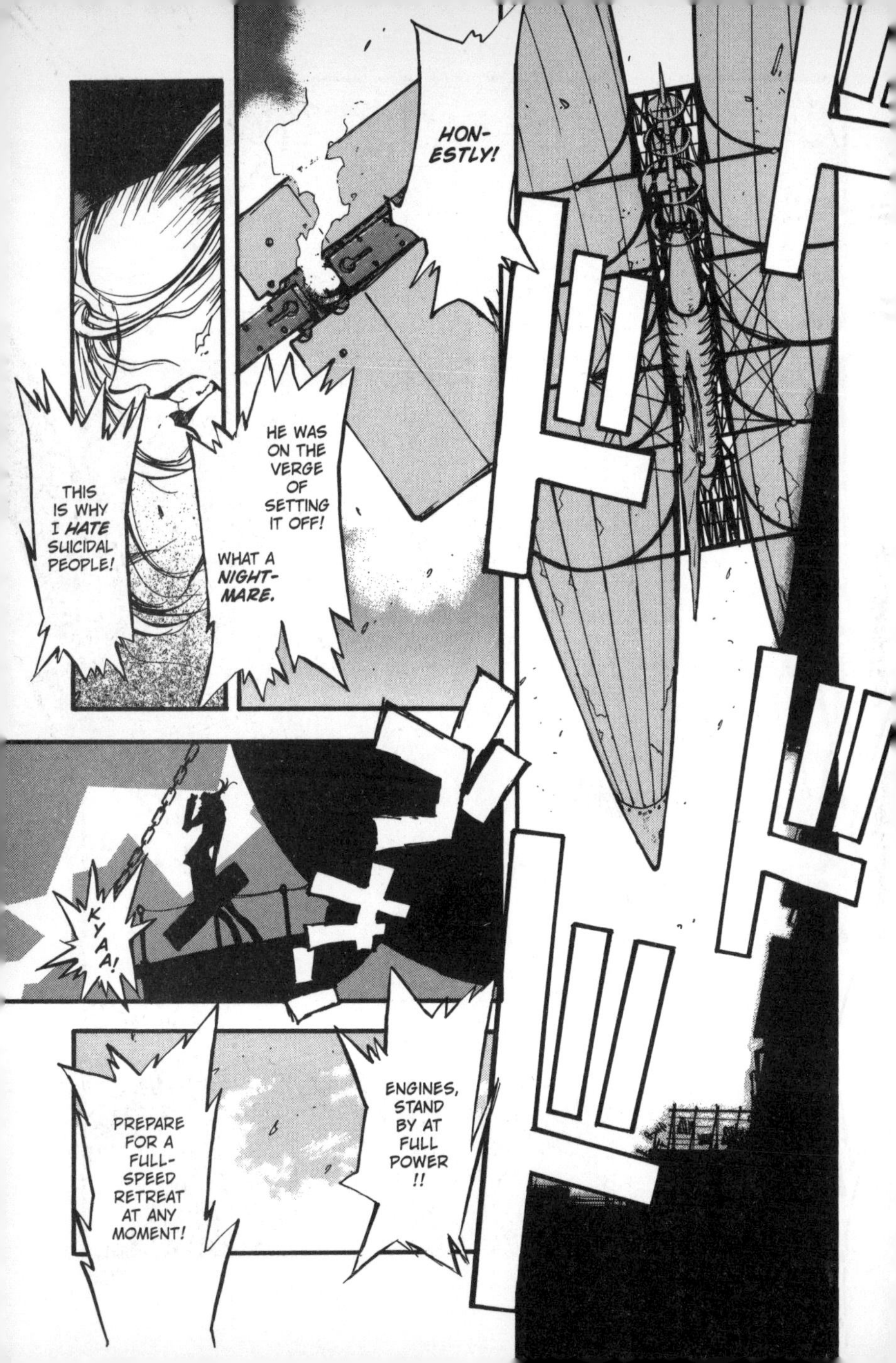

HON-ESTLY!
HE WAS ON THE VERGE OF SETTING IT OFF!
WHAT A NIGHT-MARE.
THIS IS WHY I HATE SUICIDAL PEOPLE!
KYAA!
ENGINES, STAND BY AT FULL POWER !!
PREPARE FOR A FULL-SPEED RETREAT AT ANY MOMENT!

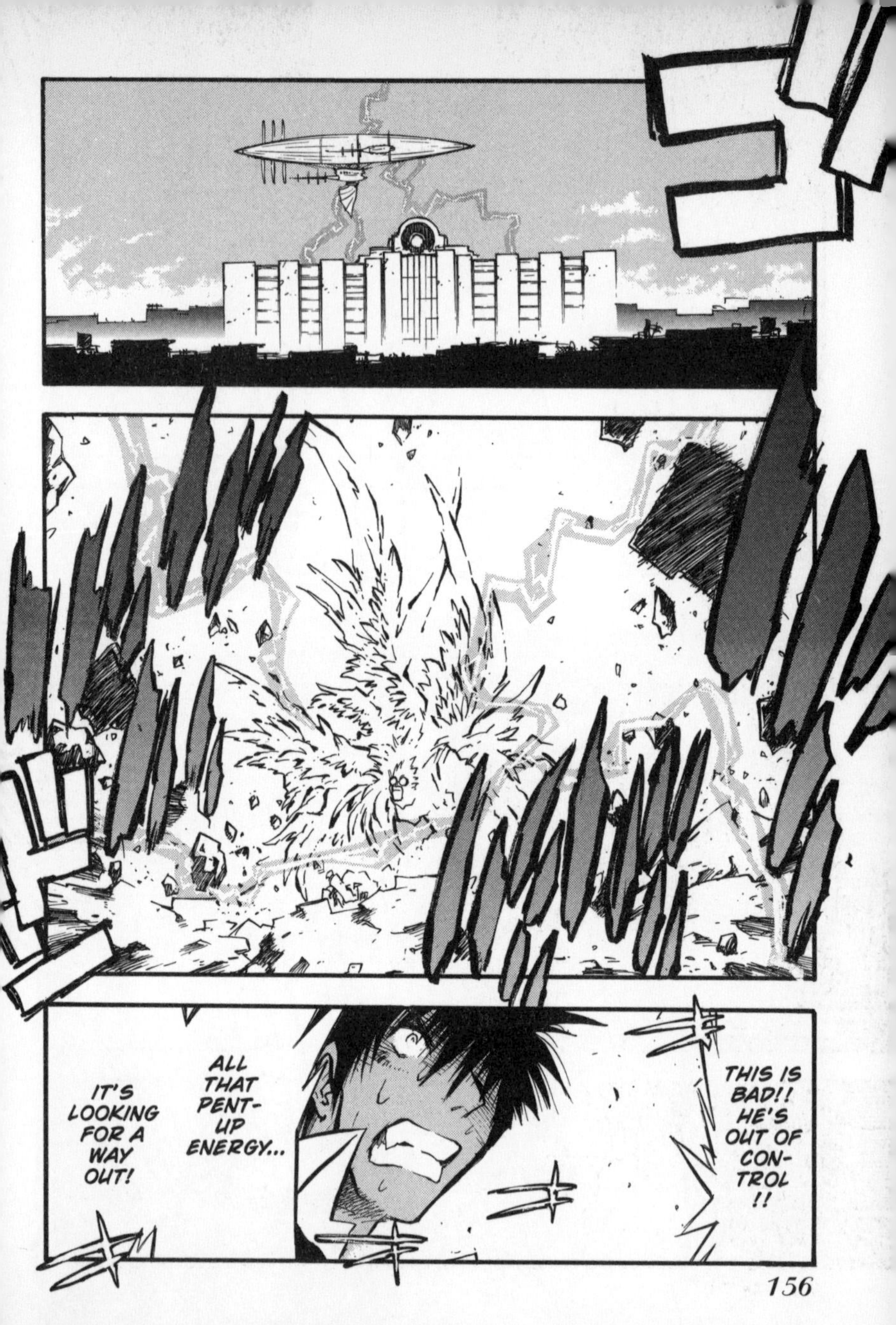
THIS IS BAD!! HE'S OUT OF CON-TROL!!
ALL THAT PENT-UP ENERGY...
IT'S LOOKING FOR A WAY OUT!

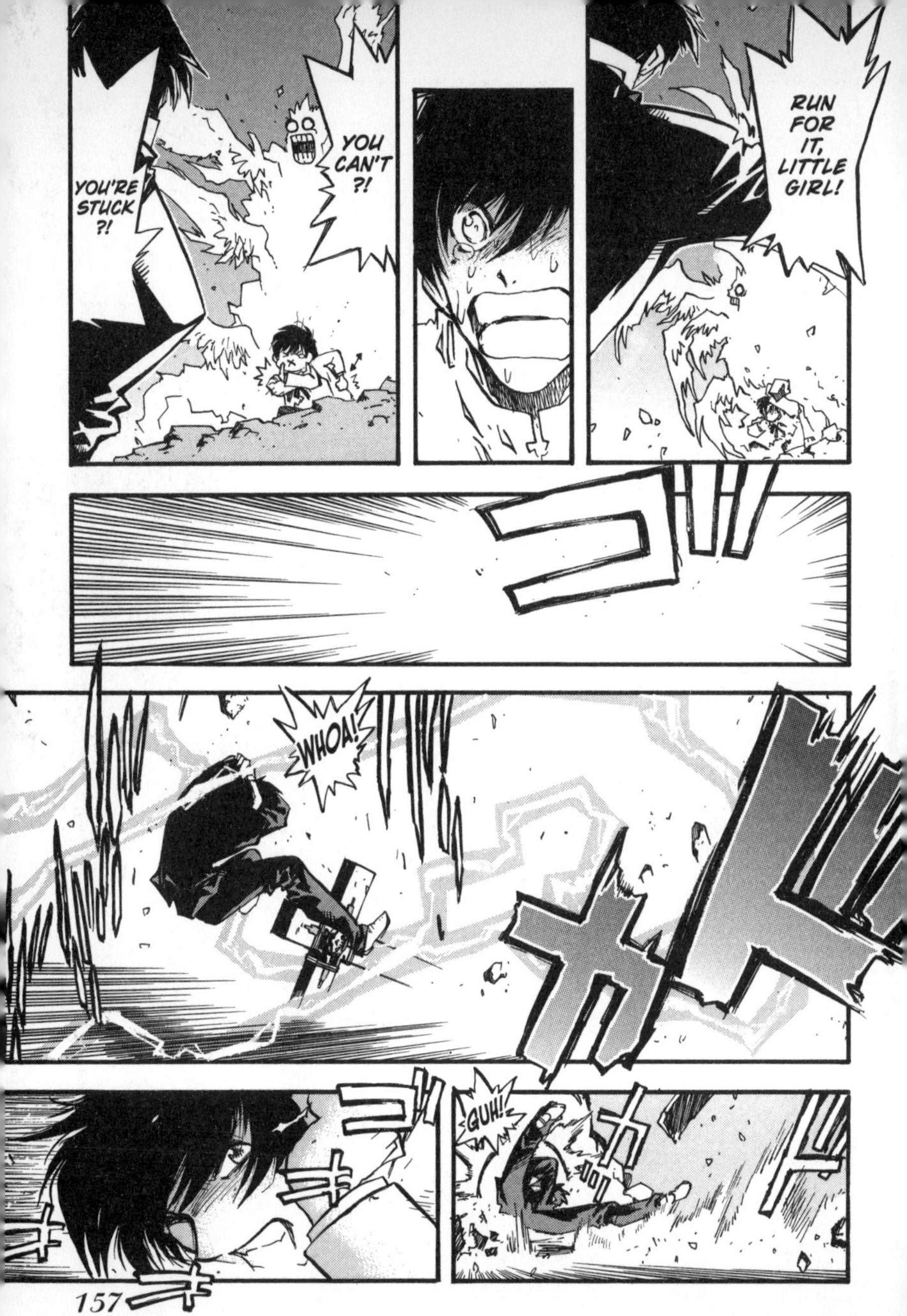
RUN FOR IT, LITTLE GIRL!
YOU CAN'T ?!
YOU'RE STUCK ?!
WHOA!
GUH!

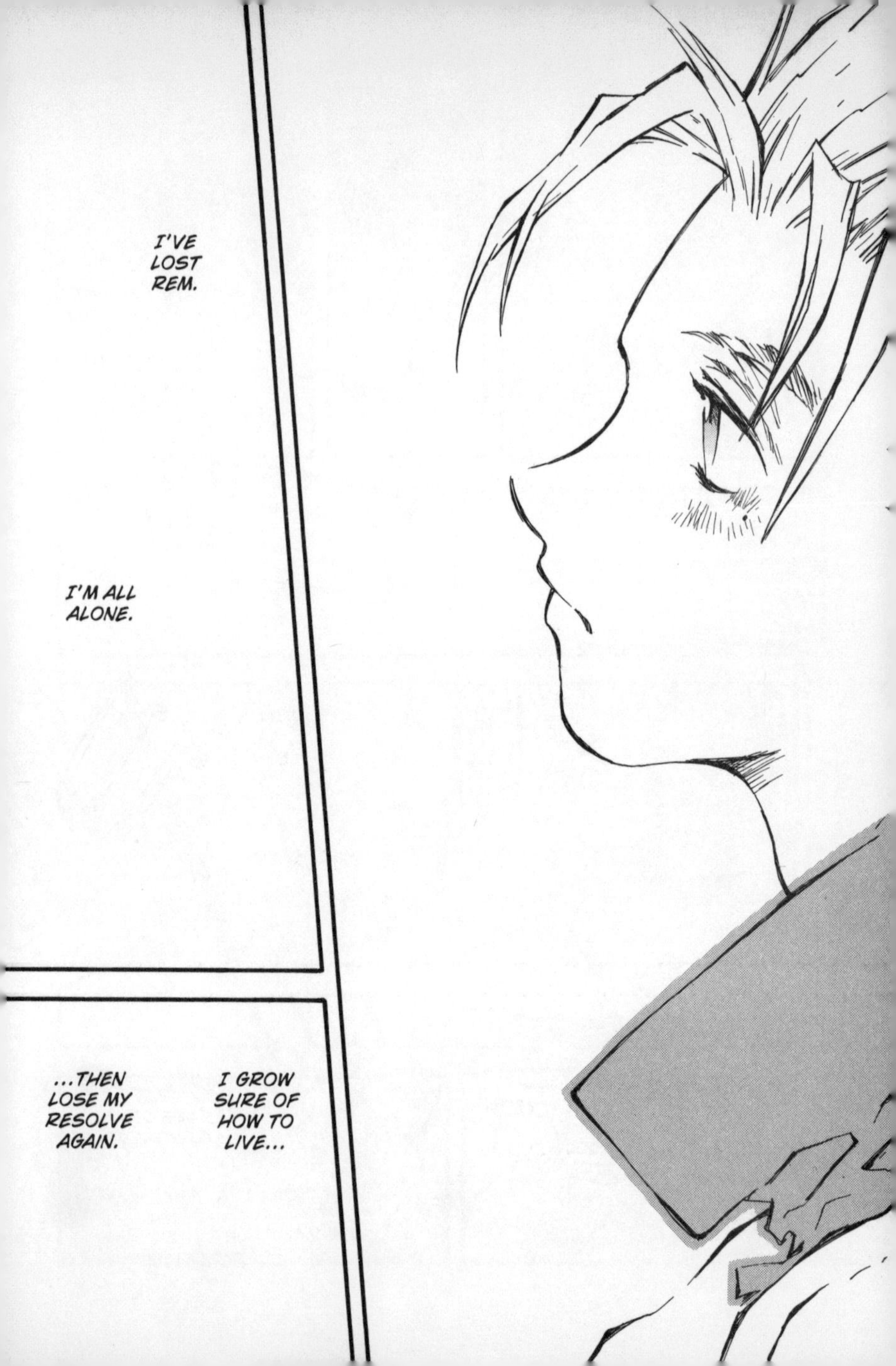
I'VE LOST REM.
I'M ALL ALONE.
I GROW SURE OF HOW TO LIVE...
...THEN LOSE MY RESOLVE AGAIN.

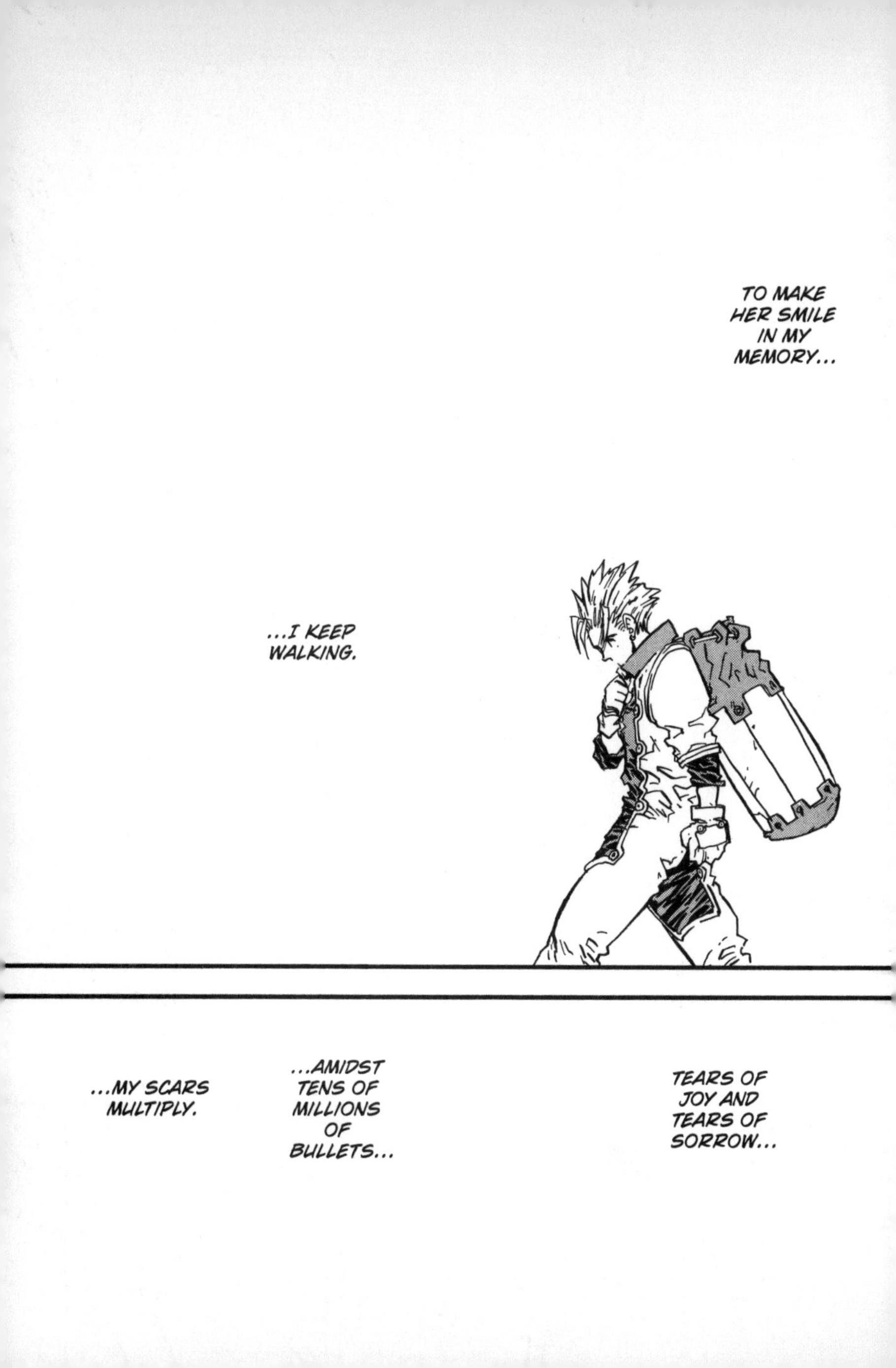
TO MAKE HER SMILE IN MY MEMORY...
...I KEEP WALKING.
TEARS OF JOY AND TEARS OF SORROW...
...AMIDST TENS OF MILLIONS OF BULLETS...
...MY SCARS MULTIPLY.

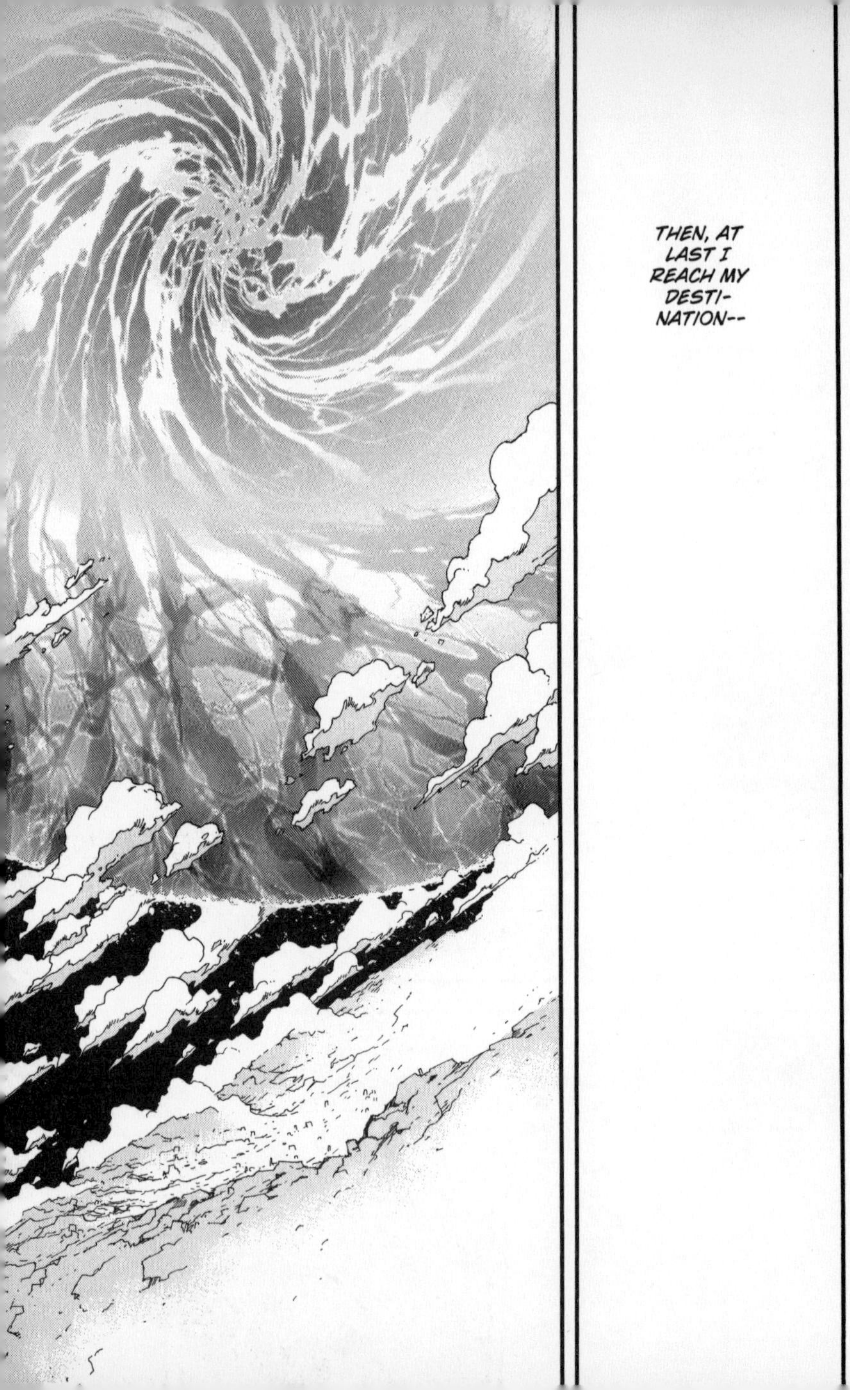
THEN, AT LAST I REACH MY DESTI-NATION--

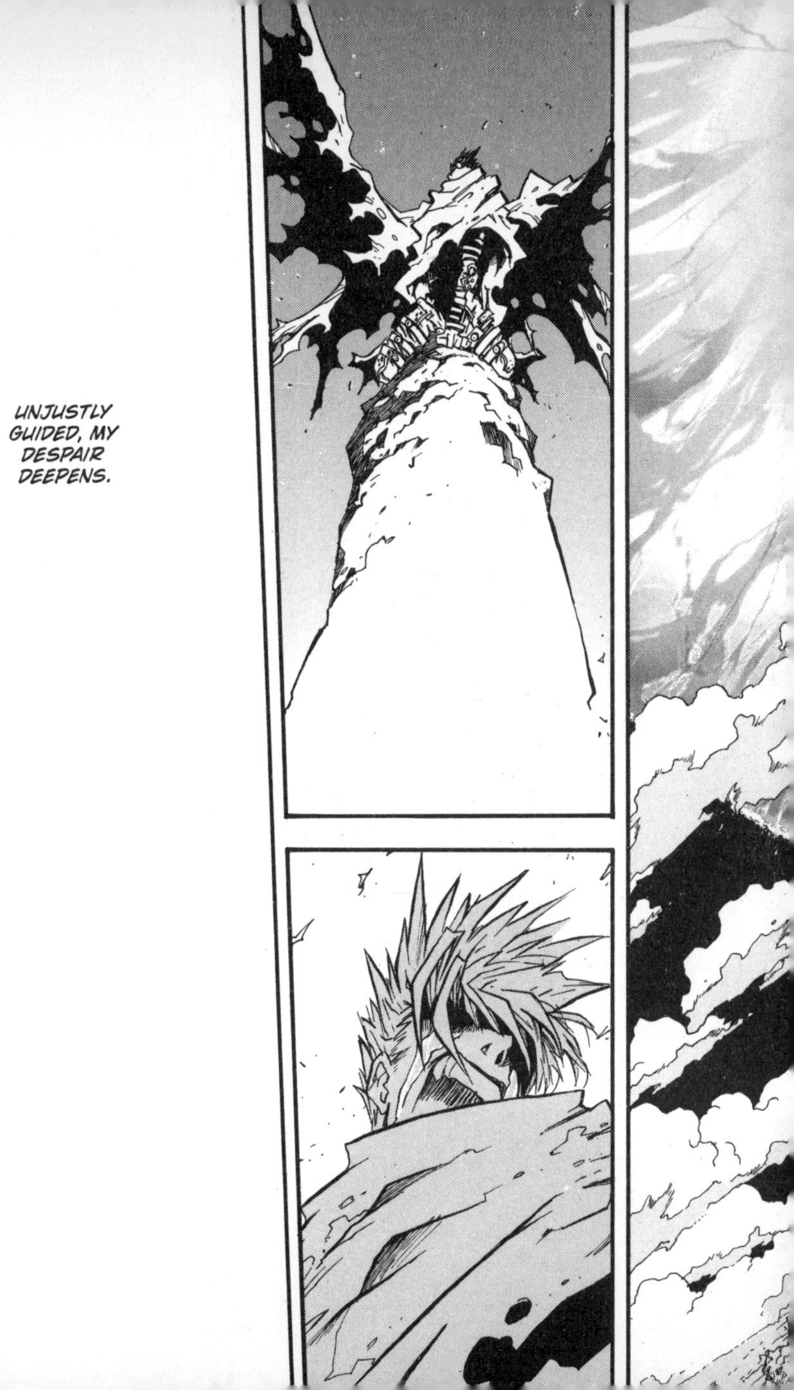
UNJUSTLY GUIDED, MY DESPAIR DEEPENS.

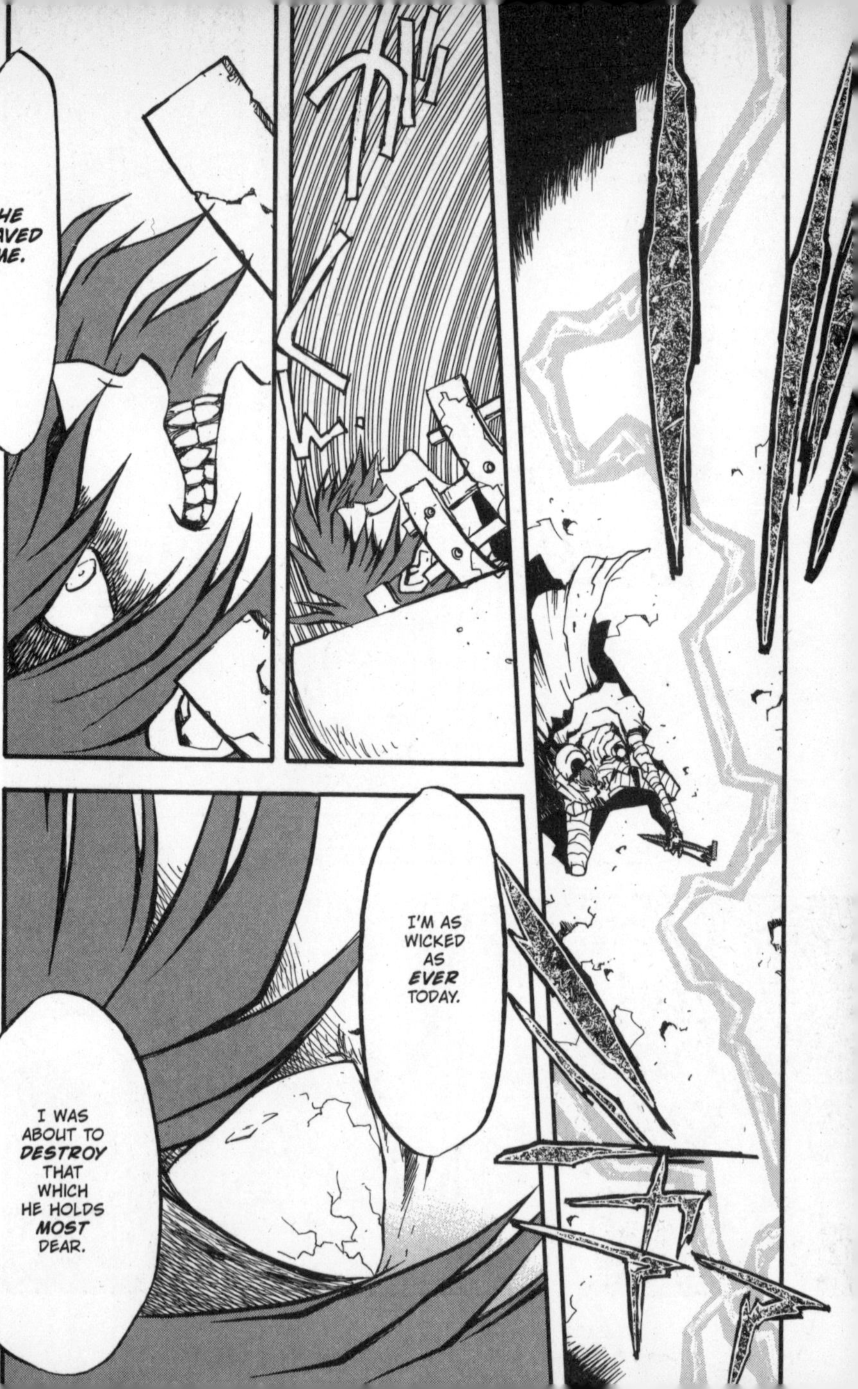
HE SAVED ME.
I'M AS WICKED AS EVER TODAY.
I WAS ABOUT TO DESTROY THAT WHICH HE HOLDS MOST DEAR.

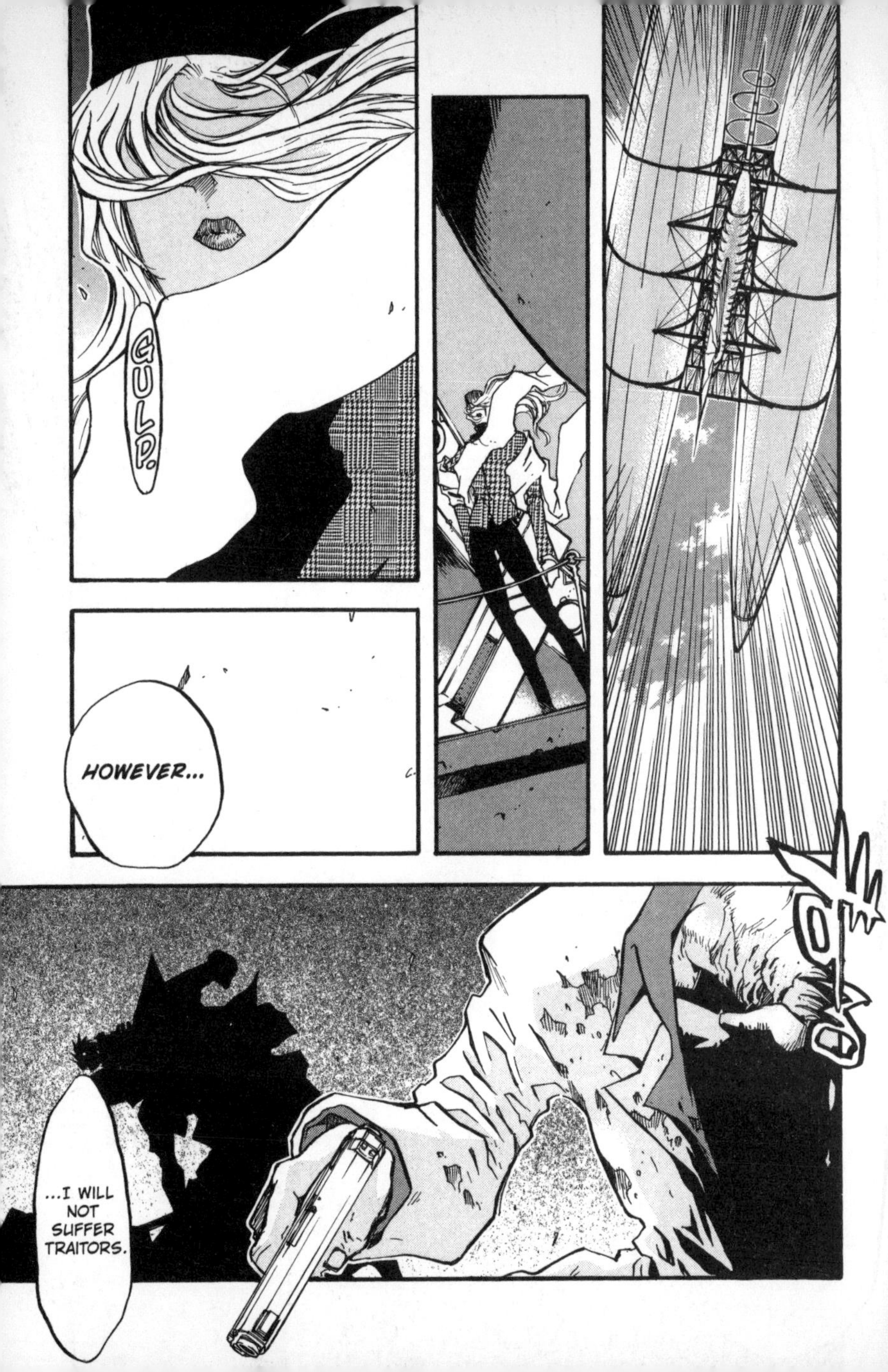
GULP.
HOWEVER...
...I WILL NOT SUFFER TRAITORS.

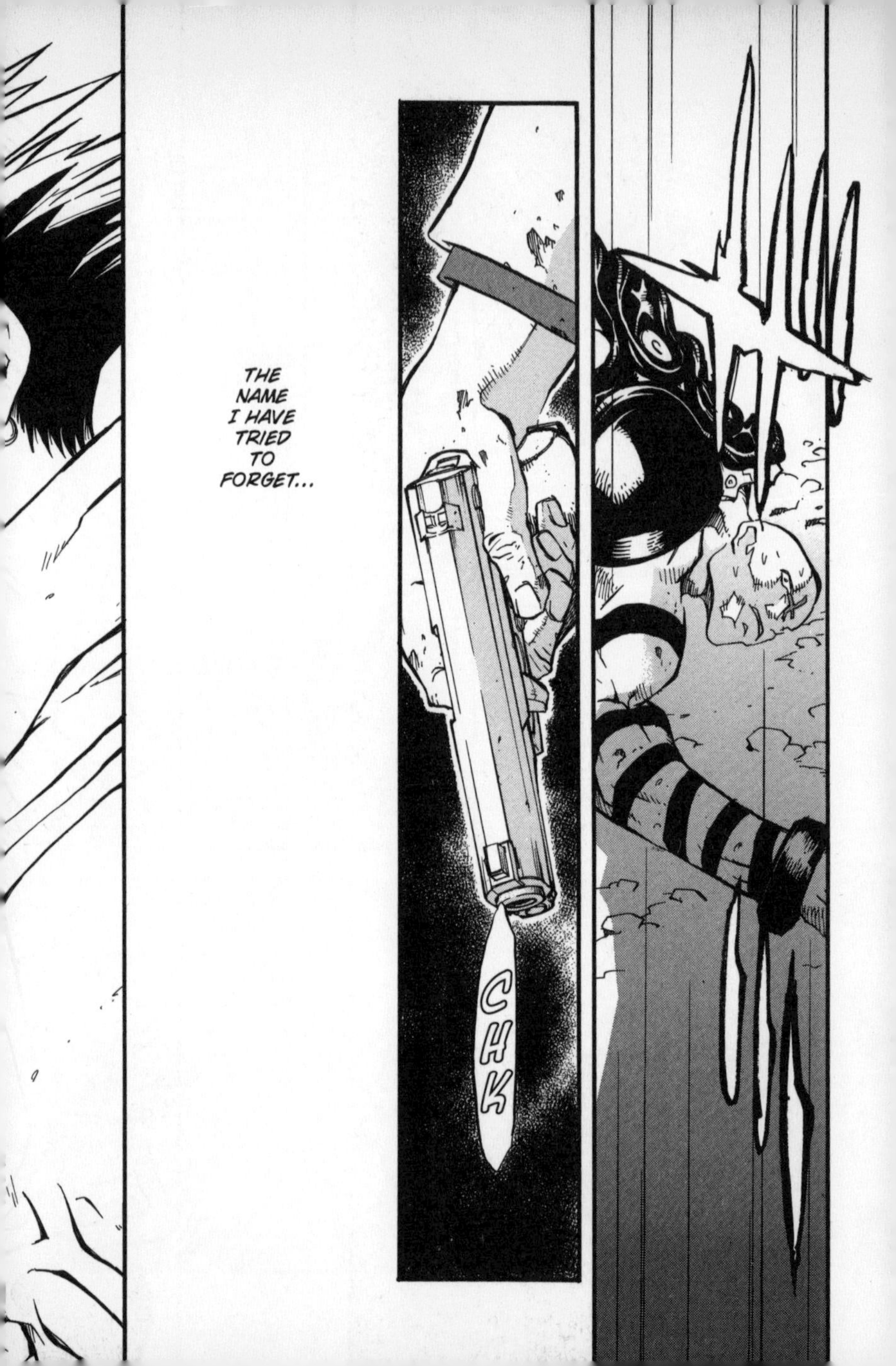
CHK
THE NAME I HAVE TRIED TO FORGET...

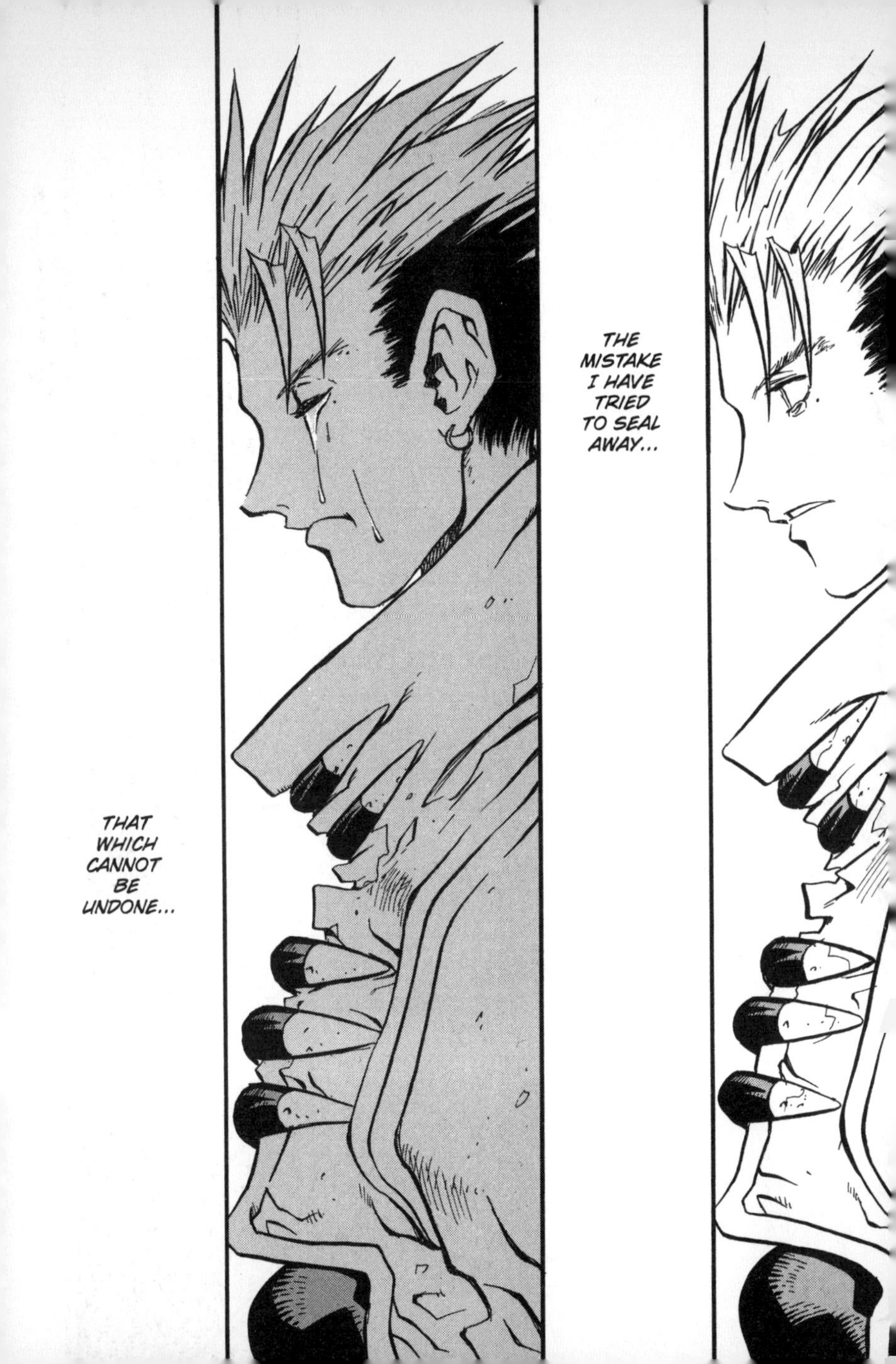
THE MISTAKE I HAVE TRIED TO SEAL AWAY...
THAT WHICH CANNOT BE UNDONE...

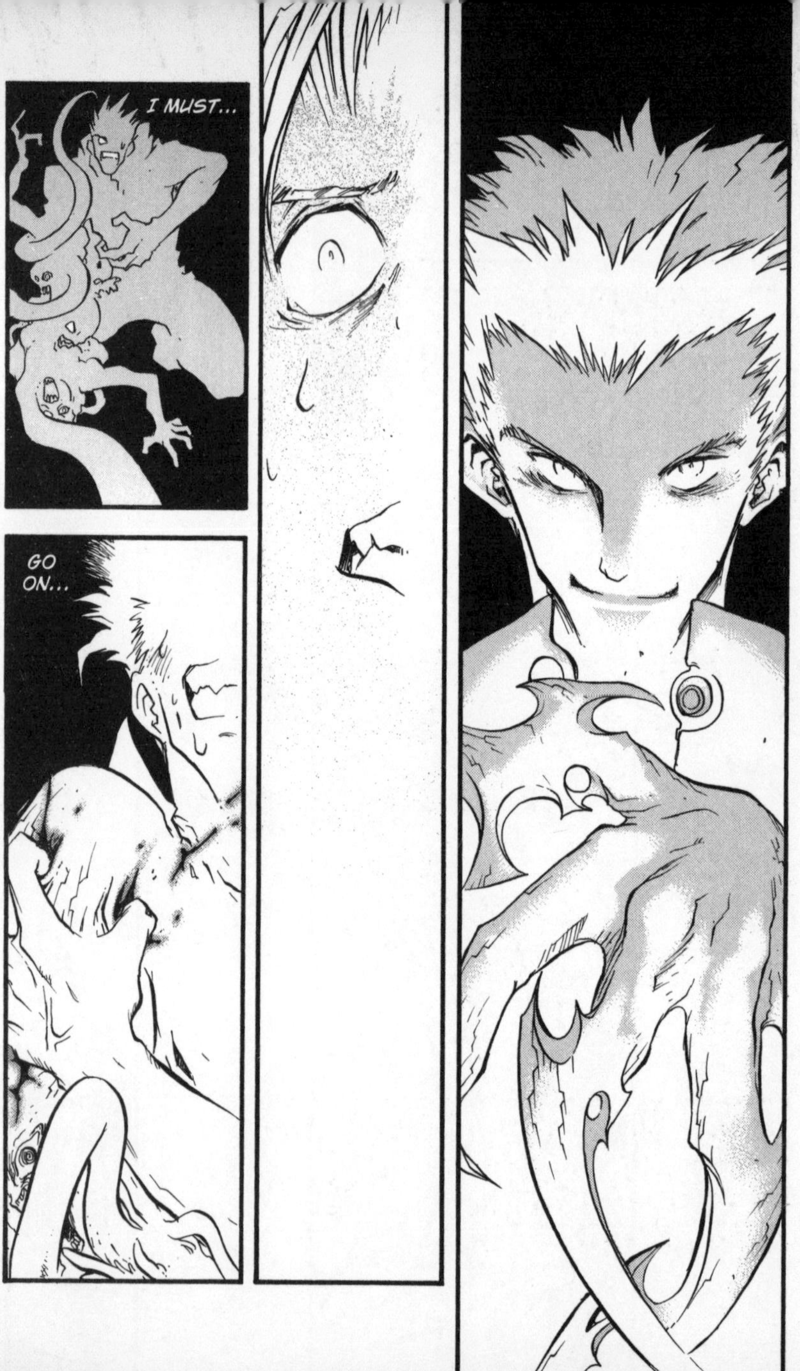
I MUST...
GO ON...

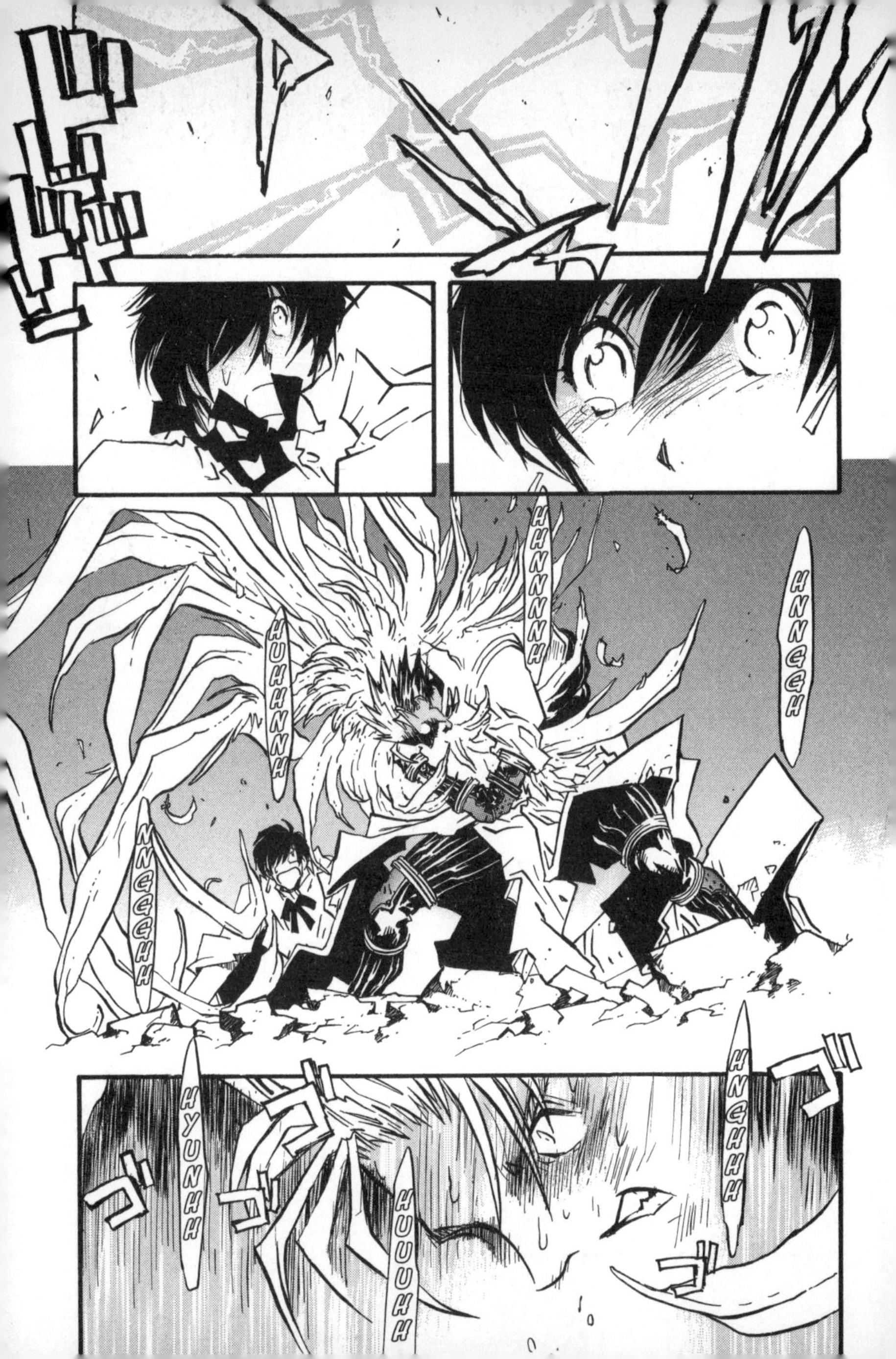
HNNNGGH
HHNNNNNNH
HUHHNNNH
NNGGGHH
HNGHHH
HUUUHH
HYUNHH

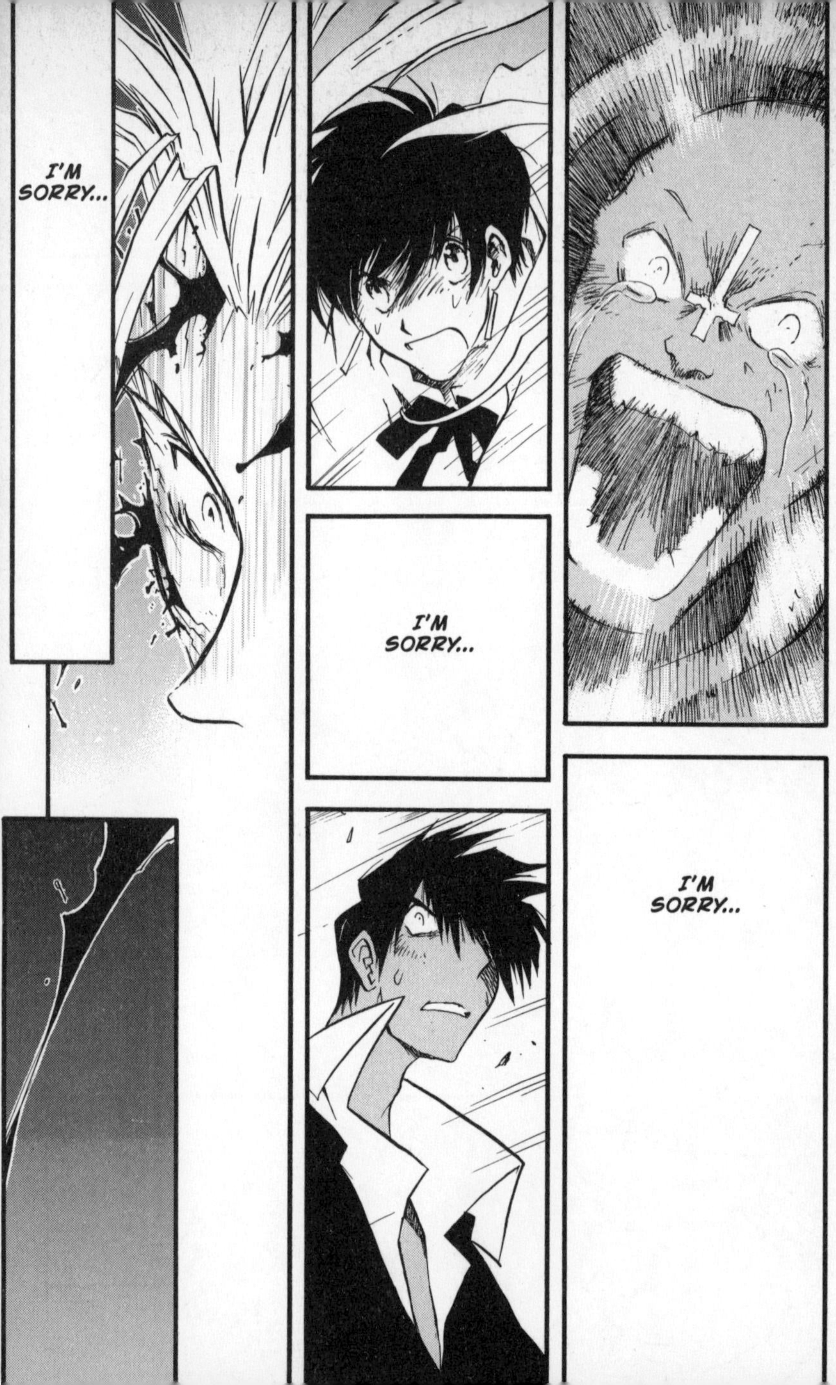
I'M SORRY...
I'M SORRY...
I'M SORRY...

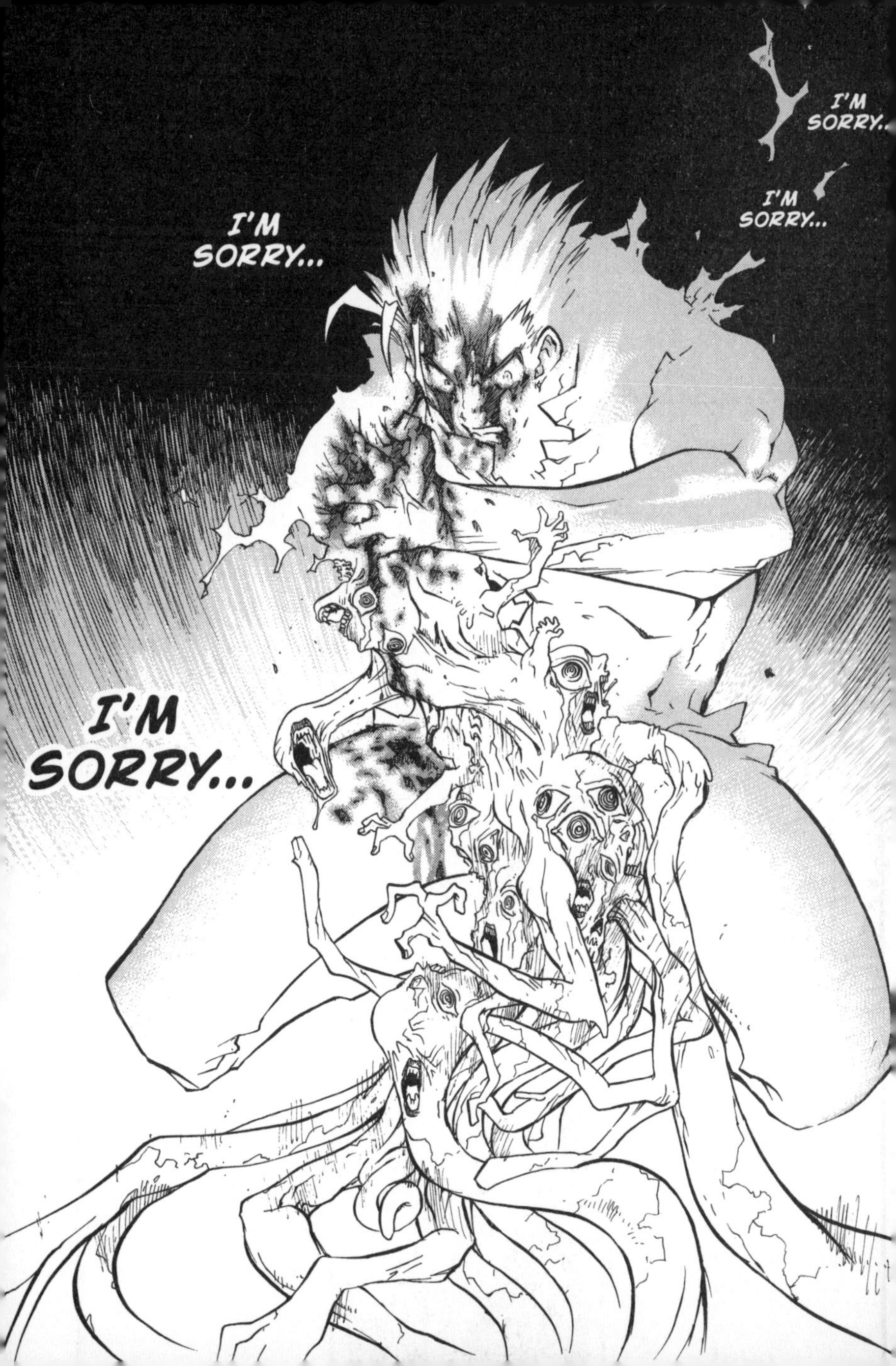
I'M SORRY..
I'M SORRY...
I'M SORRY...
I'M SORRY...

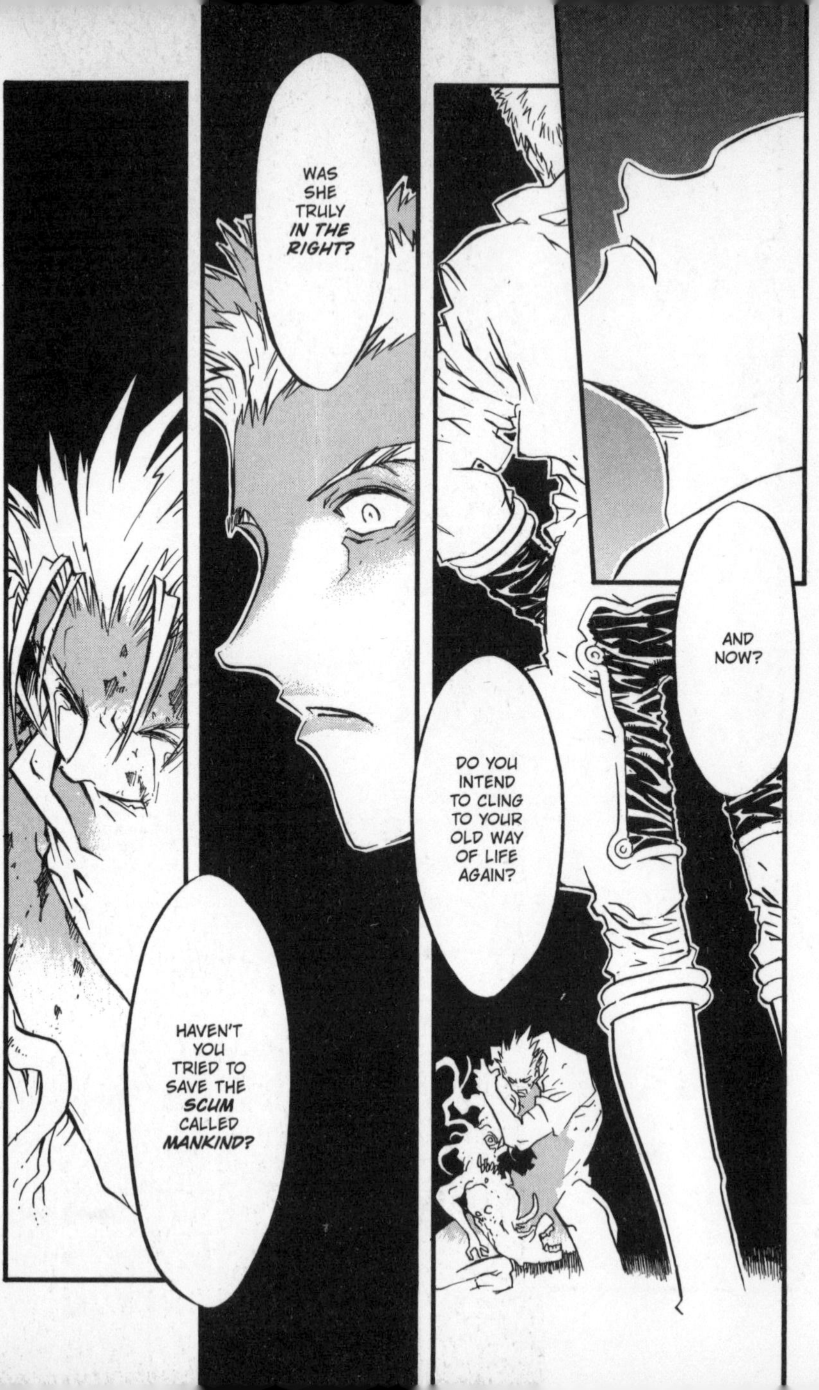
AND NOW?
DO YOU INTEND TO CLING TO YOUR OLD WAY OF LIFE AGAIN?
WAS SHE TRULY *IN THE RIGHT?*
HAVEN'T YOU TRIED TO SAVE THE *SCUM* CALLED *MANKIND?*

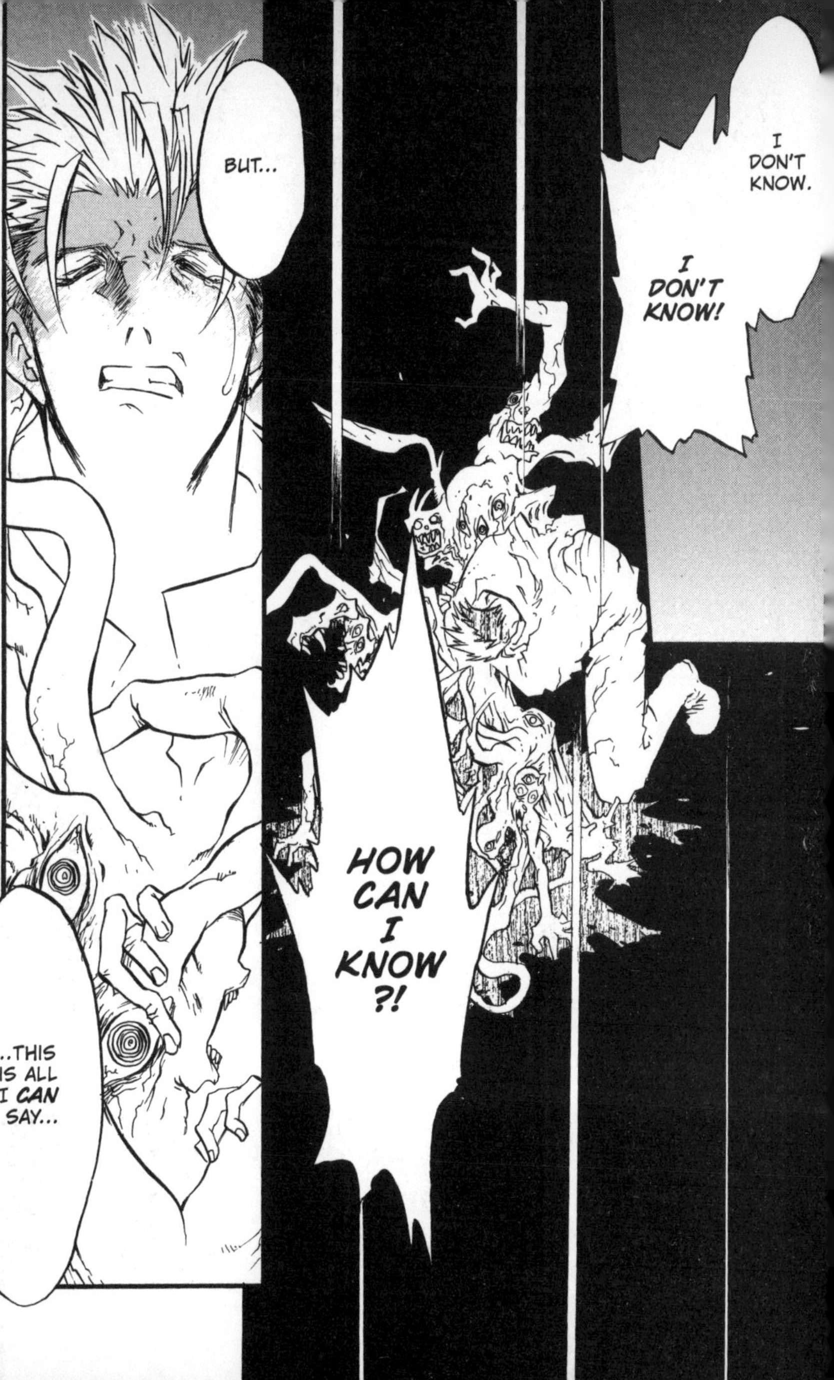
I DON'T KNOW.
I DON'T KNOW!
HOW CAN I KNOW?!
BUT...
...THIS IS ALL I CAN SAY...

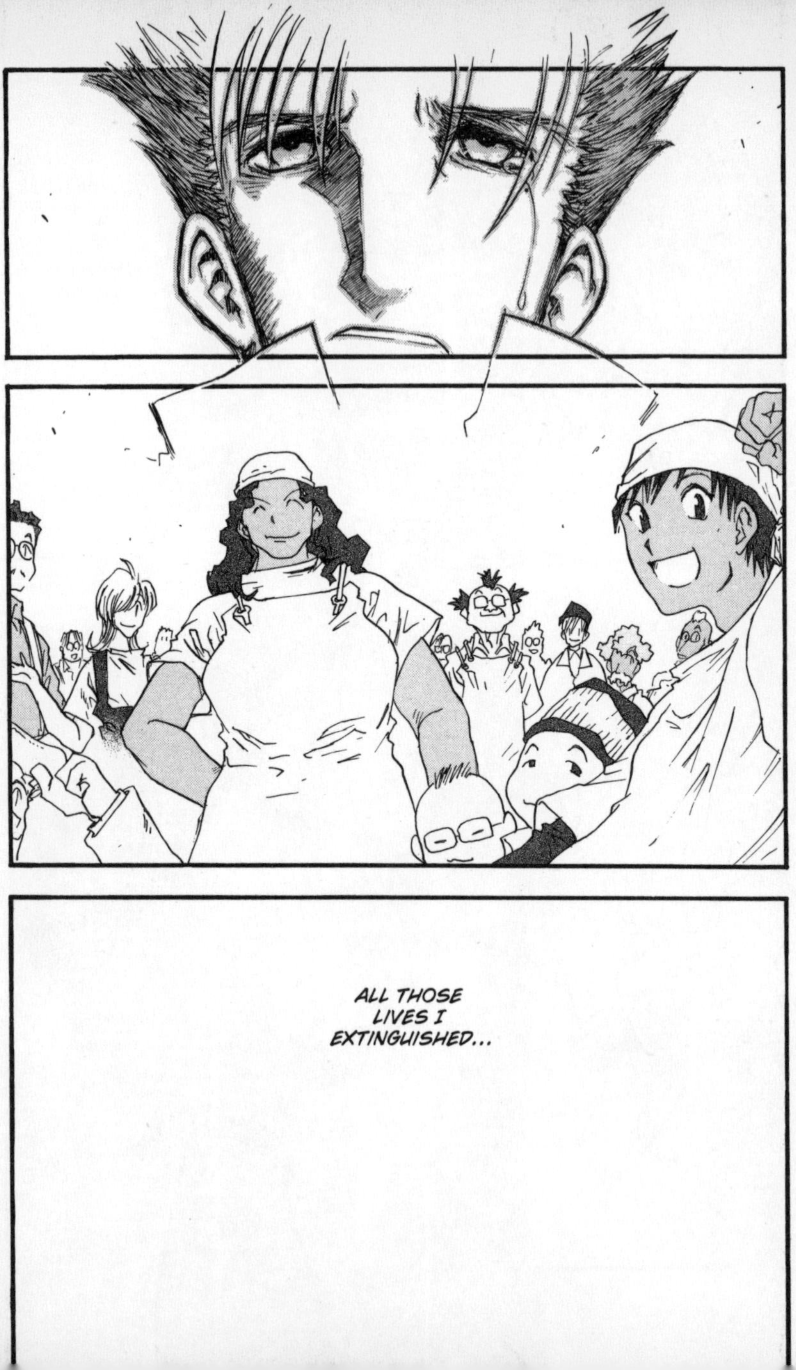
ALL THOSE LIVES I EXTINGUISHED...

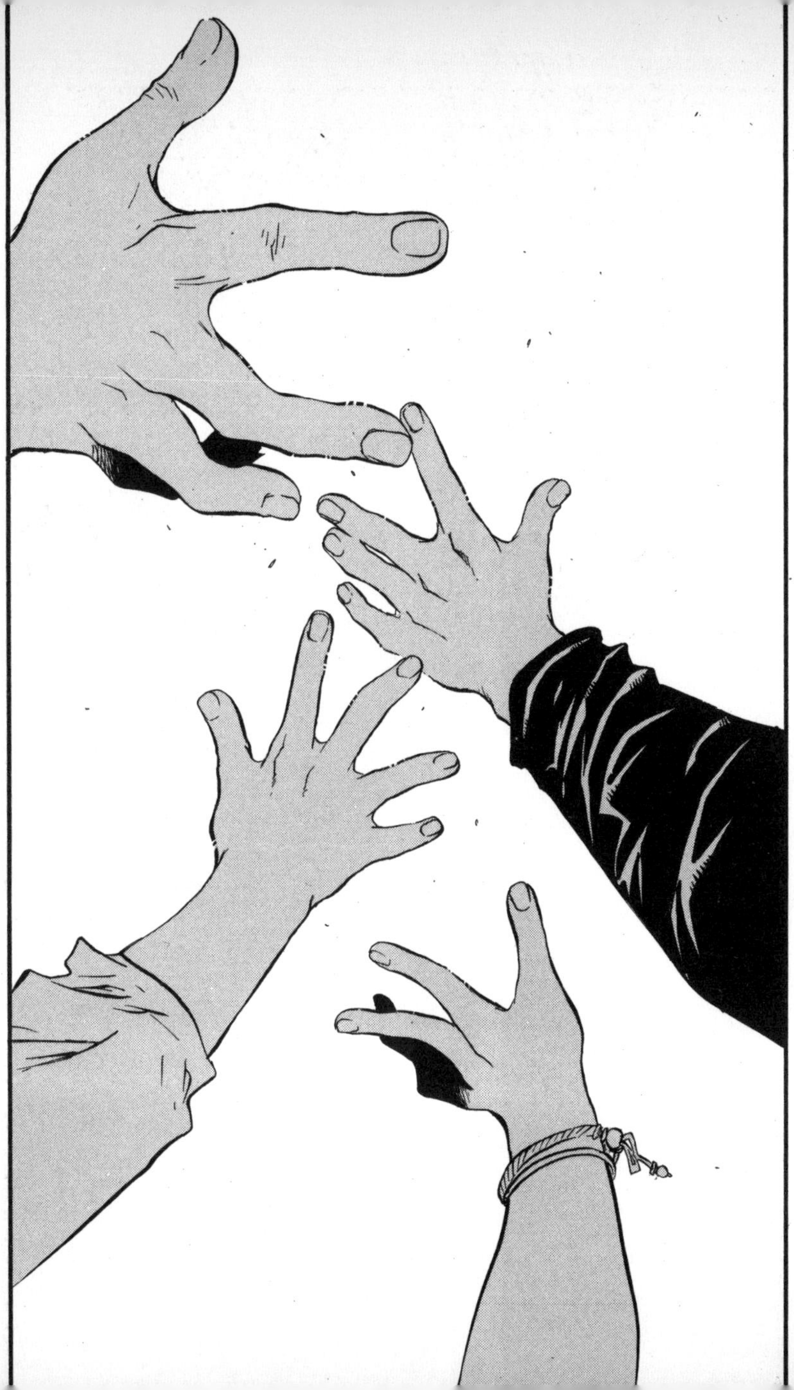

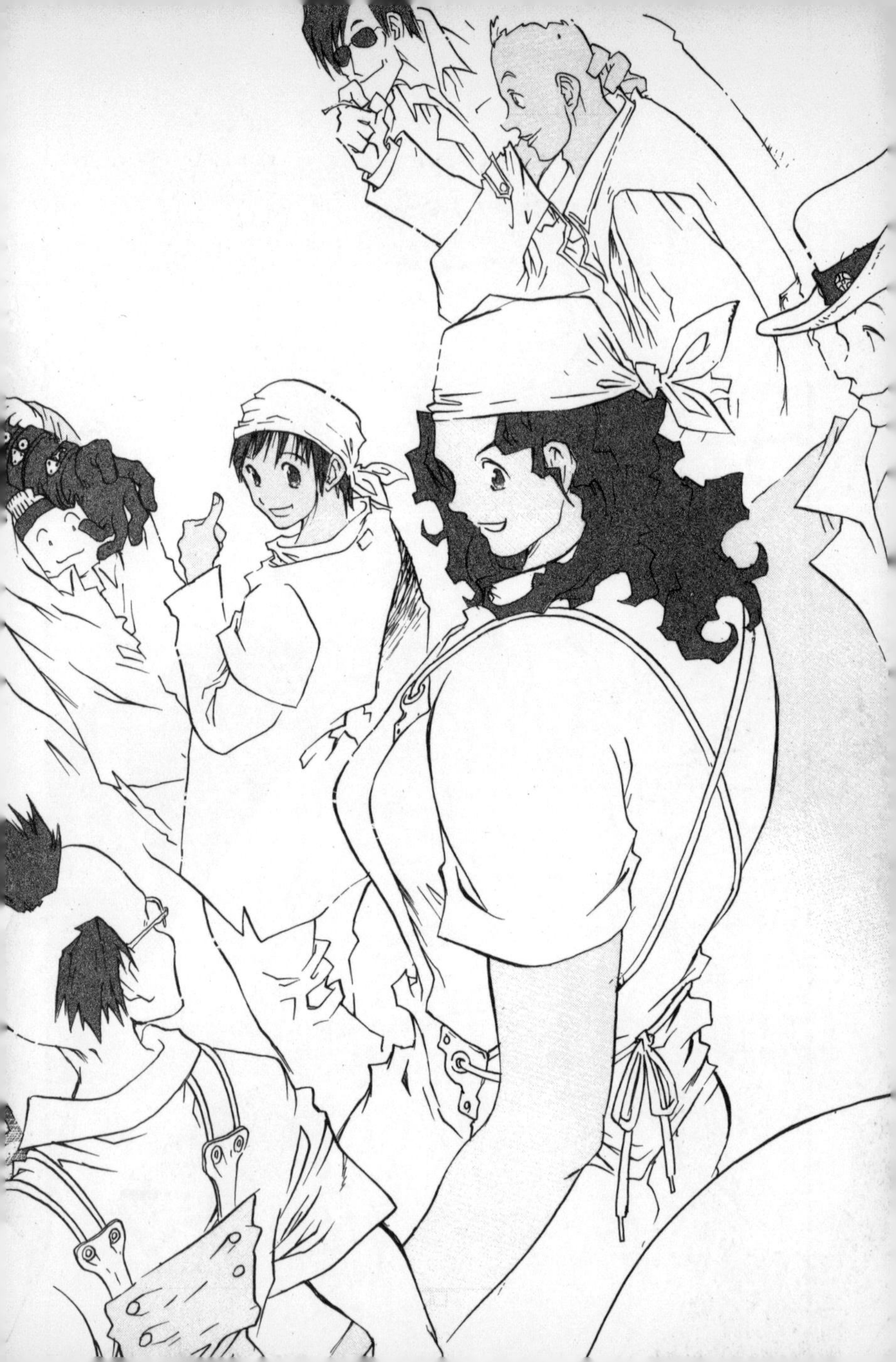

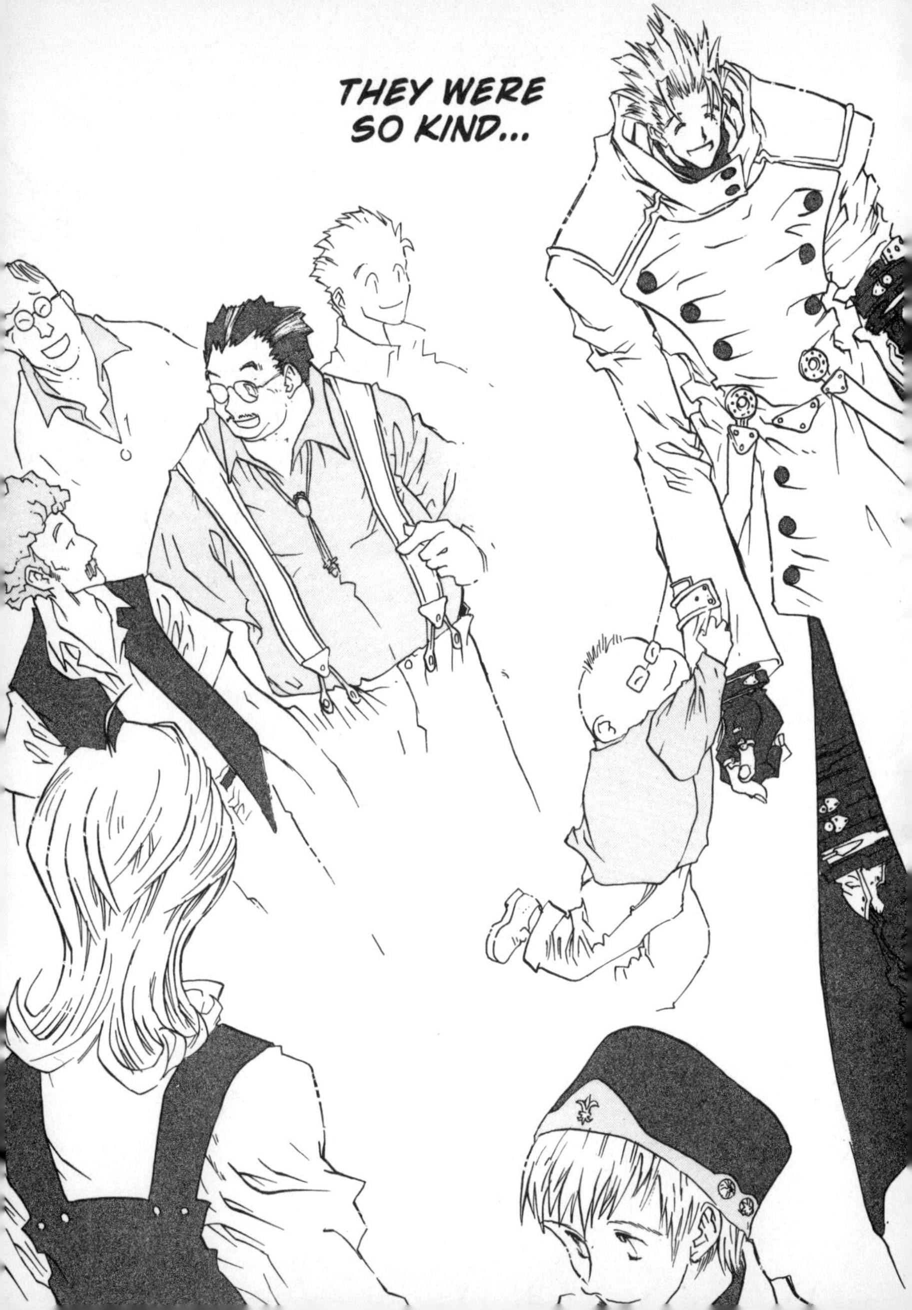
THEY WERE SO KIND...

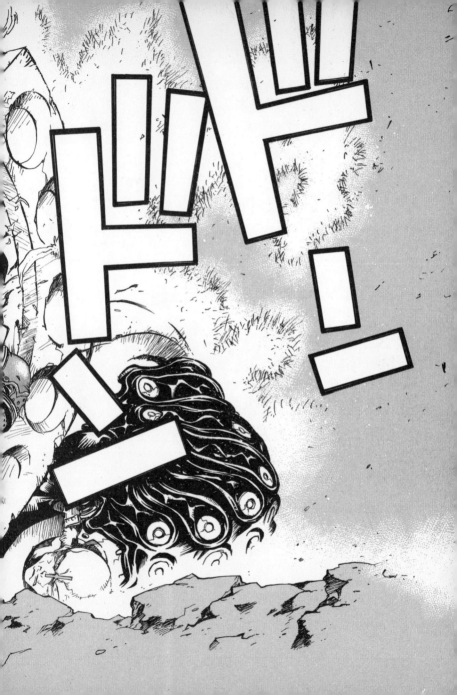

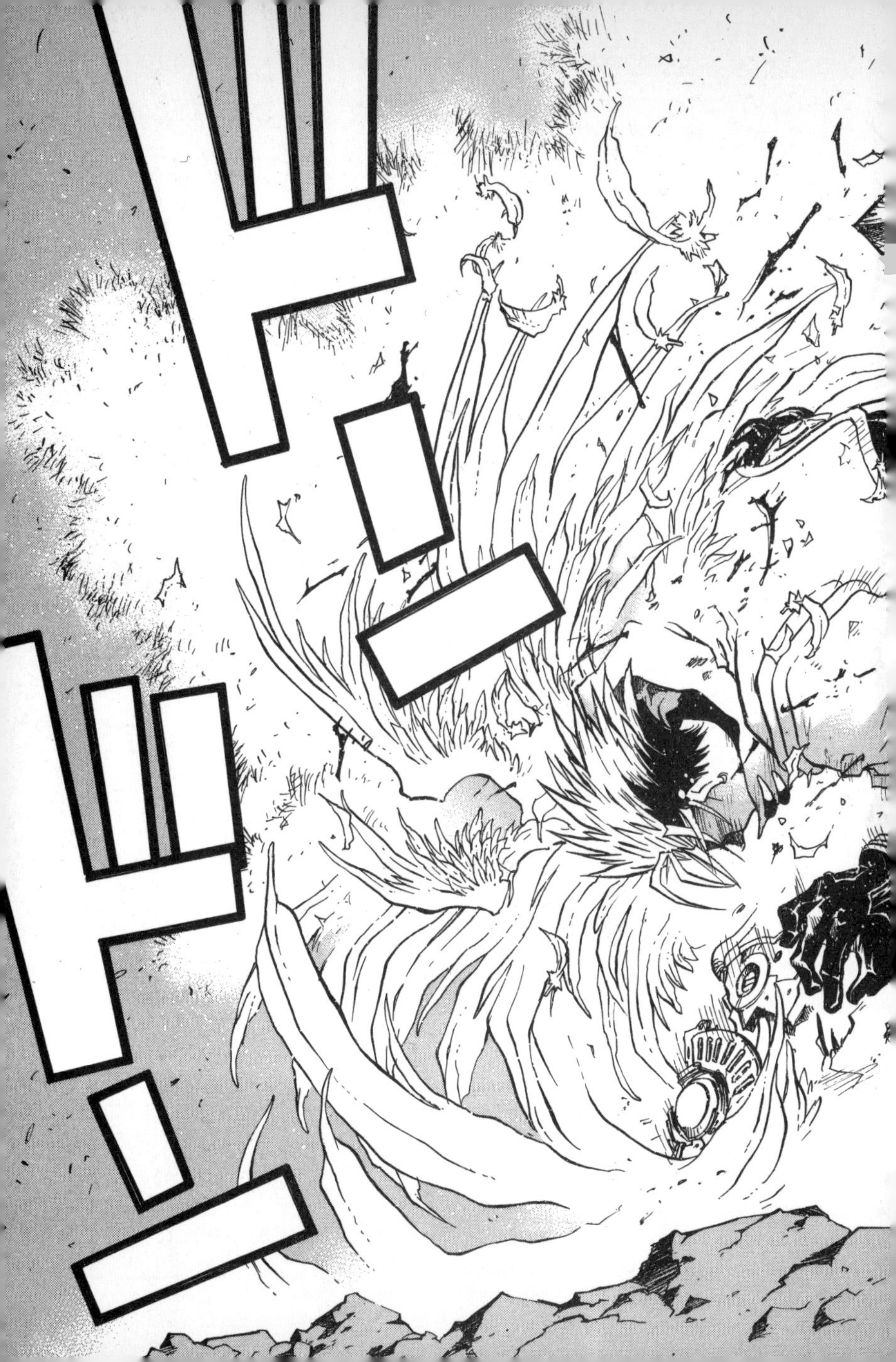
ドン
ドン

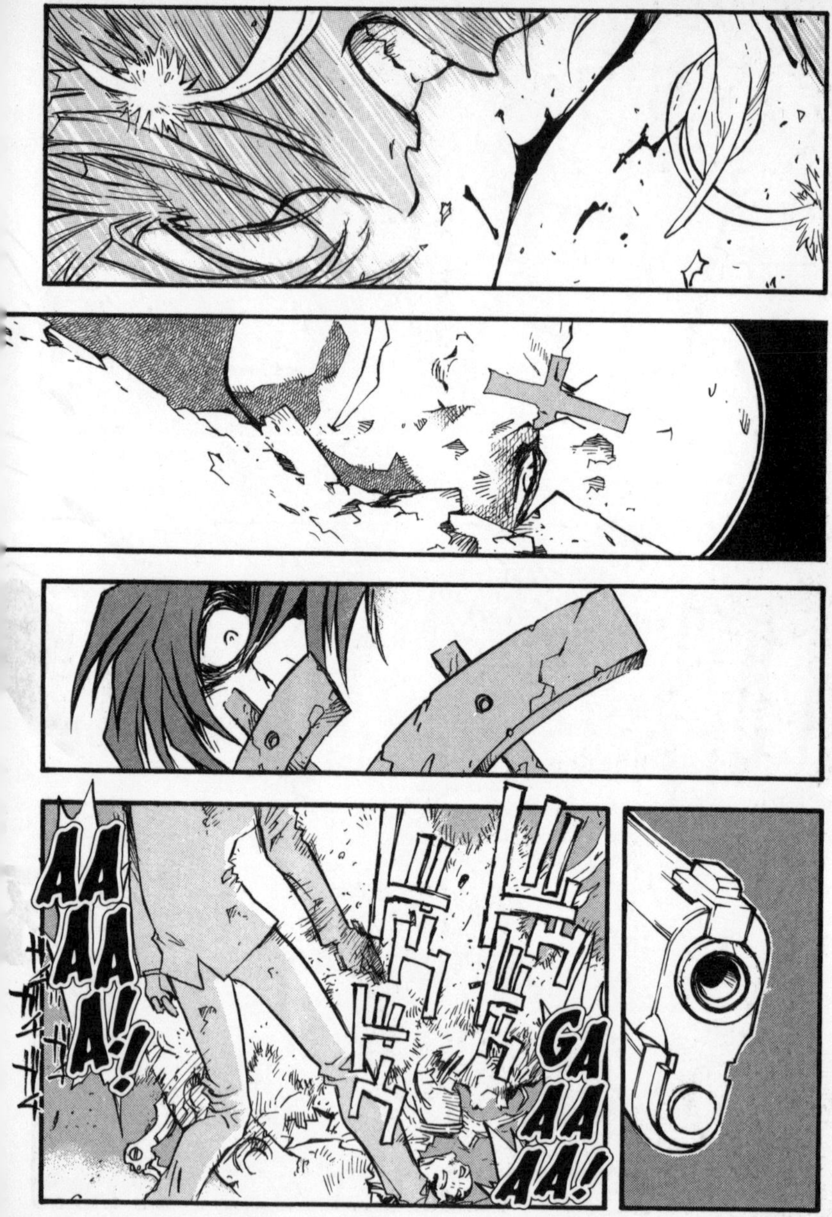
GAAAAA!
AAAAA!

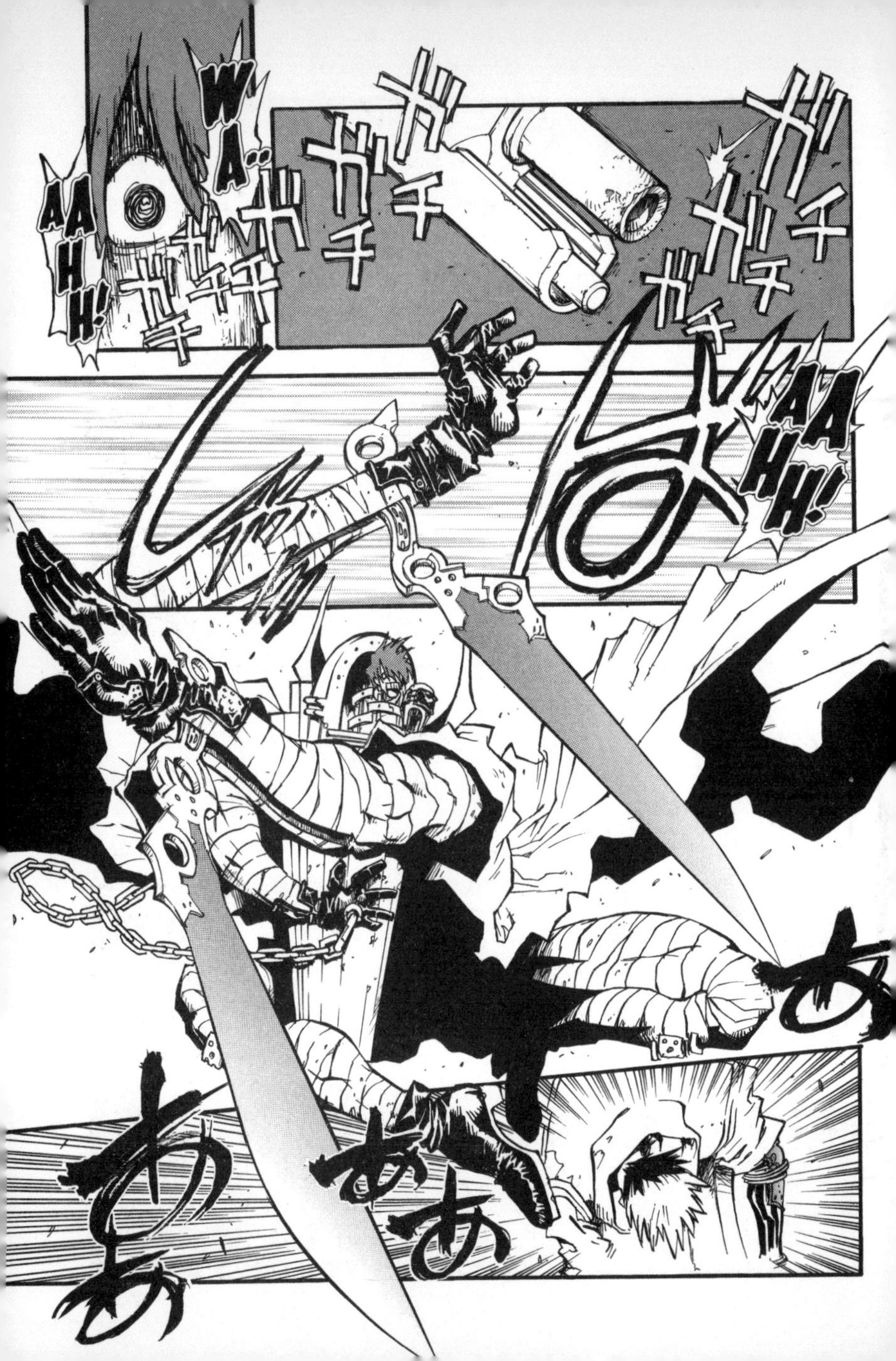

ガチガチ
ガチガチ
WAA..
AAHH!
AAHH!

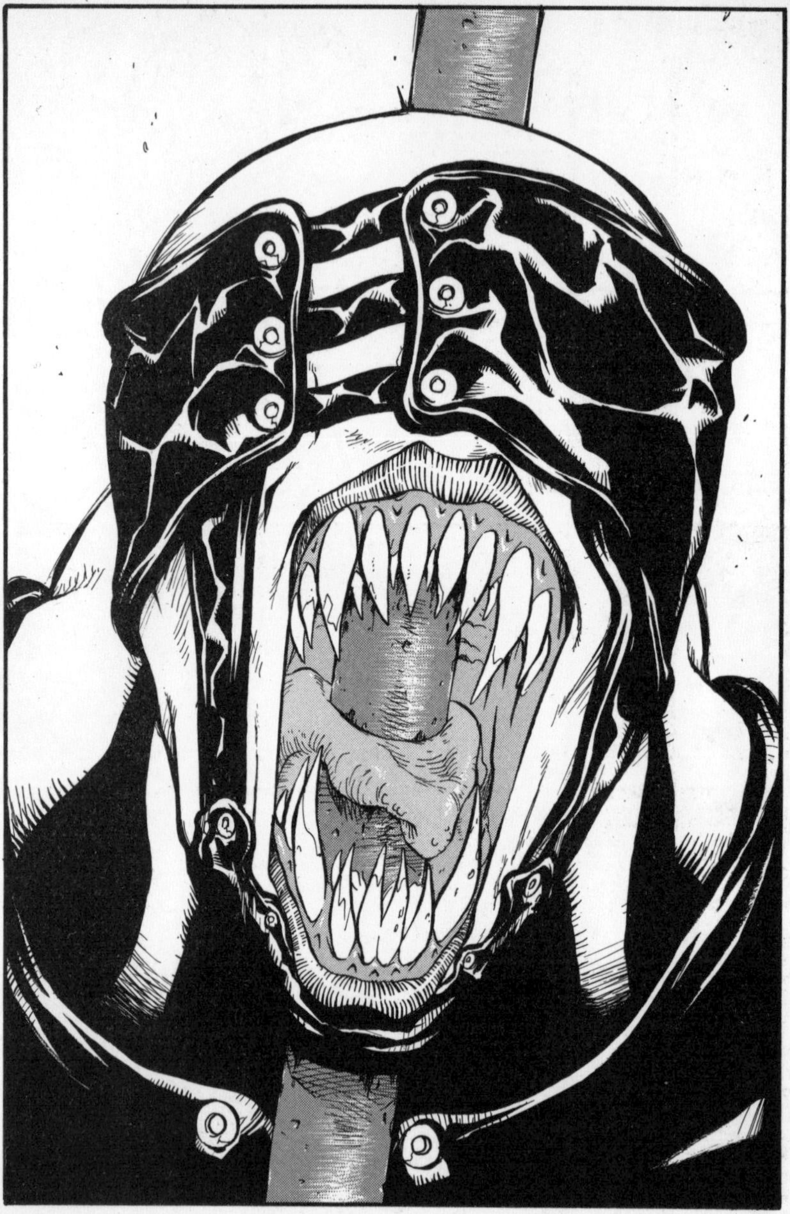

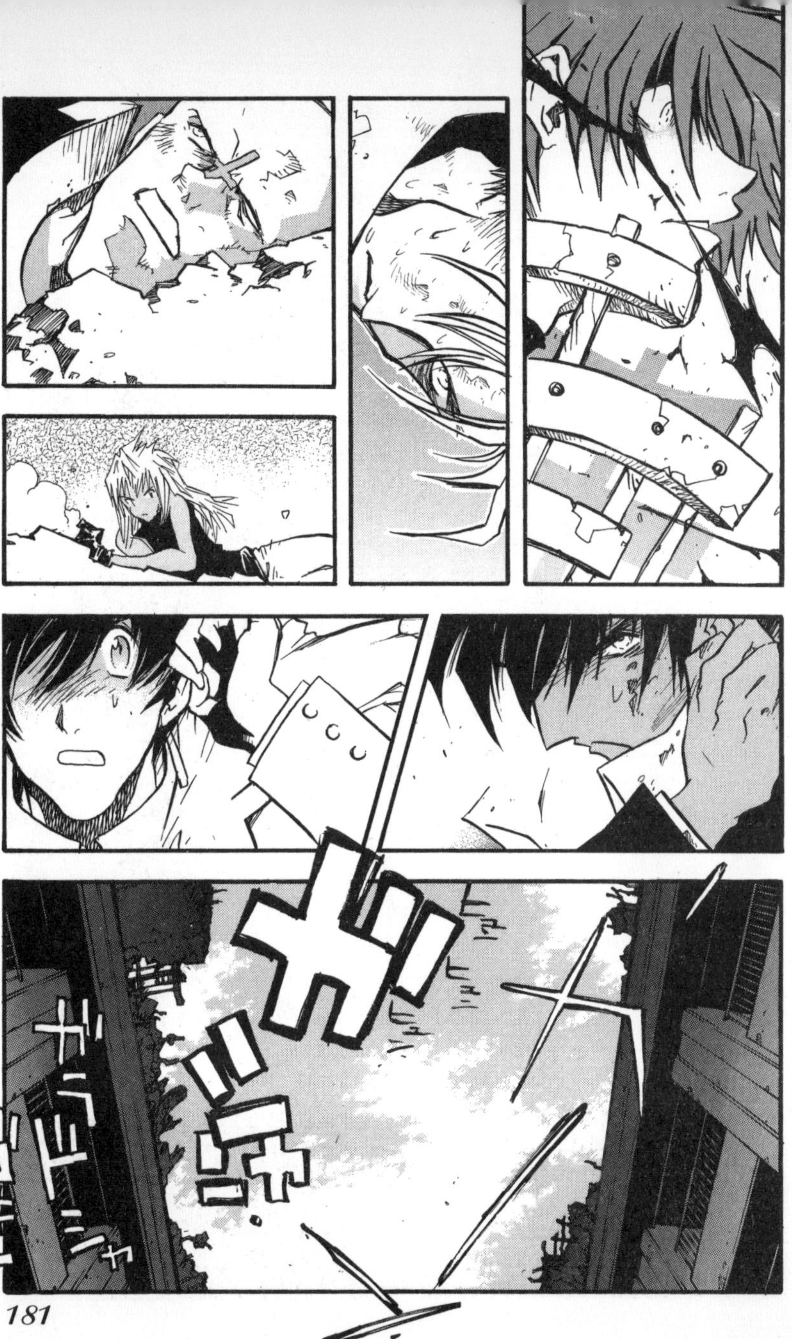

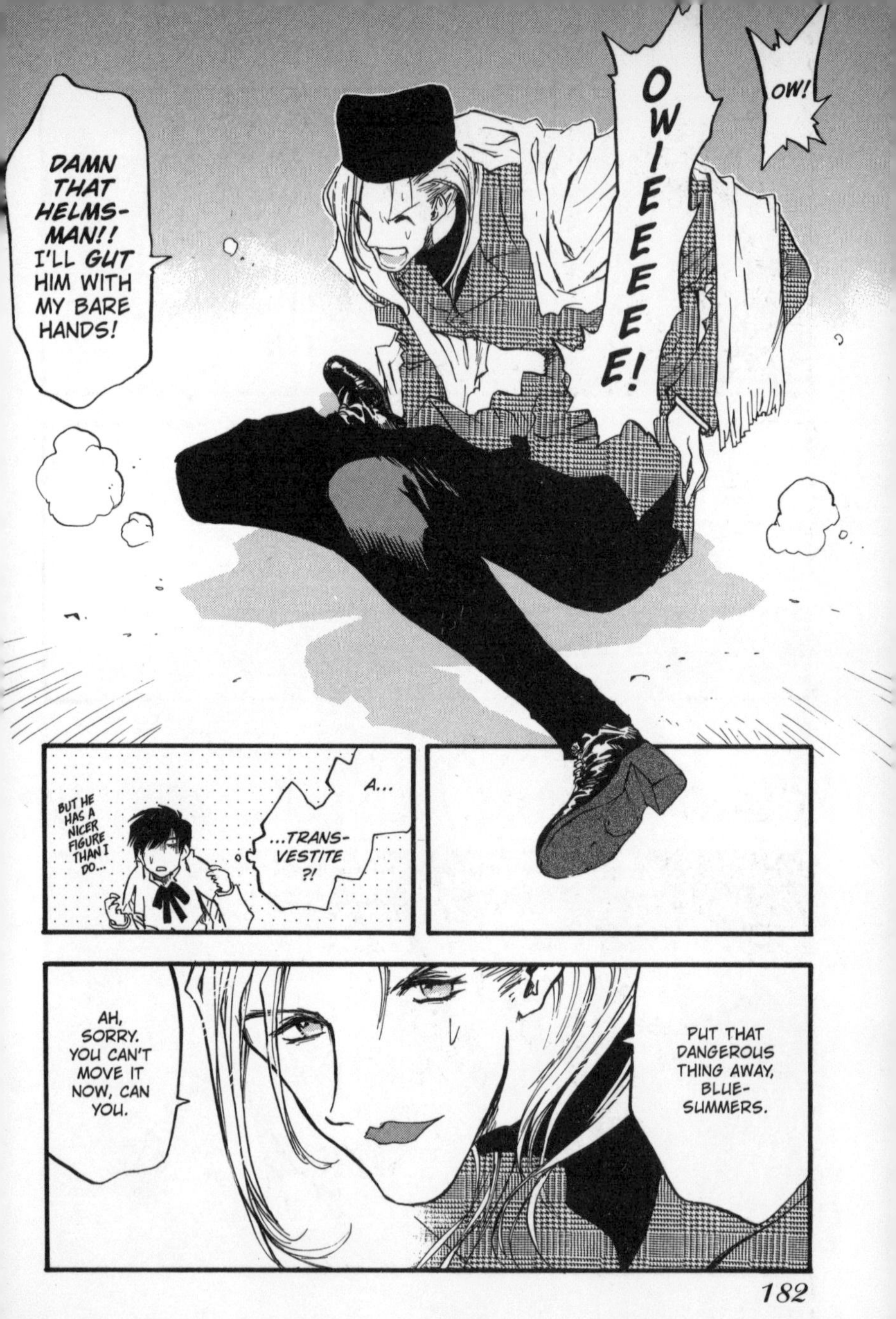

OW!
OWIEEEEE!
DAMN THAT HELMSMAN!! I'LL GUT HIM WITH MY BARE HANDS!
A... ...TRANSVESTITE?!
BUT HE HAS A NICER FIGURE THAN I DO...
PUT THAT DANGEROUS THING AWAY, BLUE-SUMMERS.
AH, SORRY. YOU CAN'T MOVE IT NOW, CAN YOU.

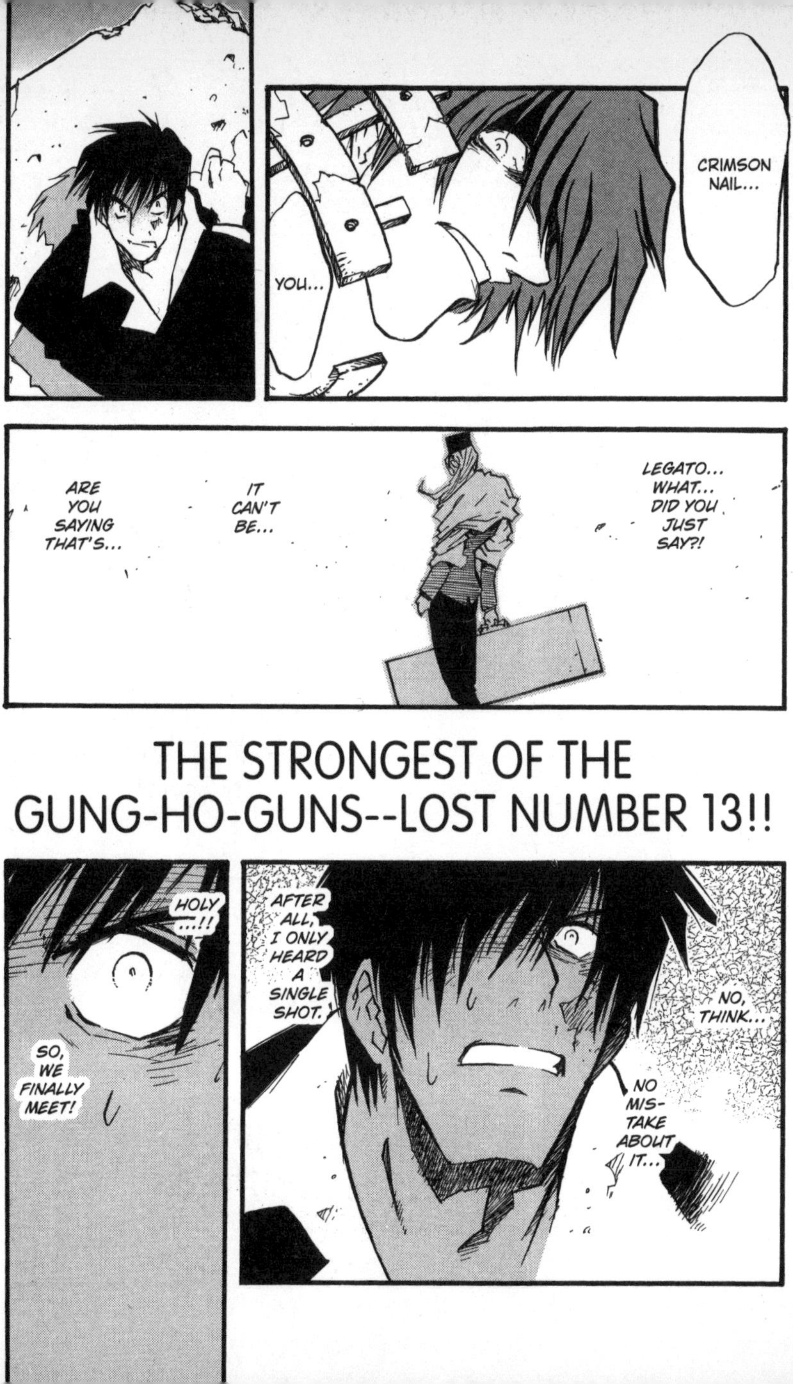
CRIMSON NAIL...
YOU...
LEGATO... WHAT... DID YOU JUST SAY?!
IT CAN'T BE...
ARE YOU SAYING THAT'S...
THE STRONGEST OF THE GUNG-HO-GUNS--LOST NUMBER 13!!
AFTER ALL, I ONLY HEARD A SINGLE SHOT.
NO, THINK...
NO MIS-TAKE ABOUT IT...
HOLY ...!!
SO, WE FINALLY MEET!

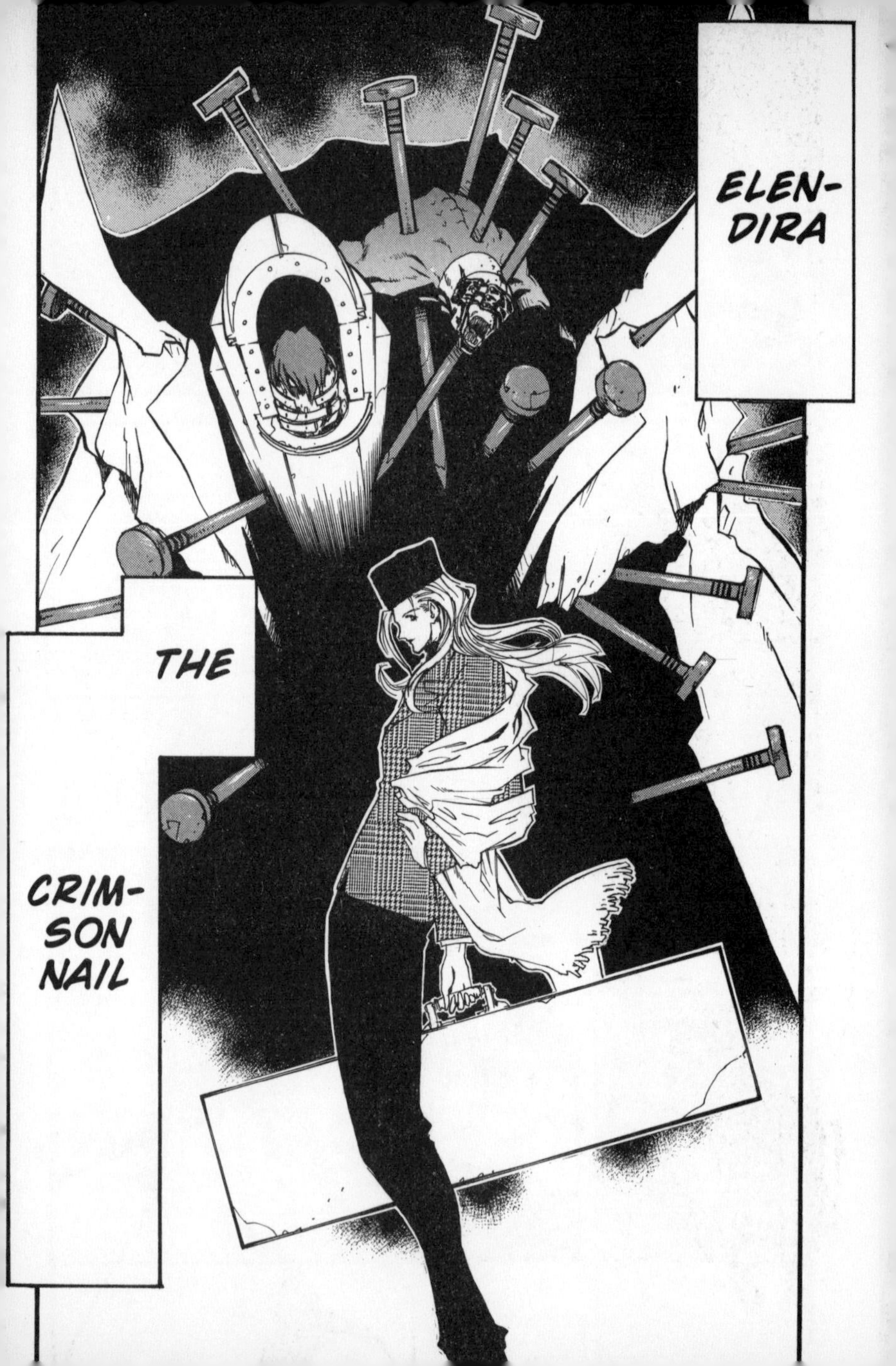
ELEN-
DIRA
THE
CRIM-
SON
NAIL

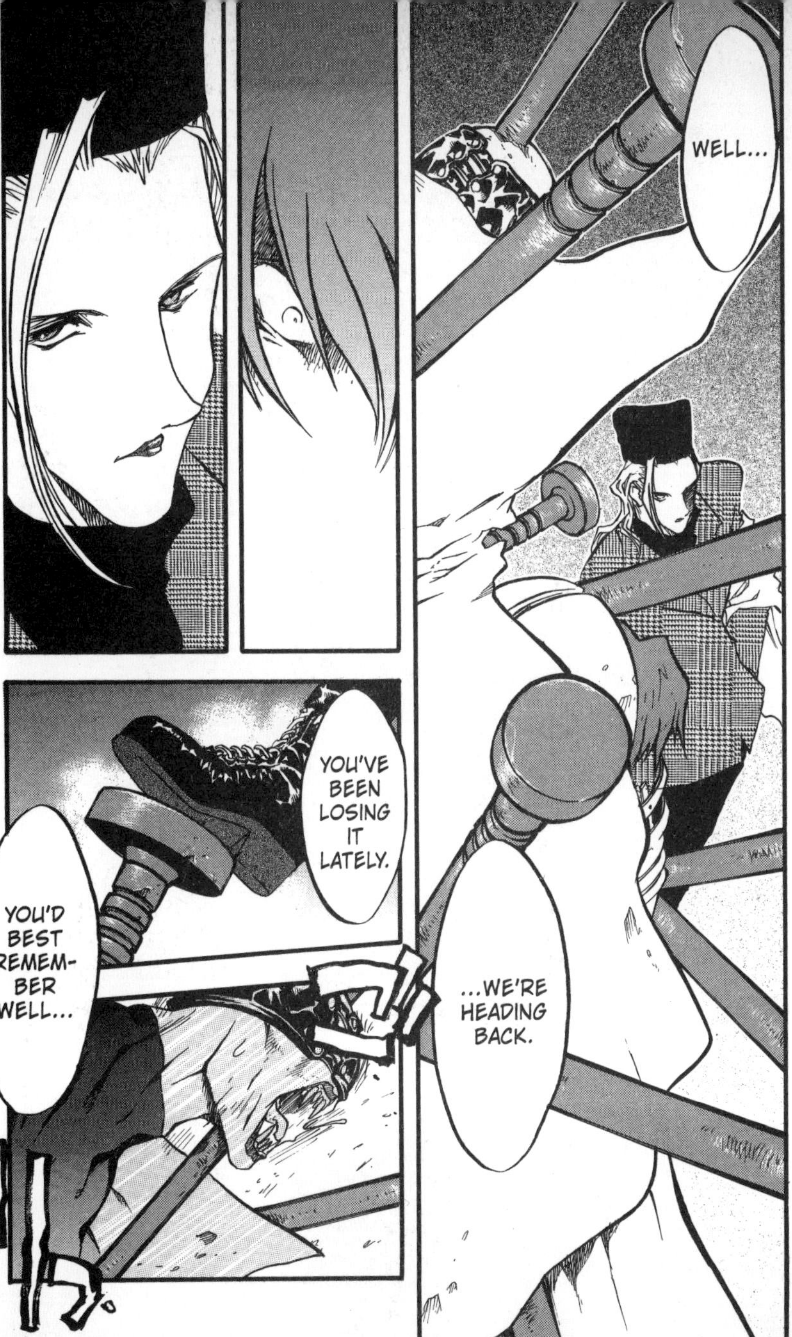
WELL...
...WE'RE HEADING BACK.
YOU'VE BEEN LOSING IT LATELY.
YOU'D BEST REMEMBER WELL...

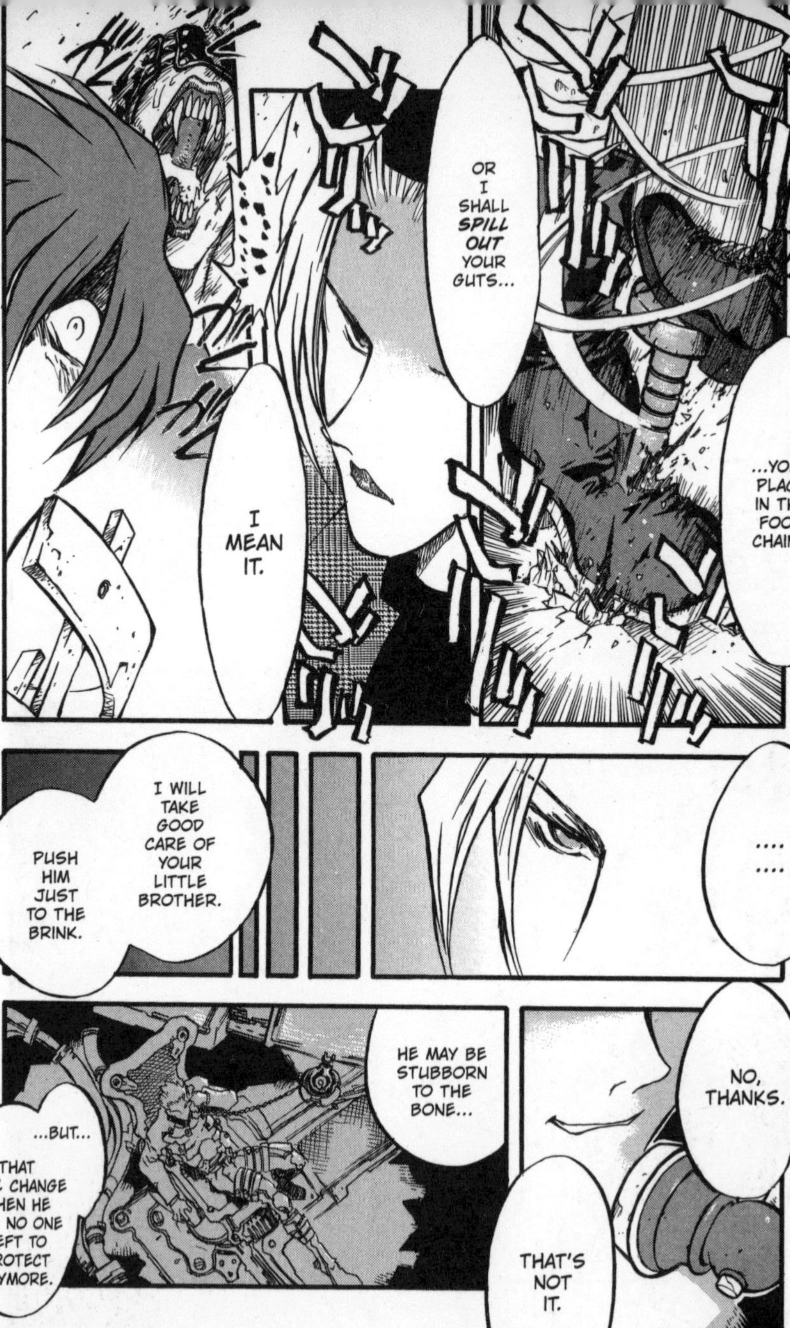
...YOUR PLACE IN THE FOOD CHAIN.
OR I SHALL *SPILL OUT* YOUR GUTS...
I MEAN IT.
....
....
I WILL TAKE GOOD CARE OF YOUR LITTLE BROTHER.
PUSH HIM JUST TO THE BRINK.
NO, THANKS.
THAT'S NOT IT.
HE MAY BE STUBBORN TO THE BONE...
...BUT...
THAT *WILL* CHANGE WHEN HE HAS NO ONE LEFT TO PROTECT ANYMORE.

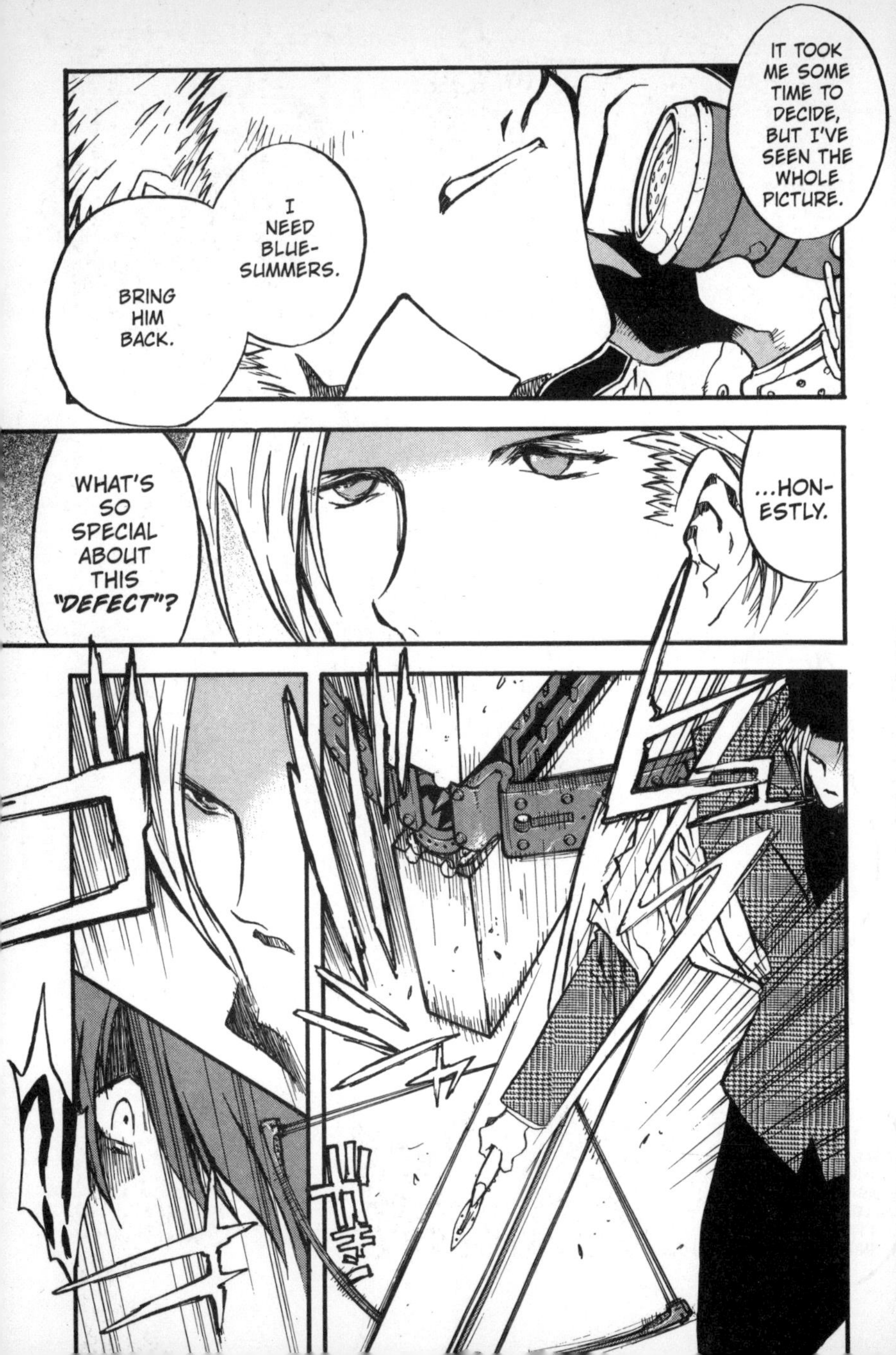
IT TOOK ME SOME TIME TO DECIDE, BUT I'VE SEEN THE WHOLE PICTURE.
I NEED BLUE-SUMMERS.
BRING HIM BACK.
...HON-ESTLY.
WHAT'S SO SPECIAL ABOUT THIS "DEFECT"?

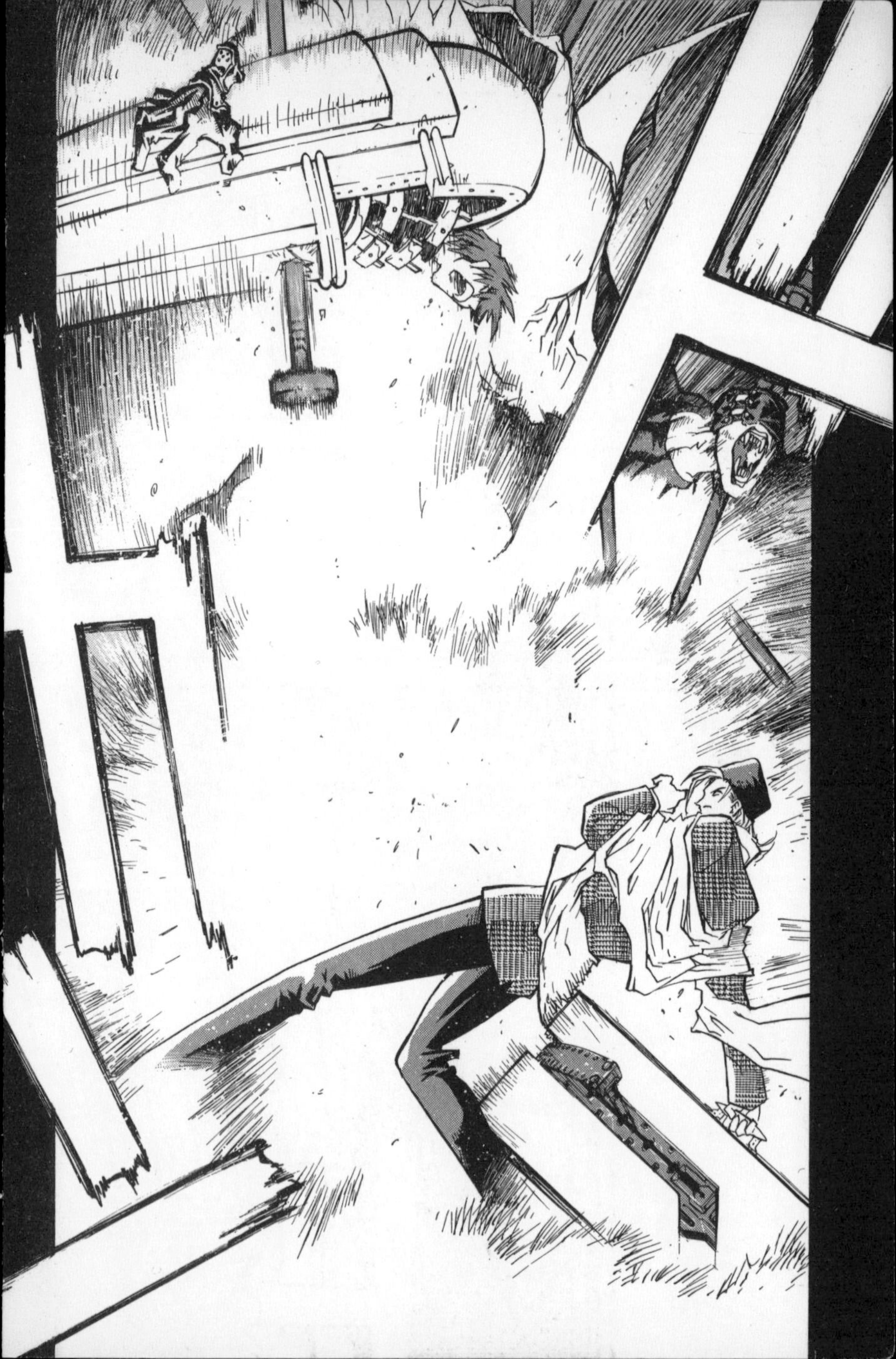

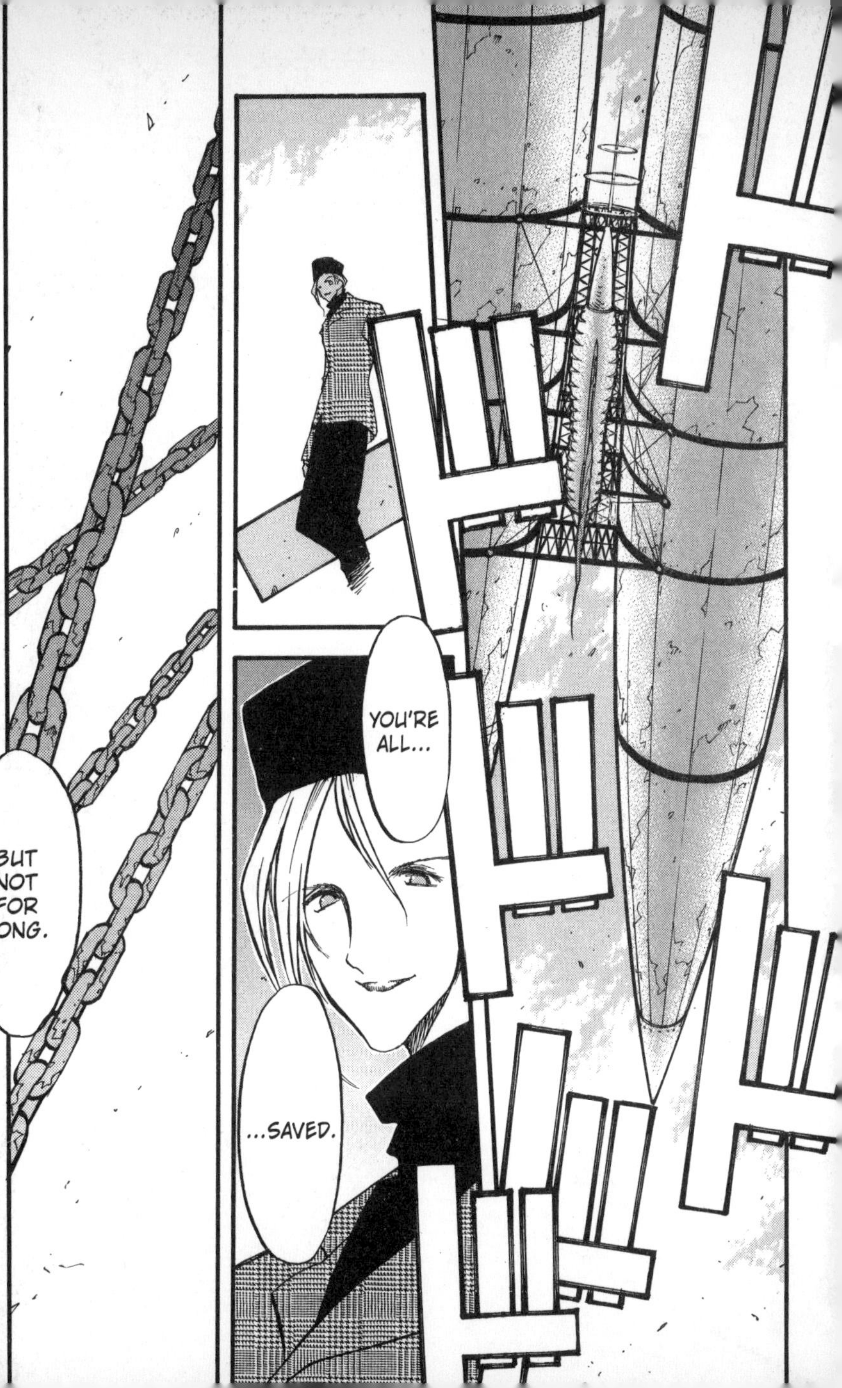
YOU'RE ALL...
...SAVED.
BUT NOT FOR LONG.

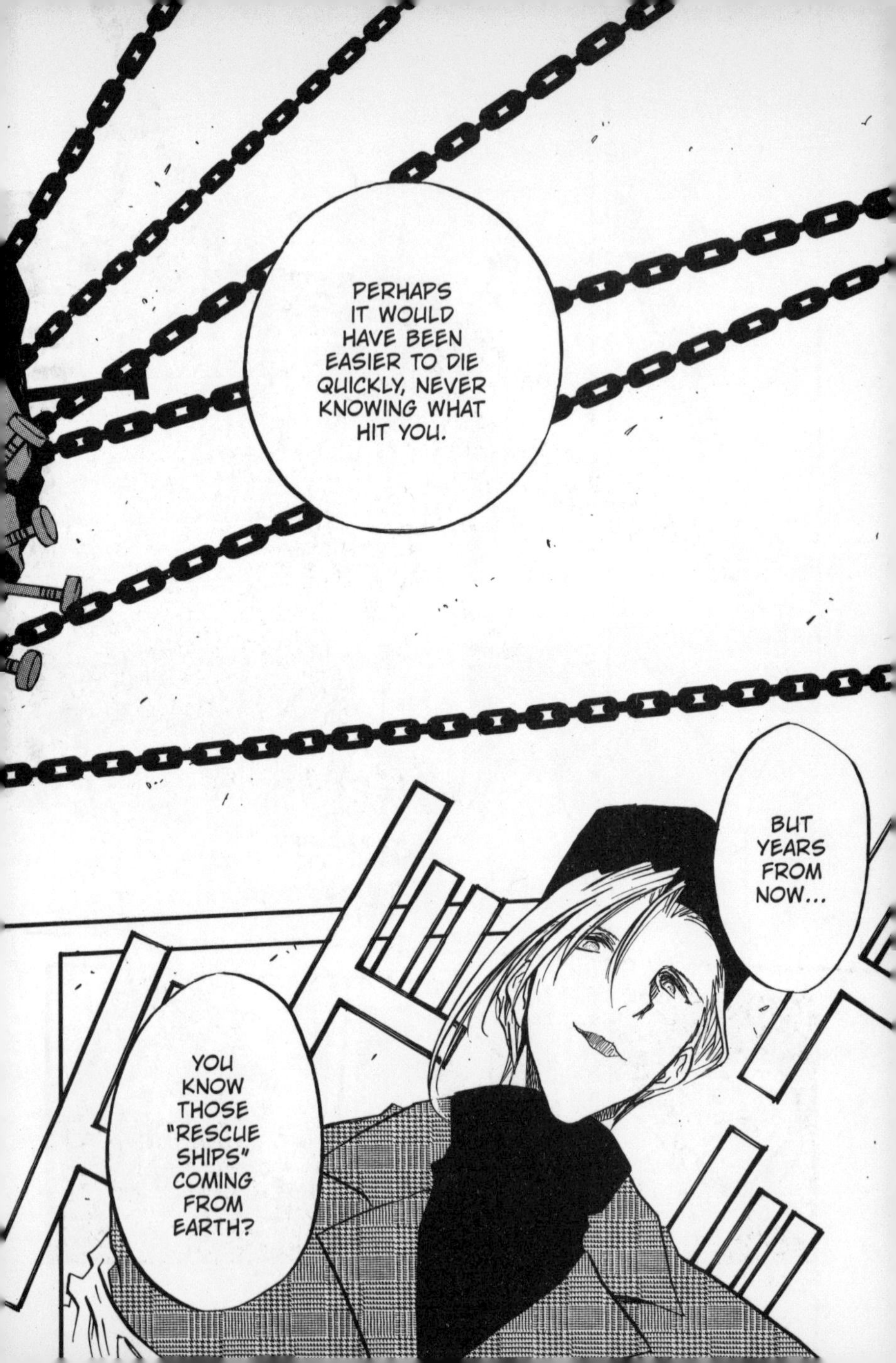
PERHAPS IT WOULD HAVE BEEN EASIER TO DIE QUICKLY, NEVER KNOWING WHAT HIT YOU.
BUT YEARS FROM NOW...
YOU KNOW THOSE "RESCUE SHIPS" COMING FROM EARTH?

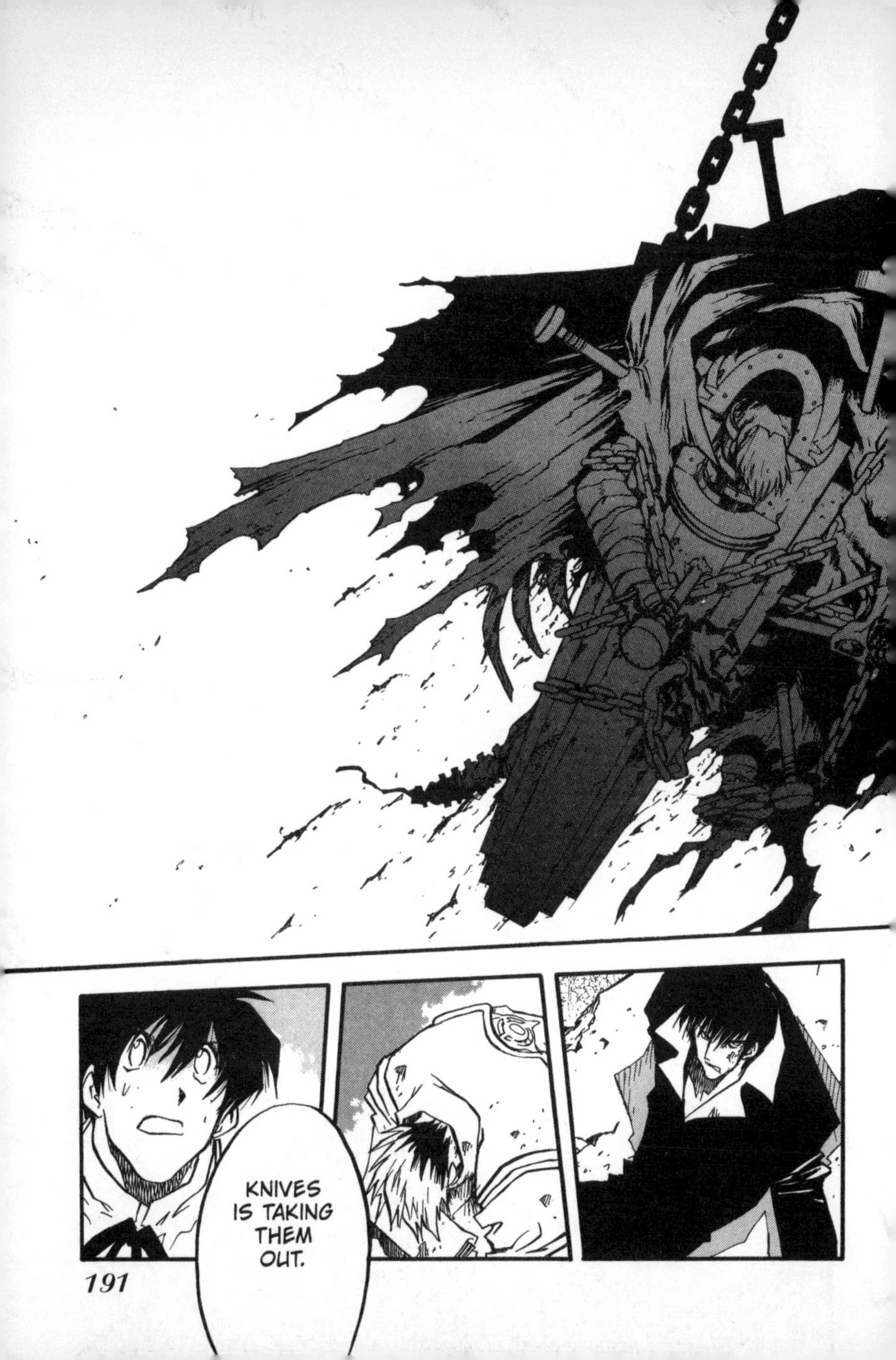
KNIVES IS TAKING THEM OUT.

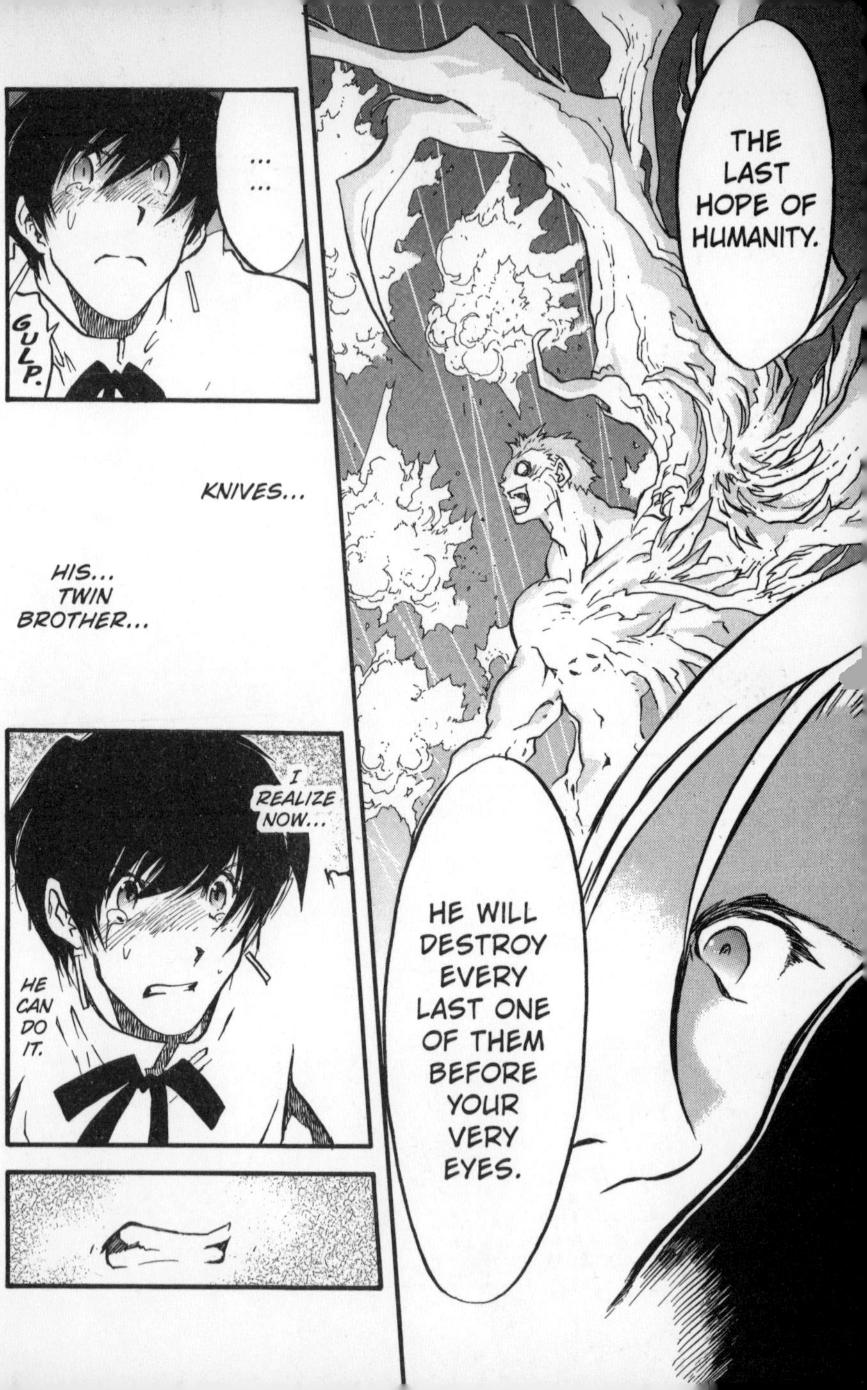
THE LAST HOPE OF HUMANITY.
HE WILL DESTROY EVERY LAST ONE OF THEM BEFORE YOUR VERY EYES.
... ...
GULP.
KNIVES...
HIS... TWIN BROTHER...
I REALIZE NOW...
HE CAN DO IT.

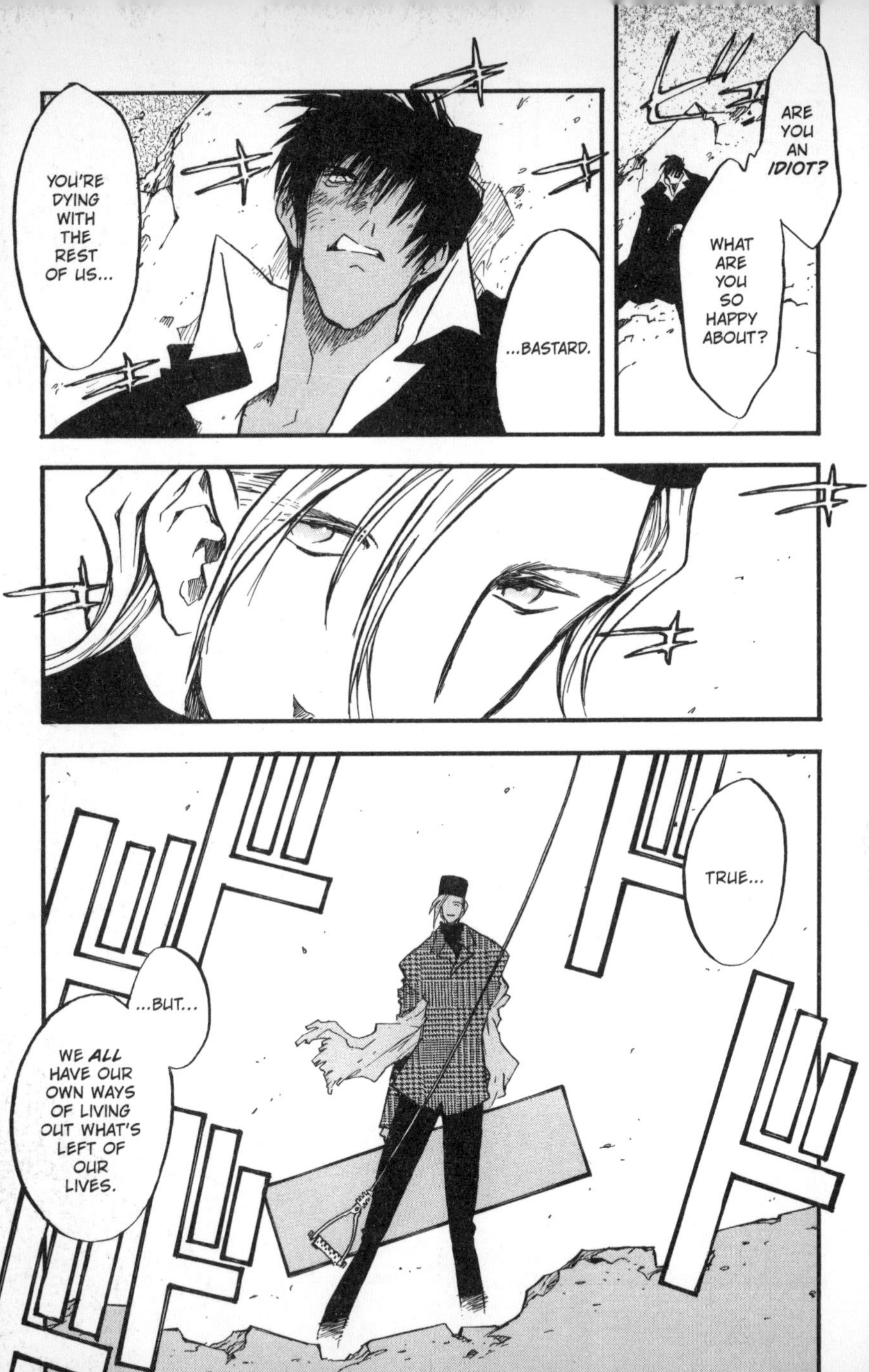
ARE YOU AN *IDIOT?*
WHAT ARE YOU SO HAPPY ABOUT?
...BASTARD.
YOU'RE DYING WITH THE REST OF US...
TRUE...
...BUT...
WE *ALL* HAVE OUR OWN WAYS OF LIVING OUT WHAT'S LEFT OF OUR LIVES.

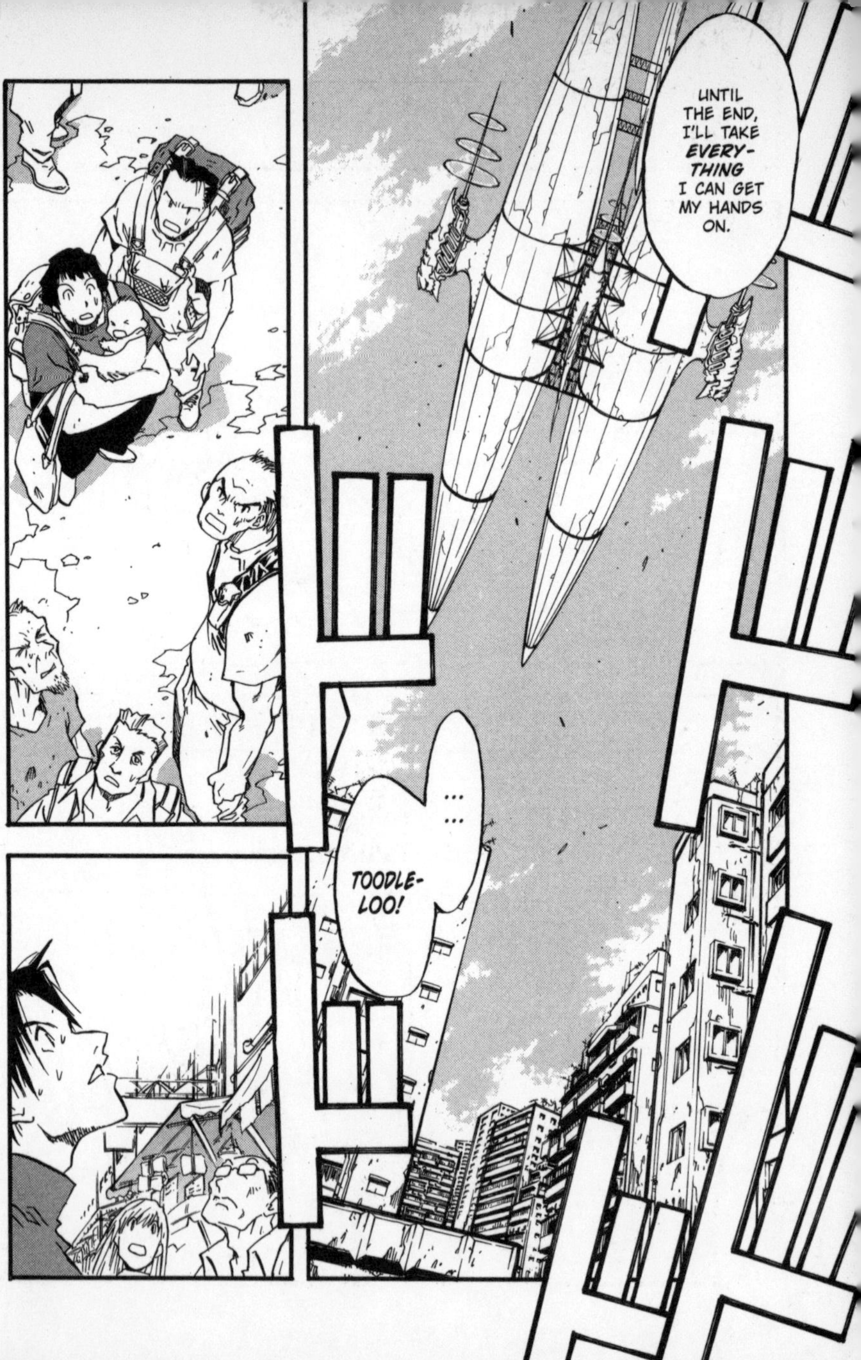
UNTIL THE END, I'LL TAKE *EVERY-THING* I CAN GET MY HANDS ON.
......
*TOODLE-LOO!*

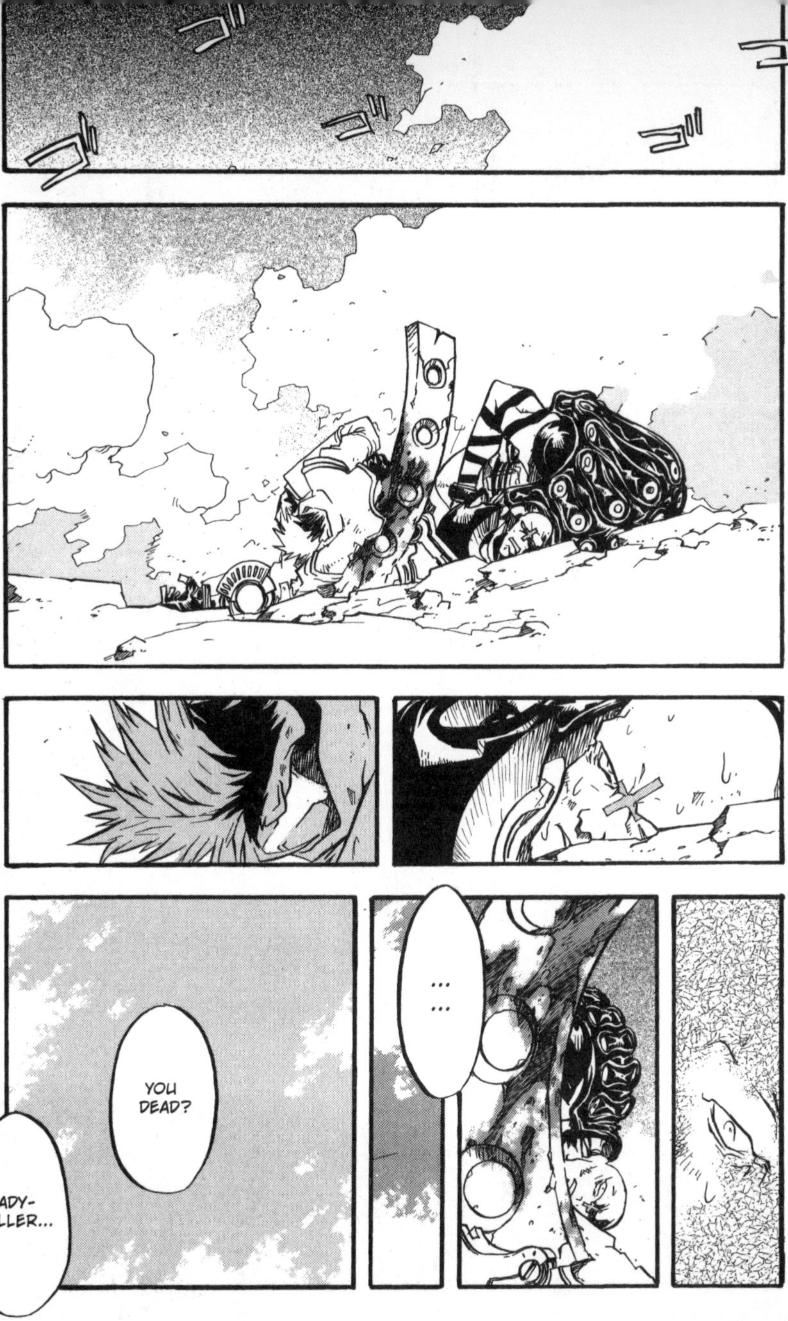
ゴゴゴゴゴ
... ...
YOU DEAD?
LADY-KILLER...

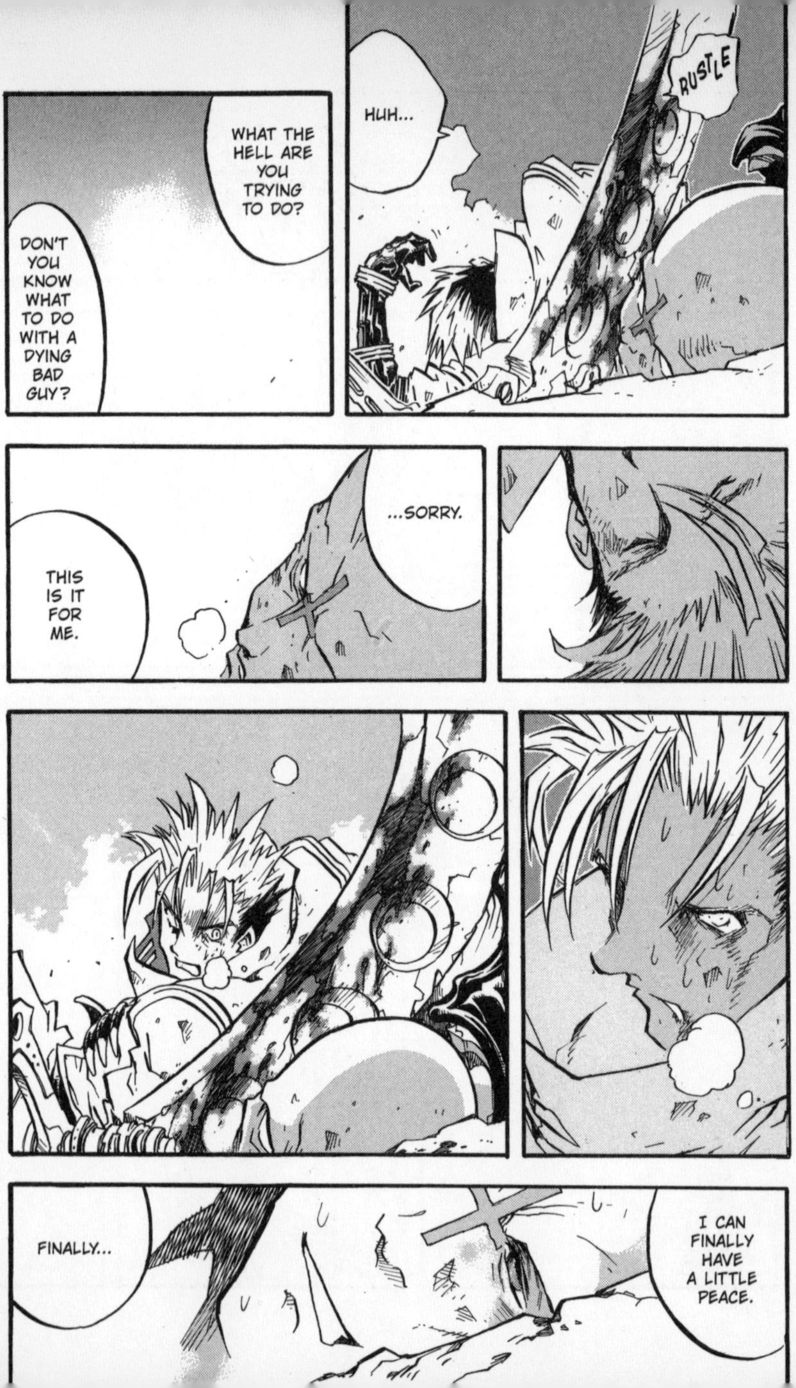
RUSTLE
HUH...
WHAT THE HELL ARE YOU TRYING TO DO?
DON'T YOU KNOW WHAT TO DO WITH A DYING BAD GUY?
...SORRY.
THIS IS IT FOR ME.
I CAN FINALLY HAVE A LITTLE PEACE.
FINALLY...

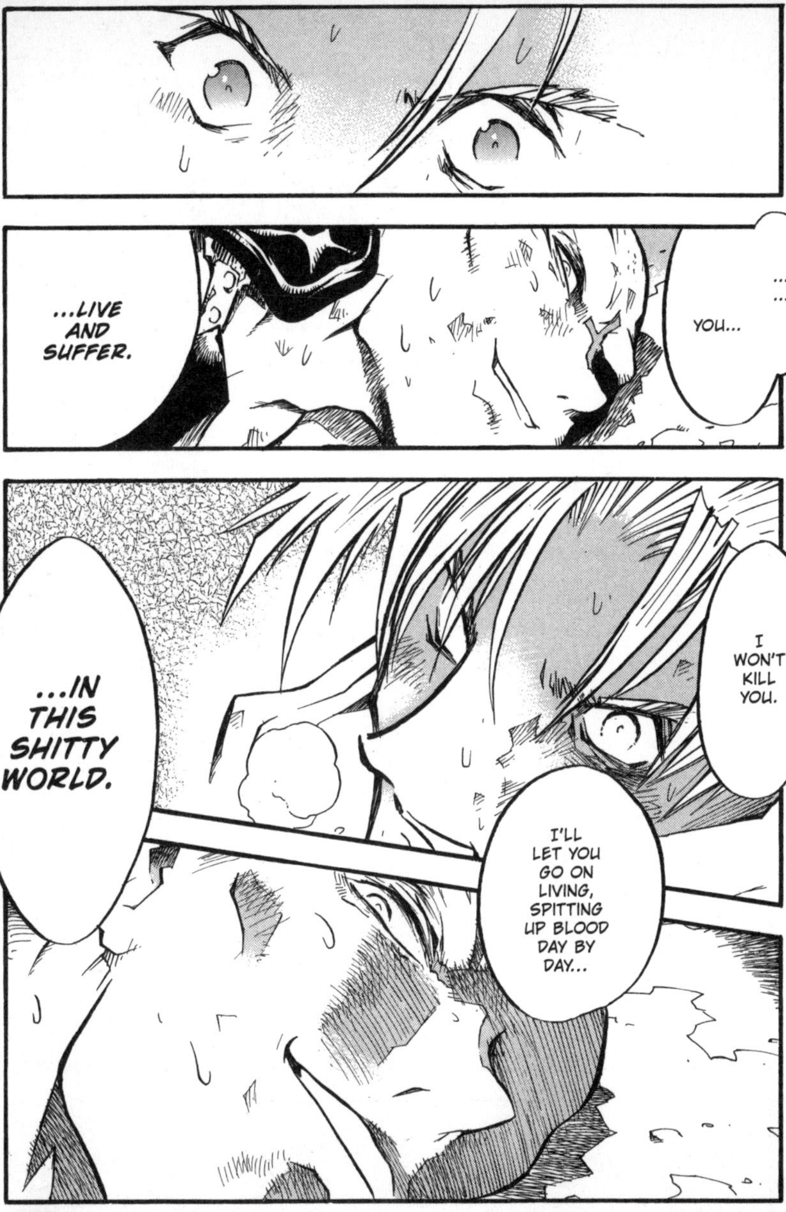
……
YOU…
…LIVE AND SUFFER.
I WON'T KILL YOU.
I'LL LET YOU GO ON LIVING, SPITTING UP BLOOD DAY BY DAY…
…IN THIS SHITTY WORLD.

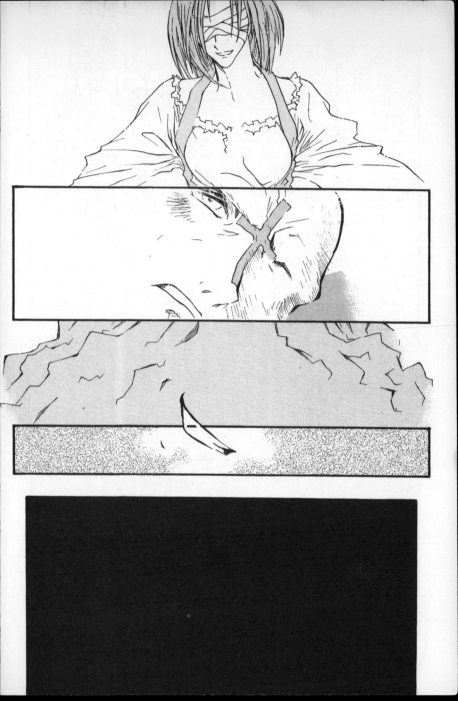

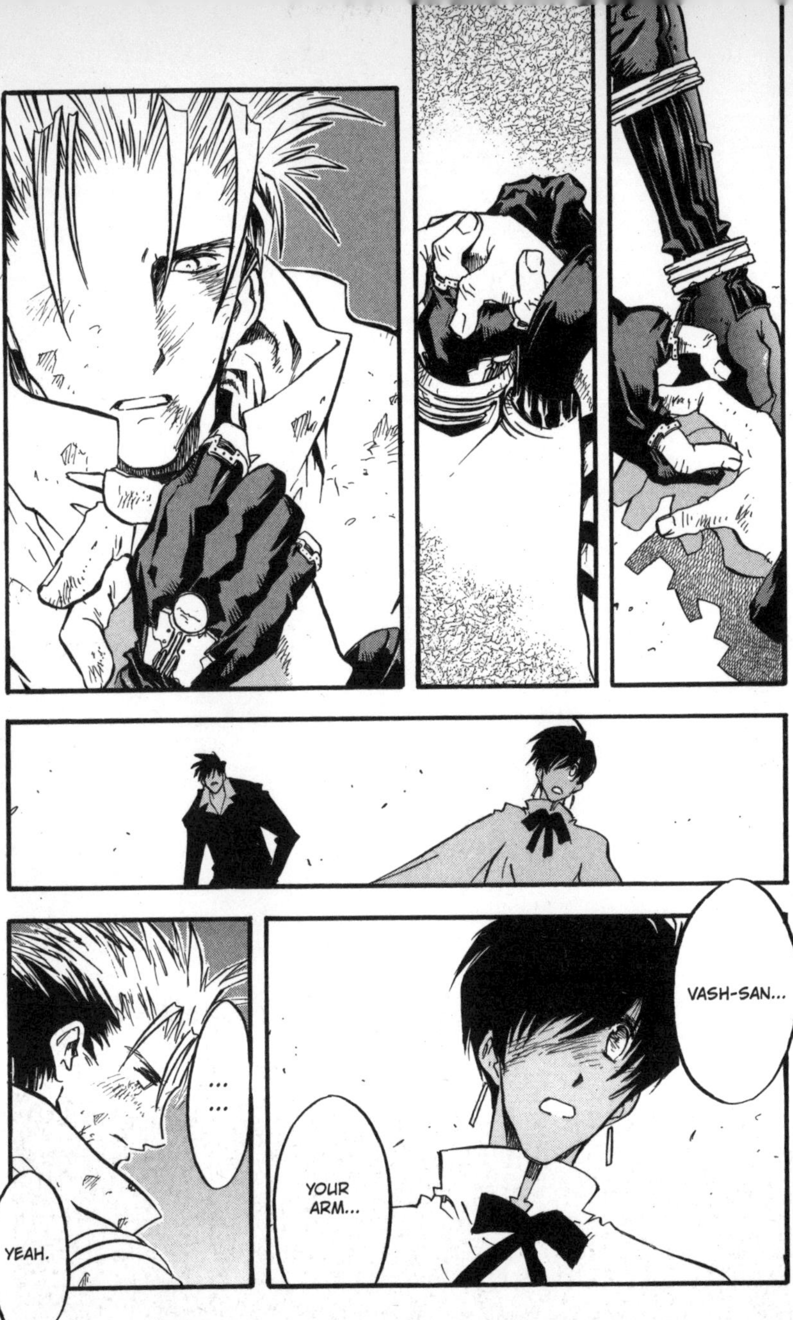
VASH-SAN...
YOUR ARM...
... ...
YEAH.

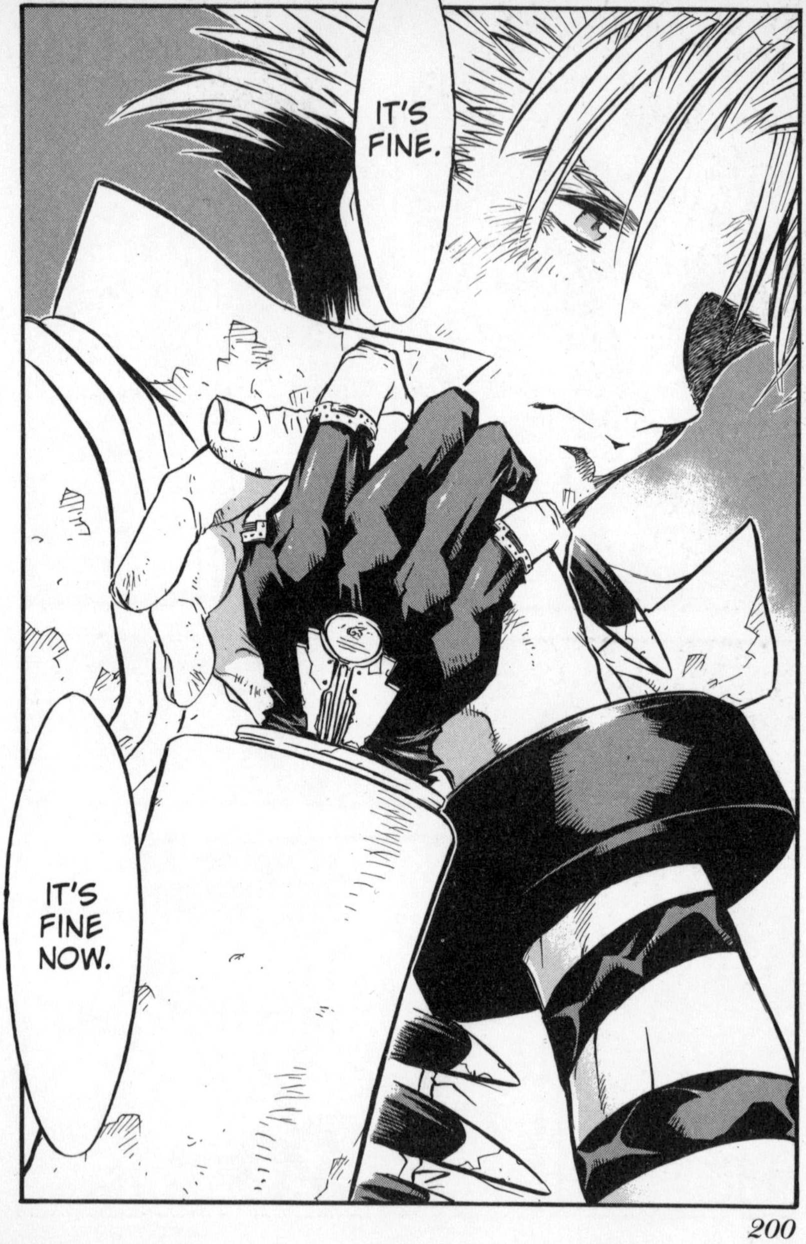
IT'S FINE.
IT'S FINE NOW.

SEMPAI!!
MILLIE! MILLIE! KYAA!!
HOW YOU FEELING, GIRL?
WE WERE WORRIED.
YOU WERE ASLEEP FOR THREE DAYS.
I SEE YOU ARE RECOVERING QUITE WELL...

THAT WAS A CLOSE ONE! THEY WERE RIGHT IN THE NEXT ROOM?!

BUT A HUMAN DOCTOR IS BEST FOR FIXING A HUMAN BODY, RIGHT?

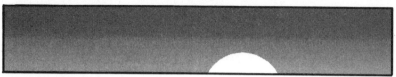

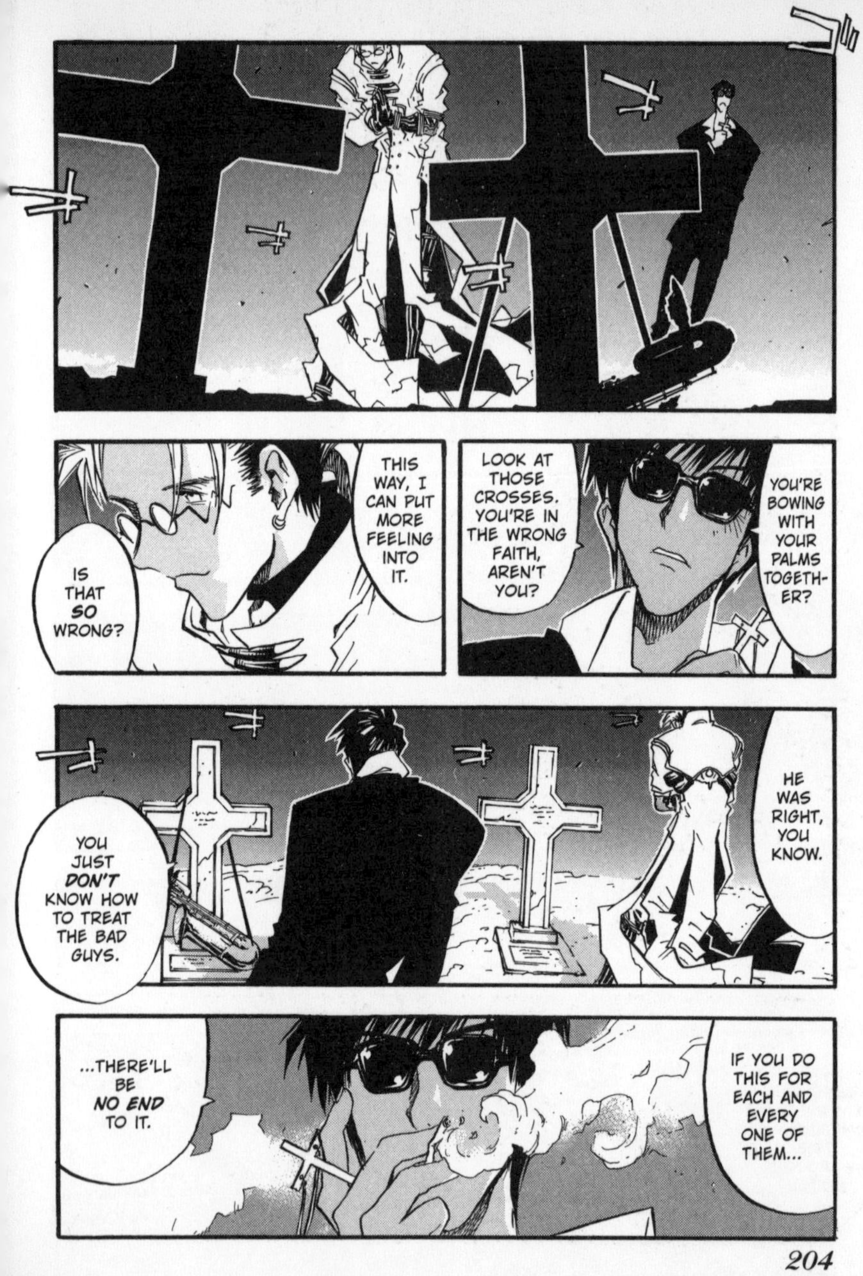
YOU'RE BOWING WITH YOUR PALMS TOGETHER?
LOOK AT THOSE CROSSES. YOU'RE IN THE WRONG FAITH, AREN'T YOU?
THIS WAY, I CAN PUT MORE FEELING INTO IT.
IS THAT **SO** WRONG?
HE WAS RIGHT, YOU KNOW.
YOU JUST ***DON'T*** KNOW HOW TO TREAT THE BAD GUYS.
IF YOU DO THIS FOR EACH AND EVERY ONE OF THEM...
...THERE'LL BE ***NO END*** TO IT.

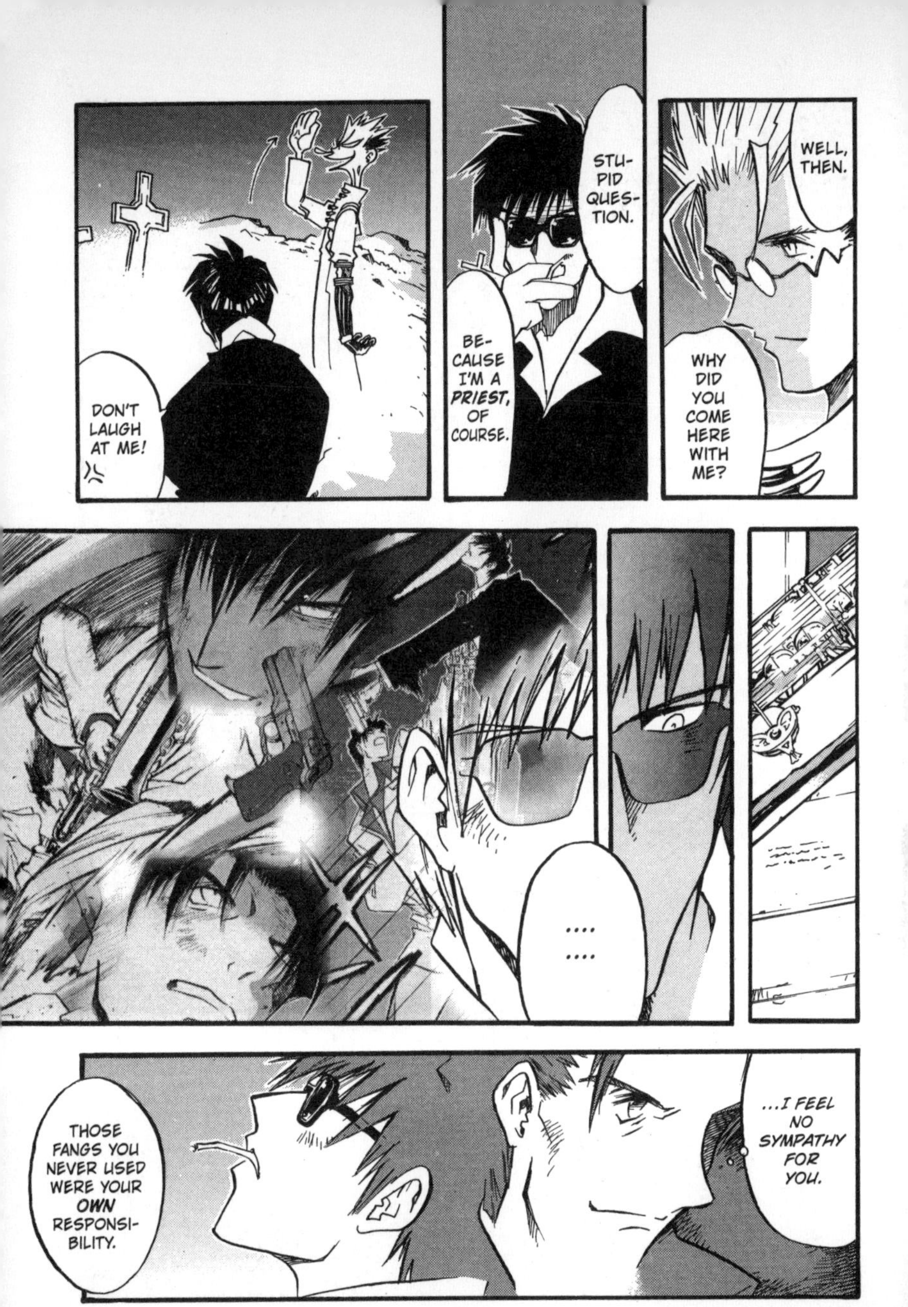
WELL, THEN.
WHY DID YOU COME HERE WITH ME?
STUPID QUESTION.
BECAUSE I'M A *PRIEST*, OF COURSE.
DON'T LAUGH AT ME!
....
....
...I FEEL NO SYMPATHY FOR YOU.
THOSE FANGS YOU NEVER USED WERE YOUR *OWN* RESPONSIBILITY.

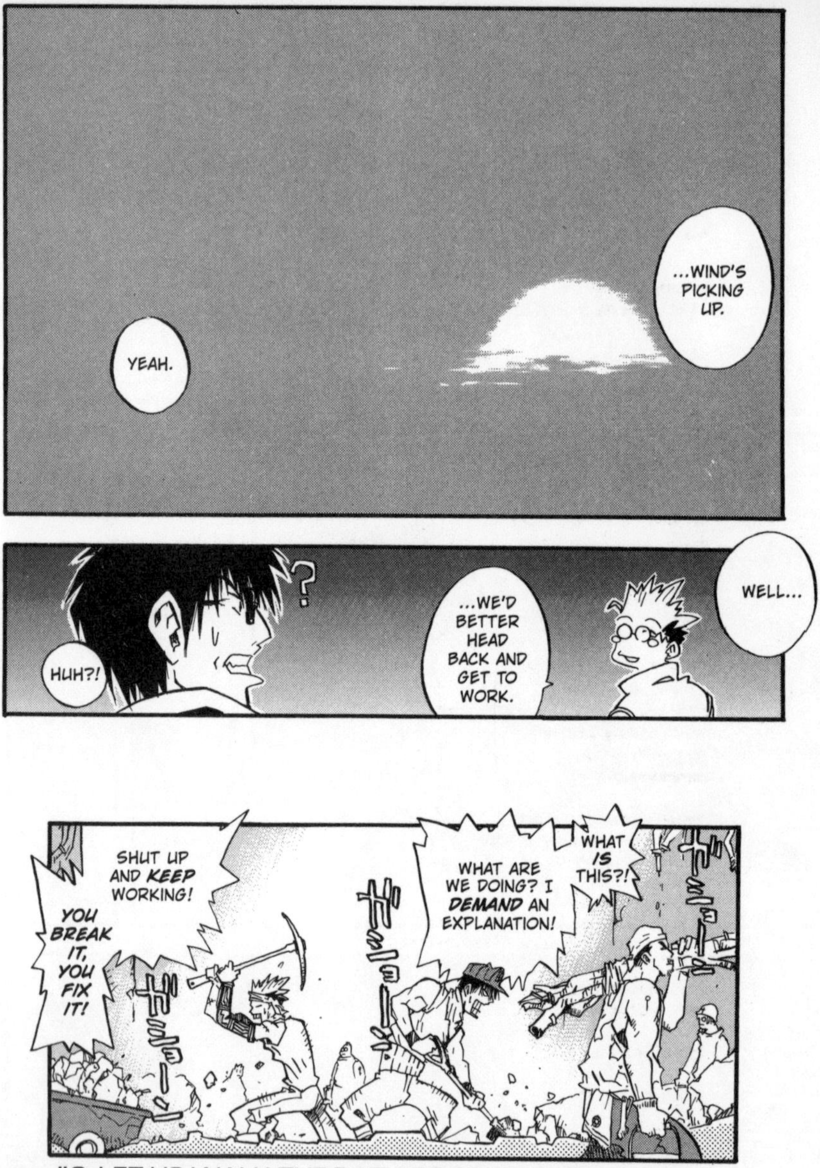
...WIND'S PICKING UP.
YEAH.
WELL...
...WE'D BETTER HEAD BACK AND GET TO WORK.
HUH?!
WHAT *IS* THIS?!
WHAT ARE WE DOING? I *DEMAND* AN EXPLANATION!
SHUT UP AND *KEEP* WORKING!
*YOU BREAK IT, YOU FIX IT!*

#6. LET US WALK THE PATH TO REDEMPTION / END

translation
**JUSTIN BURNS**

lettering
**STUDIO CUTIE**

publishers
**MIKE RICHARDSON** and **HIKARU SASAHARA**

editors
**TIM ERVIN** and **FRED LUI**

collection designers
**DAVID NESTELLE** and **JOSH ELLIOTT**

English-language version produced by DARK HORSE COMICS and DIGITAL MANGA PUBLISHING.

**TRIGUN MAXIMUM vol. 5**

© Yasuhiro Naito 2001. Originally published in Japan in 2001 by SHONEN GAHOSHA Co., Ltd., TOKYO. English translation rights arranged with SHONEN GAHOSHA Co., Ltd., TOKYO through TOHAN COPORATION, TOKYO. English-language translation © 2005 by Dark Horse Comics, Inc. and Digital Manga Publishing. All other material © 2005 by Dark Horse Comics, Inc. All rights reserved. No portion of this publication may be reproduced, in any form or by any means, without the express written permission of the copyright holders. Names, characters, places, and incidents featured in this publication are either the product of the author's imagination or are used fictitiously. Any resemblance to actual persons (living or dead), events, institutions, or locales, without satiric intent, is coincidental. Dark Horse Manga is a trademark of Dark Horse Comics, Inc. Dark Horse Comics® is a trademark of Dark Horse Comics, Inc., registered in various categories and countries. All rights reserved.

published by

**Dark Horse Manga**
a division of Dark Horse Comics, Inc.
10956 S.E. Main Street
Milwaukie, OR 97222
darkhorse.com

**Digital Manga Publishing**
1123 Dominguez Street, unit K
Carson, CA 90746
dmpbooks.com

To find a comics shop in your area, call the Comic Shop
Locator Service toll-free at 1-888-266-4226

First edition: May 2005
ISBN: 1-59307-344-5

10 9 8 7 6 5 4 3 2 1

Printed in Canada

# STOP

## This is the back of the book!

**This manga collection is translated into English but oriented in right-to-left reading format at the creator's request, maintaining the artwork's visual orientation as originally published in Japan. If you've never read manga in this way before, take a look at the diagram below to give yourself an idea of how to go about it. Basically, you'll be starting in the upper right corner and will read each balloon and panel moving right to left. It may take some getting used to, but you should get the hang of it very quickly. Have fun!**



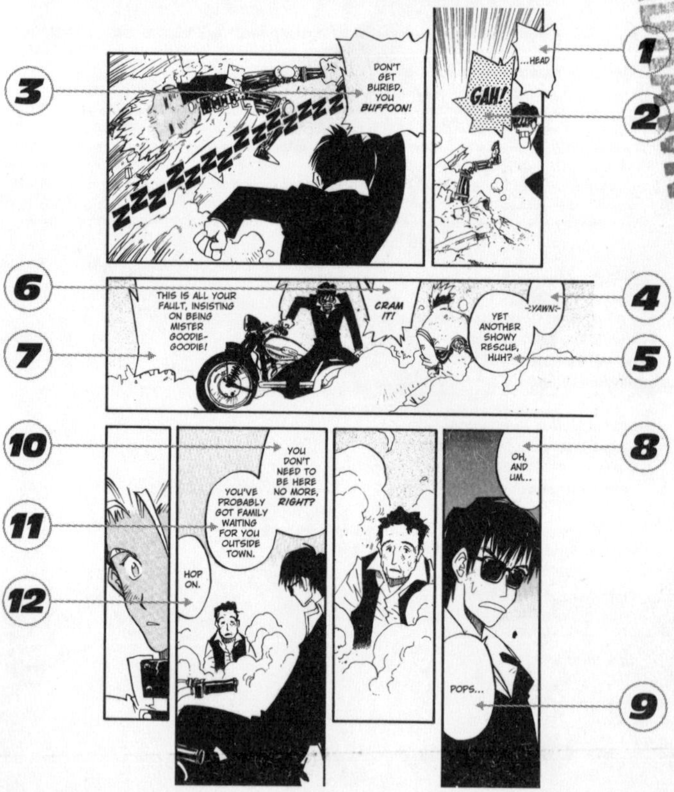
...HEAD
GAH!
DON'T GET BURIED, YOU BUFFOON!
~YAWN~
YET ANOTHER SHOWY RESCUE, HUH?
CRAM IT!
THIS IS ALL YOUR FAULT, INSISTING ON BEING MISTER GOODIE-GOODIE!
OH, AND UM...
POPS...
YOU DON'T NEED TO BE HERE NO MORE, RIGHT?
YOU'VE PROBABLY GOT FAMILY WAITING FOR YOU OUTSIDE TOWN.
HOP ON.